# Dispositif of Raciality

**Critical South**

***The publication of this series is supported by the International Consortium of Critical Theory Programs funded by the Andrew W. Mellon Foundation.***

Series editors: Natalia Brizuela, Victoria J. Collis-Buthelezi and Leticia Sabsay

Mário Pinto de Andrade, *The Revolution Will be a Poetic Act*
Leonor Arfuch, *Memory and Autobiography*
Hélé Béji, *We, the Decolonized*
Maurits van Bever Donker, *Texturing Difference*
Paula Biglieri and Luciana Cadahia, *Seven Essays on Populism*
Antônio Bispo dos Santos, *The Earth Gives, the Earth Wants*
Sueli Carneiro, *Dispositif of Raciality*
Gisela Catanzaro, *Spectrology of Authoritarian Neoliberalism*
Aimé Césaire, *Resolutely Black*
Aimé Césaire, *Toussaint Louverture*
Victoria J. Collis-Buthelezi and Aaron Kamugisha (eds.), *The Caribbean Race Reader*
Bolívar Echeverría, *Modernity and "Whiteness"*
Diego Falconí Trávez, *From Ashes to Text*
Celso Furtado, *The Myth of Economic Development*
Eduardo Grüner, *The Haitian Revolution*
Francisco-J. Hernández Adrián, *On Tropical Grounds*
Ailton Krenak, *Ancestral Future*
Ailton Krenak, *Life is Not Useful*
Premesh Lalu, *Undoing Apartheid*
Karima Lazali, *Colonial Trauma*
María Pia López, *Not One Less*
Achille Mbembe and Felwine Sarr (eds.), *The Politics of Time*
Achille Mbembe and Felwine Sarr (eds.), *To Write the Africa World*
Valentin-Yves Mudimbe, *The Scent of the Father*
Pablo Oyarzun, *Doing Justice*
Néstor Perlongher, *Plebeian Prose*
Bento Prado Jr., *Error, Illusion, Madness*
Nelly Richard, *Eruptions of Memory*
Silvia Rivera Cusicanqui, *Ch'ixinakax utxiwa*
Suely Rolnik, *Spheres of Insurrection*
Rita Segato, *The War Against Women*
Tendayi Sithole, *The Black Register*
Maboula Soumahoro, *Black is the Journey, Africana the Name*
Fatou Sow, *Feminism in Africa*
Javad Tabatabai, *Ibn Khaldun and the Social Sciences*
Dénètem Touam Bona, *Fugitive, Where Are You Running?*

# Dispositif of Raciality

## The Construction of the Other as Non-Being

Sueli Carneiro

Translated by Lanie Millar

polity

Originally published in Portuguese as *Dispositivo de racialidade: A construção do outro como não ser como fundamento do ser* by Companhia das Letras. 

Polity Press
65 Bridge Street
Cambridge CB2 1UR, UK

Polity Press
111 River Street
Hoboken, NJ 07030, USA



ISBN-13: 978-1-5095-6458-3 – hardback
ISBN-13: 978-1-5095-6459-0 – paperback

A catalogue record for this book is available from the British Library.

Library of Congress Control Number: 2025948944

Typeset in 10.5 on 12pt Sabon
by Fakenham Prepress Solutions, Fakenham, Norfolk NR21 8NL
Printed and bound in Great Britain by Ashford Colour Ltd.



For further information on Polity, visit our website:
politybooks.com

# Contents

## Part III Education and Care of the Self

# Foreword

I first met Sueli Carneiro in 2020 when I invited her to participate in the conference "Black Women's Intellectual Contributions: Perspectives from the Global South," which I organized with Lorraine Leu at the Teresa Lozano Long Institute for Latin American Studies (LLIAS) at the University of Texas at Austin. Our vision was to bring together Black women intellectuals from across the southern Americas to reflect on and discuss "the unique and dynamic ways Black women contribute socially, culturally, politically, and theoretically to the Americas, and why it is important to recognize these contributions." Engaging with Black feminist thought was essential to this project, so, we made a dream list of invitees whom we wanted to engage in dialogue. Sueli Carneiro was at the top of this list.

Widely regarded as one of the most influential Black feminist intellectuals alive today, Sueli Carneiro is a stalwart grassroots organizer, fierce political strategist, and brilliant analytical thinker. A key political voice in the fight against racism and sexism in Brazil, she is not only the godmother of contemporary Black feminism in that country, but also one of its most important public intellectuals.

Carneiro began her intellectual career as a philosophy student at the University of São Paulo (USP) in 1971 during the height of Brazil's military dictatorship – a dangerous time of censorship and extreme repression.[1] She became involved with the Centro de Cultura e Arte Negra (Black Arts and Culture Center), led by another intellectual giant in the history of Brazil's Black feminist movement,

Thereza Santos, who would be one of her primary mentors.[2] A few years later, in 1978, Carneiro was one of the hundreds of people in the crowd at the public protest that inaugurated the establishment of the Movimento Negro Unificado (MNU, Unified Black Movement) in Brazil. This period of activism also led her to acquire another significant mentor: the great Black feminist organizer and anthropologist Lélia Gonzalez.[3] In 1983, Carneiro joined with Marta Arruda, Solimar Carneiro, Sônia Nascimento, Edna Roland, Thereza Santos, Vera Saraiva, and other Black women to create the Coletivo das Mulheres Negras (Black Women's Collective), the first Black women's organization with an explicit mandate to address Black women's issues in São Paulo.[4] The organization came about after the government of São Paulo convened the Conselho Estadual da Condição Feminina (State Council on the Condition of Women) and did not include any Black women.[5] São Paulo's council was the first in Brazil, and Black women who were active in the Black Movement and becoming engaged in feminism wanted a seat at the table. The Colectivo das Mulheres Negras was their response. After much organizing and lobbying, the collective become part of the state council. The collective's membership in the council resulted in the production of the first intersectional research study on the condition of Black women in Brazil, *Mulher negra* (Black Woman), by Carneiro and Thereza Santos, published in 1985.[6] Three years later, Carneiro founded Geledés – Instituto da Mulher Negra (Geledés – Black Women's Institute), which would become one of the most enduring and most successful Black women's organizations in the country.[7]

Throughout the 1980s and 1990s, Carneiro expanded her engagement with Black feminism through grassroots organizing and intellectual production. She was deeply inspired by her mentor Lélia Gonzalez during this time. Simultaneously, Carneiro became an active member of the MNU and a feminist, organizing on both fronts in the relentless pursuit to end racism and sexism. On this path, she continually sharpened her critiques of the entrenched anti-blackness and misogyny of Brazilian society, focusing primarily on the ways that Black women's experiences reveal our inability to separate racism and sexism from one another because they are indeed interlocking forms of oppression. And as she deepened her analysis and diagnosis of inequality and violence in Brazil in the trenches of movement organizing, she simultaneously began to probe the question of race as a social problem, and develop theoretical analyses of the relationship between race and nation in the country.

Enter *Dispositif of Raciality*. In addition to her keen insights into Black feminist thought, Carneiro has demonstrated her intellectual prowess on the question of raciality and its epistemological and ontological dimensions. Trained in philosophy, and deeply committed to critical analysis and theoretical exegesis, Carneiro has spent decades querying the question of race, and specifically thinking about the ways that race – or, more specifically, *raciality* – "produces power, knowledge, and subjectivities"[8] through its function as an ontological apparatus for the construction of Being. Raciality, a colonial project that emerges alongside transatlantic slavery, is, argues Carneiro, the foil that is needed to articulate the relationship between whiteness and Being. Carneiro begins to engage with Michel Foucault's critique of the modern nation-state and his discussions of biopower and the state apparatus as a graduate student in the 1980s. She considers what it would mean to apply Foucauldian approaches to structure, power, and the state to Brazil. As a result, she begins to theorize the necessarily dialectical relationship between whiteness as Being and blackness as non-Being that gives birth to the racial apparatus and develops the argument that it is the ontological apparatus of racialized Being that comes to define the social contracts that undergird the modern Brazilian nation state project. Building out of her practical experience with on-the-ground organizing against anti-Black racism and sexism, she carefully and thoughtfully crafts a sagacious and pathfinding critique of Brazilian racism that moves away from oversimplified and reductionist discussions of color prejudice and interpersonal relations and moves toward and engages with a deep structural, historical, and philosophical analysis of how and why Brazil has emerged as a gendered anti-Black state. What do the structures of this gendered anti-blackness tell us about the apparatus of raciality as a paradigm of our modern world?

It is useful to take a pause here to retrace how we got to this point. In the 1980s, Carneiro began to pursue her master's at the University of São Paulo. It was during this time, as she notes in *Dispositif of Raciality*, that she began to engage with Foucault. As she writes here, "The intuition that gave rise to this study came about in 1984 while I was writing the final paper for a master's course taught by Professor José Augusto Guilhon Albuquerque in the School of Philosophy, Literature, and Humanities at the University of São Paulo (FFLCH-USP)." This intuition was to apply "Foucault's concepts of the apparatus and biopower to the domain of raciality in Brazil."[9] This intuition led to approximately two decades of critical engagement, resulting in the 2005 defense of her dissertation in educational philosophy, *A construção do outro como não-ser como fundamento do ser* (The Construction of the Other as Non-Being as the Foundation of Being). This dissertation eventually evolved into the publication of her book *Dispositivo da racialidade*, of which this is the first English translation.[10]

It is important to note the extreme importance of this intervention. I began my doctoral studies in 2001 at Stanford University in the then Department of Cultural and Social Anthropology. Like many doctoral students of that generation, my graduate education was greatly defined by Foucauldian thought. I clearly remember the first graduate class that I took with anthropologist Ann Stoler, who was a visiting professor at Stanford at that time. She was finishing her 2002 book *Carnal Knowledge and Imperial Power*. In that class, we spent hours and hours reading and analyzing Foucault from every possible angle, thinking specifically about structures of power and questions of the relationship between the state and the body.[11] In that moment of post-structuralism, when post-modernism was still in vogue, race was very much perceived to be a "*passé* topic" that harkened back to an old essentialism that we had moved beyond in our great theoretical brilliance and wisdom. Nevertheless, as a student of Duboisian Pan-Africanism and African diaspora studies, I found myself insisting on trying to understand Foucault's thinking in terms of race, especially regarding questions of biopower, and particularly after reading the introduction to *Discipline and Punish* and wondering curiously, like so many others, why lynching and colonial violence seemed to have slipped his mind.[12] This, of course, was two years before the publication of the first English edition of his *Society Must be Defended*, where we English-speakers finally came to understand a bit more about his racial politics.[13] Nevertheless, the seeds of curiosity and reflection had already been planted in my emerging intellectual mind, and the relationship between Foucauldian thought and race would come to be a defining dimension of my conceptual thinking. I would spend much of my graduate student and early faculty career thinking more deeply about the questions that sparked my curiosity in 2001, seeking to resolve this question of how race fits into the Foucauldian conceptualizations of structures of power and dominance. Gradually, I discovered that there was a cohort of us in the United States who were thinking about Foucault in this way. However, it was not until I met Carneiro in 2020, after she graciously and patiently accepted our very insistent invitation to participate in the LLILAS Conference, that I discovered her dissertation.

Reading Carneiro's dissertation was like finding an old friend. After nearly two decades of doing work in Brazil in collaboration with Black Movement organizers and getting to know her reputation as a preeminent Black leader from afar, I was absolutely awestruck when, upon returning from our conference, she sent me an email sharing her dissertation and asking me to read it and tell her what I thought. Words cannot express the sheer terror and joy I felt at reading this email. I was at once elated by the opportunity to engage with Carneiro intellectually and intimidated by the invitation to dialogue with her as an intellectual peer. It was not until 2023, when I hosted Carneiro as our Tinker Visiting Professor at LLILAS for the fall semester, that I mustered the courage to answer her call to engage in a dialogue with her about her dissertation, which was by now revised and published as the book *Dispositivo de racialidade*. However, our conversation had now taken on new proportions. Instead of being an email or a conversation over coffee, it turned into a semester-long collective conversation with students at LLILAS as part of her university graduate course "Black Feminist Epistemologies" – the first formal university course that she had ever offered. Over the semester, the students and I listened to, learned from, and engaged with Carneiro regarding the ideas she outlines in her work on the racial apparatus, and the genealogies of thought and Black feminist organizing that led her to these research conclusions. This time was indescribably transformative for me and for the students. Not only did we learn a great deal about Carneiro's intellectual journey, but we also began to understand more clearly why *Dispositif of Raciality* changes the way that we think about and theorize not only race in Brazil, but also race as a global phenomenon.

I would encourage the reader to return to Foucault's debate via Carneiro with fresh eyes. Our global society now stares at the face of an AI revolution, one that threatens to further sophisticate state politics of biopower through the neoliberal proxy of multinational corporate greed. As Carneiro writes of the state's shift to biopower, "This 'massifying' seizure of power can only take place by regulating life processes – birth, death, longevity – which come to be statistically measured and programmed."[14] There are lessons to be learned here as we grapple with the new world order that faces us. The work of philosopher Charles Mills informs Carneiro's conversation on the racial apparatus as she thinks through his theorization of the racial contract, and how the racial contract, like Carole Pateman's understanding of the sexual contract, can bolster our understanding of the unspoken politics of our modern political social thought, particularly under democracy. Specifically, Carneiro argues that the racial apparatus defines Being as we know it (consider, particularly, our normalization of the concept of the human (being) in popular discourse) according to racial logics. Her words are worth quoting at length here:

> The apparatus of raciality, by designating humanity as synonymous with whiteness, goes on to redefine all remaining human aspects and hierarchize them according to their proximity to or distance from this standard. In this way, white becomes the ideal Being for the Others, and the white woman a figure of mystique for non-white people. This way of affirming the bourgeoisie determined the desirable aesthetic standard for everyone, the form of love and sexuality, and corresponding morality, since the body was the expression of self-affirmation; after all, "the body functions as the mark of social values; it is in it that society fixes its meanings and values. Socially, the body is a sign."[15]

We can read Carneiro's understanding of the body as a sign in conversation with Stuart Hall's readings of Foucault regarding representation, for example. The idea that the body is a sign replete with racialized meaning is one that Hall addresses extensively in his engagements with Foucauldian thought.[16] Carneiro adds a dimension to this conversation, however, by engaging with these concepts within the context of Brazil. Historically, as students of Brazilian history well know, Brazil has touted itself as a racial democracy – a racially harmonious nation with relatively fluid racial categories. Beginning in the 1950s, at the behest of the United Nations in its desire to address the problem of racism that gave rise to the genocidal acts of the Nazis during World War II, Brazil began to conduct research on its alleged racial democracy as a way to replicate this harmony elsewhere. Much to the world's chagrin, however, the researchers of the São Paulo School revealed that in fact Brazil was a racially stratified nation along Black/white lines, and racism was alive and well. As a result, over the subsequent decades, cadres of scholars investigating the question of race began to produce scholarship demonstrating, definitively, the existence of racial inequality in Brazil. We can count Carneiro's early work with the Coletivo das Mulheres Negras as part of this wave of scholarship, particularly the publication of *Mulher negra*. Carneiro's thoughts in *Dispositif of Raciality* take this conversation several steps further, however, by moving beyond a quantitative analysis of racial inequality toward a diagnosis of the philosophical and political logics that permit and perpetuate this inequality. Moreover, her attention to the role of the state in the reproduction of the racial apparatus clearly demonstrates that the racial apparatus is also a *state apparatus*, and therefore evidence of the construction of the nation state according to the logic of gendered anti-blackness.

For those reading this translation from the global North, there are many entry points in the conversation about Brazil that invite comparison. For example, Carneiro's discussion of Black maternal death as a dimension of the apparatus of raciality (state power over life and death) should be familiar. Brazil, like the United States, holds the unfortunate status of being a country compounded by race/gender inequality. This inequality manifests readily in the rates of Black maternal mortality, where Black women's death rates far exceed white women's death rates, producing a two-nation reality: one nation living in the first world and one nation living in the third world.[17] The global nature of gendered anti-blackness is a lived reality that affects us socially, politically, and ontologically. I would strongly encourage the reader to read this book both for its insights into Brazilian society and for its insights into the very nature of the global idea of race itself. *Dispositif of Raciality* can be read in conversation with works like Charles W. Mills's *The Racial Contract* or Achille Mbembe's *Necropolitics*.[18] This is not to equate or even compare these works, but rather to suggest that Carneiro's thoughts are part of a wider discourse of race and power that is steeped in the discussion of political thought and our social world.

I want to close by making an appeal to the reader on how to approach this book. It is the case that we English speakers of the Northern academy often relegate scholars of the global South to the realm of informant rather than theoretical interlocutor.[19] As Carneiro eloquently articulates, there is a need to address the question of epistemicide in the global South by seriously engaging with Black intellectuals as critical thinkers. In *Dispositif of Raciality*, she writes:

> Black activists, with a few notable exceptions, are treated by specialists in racial issues as *sources of knowledge*, but not as authorities on the topic. Black researchers are also reduced to the role of sources and are not considered interlocutors in academic dialogues, especially when they are not limited exclusively to the topic of Black people.[20]

However, Black people are not only producers of knowledge but also critical thinkers and theorizers. And if we are to take seriously the task of disrupting the epistemological erasure of Black voices in our pursuit of more equitable engagements with knowledge, we must not only take Black intellectuals seriously, but we must also seek to do so in ways that are anti-imperialist and recognize the historical factors that have led to the erasure of Black intellectual voices from the global South because of the hegemonic dominance of the English language and Western thought in the academy. Decolonizing Black studies must also play a critical role in this project. For us to truly engage in the transnational project of Black studies, we must expand our engagement with Black thinkers from the global South who write in languages other than English and take this work seriously. Translation plays an important role in this political project.[21] And although there is a longstanding history of engaging with critical Black thought translated from French (Aimé Césaire, Frantz Fanon), there is less engagement with critical Black thought translated from Portuguese and Spanish (for a series of historical political reasons). This book is an invitation to break with this pattern. Specifically, I would encourage the reader to consider Carneiro to be part of the larger global Black radical tradition, as defined by Cedric Robinson and expanded upon by scholars like Robin D. G. Kelley and Carole Boyce Davies.[22] Indeed, as you read, you will begin to see the many reasons why this is both relevant and necessary. Sueli Carneiro is one of the most important Black political philosophers of our time.

Christen A. Smith, New Haven, Connecticut, December 2025

# Translator's Note

Sueli Carneiro's extraordinary erudition as well as her deft relay between the lived experience and the vast array of philosophical concepts she incorporates in *Dispositif of Raciality* represented a unique challenge in translating this work. Michel Foucault's thought anchors Carneiro's exploration of raciality in Brazilian society, and she incorporates conceptual vocabulary drawn from Foucault throughout the text. In addition to the concept of the *dispositif*, translated in Portuguese as *dispositivo* and most widely in English as *apparatus*, Carneiro interrogates other key Foucauldian concepts such as the *interdit/interdição*, translated by Rupert Swyer in "Orders of Discourse" as "prohibitions,"[1] which Carneiro explores in terms of the prohibitions placed on Black people as subjects, and the notion of "power tak[ing] hold over life."[2] As Foucault explains in *Society Must Be Defended*, he refers to the emergence of biopower, of "the acquisition of power over man insofar as man is a living being, that the biological came under State control."[3] Resistance to this hold over Black life, she shows us, emancipates us all. Throughout Carneiro's work, I have sought consistency in this terminology with the published translations of Foucault.

The nuance and specificity of racial vocabulary referring to people of African descent in the Brazilian context represented another challenge. There are instances where I have kept especially historical terms in Portuguese, with explanatory notes, because they have no easy conceptual equivalents in English. This is also a work deeply founded in activist practice and lived experience. Carneiro emphasized to me in conversation the importance that the term *negro* (Black) as a racial category carries for Brazilian activists of her generation as an insurgent declaration of a collective political identity. As she explores in the work, this is particularly important in a social and historical context of Brazil's emphasis on a myth of racial harmony and a proliferation of identity categories that value degrees of proximity to whiteness. The strategy we agreed on was to signal this valence of the term *negro* the first time it appears in each chapter. I have thus included a note with an explanation especially when it appears in the context of other words that refer to blackness.

Finally, I would like to offer a brief thanks to the many people who helped with the translation, starting with Sueli Carneiro herself, who graciously agreed to consult on the work. I am so grateful for what I have learned through such a close engagement with Carneiro's thought. I would also like to thank Janaina Higino Martins and Julia Wähmann for facilitating our conversation, as well as Elise Heslinga at Polity for bringing the project to me. Amanda Doxtater, Karen Emmerich, and Leah Middlebrook read many drafts and offered invaluable counsel. The anonymous reviewer's insightful suggestions made the work much stronger. The translation also benefited from suggestions and conversations with Mayra Bottaro, Cristina Carnemolla, Roy Chan, Marc Schachter, and Miguel Valerio. Thank you!

# Prologue

## Emancipation For All

I will speak from the position of the enslaved woman. From the place of those excluded from the *res publica*/Republic. Of those who, as non-citizens, were dispossessed of the right to an education.

I speak to you, hegemonic I, from the place of the "paradigm of the Other," conscious of the fact that you have inscribed me within this paradigm, and that, "thanks" to it, expectations were created for me. I am conscious of the fact that even if I try to defy them, they could still be met, since I find myself conditioned by a "historically and pedagogically prior unit"[1] of which I would be an application.

I am a historical application whose conscience perennially renews itself through the memory of slavery's soul, inherited from my ancestors and, even before that, from the negative representations that were long associated with my Black body. I am also a historical application of the Western modernity that scientifically dissected my natural inferiority, an inferiority that today constitutes the spectacle of human indigence that I exhibit to the world.

Subjugated as I am by DPS syndrome (Discrimination, Prejudice, Stigma; Roseli Fischmann's coinage, you know her but I don't think you like her),[2] I search for you, hegemonic I, but not to get true education from you. Just like the truth, as an African philosopher said (pardon the heresy), true teachings boil down to three: mine, yours, and the Truth that's unattainable for both of us. I aspire to the teaching that will result from an encounter between our experiences of learning. As far as I'm concerned, I've learned about them from the first instant that I encountered you. Perhaps instruction that can reconcile the two of us will result from our dialogue, a reconciliation within that human indivisibility where nothing that is human will be foreign to us.

I am also a pedagogical application, because the representations associated with my body have been reiterated for centuries through academic instruments and many other educational processes. Beyond reinforcing and reflecting these representations in all corners of the world, they have explained my martyrdom through religion – as a form of atonement for my sins, the greatest of which is my dark skin, inherited, as they taught me, from Cain, from fratricide, as well as my paganism, a word I came to know with you – and thus I deserved enslavement, the *only* way I could be brought close to the threshold of civilization and achieve the salvation of my soul.

Later, the sciences, bless them, would find a scientific explanation for my faults: proclaiming my natural inferiority to other humans by measuring my brain, they found me certifiably incapable of intellectual activity. By evaluating my culture, they determined that I lack sufficient capacity for self-governance and self-determination. They noted the absence of recognizable forms of social organization in my societies of origin. They proved my ignorance through the absence of writing to record my achievements (today as unknown to me as they are to you), and they revealed my primitivism through the fetishes that I worship, which do not rise to the level of true religion.

To convince you to accept this encounter, I searched for concepts (which you appreciate so much) to demonstrate the displacement of the human that you imposed on me, expelling me far away, very far away, to the dwelling place of an alterity situated in the confines of non-being, apart from those Others who were admitted to your intimacy, though with reservations. I am not speaking out of spite or envy. I can live perfectly well without you. What bothers me is only the discomfort of the living conditions that you consigned me to and which, by the way, I have only come to know by finding you.

Though exiled to the domain of particularities, of contingencies, or exteriorities of the being in which you confined me, you pulsate in me, repelling this *ontic* to which you reduced me, ontological remains that search for a dialogue that can repair the double mutilation you carried out on both of us. You find yourself imprisoned in the contemplation of the Idea you have of the world, and I, a fallen angel residing in this world, invite you to look at it with eyes that allow you to see in it a reflection of your own face.

Only I can offer you this look in which the plenitude of your being is manifest.

For this ocular operation to be as painless as possible, I have collected some of the repertoire of tricks the gods require you to perform, like a trap to which your envy of your creator condemns you. I must also point out that I'm provisionally assuming your definition of me, laying out exactly the meaning that this definition assigns to me, as an opening. Thus, you can also rehabilitate your onticity as the initial premise of a dialogue between equals that, if successful, will vault us both to the realization and celebratory contemplation of our being-there.

In addition, as the person speaking to you, I must unequivocally reveal my identity. These are not my definitions, but I am adopting them because I agree with them and because I'm sure that they will facilitate your comprehension. As I previously stated, I am *negra*, a Black woman, a combination of *pretos* and *pardos*.[3] Now, don't ask me to explain things you invented, like "*pardos*." I only know that every day that goes by they become blacker.

I bring up notions that should be familiar to you (social apartheid, class struggle) and I contest them, under certain circumstances, so as to leave no doubt about my points of view. These are ways to deal with certain issues in which I have the impression that I am subsumed: that is, those in which I and those like me are made invisible.

Before beginning this dialogue, we must get rid of anything that could interfere with our communication. That is why I seek, first and foremost, to pinpoint the strategies that have led to the profound delusion of us being bound to one another in what someone once called the master–slave dialectic, in the hope that we can cooperate for our mutual liberation. I am speaking above all of a racialism on which you once bet all your cards.

For us to liberate ourselves from each other, I assure you that you will have to make concessions. The primary one will be to give up the pleasure of creating my replicas: that is, to stop endlessly reproducing me. This will require you to sin before God and the men also endlessly practicing and teaching this witchcraft. And they call me a witch! I am tired of your self-fulfilling prophecies! Oh, I forgot to let you know about Afrodescendants; that's the new way to refer to Black people, that is, *pretos* and *pardos*.

We need help with this difficult task I'm inviting you to undertake. So, I've called up Michel Foucault, yes, the French philosopher. I know he has your confidence and my sympathies. He is a reasonably reliable mediator for our potential disputes. Since he is a border-dweller, he converses well with everyone.

A warning: the domain to which I will refer from now on doesn't concern any territory of yours that I am seeking to appropriate. It's still the French guy's. He's referring to the social setting in which we play parts – pardon my frankness – for which you wrote the script.

There's one thorny issue. Perhaps one day we can come to agree that a crime was committed of radical proportions and consequences, but at present we are still in the realm of conjecture, so don't be afraid of the witnesses I have called. Yes, they could make up a simulated jury through which we could atone for our guilt, shielded by the safety of its virtual nature. It's a basic principle of reconciliation, about which I await your consideration.

I invite you to this dialogue with an open spirit, confident that it is possible to conquer hearts and minds, even among those who – like you – reject the sound of subaltern voices, in order to construct settings and scripts that perform emancipation for all.

# Introduction

## Being and Other

This study aims to demonstrate, in a reflective and speculative way, the potentiality of Michel Foucault's concept of the *apparatus* (*dispositif*) to understand the dynamics of racial relations in Brazil. Inspired by the French philosopher, I seek to reveal the existence of an apparatus of raciality operating in Brazilian society that, by articulating multiple elements, configures raciality as a domain that produces power, knowledge, and subjectivities through the negation and prohibition of power, knowledge, and subjectivities. One could say that the apparatus of raciality ultimately establishes an ontological division, since white people's affirmation of being results from the negation of the being of Black people. Or, to state it another way, the superiority of the hegemonic I, the white I, is obtained in contradistinction to the Other, who is Black.

The apparatus of raciality acquires a specific dimension by operating in conjunction with biopower and by being instrumentalized by it. In combination with racism, biopower promotes the life of the race considered healthier and purer and promotes the death of the race considered inferior. After all, as Foucault says, "once the State functions in the biopower mode, racism alone can justify the murderous function of the State."[1] However, for those who survive, the apparatus of raciality has other strategies of subjection in store. Among its constitutive elements, I highlight epistemicide, a concept I borrow from Boaventura de Sousa Santos to demonstrate the role of education in the reproduction and continuity of power, knowledge, and subjectivities that the apparatus itself produces. Through epistemicide – which is a form of sequestration, debasement, or assassination of reason – Black people are invalidated as knowing subjects and cast as intellectually inferior. I also highlight the multiple prohibitions Black people face within the apparatus of raciality's elements. In addition to being intellectually assassinated, Black people are prohibited from attaining the status of human beings or moral, political, or legal subjects. These prohibitions function as exclusion, and are as present in discourse as in social practices. They promote the inclusion of individuals and groups in the ambit of abnormality, in the sphere of non-being, nature, and unreason. They thus contribute to the formation of a social imaginary that naturalizes the subalternity of Black people and the superiority of white people.

Nevertheless, this book does not limit itself to investigating the apparatus of raciality's multiple strategies. It also seeks to deal with Black resistance, understood through the voices and testimonies of insurgents against subordination, epistemicide, and other "cides" to which blackness finds itself subjected in Brazil. Their words reveal that it is from the strength of self-esteem, from the recognition of their own autonomy, from examples, from the triumph of memory and collective action, that the sap of resistance is extracted. The way out is through the collective, where care of the self and care of the other merge in the search for emancipation.

In the dialogue between Foucault and Gilles Deleuze in "Intellectuals and Power," Deleuze states that "Practice is a set of relays from one theoretical point to another, and theory is a relay from one practice to another. No theory can develop without eventually encountering a wall, and practice is necessary for piercing this wall."[2] In this sense, this book is the result of a reflection that integrates theoretical action and practical action in the form of activism on the racial issue in Brazil. It is the product of struggles, reflections, achievements, of old problems. It emerges, above all, from a series of doubts that I have faced throughout my life, whether as an individual upon whom raciality imposes subjection, or as a political subject constituted through resistance to this mode of subjectification. These doubts are situated in the ambit of racial relations in Brazil, in which a specific dynamic was established with such a degree of contradiction that, in some cases, it takes the form of paradox or unreason.

These are doubts that result from concerns about the permanence of ideas and practices of racial discrimination in a context in which various fields of knowledge discredit them; in which the historical conditions that constitute their locus of legitimation were supplanted and the very status of subject to which they were addressed was modified. If, as common sense dictates, racism and prejudice are the result of ignorance, there would be no lack of sufficiently widespread knowledge to discredit discriminatory practices based on race.

What concerns me even more is the denial of empirical evidence of the unequal treatment to which Black people are subject in Brazilian society, as revealed by statistical surveys and academic studies that proliferate in Brazil in various areas. Despite the recognition of discriminatory practices stemming from race, this denial imposes barriers to the adoption of measures that could curb the process of social exclusion of Black people, especially regarding access, retention, and success in the educational system.

From denying the problem to fully admitting it, passing through its relative acceptance, a scenario of disputes is uncovered about the problem of raciality on the level of both theory and political action. This scenario is most explicit in the polarization that thwarts the implementation of public policies that could reverse the unfavorable conditions of life into which Brazil's Black populations are plunged.

Taking these issues as a backdrop, this book is divided into three parts. The first is composed of four chapters. Chapter 1 introduces the concept of the apparatus in Foucault from its application to sexuality, on which I base my proposal of the concept of the apparatus of raciality. Chapter 2 describes the concept of biopower in order to show how it explains the differentiated processes of living and dying according to raciality as they manifest in Brazilian society. Chapter 3 shows that the apparatus uses epistemicide to bring about strategies of intellectual inferiorization of Black people and their invalidation as knowing subjects, which are forms of sequestering, debasing, or assassinating reason. At the same time, on the other hand, it does so while consolidating the intellectual supremacy of white raciality. Chapter 4 analyzes how the apparatus of raciality, by acting on Black raciality, sets off a series of prohibitions that function as procedures of exclusion.

The second part considers testimonies that, in the context of the apparatuses of power for Foucault, correspond to the fields of resistance that any apparatus of power produces. The witnesses are Edson Cardoso, Sônia Maria Pereira Nascimento, Fátima Oliveira, and Arnaldo Xavier (in memoriam).

Part III, "Education and Care of the Self," analyzes the testimonies presented in Part II through the theoretical frame presented in the first part, with attention to the repercussions of the dynamic established by the apparatus of raciality on formal education and the educational role that Black resistance plays in this context.

I do not propose to present the state of the field for the study of race in Brazil or of studies on Black people and education, nor to systematically rehearse the debate around the construction of racial democracy, which has been done in different and relevant forms by other authors. I understand, with Thomas Kuhn,[3] that the academic's task is the historical accumulation of knowledge proposed, questioned, and reconstructed. It would be foolhardy to turn every work into a resumption of the historical trajectory on the topic, at the risk of there being many arbitrary choices and involuntary omissions. What I present here reflects my principal intention: that this book be an exercise in applying Foucault's concepts of the apparatus and biopower to the domain of raciality in Brazil.

The intuition that gave rise to this study came about in 1984 while I was writing the final paper for a master's course taught by Professor José Augusto Guilhon Albuquerque in the School of Philosophy, Literature, and Humanities at the University of São Paulo (FFLCH-USP), when I first came into contact with Foucault's thought. At that time, the concept of the apparatus was a revelation to me, such was its potential for comprehending the dynamic that drove and configured racial relations in Brazil. The final paper I wrote at the conclusion of the course consisted of developing a flowchart, reproduced at the end of this book, that traces a simplified synthesis of the practical articulations among knowledge, resistance, and race as effects of the power of racism and racial discrimination. Various personal issues kept me from finishing the master's at that time, and I postponed revisiting and deepening that first intuition for almost two decades. It continued, however, to be nourished in my empirical observation and activism combating racism and racial discrimination.

When I returned to graduate study, in the School of Education in 1999, I took on the challenge in my doctoral work, completed in 2005 with the title of *A construção do outro como não ser como fundamento do ser* (The Construction of the Other as Non-Being as the Foundation of Being), now turned into a book over forty years after my initial intuition and twenty years after the defense of my doctoral dissertation.

As Roseli Fischmann argues, drawing from Emmanuel Levinas, true education comes from contact with the Other and the search for the Absolute Other. What better topic could there be for a contribution to education, she asks, "than the search for an objective understanding of how the negation of the Other happens through prejudice, discrimination, and stigmatization?"[4] This refers us to a "historically and pedagogically prior unit," or to the context of African slavery and to the discourses that were produced about it with the intention of legitimizing it. This was a discourse indebted to a long tradition theorizing human slavery, which was reappropriated and redesigned in the context of the conquest that took place from the end of the fifteenth century onward, and which resulted in the set of values that justified the West's continuation of African slavery for almost four centuries.

David Brion Davis lays out a central issue: the fact that since Antiquity, the topic of slavery has been bound up with religious concepts derived from Judaism or Greek philosophy. From this perspective, the slave is seen as "a Canaanite, a man devoid of Logos, or a sinner who scorned the truth."[5] Second, Davis highlights that slavery is conceived in the philosophical tradition as an integral part of a model of social hierarchy. In this sense, according to him, in Plato, Aristotle, and St. Augustine, slavery "was a necessary part of a world that required moral order and discipline; it was the base on which rested an intricate and hierarchical pattern of authority."[6] Third, slavery was thought of as a necessary condition for a redeeming mission:

> It was from slavery that Hebrews were delivered and from which they acquired their unique mission. It was slavery to desire and social convention that Cynics and Stoics sought to overcome by self-discipline and indifference to the world. And it was from slavery to the corrupted flesh of Adam that Christ redeemed mankind. For some two thousand years men thought of sin as a kind of slavery. One day they would come to think of slavery as sin.[7]

The search for a historical understanding of the ways in which the negation of the Other comes about cannot neglect the context of Western modernity, in which the ideas of autonomy, secularization of life, and the affirmation of the individual are contradictorily articulated with African and indigenous enslavement. Later, they are articulated with abolitionist movements and the processes of liberation from slavery as well as the emergence of scientific racism, inaugurating new forms of racial subjection.

In the philosophy of Martin Heidegger, there is an ontological definition of Being that is productive for the purposes of this book.

Heidegger distinguishes between categories of the ontic and the ontological: the ontic refers to particular beings or to the determination of the being, whereas the ontological refers to being as being.[8] Thus race, color, culture, religion, and ethnicity would pertain to the ontic order, to the being's particularities. The human being, specifically, would register in the ontological dimension. This allows us to presume that racism reduces beings to their ontic dimension, denying them the ontological condition and leaving their humanity incomplete.

Thus, for Heidegger, man is himself a being (Heidegger designates him with the category of *Dasein*, there-being) who coexists among other beings. However, this particular being, man, has a unique status among other beings, insofar as in him the ontic and the ontological coincide. In my interpretation, it is the idea of universality that emancipates the individual and allows them to express their specificity. Conversely, it is the idea of particularity that imprisons them, reducing their being to this particularity that imprisons the Black individual in their specific group. By making the ontic the ontological of the Other, the hegemonic I lowers the status of being of this Other.

## Race and Racism

It is important to clarify the concepts of race and racism with which this study deals. Beginning in the 1970s, studies of racial inequalities redefined the concepts of race and racism, and the weight that these factors have in social stratification. It is in this context that "*pretos*" and "*pardos*" were grouped together in the category of "*negros*," Black people,[9] justified by the similarity among the social indicators found for both in official census data and that were significantly different from self-declared white groups. This is the understanding of *negro* (Black) as an analytical category that this work assumes, following the majority of contemporary studies of the term.

In agreement with Antonio Sérgio Guimarães, we consider that race is

> a concept that does not correspond to any natural reality. On the contrary, it is a concept that merely indicates a form of social classification, founded in a negative attitude toward certain social groups, and informed by a specific notion of nature, as something self-determined. But as much as we may loathe the trickery that the concept of "race"

> allows – that is, to pass off negative and baneful prejudice, interests and social values as natural reality – the concept of race has a clear social reality, and resistance against the social conduct that it brings about is impossible to undertake without recognizing the social reality that only the act of naming allows.[10]

From this perspective, color – as a racially defined concept – can only be a factor that explains existing social differences between Black and white people as long as a preexisting conception of race exists, to which color is indebted, and as long as it is possible to establish racial differentiation from it. Thus, Guimarães defines racism as "a rather specific way to 'naturalize' social life: that is, to explain personal, social, and cultural differences from differences assumed to be natural."[11]

It is my presupposition that race is one of the structural elements of multiracial societies that originated in colonialism. The notion of social *apartheid* and the supremacy of the concept of social class championed by leftist thinkers, inheritors of historical dialectical materialism, do not account for – on the contrary, they erase or mask – the racial contradiction present in multiracial societies, considering that in such societies race/color/ethnicity (especially in Brazil) are variables that impact the very structure of classes. Racism, as a pseudoscience, seeks to legitimate the production of symbolic and material privileges for the white supremacy that engendered it. It is these privileges that determine the persistence and reproduction of racism as an instrument of domination, exploitation, and, more contemporaneously, social exclusion to the detriment of all the scientific evidence that invalidates any support for the concept of race.

Support for racist ideology depends on its capacity to naturalize its conception of the Other. It is crucial for this dominated, defeated Other to express in their concrete condition that which racist ideology attributes to them. Words and things, form and content, must coincide so that the idea can be naturalized. A self-fulfilling prophecy – which confirms negative expectations for Black people – is indispensable to justifying inequality. In this sense, the poverty to which Black people in Brazil are condemned is part of the racist strategy of naturalizing the social inferiority of dominated groups – Black people, Afrodescendants, and indigenous people. Hence the necessity to establish a theoretical perspective oriented toward non-white people. As Carlos Hasenbalg says, "if the processes of social competition [. . .] operate to the detriment of the subordinated racial group, then the focus of analysis must shift to the forms of political mobilization of non-whites and to interracial conflict."[12]

## Raciality: Power, Knowledge, and Modes of Subjectification

Foucault cautions in the *The History of Sexuality. Volume 1: An Introduction* that his investigation into sexuality is directed more toward an *analytic* of power and less toward a *theory* of power.[13] I understand that by defining his approach to power in this way, he seeks to understand not what power is, but rather the way in which power is realized and manifests. It is not the nature of power that interests him, but the way that it operates. An analytic of power targets relations of force, or, as Foucault prefers, the co-relations of force that power engenders. He aims, therefore, to reveal the network of knowledge and power, but above all the strategic objectives, that a particular field of power seeks to realize. He ultimately tries to illuminate the game that society plays in relation to a field of power.

This analytical option would allow the undertaking of an archeology of knowledge and a genealogy of power that the apparatus produces and reproduces. Obviously, the modest intent of this study eschews any pretension of carrying out an archeology of knowledge and a genealogy of power as regards racial relations in Brazil. It is limited to presenting some of the discourses and practices that configure raciality. The domain to be analyzed is comprised by racial relations engendered in Brazil by the apparatus of raciality and also encompasses knowledge produced about it. Note that the term "domain" already presupposes a field of power or of domination. It is not by accident that we say that "someone masters [*domina*] a particular issue."[14]

From a Foucauldian perspective, I understand racial relations in Brazil as a domain that produces and articulates power, knowledge, and modes of subjectification. As Foucault declares in the case of sexuality, if raciality is presented as a domain to be understood, it is because power relations "had established it as a possible object; and conversely, if power was able to take it as a target, this was because techniques of power and procedures of discourse were capable of investing it."[15] First and foremost, raciality is understood here as a relational notion that corresponds to a social dimension, which emerges from the interaction of racially demarcated groups burdened by conceptualizations of human diversity that are historically and culturally constructed. From this notion stems the idea that white beings and Black beings are considered polarities that contain, respectively, cultural values, privileges, and prejudices that arise from belonging to each of the two poles of raciality.

My objective is thus to investigate discourses and practices produced in Brazil about raciality, which operate in particular detriment to the Black pole. Therefore, beyond the relevant primary bibliography, we will consider political discourse and the actions of activists and Black militants, as well as everyday occurrences recorded by the mainstream press about the racial issue and records of the life stories of Black people.[16] Finally, and no less importantly, the third part of this book adopts the resource of testimonials in agreement with Foucault regarding the "indignity of speaking for others."[17]

# Part I

## Power, Knowledge, and Subjectification

# 1

# On the Apparatus

## Foucault's Concept of the Apparatus

For Foucault, an apparatus is always an apparatus of power, which operates in a determined field and is revealed through the articulation that is produced from a multiplicity of elements and by the relation of power that is established among them. In addition, the apparatus expresses a strategic objective that responds to a historical urgency. Foucault says the following about his notion of the apparatus:

> What I'm trying to pick out with this term is, firstly, a thoroughly heterogeneous ensemble consisting of discourses, institutions, architectural forms, regulatory decisions, laws, administrative measures, scientific statements, philosophical, moral and philanthropic propositions – in short, the said as much as the unsaid. Such are the elements of the apparatus. The apparatus itself is the system of relations that can be established between these elements.[1]

Once it is constituted, an apparatus is available to be operationalized in different circumstances and moments, reproducing itself by means of its strategic fulfillment. If, in the constitution of an apparatus, the first step is to distinguish its heterogeneous elements, the second is to "identify in this apparatus [. . .] precisely the nature of the connection that can exist between these heterogeneous elements."[2] A discourse, continues Foucault, "can figure at one time as the programme of an institution, and at another it can function as a means of justifying or masking a practice which itself remains silent, or as a secondary re-interpretation of this practice, opening out for it a new field of rationality."[3] The point is that among these elements, discursive or not, "there is a sort of interplay of shifts of position and modifications of function which can also vary very widely."[4]

With a principal function of responding to some urgency in a determined historical moment, "the apparatus thus has a dominant strategic function."[5] My proposal is that this notion of the apparatus offers theoretical resources that are able to apprehend the heterogeneity of practices that racism and racial discrimination engender in Brazilian society, the nature of these practices, and the way in which they are articulated and are sustained or realigned to comply with a certain strategic objective. In synthesis, for Foucault, the apparatus consists of "strategies of relations of forces supporting, and supported by, types of knowledge."[6]

For my purposes here, it's especially important to underline that upon instituting a new field of rationality in which relations of power, practices, and knowledge are articulated, an apparatus establishes a division that has ontological effects, constituting subjects through enunciations about the Other.

Taking the production of madness as one of his examples, Foucault shows that the apparatus establishes a division by separating the normal from the pathological. To demonstrate this division, he undertakes a meticulous archeology of the constitution of madness at different historical moments prior to Western modernity, in which the mad were considered sacred. It was in the time of Descartes when madness would be considered an experience of "unreason"; from there the concept evolved to one of insanity, and finally to mental illness. In the case of the apparatus of mental health, two subjects emerge: the normal and the pathological.

This is the divisive practice that an apparatus institutes in the ontological field: the constitution of a new unit in whose nucleus is housed a new standard identity, and outside of it an opposite externality, but essential for the affirmation of that nuclear identity. Mental illness makes the normal person possible. Thus, if the normal person has to publicly say what they are, they will assert themselves through negativity: "I am not mentally ill." They define themselves in relation to the Other, who is constructed negatively to affirm the positive dynamic of the Self. That is, the Other established by the apparatus is presented in static form, which is opposed to the variation that is ensured to the Self. The dynamic instituted by the apparatus of power is defined by the dynamism of the Self in contraposition to the immobility of the Other.

By applying the notion of the apparatus to the domain of sexuality, Foucault attempted to understand why it was possible, from a particular historical moment onward, for sexuality to be considered as the privileged place of "our truth." The fact is that "Since Christianity, the Western world never ceased saying: 'to know who you are, know what your sexuality is.' Sex has always been the forum where both the future of our species and our 'truth' as human subjects are decided."[7] For an analysis of the domain in question, it is imperative to study its formation and development through the strategies that correspond to it, and Foucault locates a motivation, a class strategy, in the formation of the apparatus of sexuality. Control of sexuality, in modernity, is related to the demarcation of an identity for the bourgeois class and its political project. This strategy created a specific investment in the female body and the woman in the bourgeois family. According to Foucault:

> The first figure to be invested by the deployment of sexuality, one of the first to be "sexualized," was the "idle" woman. She inhabited the outer edge of the "world," in which she always had to appear as a value, and of the family, where she was assigned a new destiny charged with conjugal and parental obligations. Thus there emerged the "nervous" woman, the woman afflicted with "vapors"; in this figure, the hysterization of woman found its anchorage point. [. . .] For their part, the working classes managed for a long time to escape the deployment of "sexuality." Of course, they were subjected in specific ways to the deployment of "alliances": the exploitation of legitimate marriage and fertility, the exclusion of consanguine sexual union, prescriptions of social and local endogamy.[8]

According to Foucault in *The History of Sexuality*, even before the repression of sex among the exploited classes, the bourgeois class's sexuality was formed, in which the apparatus of sexuality was first established "as a new distribution of pleasures, discourses, truths, and powers."[9] That is, he suspects that before functioning to subject one class to another, the apparatus of sexuality functioned for the self-affirmation of the bourgeoisie, "a defense, a protection, a strengthening, and an exaltation that were eventually extended to others – at the cost of different transformations – as a means of social control and political subjugation."[10] Foucault continues: "With this investment of its own sex by a technology of power and knowledge which it had itself invented, the bourgeoisie underscored the high political price of its body, sensations, and pleasures, its well-being and survival."[11]

This conception of the construction of the bourgeois body signals the repercussions that the apparatus of sexuality will produce in the ontological field. The investment in the bourgeoisie's own sex will perhaps be implicated in a greater investment in its own bodies. That body will contain a new set of cultural meanings that, in turn, will turn the bourgeois body into a paradigm of humanity and the ideal of Being for the other classes.

Following the path of Foucault's observations about the strategy of affirming the bourgeoisie as the hegemonic class, I propose that we consider the process of class self-affirmation, beyond the constitution of the apparatus of sexuality, as accompanied by the emergence or operation of the apparatus of raciality, in which skin color would acquire a new status. There is something unsaid in Foucault's formulation: the imbrication of the apparatus of sexuality with that of raciality, the latter of which covers a greater territory than sexuality, because of the status that skin color has within it.

It is important to note here that Foucault's approach opens the possibility of an analysis which, by focusing on the domain of raciality, investigates the supposedly essential attributes of the hegemonic Self – which is therefore white – and of the Other. Recall that the Self is endowed with rationality because it has produced the mad; with normality because it has produced the abnormal; and with vitality because it has inscribed the Other with the sign of death.

My proposal is complementary to Foucault's vision by claiming that this Self, in its encounter with raciality or ethnicity, produced itself as superior by producing others as inferior, claiming rationality, normality, and vitality solely for itself because of its superior nature. The apparatus of raciality also produces a duality between positive and negative, where skin color is the factor that identifies the normal, represented by whiteness. Thus, an ontology of being and an ontology of differences are constituted. As Isildinha Baptista Nogueira states: "'Whiteness' comes to be the measure of artistic purity, aesthetic nobility, moral majesty, scientific wisdom, etc. Thus, the white person incarnates all virtues, the manifestation of reason, of the spirit, and of ideas: 'they are culture, civilization; in a word, humanity.'"[12] But for this construction to function, it requires the possibility of producing its own counterpoint, its negative, which is rejected "in order to establish the positive as desirable." This is the process that "inscribes Black people in a paradigm of inferiority in relation to white people."[13]

The apparatus of raciality, by designating humanity as synonymous with whiteness, goes on to redefine all remaining human aspects and hierarchize them according to their proximity to or distance from this standard.[14] In this way, white becomes the ideal Being for the Others, and the white woman a figure of mystique for non-white people. This way of affirming the bourgeoisie determined the desirable aesthetic standard for everyone, the form of love and sexuality, and corresponding morality, since the body was the expression of self-affirmation; after all, "the body functions as the mark of social values; it is in it that society fixes its meanings and values. Socially, the body is a sign."[15]

For Foucault, morality as dictated by the bourgeoisie is "a political ordering of life, not through an enslavement of others, but through an affirmation of self."[16] For, in order for this affirmation of the Self to become consistent, it must demarcate the difference between a new subjectivity and the rest. That is the basis of the common sense that claims that the lives of white people are worth more than those of other human beings. We can confirm this effect in the difference between how society reacts to cases of violence against white people of the hegemonic classes, which troubles them, while it responds with indifference to the genocide of Black and other non-white people. This is the origin of the white bourgeoisie's self-esteem and its role as representative of what is good and desirable in the world, establishing it as an aesthetic paradigm for everyone. This is also the source of racist biological theses that discuss racial mixture as a problem and a corrupting factor for nations and peoples, a topic I will return to in Chapter 10.

By appropriating sex and sexuality, constituting for itself a "'class' body with its health, hygiene, descent, and race,"[17] the bourgeoisie stakes out its distinction from and proclaims its superiority to the monarchy, then identified as degenerate, while affirming the legitimacy of its hegemony just at the moment of imperialist expansion to conquer non-white peoples.

The articulations between racism and sexuality that will be carried out are announced via the topics of progeniture and descent. Note that Foucault recognizes the historical trajectory of the topics of madness, sexuality, or racism, but what he is fundamentally interested in is determining the new reformulation and tactical functions they acquire as part of the strategic objectives pursued by disciplinary societies and subsequently by regulation societies[18] instituted by Western modernity.[19] In different ways, a process is developed of "purging" disease from the white body to deposit it in "other bodies." In Brazil and in other places in the world, various kinds of experimentation and research used Black and indigenous people as guinea pigs for the development of technologies for the wellbeing of white bodies. As we will see in Fátima Oliveira's testimony in Chapter 7, this has not ceased and continues until the present day.

Foucault locates the moment favorable to the resurgence of apparatuses in the eighteenth century, apparatuses that operate in the ontological field to construct the Other as a non-being.[20] For him, that is when new technologies of power are produced and put into circulation, technologies that, informed by a certain vision of ethnicity or raciality, will emerge as demands of the regulation society. I understand, therefore, that the constitution of the apparatus of raciality originates in a time before the emergence of the disciplinary society, in which it will acquire new meanings. This is what I demonstrate in what follows, supported by Charles W. Mills's theory of the racial contract.

## The Apparatus of Raciality, Whiteness, and Power

The theory of the racial contract outlined by the Black American philosopher Charles W. Mills creates the conditions for establishing a dialogue between Foucault's genealogical perspective and the construction of raciality as an apparatus of power. Mills locates the emergence of the racial contract at the end of the fifteenth century – first with the expeditions of conquest and then with European imperialism. In my view, the racial contract is what structures the apparatus of raciality.

In his 1997 book *The Racial Contract*, Mills maintains that the celebration of the ephemerides linked to Columbus's voyage and the critical evaluations and historiographic revisions of these events revealed the civilizational malaise according to which the world in which we live "has been foundationally shaped for the past five hundred years by the realities of European domination and the gradual consolidation of global white supremacy."[21] In Foucauldian language, we could say that the process that is customarily called "Discovery" caused the emergence of a new triad of power, knowledge, and subjectivities informed by raciality, yielding new subjects: men, natives, white, and non-white people.

Mills additionally unveils the existence of a political system unnamed by political theorists oriented toward an analysis of notions of democracy, liberalism, and representative governance "that has made the modern world what it is today,"[22] namely, white supremacy. This omission is not accidental but rather reflects the fact that the majority of political theorists are white, and do not see that their racial privilege is political and therefore "a form of domination."[23] A theoretical approach that challenges traditional political philosophy and incorporates questions of race and racism is therefore urgently necessary. In other words, it is necessary to recognize that racism – or, as Mills puts it, global white supremacy – is itself "a political system, a particular power structure of formal or informal rule, socioeconomic privilege, and norms for the differential distribution of material wealth and opportunities, benefits and burdens, rights and duties."[24]

This discourse of the social contract is the "political lingua franca of our times"[25] and maintains that the legitimacy of the government is ensured by the consent of individuals considered equals. To question this idea and reveal the extent to which it hides the reality of the modern world, Mills uses a particular contract, the racial contract. This is not a contract made between all individuals, but rather one "between just the people who count":[26] that is, white people. The specificity of the racial contract consists in the fact that it is a contract restricted to the racially homogeneous, in which racial violence toward the racially different is an element that sustains the contract itself, displacing those who are different to a state of nature. That is, the racial contract is a contract signed among equals "who count," in which those designated as not equals are included as objects of subjugation. This is why violence is what sustains it. Under the aegis of an ideal and supposedly neutral social contract, the racial contract establishes

> a racial polity, a racial state, and a racial juridical system, where the status of whites and nonwhites is clearly demarcated, whether by law or custom. And the purpose of this state, by contrast with the neutral state of classic contractarianism, is, inter alia, specifically to maintain and reproduce this racial order, securing the privileges and advantages of the full white citizens and maintaining the subordination of nonwhites.[27]

Contrary to the classic contractarianism of Thomas Hobbes, John Locke, Jean-Jacques Rousseau, and Immanuel Kant, oriented toward normative and factual questions regarding the origins of society and of governance, contemporary contractarianism, primarily adopted by John Rawls, is limited to the field of the normative and to justifying the basic structure of society.[28] For Mills, the Rawlsian version of the social contract abandons the historical and descriptive approach of classical contractarianism, aspects that he attempts to recuperate in his theory. He therefore returns to the classic theorists, for whom the social contract, in addition to being a normative instrument, is one which explains "the actual genesis of the society and the state, the way society is structured, the way the government functions, and people's moral psychology."[29] Following Rousseau's example in his *Discourse on the Origin and Basis of Inequality Among Men* – the most emblematic case of a contract theory to explain the emergence of a non-ideal society – Mills proposes not just an ideal approach to determine how a just society should be formed, but one that is also able to explain how, in reality, an unjust society comes to exist. By situating the racial contract in this non-ideal dimension, Mills does not negate its normative function, but this function shifts to its capacity to help us understand political reality and the way in which these very theories work to rationalize oppression. In this sense, says Mills, the racial contract approach should be enthusiastically welcomed by all those engaged in refining theoretical instruments and instruments of political action able to relate the ideal social contract to the real social contract. For him,

> The "Racial Contract" [. . .] is intended as a conceptual bridge between two areas now largely segregated from each other: on the one hand, the world of mainstream (i.e., white) ethics and political philosophy, preoccupied with discussions of justice and rights in the abstract, on the other hand, the world of Native American, African American, and Third and Fourth World political thought, historically focused on issues of conquest, imperialism, colonialism, white settlement, land rights, race and racism, slavery, jim crow, reparations, apartheid, cultural authenticity, national identity, *indigenismo*, Afrocentrism, etc. These issues hardly appear in mainstream political philosophy, but they have been central to the political struggles of the majority of the world's population. Their absence from what is considered serious philosophy is a reflection not of their lack of seriousness but of the color of the vast majority of Western academic philosophers (and perhaps *their* lack of seriousness).[30]

Mills goes on to maintain that, contrary to the ideal social contract, which establishes a civil society and a government to protect its signatories constructed through metaphors like the state of nature, the racial contract is historically datable and localizable in historical events such as colonialism and European imperialism's expeditions of conquest. The result, according to him, is a world "foundationally shaped for the past five hundred years by the realities of European domination and the gradual consolidation of global white supremacy."[31] The repercussions of this unnamed political system are evidenced in the white hegemony of societies founded through colonialism and white, Western imperialism.

For Mills, even if there is no formal act that substantiates the historical reality that is white supremacy, it can nonetheless be detected in innumerable acts that, as we have seen, take place in the way Foucault understands them.[32] Though Foucault does not serve as a reference for Mills, we can detect points of contact in his reflections, especially regarding the multiplicity of heterogeneous elements that constitute an apparatus of power and the network that develops among them, including what is said, what is not said, and the proliferation of discourses associated with raciality, which Mills detects in a variety of actions:

> papal bulls and other theological pronouncements; European discussion about colonialism, "discovery," and international law; pacts, treaties, and legal decisions; academic and popular debates about the humanity of nonwhites; the establishment of formalized legal structures of differential treatment; and the routinization of informal illegal or quasi-legal practices effectively sanctioned by the complicity of silence and government failure to intervene and punish perpetrators – which collectively can be seen, not just metaphorically but close to literally, as its conceptual, juridical, and normative equivalent.[33]

In this sense, the apparatus of raciality, as I understand it, benefits from the representations of Black people constructed during the colonial period which deal with the discourses and practices that justify the constitution of masters and slaves, articulating them and giving them new meaning in light of the racialism in effect in the nineteenth century. It is in this period that such representations begin to constitute an ideology, according to Hannah Arendt. As ideology was a political weapon of European imperialism that was consolidated in the period of the "scramble for Africa,"

> When the European mob discovered what a "lovely virtue" a white skin could be in Africa, when the English conqueror in India became an administrator who no longer believed in the universal validity of law,

> but was convinced of his own innate capacity to rule and dominate, when the dragon-slayers turned into either "white men" of "higher breeds" or into bureaucrats and spies, playing the Great Game of endless ulterior motives in an endless movement [. . .] the stage seemed to be set for all possible horrors.[34]

For my purposes, it is important to note that for Arendt, "Race-thinking, rather than class-thinking, was the ever-present shadow accompanying the development of the comity of European nations, until it finally grew to be the powerful weapon for the destruction of those nations."[35] What happened had repercussions for all multiracial societies founded by European colonialism and imperialism, which would produce patterns of social hierarchy that take raciality as their fundamental differentiator, as Mills shows.

## The Apparatus of Raciality in Brazil

In order to discuss the topic of the apparatus of raciality in Brazil, it is useful to note that Foucault understands discourse as a social practice that emanates from all points of power. Discourse contains the sense of the relations of power that engender it, but from Foucault's point of view, it is not legitimate to look for some hidden meaning in it, to the extent that this meaning is explicit in the knowledge that discourses produce.[36] Thus, social practices would be constituted discursively and discourses would form subjects and objects that adapt, move, multiply, or invert positions. What propels this dynamic, according to Foucault, is the subject's will to know the truth, instituting it as the place of truth.

If, as Foucault shows in the *History of Sexuality*, sex is what delimits a truth about the subject that defines its normality or abnormality, race also, in my understanding, delimits our apprehension of this truth. It is through race that the value of each human group is demonstrated, its humanity measured, its normality determined. Thus, knowledge about Black people is considered a discursive practice of differentiation according to raciality, which allows each individual to be socially determined through discourses of race produced within relations of power.

As Daniella Georges Coulouris explains,[37]

> The concept of power developed by Foucault is articulated with the idea of discourses. Discourses are formed within knowledge that is

> characterized by the mastery of certain objects and by the production of enunciations that claim to be more valid than others. There is no knowledge without power, just as there is no knowledge without conflict, without a clash among various different positions. Science institutionalizes the production of truths by retaining the power to produce and distribute true enunciations, and also by excluding, marginalizing, whatever might be outside of this world of reason and order. That is, the production of a truth is always confrontational.[38]

For Coulouris, the term "gender" has a theoretical as well as a political valence, insofar as it allows us to understand unequal social relations, as well as the idea that research on the topic works to modify undesirable gender relations.[39] In my understanding, the term "race" doubles this perspective. As a methodological instrument, it seeks to make possible a comprehension of the unequal relations between different human groups, more specifically the unequal treatment and unequal social conditions we see between Black and white people in Brazil. As a discursive practice, studies in this area aim to modify the social relations that produce racial discrimination and asymmetries. Nonetheless, there is a fundamental difference between race and gender in the academic realm, since, as Coulouris points out, "gender" is a term that "has always been articulated, directly or indirectly, with the questions reclaimed by feminists. Therefore, this knowledge cannot be understood as separate from political activism, because it comes out of problems posed by the European and North American feminist movement."[40]

For feminists, this identification between subject and object constructs the authority of speech or of feminist discursive practice, which is different from what happens with knowledge produced about Black people. Such knowledge is largely constructed as disconnected from Black people and their demands, even if it is possible to identify in many studies the intent to transform the social conditions that produce social inequality.[41] This absence of Black people in discursive practice is changing, though still tentatively. Areas of knowledge that specialize in "knowing the Other" have been created. The difference is then made into a topic of investigation, of the production of knowledge, of degrees, of recognition – power, that is – and additionally produces the insurgent knowledge that emerges from fields of resistance, disputing the production of truth about the dominated raciality.[42]

The first dissonant voice that emerges from this discursive realm is that of Guerreiro Ramos, who reclaims the place of subject in this field of thought from his position of belonging to the subalternized raciality. Before him, Luiz Gama had expressed another moment of self-affirmation as subject in the abolitionist debate and thought in which he saw himself implicated. Gama's inheritor in the twentieth century is the insurgent figure of Abdias Nascimento, whose vast theoretical production has never received its due recognition in Brazil, though he has been included internationally among the great figures of Pan-Africanism.[43] The reactions to these Black thinkers (all of whom have limited visibility in the field of race studies) demonstrate that the position of fully reflective subject is historically denied to them, just as Black vindication is discarded, in opposition to what takes places with knowledge about gender. According to Coulouris, in the field of gender studies, "the necessity to preserve the field of knowledge was combined with the defense of feminism's political goals."[44] Until recently, knowledge about Black people, knowledge about race, and the necessity to preserve this field were undertaken without the assistance of the interests, goals, and demands of Black social movements. In many cases, they were decidedly in opposition to these interests. Ari Lima identifies the displacement that historical subjection of Black people has produced in the production of knowledge:

> My subaltern voice thus speaks not just of economic and racial oppression, but also of a historical past where I lacked access to legitimated fields of knowledge and power, of the containment of Black-African symbols and values, of restrictions on speech, and of the difficulty in using categories and concepts that translate my experience as a Black intellectual to the Brazilian academy.[45]

In this sense, as Coulouris affirms, "central concepts for a theoretical consideration of gender – like the concepts of power, domination, ideology and discourse"[46] – are mostly absent as instruments of analysis in the majority of studies.

As far as studies about Black people in Brazil are concerned, Kabengele Munanga, the author of *Cem anos de produção bibliográfica sobre o negro no Brasil* (One Hundred Years of Bibliography about Black People in Brazil), signals in the preface that

> In fact, despite the chronicles of some Western voyagers in the seventeenth and eighteenth centuries about Black presence in Brazil, such presence was considered an "object" of academic investigation only at the end of the nineteenth century thanks to the pathetic appeals of Sílvio Romero. We had to wait almost half a century for the psychiatrist

> Raimundo Nina Rodrigues to respond to Sílvio Romero's pleas and initiate the first studies about Black people in Bahia, crowned by the publication of the work *L'animisme fétichiste des nègres de Bahia* [The Fetishist Animism of Blacks in Bahia] in Paris in 1900. Despite the slow pace and the lack of interest that characterized the first phase of research on Black people in Brazil – after Nina Rodrigues's death there was another period of silence, broken by his disciple Artur Ramos – studies about Black people began to diversify primarily in the 1950s. Black people went from being seen historically through the slave trade, slavery, and abolition, to merely biologically through physical differences. As the producers of an unequal culture, they came to be regarded as a social problem subject to sociological analysis within the anti-racist discourse of the time. [. . .] From the 1970s on, new areas of research emerged with the development of Black consciousness in social movements, enriched by discussions about reclaiming identities and strategies of social inclusion and participation, among other topics. Slowly and arduously, a few rare Black people began to penetrate the conceptual space of the human sciences, fomenting new lines of research into the problems of education, multiculturalism, and public policy within the context of affirmative action inspired in the United States and post-apartheid South Africa.[47]

Ari Lima points out the limits and contradictions in which Black intellectuals become entangled in academic spaces: would such spaces offer the possibility of denying the intellectual inferiority attributed to Black people, be spaces for confronting enshrined ideas, or merely be a strategy for assimilation? A similar list of questions to those Ari Lima poses could be situated – in the same analytical sphere as Charles Mills's analysis of African Americans – as another expression of the epistemological dimension of the racial contract, in racially hegemonic peoples' control of analytical categories essential to non-white peoples. For Mills, the question of the scientific objectivity of Black academic production is part of the general framework of scientific validation that upholds power in the academic sphere, and that derives from a "conceptual array and a standard repertoire of concerns whose abstractness typically elides, rather than genuinely includes, the experience of racial minorities."[48] The strategy is to obstruct the emergence of alternative conceptualizations. The result, in Mills's view, is the fact that, particularly in political philosophy, "Those African American philosophers who do work in moral and political theory tend [. . .] to produce work indistinguishable from that of their white peers."[49]

As I have indicated, by formulating the theory of the racial contract, Mills has the perspective or objective of establishing a conceptual bridge between hegemonic political philosophy, which, according to him, is sustained by abstractions about justice and rights, and the conceptual and political agenda resulting from the concrete history of non-white peoples. The new generation of Black intellectuals who broke the barriers that historically limited, impeded, and closed off Black people's access to institutions of higher education turn these same conditions into a strength, contributing new questions that their academic disciplines had not tackled in their entire history. As Osmundo de Araújo Pinho and Ângela Figueiredo declare in their provocative article "Ideias fora de lugar e o lugar do negro" (Ideas Out of Place and the Place of Black People):

> The field of Brazilian social sciences, especially that which deals with the study of racial relations, forms part of the history of race relations in Brazil. It both feeds the interpretations that enter into actual discussions, going beyond the academic field per se, and, by constituting legitimated models of reading reality, helps to hide what it should illuminate: the relations between the production of knowledge and the unequal structure of Brazil's racially marked society. [. . .] What seems out of place are not necessarily the ideas, but Black people when they are not pinned down into a category, subjugated as an object, or represented as an allegory.[50]

My premise is that in the context of Western modernity, raciality has come to be constituted as an apparatus as conceived by Foucault. Raciality is understood as a notion that produces an ontological field, an epistemological field, and a field of power, consequently shaping knowledge, power, and modes of subjectification whose articulation institutes an apparatus of power.[51] To understand how this happens in Brazil, we must remember that slavery corrupted the value of work: since work was compulsory for the slave, there was no way for it to be considered positive for the white master. Freed from work by the existence of the slave, he became addicted to idleness. Manual labor was stigmatized by the equally stigmatizing tradition of slavery. In this context, abolition would represent the moment of Black people's emergence into the new disciplinary order introduced in Brazil, when the economy based on slave labor transitioned to one based on free labor. The apparatus of raciality, as an apparatus of emerging disciplinary power, will demarcate this new status in theoretical acts of subjection, similar to what Muniz Sodré, in a different context, identifies as "a kind of ontological symbol of the subaltern economic and political classes."[52]

This is how Black people emerge from history to enter the sciences; the passage from slavery to freedom represented the passage from object of work to object of study. The invisibility of Black presence that gradually unfolds in Brazil contrasts with the vast academic production that would develop around this new condition as an object of study. It is an epistemicide that constructs a field of knowledge founded in a manifesto, a convocation, as we could consider Sílvio Romero's call to be. Its counterpart is also the increasing whitening of social representation. These are two strategies that at the level of the construction of the country's social imaginary promote the whitening of all dimensions of social life.

## Black People as Objects of Science

As could be anticipated by the references to Osmundo de Araújo Pinho and Ângela Figueiredo – whose work demonstrates the conflicts that currently envelop white and Black intellectuals in academic production about racial relations – even after investigation of these topics intensified, Black people were absent as subjects of knowledge. This extraordinary production about them as objects occurred by considering them field informants, and thus without welcoming them as political subjects and subjects of knowledge. Many times, Black resistance was disqualified via an appeal to raciality as a factor of subordination and social exclusion, prone to being mobilized to overcome socially constructed racial differences. This negation reiterates the reified character that Black people have acquired in society and the relations of power that are imbricated in this process of objectification, adjusting to Foucault's view that knowledge and power are mutually implicated, since, after all, "there is no relation of power without the constitution of a field of knowledge, just as, reciprocally, all knowledge constitutes new power relations."[53]

Sílvio Romero offers, in my view, the best expression of the process of objectification of Black people in Brazilian sciences:[54]

> It is shameful for Brazilian sciences that we have not dedicated more of our works to the study of African languages and religions. [. . .] When we see men like Bleek[55] hiding out for dozens and dozens of years in the middle of Africa just to study a language and document a few myths, we who have material at home, have Africa in our *kitchens*, as we have America in our *forests*, and Europe in our *salons*, we have produced

> nothing in this regard. It is a disgrace. [. . .] Just as the Portuguese remained in India for two centuries and discovered nothing scientifically extraordinary, leaving the glory of the revelation of Sanskrit and the Brahmic scripts to the English, so we foolishly allow our Black peoples of the Coast to die as worthless, and we will leave the study of so many African dialects that are spoken in our *senzalas*[56] to others! *Black people are not just an economic machine; they are, above all, and despite their ignorance, an object of science.*[57] [. . .] Specialists should make haste, seeing as the poor *moçambiques*, *benguelas*, *monjolos*, *congos*, *cabindas*, *caçangas*[58] [. . .] are dying. The best opportunity, one could say, is passing with the merciful extinction of the slave trade. Make haste, lest you lose them completely.[59]

In this text from 1888, Sílvio Romero makes explicit the strategic objectives that the apparatus of raciality harbored up until his time. The first strategic objective to which the apparatus of raciality lent itself was justifying the transformation of Africans into an "economic machine." Articulated within the periodization Dante Moreira Leite proposes,[60] this would be in the nativist phase. Once the phase of exploiting slave labor for the primitive accumulation of wealth and capital had passed, the establishment of a field of knowledge about the diversity that racialism instituted turned Black people into objects of scientific study, possible sources for understanding of human evolution, and for scientific experimentation.

Romero also makes clear the admission of a field of power in which this knowledge that would be constructed about Black people should emerge – whether touching on language or religion – from the unexploited raw material in our *senzalas* and kitchens. This is what he compares to the "glory of the revelation of Sanskrit and the Brahmic scripts." He contrasts the academic discipline of the English to the indigent contribution of the Portuguese to the sciences. And he especially expresses the conviction that Black people are doomed to extinction, given that their condition of "economic machine" has been left behind due to the exhaustion of the economic model based on slavery and the criminalization of the slave trade. Black people have no place in the emerging economic order and, due to their ignorance, present limited characteristics that make them suitable objects of science. Thus, Brazilian "men of science" should be diligent in their scientific dissection. Romero makes clear that there is a field of knowledge that also institutes a field of dispute and of power at an international level, into which Brazilian researchers should enter. Therefore, with the selection of Black people as an "object of science," a field of knowledge is established that institutes a field of power, prestige, and glory. Above all, it is constituted as a space where knowledge and power are disputed by and among white people, which, conversely, excludes Black people from being producers of knowledge and wielders of power.

Romero would not appeal in vain, and from the end of the nineteenth century on, we would see a growing objectification of Black people in Brazil's social sciences. At first, studies of Black people were driven by anthropology, but other disciplines got involved as the scope expanded to studies of racial relations and racial inequalities; it thus also became a field of dispute for Black intellectuals and activists.

Amid all this vast theoretical production about Black people, the year 1988 presents us with a second situation: in the year of the Centenary of the Abolition of Slavery, a commission of notable Brazilian intellectuals and researchers who were specialists in racial topics was formed without the presence of a single Black person. The coordinator of the commission explained the flagrant absence in the following terms: "The problem is that as of now we have not found anywhere in an elitist country such as ours a single Black PhD in history, however hard we searched."[61]

Throughout the twentieth century, there was an intense production of knowledge about Black people, with a proliferation of research institutes and centers of African studies and of racial relations across the country, which granted degrees and made white researchers and intellectuals famous as "specialists in Black people," confirming Romero's prediction. It was a case of knowledge and institutions appropriated by white people who shaped interpretations and modes of subjectification for Black people. This was the state of affairs that explains why a century after Abolition, the nation's "intelligentsia" was incapable of finding a Black historian in a setting in which there was ample historiographic production available from the likes of Joel Rufino, Clóvis Moura, and Milton Santos.

In its more contemporary version in Brazilian universities, epistemicide – a discussion of which we will delve into more deeply later on – also manifests in the antagonism between activist discourse and academic discourse, through which Black activist thought is disqualified as a source of authority in knowledge about Black people, while white people's discourse about Black people is legitimated. As a general rule, white and hegemonic production about racial relations dialogues with itself, delegitimating the production of Black researchers and activists about the topic. This is patent in the bibliographic references used in academic publications, in which non-Brazilian Black authors figure, and also in the fact that few Black Brazilian intellectuals achieve national and international prestige.

Black activists, with a few notable exceptions, are treated by specialists in racial issues as *sources of knowledge*, but not as authorities on the topic. Black researchers are also reduced to the role of sources and are not considered interlocutors in academic dialogues, especially when they are not limited exclusively to the topic of Black people. Black people's progress in racial relations has promoted some Black activists from the role of mere object to that of primary source, with a certain incipient status of primary manifestation of the issues that justify the field.

Let us now return to Foucault's analysis of the domain of sexuality: "One must not suppose that there exists a certain sphere of sexuality that would be a legitimate concern of a free and disinterested scientific inquiry were it not the object of mechanisms of prohibition brought to bear by the economic or ideological requirements of power."[62]

Here, let us substitute the term "raciality" for "sexuality." Along the same lines, continuing the parallel with Foucault's thinking, if raciality is constituted as a domain of knowledge, this constitution took place as a result of the relations of power that instituted it as a possible object. In exchange, if power could take it as a target, this was because it became possible to invest in raciality via techniques of knowledge and discursive procedures in the service of colonization, domestication, eugenics, or repression, as other scientific disciplines also did (psychiatric forensic medicine, anthropology, criminology, craniology, etc.). Each one constituted a domain in which raciality was studied to the detriment of Black raciality and non-white raciality in general. The case of Black raciality in Brazil was no exception.

To sum up, ever since Romero's call, the Brazilian intelligentsia, as Foucault describes, has not ceased interrogating this "object," while simultaneously excluding it as a subject of knowledge. The lack of recognition of Black intellectuals and the objectification of Black activists as primary sources of research anticipate the topic of epistemicide that operates in strict consonance with the apparatus of raciality.

## The Grand Narrative

As Foucault says, "speech is no mere verbalisation of conflicts and systems of domination, but [. . .] it is the very object of man's conflicts, the power that we wish to seize."[63] He indicates that the internal order of discourse is derived from discourse itself, since "we can isolate another group: internal rules, where discourse exercises its own control; rules concerned with the principles of classification, ordering, and distribution. It is as though we were now involved in the mastery of another dimension of discourse: that of events and chance."[64]

In the Brazilian case, the discourse that molds racial relations is the myth of racial democracy. Its construction and persistence until today in themselves evidence its strategic function, which is above all to appease racial-ethnic tensions.

For Jessé Souza, racial democracy is our foundational myth, which aspires to offer the perspective of "the development of a superior civilization in a mixed-race land." Nevertheless, he continues, this would be "a contradiction in terms, given that the superior intellectual and moral functions that allow 'civilization' were attributes of the white *race*."[65] Grounding his analysis in empirical studies, Souza demonstrates that racism was the only "prejudice whose explicit and wide denial by the majority was shared by all classes without distinction."[66] Souza goes on to argue that if it is undeniable that there is no real racial democracy in Brazil, on the other hand we must consider the wide rejection of racial prejudice as an indication that "racial democracy is, in some measure, a project nourished by all social strata."[67] Unfortunately, he disregards the complex mechanisms that historically determine the silence, denial, and invisibilization of the racial problematic.

This is what perhaps makes the myth of racial democracy a grand narrative that reveals the existence of an agreement to accept this discourse with all its consequences.[68] It is illustrative of what ex-president Fernando Henrique Cardoso says in the opening speech of the International Seminar "Multiculturalismo e Racismo: O papel da ação afirmativa nos estados democráticos contemporâneos" (Multiculturalism and Racism: The Role of Affirmative Action in Contemporary Democratic States), organized by Brazil's Secretaria Nacional de Direitos Humanos (National Human Rights Agency) in July 1996. He states:

> I always remember – and I've referred to this on more than one occasion – a meeting that took place many years ago in the Ministry of Foreign Relations in Rio de Janeiro. I was a sociology assistant and I worked with professors Florestan Fernandes and Roger Bastide, two eminent sociologists whose work was dedicated to the problem of relations between Black and white people in Brazil. And, perhaps with a certain ingenuousness, I referred to the fact that there is, in fact, prejudice in our country. At the time, saying that was like making a statement against Brazil. The person moderating the panel – someone highly respected – was bothered by the statement, and at the end, they confessed that they had almost asked me to remove myself from the meeting. They then gave me a few compliments to compensate for having revealed their deep displeasure with the fact that I had said that there was color-based prejudice in Brazil.[69]

At another point in the speech, Cardoso continues: "up until the 1950s, Brazil believed itself to be a racial paradise. From then until now, however, many things have changed; indeed, we have discovered that we are not as given to tolerance as we believed."[70] He then warns:

> Nonetheless, we should not exaggerate this criticism and self-criticism, since it is true that, on the one hand, hypocrisy exists, and, on the other, openness. Such ambiguity coexists in our cultural character, and it is necessary to take advantage of it. Perhaps due to my temperament, I am not very Cartesian. In my understanding, a certain dose of confusion and ambiguity improves things and makes them easier; indeed, an excess of clarity is sometimes divisive.[71]

As we have contended in previous work,[72] it is important to remember two elements from the ex-president's speech: the *divisive* character that the admission of racism or of racial prejudice has in our cultural tradition, which has reached the point that such an admission is considered "a statement against Brazil" or almost a question of national security; and the *naïveté* that certain people incur when they dare to express that racism exists in our country, in the face of the pact of silence in which this problem is immersed.

The myth of racial democracy corresponds to a desire for society's self-representation and a positive portrayal of the country in the presence of an "internalized and scientifically legitimated inferiority complex."[73] It lends itself to the construction of a positive identity for a country whose concrete reality impedes it from actually realizing Westernization, whether racial or cultural. As Sílvio Romero declares in the *História da literatura brasileira*

(History of Brazilian Literature), "All Brazilians are *mestiço* [mixed-race], if not by blood, in our ideas. [. . .] There's no point in arguing if this is good or bad; it's a fact and that's that."[74]

In an article that I published in *Correio Braziliense*[75] in 2000, I asserted that the racial miscegenation present in our society has lent itself to different political and ideological uses.[76] First of all, miscegenation has been used to support the myth of racial democracy, inasmuch as sexual intercourse among white, indigenous, and Black people would be the principal indication of our "racial tolerance." This is an argument that leaves out the colonial rape practiced by the colonizer against Black and indigenous women, the scope of which is being revealed by genetic research that indicates that more than half of those in Brazilian society who suppose themselves to be white carry some genetic marker of Black or indigenous ancestry.[77]

Second, miscegenation has become an effective instrument for whitening Brazil, through the institution of a chromatic and phenotypical hierarchy with dark-skinned Black people at the bottom and *brancos da terra* ("whites of the land"; native-born whites) at the top. It offers the symbolic benefit of proximity to the human ideal – which is white – to everyone in between. This has particularly impacted Black Brazilians, considering that this social imaginary implies a supposedly greater social acceptance of lighter-skinned people compared to those with darker skin, and it appears to explain the diversity of expressions that Black people and their mixed-raced descendants adopt to describe themselves racially, such as: dark brown, light brown, golden brown, chocolate brown, mulatto, *mestiço*, *caboclo*, *mameluco*, *cafuzo*, that is, confused, such that all are put together in the IBGE's official category, *pardo*![78] And "*pardo*" is something that no one manages to define, either as a race or as a color. Perhaps the term is only useful to describe all those whose ethnic and racial identity was destroyed by racism, discrimination, or the symbolic social burden that blackness carries with it, and who no longer know what they are or simply don't want to be what they are.

This kind of differentiation has been efficiently working to fragment Black identity and prevent those who identify as Black from joining together politically to collectively demand racial equity, given that, contrary to what the social imaginary would imply, *pretos* and *pardos* (to use the IBGE nomenclature) comprise a group that according to social indicators have similar and equally inferior living conditions when compared with white people. This is the reason that today the category of *negro* is defined politically and sociologically as the sum total of those whom the Census classifies as *pretos* and *pardos*.[79]

Yet, the extensive miscegenation and praise of racial mixing have not been able to change Brazilian society's historically produced desire to whiten everyone. As Kabengele Munanga states:

> Despite the failure of society's process of physical whitening, the white ideal inculcated by means of psychological mechanisms that it could not explain remained intact in the Brazilian collective unconscious, always whirling in the heads of Black and mestizo people. This ideal hinders any effort to form an identity based on "blackness" and "racial mixing" since everyone dreams of one day being admitted to the white identity, which they consider superior.[80]

An article by Otávio Frias Filho also measures the imposition of this mode of subjectification on those who suppose themselves to be white[81] as well as their consciousness of the precarity of their whiteness. The article shows that "the solid presence of blonde women in the media's and showbiz's imaginary is not such a frivolous or gratuitous phenomenon. [. . .] It is sufficient to page through luxury magazines' displays of wealth and leisure to verify the advance of 'blonding' as the next phase of 'whitening.'"[82] "Blonding" is that which, as Frias continues to note, is "motivated, perhaps, by progress in cosmetics which facilitates chromatic change."[83]

The whitening ideal has not been abandoned. It is imposed on the social imaginary by the dominant culture through the permanent exhibition of its symbols, which express their material and symbolic success as a demonstration of their "natural" superiority, systematically compared with the symbols of the stigmatization of blackness – their necessary counterpoint. The media, "in order to portray poverty, misery, delinquency, illiteracy, ignorance, human indigence, make abundant use of Black people."[84] And in order to prop up the myth, they promote a minimal and subordinate integration of Black people who do not comply with the stereotypes established in the images circulated by mass media, especially in advertisements. The very exceptionalism of this integration reiterates the arbitrary rule.[85]

Racial mixing has been used to bar the implementation of policies that promote social equality for Black people, such as affirmative action. Among the arguments made against these policies, a key one is the impossibility of determining who is Black in Brazil, considering, again, racial mixing.

Critics of the Black Movement's[86] position challenging the myth of racial democracy and its contraposition to the North American model of racial relations – which, in its forthright and explicit institutionalization, is considered by activists as less harmful than the Brazilian model – look in different ways to redeem the positivity of the idea of racial democracy. Jessé Souza seems to validate the myth with the following argument: "Since myths have nothing to do with falsehood, but rather with the hopes and real desires of human communities, we don't see how the Brazilian myth of racial democracy shouldn't be considered an interesting sociopolitical project."[87]

The consequence of this view, for Souza, is that "to reject it as pure lies is more than unwise, it is dangerous. It is to choose the isolation of a discourse of the resentful that is founded on the unstable efficiency of taking political advantage of a guilt complex."[88] As a result, the Black Movement's political criticism of the fallacy of Brazilian racial democracy is de-authorized, first, as the result of ignorance or the lack of knowledge made clear in the inability to understand the dialectical articulations between myth and reality; and, second, through an alleged pathology in the political behavior of those who position themselves in such a way, a type of unreason, founded in resentment. Souza also brings up the implicit idea that unmasking the myth as a historical and social untruth seeks to assign blame that, besides being ineffective, reveals political opportunism. In addition, he gives a warning that could sound like a threat, because the "isolation of a discourse" he refers to could be translated to political isolation, since it makes alliances invisible – alliances without which change would not be possible. It requires us to presume that in the negotiation of a new agenda for racial relations, the cultural patrimony of the myth should be preserved.

The big question to be raised is the following: why do so many intellectuals, the majority of whom are white, strive with such determination to "defend" the myth of racial democracy, while an inverse ratio of Black people, especially activists in the anti-racist struggle, endeavor to condemn it? Souza gives us other clues: "in the context of the inferiority complex, internalized and 'scientifically' legitimated, the myth of racial democracy becomes a fundamental compensatory feature."[89] He is referring to nineteenth-century racist paradigms, especially those related to racial mixing, which were fundamentally pessimistic about the possibility of "the development of a superior civilization in a land of mixed-race people,"[90] as we have previously cited.

Souza thus understands that these negative characteristics attributed to a mixed-race society like ours would be "counterbalanced" by the racial tolerance we have achieved, which would offer us a moral reserve in relation to civilized countries: an unforeseen civilizing capacity, the offer of a new paradigm to the world through which to consider the question of human diversity. The valorization of our cultural character produced a civilizing view such that "all the positive ideas that Brazilians associated with themselves are represented in this myth: sensuality, affection, tolerance, cordiality, etc."[91] And, principally, our aptitude for peace, above all understood as the absence of racial conflict.

The myth of racial democracy opens a critical dialogue between Brazil and dominant countries, in which tolerance and the absence of racial conflict are indicative of other potentialities that our country would offer as proof of the promise of economic and cultural power on the world stage.

A second and recurring criticism levied by white intellectuals against Black activists' efforts to unmask the myth of racial democracy consists of casting their position as "subservient to the methods and instruments adopted in the United States, as though their situations were the same."[92] This argument implies, on the one hand, a condemnation that affirms a nationalist perspective of Black people, who should value the "cultural ambiguities" specific to our character. On the other, it refuses to recognize that the Black diaspora shares a common historical situation of enslavement and racial oppression, as well as a cultural ethos determined by the subjective and objective forms of resistance to this oppression. Above all, the Black diaspora shares the challenge of collective emancipation across all the societies of the world where it is distributed. This makes Black culture, wherever it manifests, part of the heritage of Black people everywhere.

Foucault also examines non-discursive elements in his analysis of power through the notion of the apparatus. His analysis considers material components, like the *architectural organization* that the apparatus engenders. And nothing could be more paradigmatic of this construction than the image of *Casa-Grande & Senzala* enshrined in Brazil's social imaginary.[93] Beyond designating a celebrated and classic work, it constitutes an architecture that continues to be re-created historically in other binaries and structures, such as skyscrapers and favelas, mansions and tenements, stilt houses, *quilombos*, *malocas*, etc.[94]

A binary that has taken on a significance independent of its empirical structure to symbolize racial asymmetries is the differentiation between the service elevator and the social elevator. Also rooted in the Brazilian imaginary is the idea of having "a foot in the *senzala*" or "in the kitchen," expressions that sometimes indicate one's class and other times indicate one's race, but which almost always mean both.

The architectural metaphor derives from a wider process of intersections between blackness and territoriality. As Luís Mir explains,

> Brazil's territory was sliced up for the purpose of colonization, and later, during Independence and Abolition, to keep Indians, Africans, and mixed-race people from improving themselves and forming a new ethnic and geographic map, of which these populations became a part. [. . .] [The] official fomentation of European emigration was the tool employed to attempt the definitive physical and economic destruction of the ex-slaves before the formal abolition of slavery in 1888, which sets off the process of Africans'extermination and social suffocation. [. . .] Colonial hubs were planned for the new inhabitants that would give rise to new Indo-European cities [. . .] and they received streets, housing developments, and abundant credit, among other benefits. The ex-slaves never received land, credit, education, or assistance in this country.[95]

These are cornerstones of the racial contract in Brazil and examples of the logic that promotes the inscription of racialities into a sphere beyond discourses, like the biopower that we will deal with hereafter.

In his analysis of racism, Foucault had in mind the German experience of the Holocaust. He did not, however, consider racism as an apparatus of power in multiracial societies with slaving pasts, in which racism operates to discipline, order, and structure racial and social relations and in which the contradictions of class and race are confused. Poverty is established as the chronic condition of Black existence, insofar as class mobility comes to be controlled by raciality. This dynamic has a paralyzing effect on the dominated group, resulting in its confinement in the lowest strata of society and producing modes of resistance that frequently function as a mechanism of inscribing the subjugated raciality in the dynamic of the apparatus, and less as a strategy of emancipation.

The field of resistance links Black people to the apparatus of raciality as its necessary counterpart, with the understanding that where a field of power is instituted, resistance is produced. And resistance creates conditions for reinsertion in the apparatus, for a negotiation with power, and for disputes about historical truth. Keeping in mind that Black people are collectively taken as non-bearers of civilizing elements and racially undesirable for the project of the nation that is designed from the Republic, the first possibility for including them in the "new" society will happen individually. It follows that individual social mobility is allowed, which is the keynote of the process of social inclusion of Black people. This social inclusion will happen by recognizing exceptionality understood exclusively in the individual sphere. And it will be even more acceptable if this exceptionality can be disassociated from the physical and symbolic markers of blackness. In this sense, de-racializing oneself – refusing or camouflaging racial identity in discourse and in practice – is an imperative condition.

The other possible reaction to the apparatus of raciality comes from the formation of a collective subject who demands their rights, who seeks recognition as a political subject. This recognition will lead to the transformation of social pacts by including Black people as a collective.

On an individual level, it is more common that Black people are considered incapable of meeting the requirements for inclusion. As a collective, we have achieved scarce social achievements throughout our history. The articulation of the individual and collective spheres has meant that the majority of Black Brazilians have remained consigned to the logic of biopower. Nevertheless, resistance need not lead only to a reinsertion in the apparatus of raciality, or mean that only exceptional individuals can be included, while the majority of Black people remain consigned to the racist logic of biopower. This is how it has been, but emancipation can and should be for everyone. And this will happen through political struggle.

# 2
# Biopower
## Blackness under the Sign of Death

This chapter demonstrates that the apparatus of raciality, which has a subalternizing function for human beings according to race, gains a specific dimension when it operates in conjunction with biopower and is instrumentalized by it. Within biopower, gender and race are articulated together, producing specific effects. As regards the female gender, this becomes evident, for example, in the emphasis on technologies of reproductive control, which manifest differently according to raciality. As regards the male gender, simple violence manifests.

Foucault shows that biopower emerges when, in the nineteenth century, power takes hold over life, and consequently there is an inclination toward "State control of the biological."[1] There is a fundamental difference between the mode in which this biopower is exercised in comparison to the mode in which the right to sovereignty used to be exercised. If the sovereign – who had as one of his fundamental attributes the right over life and death – could "have people put to death or let them live," biopower is constituted as the power to "'make live' and 'let die'." The former concerns death, since, after all, "it is at the moment when the sovereign can kill that he exercises his right over life,"[2] while the latter principally comes to concern life and to regulate it in different and ever more comprehensive ways:

> Beneath that great absolute power, beneath the dramatic and somber absolute power that was the power of sovereignty, and which consisted

> in the power to take life, we now have the emergence, with this technology of biopower, of this technology of power over "the" population as such, over men insofar as they are living beings. It is continuous, scientific, and it is the power to make live. Sovereignty took life and let live. And now we have the emergence of a power that I would call the power of regularization, and it, in contrast, consists in making live and letting die.[3]

The transformation that Foucault refers to here takes place, above all, in the ambit of the technology of power: in seventeenth- and eighteenth-century disciplinary societies, the techniques of power were essentially focused on disciplining the body of the individual (the "man-as-body"), while in biopolitics they operate upon a multiplicity of people (the "man-as-species"): that is, on human masses and populations.[4] This is not, in fact, substituting the regulation of the population for the discipline of the individual, but rather a complementary relationship, since the technique of discipline – which surveils, trains, and punishes bodies – shows itself to be insufficient to govern the economic and political body of a society "that was undergoing both a demographic explosion and industrialization":[5]

> To be more specific, I would say that discipline tries to rule a multiplicity of men to the extent that their multiplicity can and must be dissolved into individual bodies that can be kept under surveillance, trained, used, and, if need be, punished. And that new technology that is being established is addressed to a multiplicity of men, not to the extent that they are nothing more than their individual bodies, but to the extent they form, on the contrary, *a global mass that is affected by overall processes characteristic of birth, death, production, illness, and so on*. So after a first seizure of power over the body in an individualizing mode, we have a second seizure of power that is not individualizing but, if you like, massifying, that is directed not at man-as-body but at man-as-species.[6]

This "massifying" seizure of power can only take place by regulating life processes – birth, death, longevity – which come to be statistically measured and programmed. The very notion of "population" with which biopolitics deals emerges in this context as a scientific and political problem, "as a biological problem and as power's problem."[7] It is less about the right to kill and more about the right to intervene to make the population's masses live. Foucault thus says that the technology of power comes to be centered on life, no longer (or not just) on the body. And since the disciplinary mechanism of the body and the regulating mechanism of life are distinct, they can be linked. This occurs, for example, in the city, where a series of disciplinary mechanisms are exercised on the body – urban spatial division, the placement of houses in the city and of the rooms in houses – and regulating mechanisms are imposed on the population: security systems; hygiene regulations to ensure longevity; regulations on sexuality and procreation, etc.[8] The society that emerges under the effects of the double wager of discipline and regulation is, in Foucault's words, a normalizing society.[9]

We must ask, however, where the exercise of the power to kill enters into the scheme that explains biopolitics – which itself acts principally upon life. How is it possible, the author asks, that in these conditions, political power comes to kill, "to call for deaths, to demand deaths, to give the order to kill, and to expose not only its enemies but its own citizens to the risk of death?"[10] It is here that racism intervenes, and while it had existed prior to the nineteenth century, it was inserted into internal state mechanisms by the emergence of biopower. Racism operates to fragment the field of the biological, which power has taken over, divide it according to "races," and thus introduce a rupture between those who should live and those who should die.

But this is not the only function of racism in biopolitics. Beyond the negative role of fostering division, racism fulfills what is in some sense a positive role: "The very fact that you let more die will allow you to live more."[11] It is true that the logic of this relationship – "if you want to live, you must take lives" – is characteristic of war, which pre-dates both the state and modern racism. State racism allows this warlike relationship to function as a biological relationship in a completely new way that is compatible with biopower. For Foucault, power's calculation happens as follows:

> The more inferior species die out, the more abnormal individuals are eliminated, the fewer degenerates there will be in the species as a whole, and the more *I – as species rather than individual – can live, the stronger I will be, the more vigorous I will be. I will be able to proliferate.*[12]

Consequently, the death of the Other – who is Other because they are degenerate and of an inferior race – allows biopower to promote the life of the healthier and purer race. In other words, racism is indispensable for power, while biopower, whose fundamental function is promoting life, takes life. "Once the State functions in the biopower mode," Foucault reminds us, "racism alone can justify the murderous function of the State."[13] As he says, the state takes life in two ways: through direct murder and indirect murder, in the latter case when it exposes someone to death, when it multiplies the risk of death, when it promotes the political death of those who are racially "inferior."[14]

It is from this perspective that I inscribe blackness under the sign of death, from an analysis of the distinctions that arise in the process of birth–disease–death or simply in the process of Black and white people's living–dying in Brazilian society. These are processes in which genetic predispositions are united with the production of differentiated living conditions, promoting, as Foucault states, caesuras within the field of the biological.[15] This is, for him, the first function of racism. The second, as we have seen, consists in the elimination of those who are inferior, impure, abnormal, or different, which is the condition of social asepsis: "something that will make life in general healthier: healthier and purer."[16]

This book proposes that multiracial societies that have resulted from colonization engender the apparatus of raciality as a disciplining and normalizing instrument of racial relations. As I understand it, this apparatus works to discipline and normalize racial relations in postcolonial societies as well as relationships of sovereignty with societies understood as racially inferior. Biopower is fundamental for this purpose; after all, it was an "indispensable element in the development of capitalism; the latter would not have been possible without the controlled insertion of bodies into the machinery of production and the adjustment of the phenomena of population to economic processes."[17]

The definition of bodies and of the parts of the population suitable to support this process of capitalist development at the time of nascent industrialization in Brazil would determine the racial stock appropriate for the task. The racial predispositions established for each human group would support these choices. Adjustments to the task of populating would take place, on the one hand, through immigration policy, as we have already discussed, and, on the other, through the racial contract, in which whitening is as much an aesthetic and eugenic project as a strategy of promoting racial groups considered suitable for supporting the process of economic modernization.[18]

To carry out this task, it became necessary to produce docile bodies, to train them, to maximize their physical profitability. But biopower doesn't stop there. In order to "make live and let die," hostility and contempt must be socially consolidated around one social group. Like a kind of associative automatism, these feelings and portrayals become sufficient to direct the distribution of social benefits. In my view, wherever biopower has no interest in disciplining, subordinating, or choosing the subordinated social segment within the power relations constructed by raciality, it comes to act as a strategy to eliminate the undesirable Other. Biopower activates the apparatus of raciality to determine who should die and who should live.

In this sense, from the nineteenth century on, Brazil would also assist in the emergence of new public health procedures into which raciality would intervene by orienting them in a corrective eugenicist direction that presumed especially promiscuity, established in slavery. Disciplinary techniques are joined to this new technology of power, with the innovation that they exercise the power to make live and let die without having to institutionalize race, but by disposing of mechanisms that can reach it wherever it may be hidden, to distribute life and death.

In this context, in the data that have been produced by various different research agencies about violent deaths in Brazil, we hear the echo of Foucault's statement that "the right of life and death is always exercised in an unbalanced way: the balance is always tipped in favor of death."[19] It is this imbalance that I will subsequently describe as a strategy of biopower.[20]

Raciality in Brazil causes the health–disease–death process to present distinct characteristics for each one of its vectors. Thus, whiteness and blackness have different conditions for living and dying. Foucault, by inscribing racism in the sphere of biopower, clarifies that the latter, as a technology of power aimed at preserving the life of some and abandoning others to die, lends itself to determining whether to let die or let live. Employing the maxim "let live and let die" as an expression of biopower, he identifies racism as what legitimates the right to kill, which will be exercised by the state through action or omission, in a direct or indirect way.

Studies of racial inequality identify the juxtaposition and/or articulation of adverse life conditions with sexism and racism as determining the situation of racial inequalities that manifest in different dimensions of social reality, and especially in the field of the Black population's health. Some authors have identified that in the last few decades in Brazil, mortality rates – for example infant mortality – have significantly changed for different social groups and ethnic/racial groupings, causing the nation to effectively see a reduction in the mortality rate of children under one year of age.

According to Estela Maria Garcia de Pinho da Cunha, in the period between 1977 and 1993, this reduction was 57%. Yet, the author cautions us about this fact that

> when the color variable is introduced, one realizes that the white infant mortality rate for children under one year of age fell by 43% in this period, while the reduction of the Black infant mortality rate was significantly less, just 25%. [. . .] A second relevant aspect is that racial inequalities were exacerbated over time. Thus, while according to the 1980 census the relative difference between mortality rates of Black and white children under one year of age was 21%, almost twenty years later, this value had risen to 40%. These findings suggest that, comparatively, the children of Black mothers increased their exposure to risk of disease and death.[21]

Thus, under the aegis of biopower on the subordinated pole of raciality, disadvantages set in from infancy, in which genetic factors accumulate with unfavorable life conditions to inscribe blackness under the sign of death. As a counterpoint, whiteness is configured as a sign embodied in greater life expectancy and lower mortality and morbidity rates as a result of privileged access to socially constructed assets. However, what we argue here is that "let live and let die" defines the conditions of life and death to which raciality will be submitted in all its vectors by the power of the sovereignty that informs it and decides on the value of each life and each death in the sphere of raciality.

In what follows, we will offer examples of recurring practices in our society that inscribe raciality in the biopower logic of "let live and let die" pervaded by processes that naturalize the value of life and death: raciality inscribes whiteness in the register of life and blackness under the sign of death.

## Black Women: On Preventable and Avoidable Deaths

> In the loneliest of places, I examine every decision I make within the light of what I've learned about myself and that self-destructiveness implanted inside of me by racism and sexism and the circumstances of my life as a Black woman.[22]
>
> Audre Lorde

In medical literature, avoidable deaths are those that should not have occurred if adequate preventative measures had been taken.

The Brazilian feminist movement has made use of this concept particularly to refer to the deaths of women from preventable disease, that is, those that could have been avoided; and when women become ill from such diseases, they should have had access to curative treatment. Thus they are deaths that should not have occurred.

In the 1980s, the feminist movement created an emblematic image illustrating the magnitude of this phenomenon across the world. They said that when a plane crashes, it creates a worldwide commotion, because in general, it is difficult for anyone to escape. Yet, although the number of women who die giving birth every day is equivalent to the number of deaths in a jumbo jet crash – an infrequent occurrence – these women's deaths don't stir public opinion in the same way.

Today in Brazil, maternal mortality is still a classic example of preventable and avoidable death. For the World Health Organization (WHO), the concept of maternal mortality encompasses deaths that take place at any phase of pregnancy, during childbirth, postpartum, and up to forty-two days after. The organization also works with the concept of late maternal mortality, that is, death that occurs up to a year after giving birth. On the WHO scale, acceptable maternal mortality is from 0 to 20 per 100,000 live births; Brazil exhibited a very poor index of around 120 maternal deaths per 100,000 live births. In developed countries and, in the particular case of Cuba, which already has the maternal mortality rate of a developed country, no more than 10 women die per each 100,000 live births.

At the beginning of the twenty-first century, Brazilian capitals had a maternal mortality rate of 74.5 per 100,000 live births, with the number one cause of maternal death being preeclampsia, or untreated high blood pressure during pregnancy. This is attributed to the quality of prenatal care offered to new mothers or to a lack of follow-up during pregnancy; it can also be attributed to malpractice, since more than 90% of births take place in a hospital. That is, in Brazil, women have children in hospitals with this unacceptable number of deaths according to WHO standards. However, according to the feminist doctor Fátima Oliveira, whose testimony we will see in Chapter 7, 96% of maternal deaths are preventable and avoidable, since pregnancy and childbirth are not diseases but, rather, physiological conditions.

When we see the racial breakdown of maternal mortality rates in Brazil, we face several problems related to gathering the color question in research, especially national studies commissioned by the Ministry of Health. In the first place, they contain estimates based on case studies. In the first of these, by Alaerte Martins,[23] the racial/ethnic breakdown is investigated in maternal deaths in the state of Paraná. Martins' data are the first that make a national projection, though they are not actually national data but rather case studies projected on a national scale that deal with the color question in maternal mortality.

The conclusions of this study are that 6.6 times more Black women die from maternal death than white women in one of the most developed states in Brazil. In addition, this study has a novel finding: self-declared Asian women in Paraná die seven times more than the others.

According to Fátima Oliveira, the higher mortality of Black and Asian women suggests the necessity for in-depth research into the racial/ethnic dimension of maternal mortality in Brazil. In relation to the unexpected data regarding Asian women, Oliveira signals that they were likely subject to the same negligence that other studies have identified in the care that pregnant Black women have received, and to the dismissal or lack of acknowledgement of the human being's biological condition in healthcare and specifically in childbirth. Proceeding with this in mind, along with Oliveira, we will leave aside the human being as concrete entity and will deal with the human as abstraction that takes white raciality as its paradigm.

Martins' findings about Asian women highlight this problem since, theoretically, Asian women exhibit a better social situation than Black and white women in terms of socioeconomic indicators, which gives them access to better-quality healthcare. Nonetheless, they show a higher mortality rate than Black women in the state of Paraná. For Oliveira, this phenomenon can be explained by the lack of attention to possible factors unique to the Asian population, unknown to healthcare professionals, since, according to her, human beings' biological conditions make them more or less biologically predisposed to certain causes of morbidity and/or mortality. Thus these unique factors should be understood in order to take preventative action when what is at stake is the protection of women's life and health.

Yet the disqualification of the importance of life according to raciality instills and prescribes this negligence, disdain, and refusal to prioritize the attempt to recognize and understand these unique factors.

The available data allow us to state that Black women have the greatest predisposition to high blood pressure (which, as we have noted, is the number one cause of maternal death in Brazil) and that during pregnancy this biological predisposition, under adverse conditions, disadvantages them. Therefore, these biological predispositions must be understood to diminish their effects in unfavorable conditions. Biological conditions that become more critical when linked to unfavorable social conditions are aggravated, inscribing Black women in a vicious circle of greater incidence and risk of maternal death.

Neglecting protection in childbirth is part of a negative dynamic of Black raciality that entraps these women in a vicious cycle of systematic violation of their reproductive rights. A study undertaken by the Oswaldo Cruz Foundation (Fiocruz) and the municipality of Rio de Janeiro identified racial discrimination in both public and private hospitals and maternity hospitals in the city of Rio de Janeiro. The study tracked 10,000 women immediately following childbirth between June 1999 and March 2001, and controlled for education level and socioeconomic class. The conclusion of this study was that there is differential treatment for Black and white pregnant women evident in less attention paid to the former. This inequality manifests in a variety of medical procedures such as: the use of pain relief during birth; fetal heart monitoring; measuring the size of the uterus during prenatal visits; responsiveness to concerns during prenatal visits; and permission to have a companion present before and after childbirth.[24]

Sharing these results, which confirm the presence of racism in healthcare as an institutional practice determined by a differential perception of the value of each life according to color, had intense repercussions in the media and provoked strong reactions from healthcare professionals, who attempted to discredit the study and alleged that the authors did not understand the procedures described within it. This reaction was based, in general, on a refutation of the facts described. The Regional Board of Medicine of Rio de Janeiro (Cremerj), through the director of the Technical Chamber of Gynecology and Obstetrics, stated that they did not believe that racial prejudice against pregnant Black women existed and that what could have happened was that

> poorer pregnant women without education do not have the financial resources or sufficient discernment to find a good healthcare facility or public hospital and end up disadvantaged. [. . .] In some places, such as

> Baixada Fluminense [on the outskirts of Rio], care in public hospitals is very poor, regardless of the color of the person. [. . .] It happens that the majority of patients in these places are poor and a large number of them are Black. Since Black pregnant women form the majority, the study ended up concluding that they received worse care, when in reality, there are few white women. [. . .] Not even today, working as I do in a private clinic, have I witnessed things of this nature. An obstetrician doesn't care about color. The pregnant woman is our patient.[25]

Kátia Rato, one of the coordinators of the study and coordinator of the mother–child sector of the Municipal Office of Health of Rio de Janeiro, rebuts this type of allegation, referring to her own shock at the results. According to her: "It was a surprise, we didn't know we were going to find this difference." The other coordinator of the study, Silvana Granado, of the Fiocruz National School of Public Health, said: "This left a great impression on us. At first we thought that we were comparing people of different socioeconomic classes and levels of education. But when we saw that the difference persisted, we were shocked."[26] Controlling for the education and socioeconomic class variables, the researchers could not find any other explanation for their results besides prejudice both in prenatal care and in childbirth. Rato also alludes to the fact that "discrimination has still not been scientifically verified because none of the doctors are aware that they are acting with prejudice."[27]

In an article about the results of this study,[28] Fátima Oliveira demonstrates the consistency of these technologies of biopower applied to the Black populations of the world and how this bias appears in health-related studies. According to her:

> I mentioned evidence of racism in research in two studies undertaken in the USA. The Canto Study, coordinated by John Canto of the University of Alabama (2000), showed that Black people, independently of sex, have much lower probabilities than white people of receiving efficacious treatment for heart attacks. The Tuskegee Experiment, a classic story of racism described in the film *Miss Evers' Boys*, reveals that from 1932 to 1972 the United States Public Health Service experimented on 600 Black men – 399 with syphilis and 201 without – to observe the evolution of syphilis in the untreated, none of whom were informed that they had syphilis nor about the effects of the disease, only that they had bad blood. In the 1950s a cure for syphilis arrived with penicillin – prohibited for the guinea pigs of the Tuskegee Experiment, in the entire USA! After forty years, there were 74 survivors. More than 100 died of syphilis or complications from it. The Centers for Disease Control and Prevention (CDC) in Atlanta was responsible for the final phase of the

study. In 1997, when Bill Clinton apologized for the errors and abuse committed by the US government, there were just eight survivors!

In the same article, Oliveira concludes with a call to action informed by other examples of abandonment and instrumentalization of life:

> It's time to act, since only the banalization of institutionalized racism tells us why, a half century after Nuremberg, British scientists' experiments with children in Sierra Leone (1994) were as cruel as the Nazi extermination camps, and explains that the fear of racial discrimination keeps the parents of Black and Hispanic children in the USA away from hospitals, as evidenced in a study by the doctors Donna Ronsaville and Rosemarie Hakim of the Health Care Finance Administration in Baltimore, Maryland (2001).[29]

The growing lack of confidence in the treatment of Black patients motivated an unprecedented complaint filed by Sueli Rocha Rodrigues. As a twenty-three-year-old pregnant Black woman at nine months of gestation, she heard racist comments in the José Soares Ribeiro general clinic, waiting for the Vespasiano Maternity Hospital, in the metropolitan region of Belo Horizonte. According to the magazine *Hoje em dia*, what happened was as follows:

> According to the chief of police Benvindo Antônio Ferreira, he [the doctor] was charged with the crime of verbal assault motivated by racism, according to the third paragraph of article 140 of the Penal Code. He will be released pending trial. The complaint was made after negative comments about poor and Black people. Sueli recounts that she went to the hospital after beginning to feel contractions. While she was waiting to be seen, she allegedly heard the doctor remark to two of the hospital's receptionists that he "hated Blacks," that they "were a wretched race" and that "Blacks and poor people had to die." According to the student, the statements were allegedly made after comments about President Luiz Inácio Lula da Silva's visit to Africa.[30]

According to Sueli's statement, in addition to her, there were two other Black youths awaiting care, and one of them allegedly left in anger after hearing the doctor's opinions. She says that:

> Since I could not leave due to my condition, I decided to call the police. I was outraged. [. . .] But what world was I bringing my child into if I didn't start to combat this type of attitude now? I had endured prejudice before, but now, because of my condition, I couldn't anymore. [. . .] I heard this doctor say he hated Black people. Have you thought about

> if something happens to me and I end up in the hands of a person like that? He could kill me through negligence, contempt, anything. I'm glad I reported him.[31]

In an interview on local radio the doctor denied the accusations and alleged that he had a nine-year-old adopted Black son at the time, as well as many Black friends. However, the receptionists who were involved in the situation and were called as witnesses confirmed Sueli's complaints. The doctor was released by the police chief to await trial after posting bail of 2,400R$ (reais).

Another area that reveals negligence in the Black population's heathcare is the lack of recognition of the issue of myomatosis, which disproportionately affects Black women. Fibroids (myomas) are tumors that occur only during a woman's reproductive years. They begin between menarche (first menstruation) and menopause, since they are estrogen-dependent tumors. Thus, menopause tends to diminish their size as a result of reduced estrogen production, and they never first appear in this phase of life. Fátima Oliveira clarifies:

> Uterine fibroids are the most common tumors among women and affect close to 20% of women during reproductive years (between the first menstruation and menopause). In general, they are "silent tumors," in that they don't have symptoms, they are benign (less than 1% of fibroids become malignant), grow slowly, and the majority shrink in size, on their own, after menopause.[32]

Oliveira points out that evidence-based medicine has robust literature about the problem of uterine fibroids and their relationship to raciality. According to her, on a national level, there are serious, important, and revealing studies of the problem, and yet the medical class and the Ministry of Health do not take them into account because these studies were not carried out by doctors.

This is the case regarding studies done by Vera Cristina de Souza during her master's and doctorate[33] on hysterectomy. It is a topic to which healthcare professionals interested in the health of the Black population have not been able to draw attention and recognition, whether for healthcare professionals – especially doctors – or for healthcare policy makers.

According to Oliveira, this is due to two factors: first, a medical culture that does not accept a non-doctor as a producer of knowledge; and, second, the fact that fibroids seem to point to a biological predisposition but that they can appear or not according to particular conditions. This preponderance of biological factors at the root of the condition, according to her, could be one of the reasons that doctors distance themselves from a discussion of fibroids and other diseases – for example, sickle cell anemia – with the same profile. Oliveira further states that there is evidence that without a shadow of a doubt points to the fact that Black women have a greater biological predisposition to developing uterine fibroids – and that the medical attention paid to white and Black women with fibroids, as for rich and poor women with the same disease, is quite different.

In *Oficinas mulher negra e saúde* (Black Women and Health Workshops),[34] Oliveira tells us that the greatest incidence of fibroids in particular racial/ethnic groups puts them in the category of racial/ethnic disease. If there are many cases in a single family, fibroids could be considered an inherited disease. There are strong indicators that the origin of fibroids is genetic, probably a polygenic condition. There are studies that demonstrate that the incidence of fibroids in Black women is high – five times greater than in white women. And it is twice as high among white Jewish women from Eastern Europe as in the remaining white population. Various studies have also demonstrated the high incidence of fibroids in Black women, and several have indicated that obesity and contraceptive pills with high doses of estrogen stimulate the appearance and growth of fibroids.

The data relayed above were collected in the United States, and indicate that Black women develop five times as many fibroids as white women; they are corroborated by studies carried out by Vera Cristina de Souza in Brazil. Considering that Black women have greater difficulty than white women in being diagnosed, the scale of the problem is frightening.

As for treatment, Oliveira points to three basic medical procedures. First, fibroids can be treated through observation: that is, the fibroids are diagnosed and then observed; the practitioner notes whether they grow or stay the same. Second, there are two surgical options: myomectomy, removal of the tumors (generally women develop more than one tumor), or hysterectomy, the surgical removal of the uterus, could be indicated. Fibroid surgery is indicated, in general, when a woman's abdomen or uterus reaches the size of a three- to four-week pregnancy, because a uterus with a tumor of this size is uncomfortable, heavy, and can lead to serious problems for the patient, such as the urgent need to urinate, recurrent bleeding, etc. Finally, there is a technique of uterine fibroid embolization, which embolizes the arteries that supply the fibroids, impeding the circulation of blood, thus causing the tumor to atrophy until it disappears. It is a highly regarded and assessed non-surgical technique, though new, but it is quite expensive (in 2003 uterine fibroid embolization cost around 8,000R$),[35] and so inaccessible for the majority of Black women.

What happens to Black women with uterine fibroids? Oliveira identifies overlapping problems associated with reproduction and raciality. The high incidence of sterilization of Brazilian women, especially Black women (*pretas* and *pardas*),[36] and the fact that hysterectomy, unlike tubal ligation, has always been paid for by the Sistema Único de Saúde (SUS, Unified Health System),[37] makes it impossible to know whether Black women more frequently undergo sterilization through the removal of the uterus or through tubal ligation.

In any case, the two techniques are carried out disproportionally on Black women, resulting in a process of population control of the Black population: that is, the application of the technology of biopower. The previously mentioned doctoral study by Vera Cristina de Souza,[38] for example, analyzes the SUS data on hysterectomy. She identifies greater relative access for Black women to hysterectomies, attributing this to political causes: the uterus of a Black woman has no value, so any presence of fibroids indicates the removal of the whole organ. De Souza shows that medical treatment of women differs depending on whether they are Black or white. Conservative treatment, the use of medication or observation, is generally indicated for white women regardless of social class; for Black women, on the contrary, hysterectomy is indicated.

But Oliveira is emphatic in declaring that Black people of all ages die prematurely in Brazil from preventable and avoidable causes. Thus the premature death of Black people lays bare the racism in medical (un)care. And what is more, making this phenomenon invisible is a time-tested and successful political strategy that is also sexist and racist. This, for Oliveira, explains the difficulties researchers face in the biomedical field and the education system related to the racial/ethnic dimensions of research and healthcare.

## Black Men: Violence as a Mode of Subjectification

> With the passage of time people have seen how Black men behaved with police and how police behaved with us. [. . .] But with Black men the police were always the same: arrest them! They knew it wouldn't be a problem.[39]
>
> José Correia Leite

In *Discipline and Punish*, Foucault demonstrates how disciplinary apparatuses, through the effects of their strategic fulfillment, created an environment of delinquency that was institutionalized in the carceral system, of which panopticism is the emblematic expression. In Brazil, the post-abolition period consolidated Black raciality as the environment of delinquency *par excellence*, even producing a legal apparatus for it, the Vagrancy Law.

In his article "Vadiagem" (Vagrancy), Lúcio Ronaldo Pereira Ribeiro demonstrates the origins and objectives of this penal apparatus. According to Ribeiro, the criminal offense of vagrancy is present in Brazil's legal system starting with the Philippine Ordinances[40] in Title LXVIII, "On Vagrants," and later appears in the Imperial Criminal Code of 1830. As Ribeiro points out,

> The Empire's characterization of Black people as criminal was subsequently maintained, augmented by an explicit link to the practitioners of capoeira, who, at that time, would be considered vagrants. It is interesting to observe that, even today, in capoeira *rodas*[41] and environments, the term *vadiar* (to loiter) is used to mean that the capoeirista is playing capoeira and that someone who is playing capoeira is a vagrant. [. . .] Here is the legal text from the Penal Code of 1890 [. . .]: "Art. 402. Engaging in public streets and squares in exercises of skill and bodily ability known by the name of *capoeiragem*; *running around*. [. . .] Penalty: 2–6 months' imprisonment."[42]

This seems to be the source of the popular saying according to which "an idle Black man is a suspect; a running one is a thief." Ribeiro exposes the meanings and the priority targets of this type of crime:

> An analysis reveals the following regarding the terms of the punishment set out by the law: at the time of the ordinances, punishment was very severe, and consisted of lashes. Nonetheless, this punishment was only applied to those who had lords and masters, from which we conclude that they were only applied to slaves. [. . .] In the Penal Code of the Republic [. . .] punishment was greater than that prescribed in the Penal Code of the Empire, consisting of forced labor and prison terms. Upon completing the sentence, the offender also had to swear that they would not remain in a situation of vagrancy.[43]

The discretionary implications of race and social class present in these prescriptions do not go unnoticed by Ribeiro and he synthesizes them in the following way:

> At the time of the ordinances, the victims of these injustices were slaves, that is, the Black, mulatto, and white people in situations with the fewest remedies. [. . .] However, not just enslaved and freed people, but all those who did not fall under the master–slave relationship. [. . .] In the code of the Republic, which followed the abolition of slavery, sentences that consisted of a prison term with forced labor were increased.[44]

This classification places into relief the symbolic character of abolition, whose promulgation on May 13, 1888, put an end to slavery. Slavery, however, would return to the legal system two years later by means of the Vagrancy Law and its punishment of forced labor and imprisonment. And this occurred in a context in which the majority of the male workforce consisted of the formerly enslaved kept out of the labor market.

The Vagrancy Law, in my view, is an example of the rule of continuous variations that Foucault mentions in his analysis of power. It promotes the institutionalization of the formerly enslaved in organs of repression, since, as Ribeiro confirms, "even after completing their sentence, the offender still remained in a way linked to the prior criminal case, because, as part of it, they would have signed the pledge to no longer engage in vagrancy – a pledge that was frequently broken."[45]

This analysis also introduces a crucial dimension which implies, on the one hand, the apparatus of raciality and demarcates, on the other, its impact under the aegis of biopower with the advent of the Republic. This is an example of the rule of double conditioning made explicit by Foucault. According to Ribeiro:

> The industrial elite, which controlled the government, preferred an immigrant labor force over the class of vagrants, of the indolent, that is, over the domestic labor force, and this is how the contingency of vagrants increased significantly. Thus the government incentivized foreign immigration. [. . .] Foreign immigrants who came to work in Brazil at the end of the nineteenth century took the place of recently freed slaves in farming. These relations were governed through the law of leasing of services – restricted to rural areas – that even prescribed a prison term to those who did not comply with the contract. As a rule, these were long-term contracts, and if the conditions were a little better than those of the enslaved, they were not good. The majority of the regular and disciplined work was done by the immigrant labor force. [. . .] Thus vagrancy was the typical crime of the formerly enslaved who wandered the streets, since they had no land, shelter, work or possessions.[46]

The availability of this sector of the population to be deployed as army reserves was therefore assured for any need or strike the capital might face:

> Without a doubt, this mechanism of control was quite an effective aggravating mechanism for controlling the poor, minority labor force, particularly Black, mulatto, *cafuzo*, *mameluco*,[47] mixed-race and poor foreign people. The description of this type of vagrancy, without considering the possibility – quite common at that time – of unemployment, principally in the case of Black and mixed-race people, would theoretically initially allow anyone who was not working to fit within this legal category, which would at a minimum result in the shame of being detained and/or taken into police custody.[48]

Coming and going did not constitute a right for these people, but rather occurred at the discretion of police repression:

> The police officer is the one who makes the initial classification, and thus finds himself with great power in his hands: the power to restrict a person's liberties every day. On the part of the detained or imprisoned person or those who could be portrayed with this profile, there was a growing expectation of vulnerability before the police, since they knew that they could always – and probably would – be approached by the police because of the characteristics that made them suspicious and dangerous.[49]

As a result, since Black men were displaced from the sphere of work after abolition, they were also excluded from the disciplinary techniques of work. Nonetheless, their social existence was still subordinated to this new technology of power. Disciplinary techniques are applicable to the body that produces, and in the post-abolition period, places of work were reserved for immigrants, not for the formerly enslaved. Fernando Henrique Cardoso's assessment is masterful in its unmasking of the intent behind this legal apparatus. Since vagrants are those who do not work,

> all that happened after abolition was the emergence of a large excluded mass, in the sense of people who no longer had a place on the social ladder. The enslaved had a terrible place, but they had a place. Emancipated people have no place. The emancipated, the formerly enslaved, and the descendants of the enslaved made up the first large marginal population. That is: the actual transition from enslaved to citizen had not occurred.[50]

The mechanisms of social control of these masses for whom there was no intention of inclusion would be inscribed in the ambit of technologies that arose from biopower, through which the state would exercise its rights to kill or "let die." In "A cor da morte" (The Color of Death), a statistical and criminological study of the victims of homicide in Brazil, the authors, Gláucio Soares and Doriam Borges, presume in the very title of the study the inscription of blackness in Brazil under the sign of death. They note regarding their findings that:

> The results demonstrate the existence of a relationship between gender, age, marital status, and skin color, on the one hand, and victimization, on the other – relationships that are repeated every year and in virtually every state [in Brazil]. The lack of more precise data makes a systematic study of these relationships in the country across decades impossible, but we can now know that death has a color. This relationship was previously suspected, but there was no way to demonstrate it, because color was absent in many Brazilian statistics. The absence of color had green and yellow tones, in a kind of patriotic fundamentalism that denied racial discrimination and its effects.[51]

The technologies of biopower delimit different forms of taking hold of the target body according to gender. As we have previously seen, control of the Black female body takes place fundamentally by "letting die" or through control of reproductive capacity. In the dimension of biopower in which the previously mentioned study is situated, the strategic target is the Black man and violence becomes the constitutive grounds for the production of the Black masculine gender.

In *Mapa da violência IV* (Map of Violence No. 4), produced by UNESCO[52] with data collected from sixty-seven countries, Brazil is in fourth place, only after Colombia, the Virgin Islands, El Salvador, and Venezuela. In Brazil, youths between fifteen and twenty-four years of age are the group most frequently killed. It turns out that when the data are disaggregated according to color, they reveal that blackness is imbricated in mortality. Among Black youths, violent deaths are 74% higher than among white youths. "Letting die" comes about, in this case, by abandoning Black youths to the war of drug trafficking, to which they contribute as soldiers destined to kill and be killed, confirming Foucault's declaration that "the right of life and death is always exercised in an unbalanced way: the balance is always tipped in favor of death."[53]

Under the sign of death, of "letting die," Silvia Ramos and Leonarda Musumeci demonstrate that urban violence in Brazil presents patterns defined by the United Nations as indicators of civil war: 350 deaths per 100,000 inhabitants, just in Rio de Janeiro, a phenomenon that is repeated at similar levels in other states.[54] The overwhelming majority of victims are young, Black, and poor, victims of lethal violence, and are murdered, as a general rule, by other young, poor, and majority Black men.

According to Ramos and Musumeci, it is a fratricidal war in which gender, race, and class violence are articulated, entrenching a true genocide of Black men. Indifference to this slaughter finds its counterpart in the indignation that assails the country when the victims of violence are white, upper-class people.

In a 1996 report from Human Rights Watch on the problem of police violence in Brazil, James Cavallaro defines as the key point a disinterest on the part of police and judicial authorities in investigating crimes, stating: "Once having established that the victim was a *marginal*,[55] the investigations were effectively closed [. . .] effort is only made when the police commit a gross error and kill a white, middle-class person."[56] When the victim is a socially well-positioned Black person, it is the wrong Black person. Such was one of the most emblematic cases of the biopower dynamic in Brazilian society: a young Black dentist murdered by military police appeared profiled in a press outlet with the epithet that I discussed in the article "O negro errado" (The Wrong Black Man), with the following allegations:

> A Black man suspected of robbery has been killed. A mistake. After all, Black people are all the same, especially in the dark! But the mistake must be corrected. It is easy to do so by reconstructing the stereotype embedded in the social imaginary: a Black individual, who is armed, resists arrest, police defend themselves, and he is killed. In his pocket is found the wallet belonging to the victim of the robbery that just took place. Mission complete. What went wrong in this case? He was a dentist, he had a military father who knew his son's character and the military's practices well enough not to believe the official police version of what had happened: resistance followed by his death and a witness who refused to be an accomplice to a summary execution, who ran the risk of becoming yet another case. They are not used to apologizing. In an editorial about the case titled "Police racism," the *Folha de São Paulo* indicates: "This time they got the wrong Black man." It is true, because it happens every day, with complete impunity and societal indifference, on the periphery of Brazilian cities where the poor, favela-dwelling

> "right Blacks" are. According to anthropologist Luis Eduardo Soares, they are subject to stereotypes created by police: "the dead youth is always a drug trafficker in confrontations with the police." The "killer kit" is always ready to plant a weapon and some drugs on the victim to reproduce the same story.[57]

He was the "wrong Black man" because he was out of place: he was educated, with a white-collar profession, and social capital that allowed him to avoid a pauper's burial. It was his military father who triggered the mechanisms that made the case impossible to ignore, leading the authorities responsible for the police's choices in action on the streets to speak out publicly. They treated the case as a mistake or a lamentable error, which disguises the fact that it is

> the result of a police culture with a Lombrosian bias, based on the principle of kill first and ask later, a permission to kill ensuing from impunity insofar as violence and people's basic human rights go, people whose rights and full humanity are not recognized. This is why some of the basic principles of human rights do not apply to Black people: those of not being arbitrarily imprisoned or detained and the presumption of innocence. Unarmed, and not resisting arrest, Flávio Ferreira Santana's body was assassinated first, followed by his character.[58]

As we have seen, Foucault lays out a distinction between technologies of power instituted by disciplinary apparatuses and the new technologies of power instituted by biopower. It is evident that apparatuses also concern technologies of power that aim to train the body, especially for work. They are techniques to control and improve the productivity of the body, as has been seen in Brazil, for example, under the aegis of the modernization effort of the post-abolition period. Thus the apparatus of raciality aimed to tame the white body, the body destined for free work, though it also reached Black bodies that eventually were able to escape murder.

I propose in this book that the mixture of the apparatus of raciality with biopower becomes a mechanism with two consequences: it promotes the lives of white people and the "multicide" of Black people in the sphere of biopower. Under the aegis of the apparatus of raciality, the majority of the racially elect are prioritized and included in the spheres of the reproduction of life, as, at the same time, are the subordinate minority of Black people who eventually survive biopower's technologies of death.

Thus, in the segments of society inscribed in the dominated pole of raciality, biopower establishes a dynamic in which the "cides"[59] await them as actions or omissions of the state, while society shows itself to be complicit, tolerant, or indifferent. In Brazil, blackness is inscribed under the sign of death through extermination, homicide, physical or moral assassination, poverty and chronic misery, the absence of policies of social inclusion, and negative differential treatment in healthcare access. As Foucault states:

> The specificity of modern racism, or what gives it its specificity, is not bound up with mentalities, ideologies, or the lies of power. It is bound up with the technique of power, with the technology of power. It is bound up with this, and that takes us as far away as possible from the race war and the intelligibility of history. We are dealing with a mechanism that allows biopower to work. [. . .] So you can understand how and why, given these conditions, the most murderous States are also, of necessity, the most racist.[60]

In this context, Black resistance is often configured as an attempt to penetrate the disciplinary society, into which the descendants of European immigrants and others are already integrated in the dimension of power. Others, such as Asians, are admitted to the privacy of hegemonic Being.[61] The majority of the time, Black resistance is configured in a dramatic effort to preserve the first and most basic of human rights, which is the right to life. But there is also another dimension of resistance, which fights for life and is not content with entering society as it is, since it signals the necessity of society's actual transformation, disarming the triggers of biopower and subjection imposed by the apparatus of raciality, as indicated by the witnesses that we will call in Part II.

# 3
# Epistemicide

Thus far I have sought to demonstrate the existence of an apparatus of raciality that operates in Brazilian society as an instrument to articulate a network of elements defined by the racial contract, and which determines the system of production's functions and activities as well as social roles. Now I will deal with locating epistemicide within this scenario as a constitutive element of the apparatus of raciality.

It is important to remember that the concept of epistemicide employed here is taken not from Foucault's theoretical apparatus, but rather from Boaventura de Sousa Santos. For him, epistemicide comprises one of the most effective and lasting instruments of ethnic and racial domination, by negating the legitimacy of knowledge produced by dominated groups and, consequently, negating the members of these groups, who come to be ignored as knowing subjects.

This concept developed by Santos makes it possible to understand the process of dismissing the Other's rationality, culture, and civilization, which took place and continues to take place in Brazil. In *Pela mão de Alice: O social e o politico na pós-modernidade* (By Alice's Hand: The Social and the Political in Post-modernity), Santos holds that epistemicide derives from the civilizing vision that informed the colonial enterprise and reached its full formulation in nineteenth-century racialism. In describing the violence inherent in the colonial process, he unveils two of its fundamental elements: genocide and epistemicide. For him,

> the genocide that so often marked European expansion was also an epistemicide: foreign peoples were eliminated because they had foreign forms of knowledge and foreign forms of knowledge were eliminated because they were sustained by foreign peoples and social practices. But the epistemicide was much more extensive than the genocide because it took place in every attempt at subalternization, subordination, marginalization, or illegalization of practices and social groups that could threaten capitalist expansion or, during a good part of the century, communist expansion (just as modern as capitalist expansion in this domain); and also because it took place in peripheral, extra-European and extra-North American spaces within the world system, such as in Central Europe and in North America against workers, Native people, Black people, women, and minorities (ethnic, religious, and sexual) in general.[1]

We can detect a link between this conceptualization of epistemicide and the status of the Other in the Western philosophical tradition, specifically the way in which this tradition excludes diversity by reserving a single destiny for the Other. We can also detect a link between Santos's conceptualization of epistemicide, the status of the Other in the Western philosophical tradition, and the model of society designed by the racial contract that Charles W. Mills describes, which presupposes the integration of Black people as subordinate or the self-fulfilling prophecy of the ideology of racism. What is in question is whether or not it is possible to break with the paradigm of exclusion and with a type of integration that means the subordinate entry of Others kept in the condition of colonization, wardship, and dependency.

In addition to invalidating and disqualifying subjugated peoples' knowledge, epistemicide implies a persistent process of cultural impoverishment. This happens by denying access to education, especially high-quality education; through the production of intellectual inferiorization; through different mechanisms of delegitimating Black people as the carriers and producers of knowledge and through denigrating their cognitive capacities; and through material deprivation and/or by compromising their self-esteem via widespread discrimination in education. These processes are necessary because it is impossible to disqualify dominated peoples' forms of knowledge without also disqualifying them as knowing subjects, both individually and collectively. They are thus denied reason, the very condition necessary to access knowledge considered legitimate or legitimated. Consequently, epistemicide is a fatal wound to the rationality of the subjugated; it hijacks their very capacity to learn. It hijacks reason in a double sense: by negating the rationality of the Other and by imposing cultural assimilation on them.

Since it is a persistent process of manufacturing intellectual inferiority or negating the possibility of fulfilling one's intellectual capacities, epistemicide is carried out on human beings instituted as different and racially inferior, as a technology that includes the apparatus of raciality and that aims to control hearts and minds.

The concept of epistemicide, thus defined, allows us to understand the multiple forms in which Black people inhabit contradictions regarding education, and especially racial inequality in education. It allows us to organize this set of issues guided by an epistemological conceptualization of the production and reproduction of knowledge that determines the relations outlined above, as well as the educational system's perception of Black students. Included within this concept of epistemicide is an interpretation of these students as knowing subjects. According to this epistemological conceptualization, these students' cultural and racial differences will influence their intellectual possibilities. This is the case, as Santos states, because "for the old paradigm, science is a very specific and privileged practice since it produces the only valid form of knowledge,"[2] and the only valid knowing subject is already determined.

For various different thinkers, reason's spheres of activity constitute the parameters for gauging judgement and validation of the quantum of rationality identifiable with each human group: self-control (mastery of the self) as a condition of the constitution of the moral subject; mastery of nature as a condition of the development of technology, progress, science, and human development. These, therefore, will be the essential axes of valuation of diverse human groups. The assumptions established by Western reason refer to the possibilities of knowing and producing knowledge and simultaneously establish doubt about the educability of each human group. In *Observations on the Feeling of the Beautiful and the Sublime*, Kant states:

> The Negroes of Africa have by nature no feeling that rises above the ridiculous. Mr. Hume challenges anyone to adduce a single example where a Negro has demonstrated talents, and asserts that among the hundreds of thousands of blacks who have been transported elsewhere from their countries, although very many of them have been set free, nevertheless not a single one has ever been found who has accomplished something great in art or science or shown any other praiseworthy

quality, while among the whites there are always those who rise up from the lowest rabble and through extraordinary gifts earn respect in the world. *So essential is the difference between these two human kinds, and it seems to be just as great with regard to the capacities of mind as it is with respect to color.*[3]

In his physical anthropology, the philosopher identifies innate differences among the races. They encompass capacities and inclinations due in great part to the environment. Thus, the tropics inhibit the development of industrious types, as seen in the case of Black people, as opposed to what happens in temperate climates, which explains the propensity of Western white peoples to be more industrious. Kant's concerns focus on determining the conditions of possibility for the development of culture and civilization, and on identifying the human groups with the greatest aptitude for this task. From the classification of the innate capacities of each of the human races, he concludes that Native Americans are too weak a people for difficult work and are resistant to culture. Asians are civilized human types, but static and lacking spirit, while Africans are the human type that represents slave culture, given that they have accepted enslavement, have no love of liberty, and are incapable of creating a civil, ordered society for themselves. These characteristics are the order of human moral character, in which the world of liberty is inscribed, a world from which Africans are excluded because of their individual nature accustomed to slavery. According to Thomas McCarthy:

> Such differences in talent and temperament are what Kant has in mind when he speaks of the "innate" [*angeboren*] differences between the races. Because racial differences are adapted in large part to geographical differences, abilities and inclinations suited to one environment may be dysfunctional in another. In particular, the weaker impulse to activity suited to tropical climes, according to Kant, renders their native inhabitants – e.g. blacks – less energetic and industrious than the native inhabitants of temperate zones – e.g. whites – and thus less capable of self-improvement. Because the growth of culture and civilization depend on such things, we can understand why, in Kant's view, the advancement of the species is, and will continue to be, centered in Europe.[4]

Negating the full humanity of the Other, imprisoning them in categories that are foreign to them, asserting their innate incapacity for human development and improvement, denying their capacity to produce culture and civilization – all this lends itself to the declaration of reason as racialized, which naturalizes and establishes the hegemonic nature of European superiority. The Non-Being thus constructed affirms the Being. That is, the Being constructs the Non-Being, denying to them the set of characteristics that define full Being: self-control, culture, development, progress, and civilization. In the context of relations of domination and reification of the Other, set up by the colonial process, the status of the Other is "a thing that speaks."

Hegel links Africans to brutality and savagery. They are incomplete humans or non-humans – in their character there is "nothing consonant with humanity." Africans are thus described:

> The African, in his undifferentiated and concentrated unity, has not yet succeeded in making this distinction between himself as an individual and his essential universality, so that he knows nothing of an absolute being which is other and higher than his own self. Thus, man as we find him in Africa has not progressed beyond his immediate existence. As soon as man emerges as a human being, he stands in opposition to nature, and it is this alone which makes him a human being. But if he has merely made a distinction between himself and nature, he is still at the first stage of his development: he is dominated by passion, and is nothing more than a savage. All our observations of African man show him as living in a state of savagery and barbarism, and he remains in this state to the present day. The negro is an example of animal man in all his savagery and lawlessness, and if we wish to understand him at all, we must put aside all our European attitudes. We must not think of a spiritual God or of moral laws; to comprehend him correctly, we must abstract from all reverence and morality, and from everything which we call feeling. *All this is foreign to man in his immediate existence, and nothing consonant with humanity is to be found in his character.*[5]

Brutal beings, dominated by passion, lacking an ethical sense – "their moral sentiments are extremely weak, or, to be more precise, they are altogether deficient"[6] – Black people need to be tamed. Though he considered slavery itself to be unjust, Hegel admitted that "slavery is still necessary: for it is a moment in the transition towards a higher stage of development."[7]

Charles W. Mills provides an epistemological explanation for how Black people are manufactured as Non-Beings. We recall that for Mills, in addition to its political and moral dimensions, the racial contract has an epistemological dimension charged with prescribing "norms for cognition to which [the racial contract's] signatories must adhere."[8] In my interpretation, this is the terrain on which epistemicide is erected.

I will take up Mills's argument again. The classical contractualist approaches find epistemological parameters in natural law. That is, the epistemology associated with classical contractualism presupposes that we can know reality, what things objectively are, and the rules of good and evil through our natural faculties. The racial contract also has an epistemological dimension, since, after all, it requires its own "norms and procedures for determining what counts as moral and factual knowledge of the world."[9] However, "things are necessarily more complicated," since officially sanctioned reality diverges from actual reality such that, to be part of the racial contract, "one has to learn to see the world wrongly."[10] This is what Mills calls an "inverted epistemology," observing that wrong perceptions are duly sanctioned by white epistemic authority:

> The requirements of "objective" cognition, factual and moral, in a racial polity are in a sense more demanding in that officially sanctioned reality is divergent from actual reality. So here, it could be said, one has an agreement to *mis*interpret the world. One has to learn to see the world wrongly, but with the assurance that this set of mistaken perceptions will be validated by white epistemic authority, whether religious or secular.[11]

It is for this reason that there are those who see racism and discriminatory practices as resulting from ignorance, since the epistemological inversion they produce (the misrepresentation of the Other) is nothing more than a perversion. The racial contract informed by this inverted epistemology leads to epistemicide, since the contract requires the epistemic authority to sanction a series of myths and false representations of non-whites and their political, moral, and cognitive capacities. Thus, Mills continues,

> *on matters related to race, the Racial Contract prescribes for its signatories an inverted epistemology, an epistemology of ignorance, a particular pattern of localized and global cognitive dysfunctions (which are psychologically and socially functional), producing the ironic outcome that whites will in general be unable to understand the world they themselves have made.* [. . .] One could say then, as a general rule, that *white misunderstanding, misrepresentation, evasion, and self-deception on matters related to race* are among the most pervasive mental phenomena of the past few hundred years, a cognitive and moral economy psychically required for conquest, colonization, and enslavement. And these phenomena are in no way *accidental*, but *prescribed* by the terms of the Racial Contract, which requires a certain schedule of structured blindness and opacities in order to establish and maintain the white polity.[12]

Thus, with the destruction or disqualification of the dominated cultures, epistemicide lays the foundation for the supposed epistemological legitimacy of the dominant culture, justifying Western modernity's hegemony. We have an even better understanding of how this happens when we perceive the strategy of producing epistemicide brought about by the hegemonic epistemological and scientific paradigm. This paradigm, as Santos says, is sustained by the distinction between appearance and reality. By identifying science with the effort to go beyond appearances and get at the truth about reality, the hegemonic paradigm leads to epistemicide, since all the forms of knowledge which are foreign to it come to be disqualified as primitive and underdeveloped because they do not reach the truth and remain on the plane of appearances.

> This presumption to know how to distinguish, to hierarchize, between appearance and reality and the fact that the distinction is necessary in all knowledge processes makes epistemicide possible. It makes possible the declassification of all forms of knowledge foreign to the paradigm of modern science, under the pretext that they are forms of knowledge merely of appearances. The attribution of appearance to knowledge forms from the South and of reality to knowledge forms from the North is the basis for Eurocentrism.[13]

Santos points out that the intentional suppression of these subjugated or buried forms of knowledge has enormous consequences for humanity as a whole, since it means "the irreversible impoverishment of knowledge's horizon and possibilities," which takes place through the "systematic liquidation of alternatives whenever these alternatives are not compatible with hegemonic practices, whether on the epistemological or practical planes."[14]

This is one of the irremediable consequences of the the racial contract's epistemological dimension. In this sense, colonialism and racism are constituted as a global apparatus which destroys bodies, minds, and spirits, by linking and subordinating the cognitive survival of dominated peoples to the parameters of Western epistemology.

## The Installation of Epistemicide in Brazil: (De)humanism and Education

In order to think about the relationship between education and raciality in Brazil, we have to investigate other elements that intervened and gave rise to this imbrication. In Brazilian society, epistemicide would first be expressed in the Catholic church's attempts to suppress, condemn, censor, and control the Black population's knowledge during a vast period of our history. With the abolition of slavery and the emergence of the Republic, Brazilian thought registers the influx of scientific racism, contributing new characteristics to epistemic processes. As emancipated people who were undesirable as citizens, Black people came to be subject to the educational procedures of containment, exclusion, and assimilation.

As Roseli Fischmann has shown, within the Catholic church, the Jesuits were characterized by a particular union of the rigors of religious life with those of military life.[15] Under the aegis of hierarchy and obedience, common to both institutions, and with the objective of combating the Reformation, the Portuguese crown took the Society of Jesus as the most trustworthy of the religious orders. Thus the king of Portugal would designate the Jesuits as responsible for education in Brazil and would keep them here with resources drawn from taxes and religious tithes paid by the crown, and passed along to the Society according to the Right of Patronage. Public education would remain under Jesuit control from 1549 to1759. During this time, Jesuit Houses spread throughout Brazilian territory, each of which provided a small library and someone who could offer basic education.

The Portuguese Enlightenment would come to education in Brazil amidst a political crisis entangled with religious issues when the Marquês de Pombal decreed that other orders of the church would take over the responsibility previously conferred on the Jesuits.[16] This was not because the Jesuits were seen as a symbol of conservatism, given that they ended up culturally developing and expanding the nation, to the extent that Fernando Azevedo declared that they were responsible for the unification of our vast territory through the colonizing and mission work of the Jesuit Houses. He also attributes to them the fact that Brazil did not break up into various different countries, as happened in Spanish America, identifying specific conditions of development by the Jesuits in the Portuguese colonies. In addition, it is important to consider that Portugal came to regard their educational work as a risk for fomenting independence movements, looking at the example of what took place in Europe, which would culminate in the French Revolution, the Minas Gerais Conspiracy, and American independence.[17] Pombal clearly identifies the crucial and even strategic role of education in the development of these events.[18]

How did the Jesuits deal with Black people? In his book *O negro e a Igreja* (Black People and the Church), J. E. Martins Terra wonders why the Jesuits accorded such different treatment to indigenous and Black people in Brazil. He answers by citing Serafim Leite:

> The answer [. . .] has been given many times, but it is important to recall it again. *Because those native to the Americas were free*. They were declared as such in canon and civil law. And the Jesuits in Portuguese America were entrusted with the defense of this *liberty*. That is the reason. Black people who came from Africa were not free, nor was the defense of their liberty entrusted to the priests. The institution of African slavery was in effect in Africa from time immemorial. Even before the foundation of the Society of Jesus, the Americas were inundated with Black slaves. The Church's laws tolerated this slavery, and the civil laws of the nations regulated it. All colonizing nations, Portugal, Spain, France, England, the Netherlands, then, and for quite a long time, and with them the independent countries of the Americas, profited from Black slavery legally, that is, according to the laws of the time. The Jesuits were never entrusted, nor could they have been, with the defense of a liberty that did not exist.[19]

The justification for Black slavery refers to the enslaved's own institutions, legitimated with the understanding that slavery was an African social institution based on Africans' supposed slave nature. Such an argument allows the Jesuits to be declared powerless before the extent of the phenomenon of African slavery. Africans themselves would not offer any assistance in questioning enslavement, since enslavement would be written in their nature and their institutions. Therefore,

> In view of the then-irremediable fact of Black slavery, the Jesuits were left with just two paths: come out against it and disappear from the face of the earth, renouncing all their other educational, cultural, and mission work, which they would no longer carry out since they would be expelled from all civilized nations, a path without any benefit for civilization since Black slavery would continue within it; or accept it and try to mitigate it, through differential treatment and the exercise of charity, constantly combating the mistreatment of Black people, respecting the human personhood within them, and also, when it was in their power, imposing such personhood on the colonists, their masters.[20]

A papal bull put an end to the possible question of whether a Black child should go to school by declaring that Black people did not have souls. Keeping in mind the indissoluble vows between the Society and Jesus and the Pope, especially with regard to their extraordinary vow of obedience, the education of Black children was entirely out of the question. The first argument affirming the non-educability of Black people was the lack of a soul, later replaced by the lack of reason in the context of the laicization of the modern state. So epistemicide would first be joined to the apparatus of raciality through the establishment of foundational ideas and discourses around the educability of Afrodescendants.

Accordingly, the history of epistemicide in relation to Afrodescendants is the history of epistemicide in Brazil, given the obscurantism into which the country had been thrown ever since its origins. The project of domination that was expressed in an extreme way for Afrodescendants is the natural offspring of the project of domination in Brazil, a complex system organizing different levels of power and privilege. The lot of Africans and their enslaved descendants was the permanent weight of exclusion and punishment.

It is important to highlight that there was a consensus among various authors that the knowledge offered by the Jesuits was profoundly humanistic in nature.[21] The papal bull that decreed that Black people had no souls is what allows the constitution of a type of *sui generis* humanism, a humanism that is constituted without Black people: because they don't have souls, because they are not human, their absence does not impede this kind of humanism.

## Disqualification of Knowledge and Subjects

On the other hand, the theoretical and philosophical matrices previously cited would have diverse translations in Brazil, in its capacity as an extra-European space, with repercussions for education. Culture, civilization, and development comprised the greatest challenges that Brazilian intellectuals confronted in the transition from the colonial system to the Republic, and in this context, progress, order, and discipline were the keywords that designated the opposition between Europeans and non-Europeans.

Thus,

> the leadership in civil society, represented, for example, by those in charge of a prominent and traditional newspaper editorial line, warned about the risks to the consolidation of the Brazilian Nation

of the assimilation of contingents recently liberated from enslavement, assigning to the schools the job of educating and leading the "uneducated masses."[22]

The above formulation by Roseli Fischmann was the starting point for my reflection on the strategic role that formal education plays in Brazil in reproducing a concept of society dictated by the country's economic, intellectual, and political elites. Within this conception, race and culture are structural categories that determine hierarchies that can only be fully legitimated – through the systematic repetition and internalization of certain paradigms (from which racist theories result) – if they can institute and naturalize in some a consciousness of superiority, and in others a consciousness of inferiority.

The European consecration of Black people's natural inferiority, and especially of their cultural and moral indigence, would be corroborated in the cultural realm, as the following passage by Raymundo Nina Rodrigues[23] shows:

> In fact, the reality of Black people's social inferiority is not under discussion. No one yet even remembers to contest it. And it is vitally important to challenge the evidence itself. However, those who make that argument consider Black people's inferiority inherent in their organic constitution, molded by a different physical and cultural habitat. It would be an actual organic or morphological incapability. For some authors [. . .], the premature ossification of cranial sutures would impede the development of the brain, with the above-mentioned consequence. And the irreparable permanence of this defect attests to Black people's incapacity, throughout all of history, not only to assimilate the civilization of the diverse peoples with whom they were in contact, but also to create their own culture.[24]

In the face of chronic cultural inadequacy, Black people's robust presence, especially before the inevitable abolition of slavery, raises the issue of the impact of this presence on the country's civilizing possibilities. Rodrigues says the following:

> What Brazil must determine is how much inferiority results from its Black population's difficulty in civilizing itself, and if this inferiority is at all compensated by racial mixing, a natural process by which Black people are integrating with the Brazilian people, for the great mass of its population of color. [. . .] Black Brazilians' cultural capacity; means for promoting or compensating for it; mixed Aryan–African people's sociological and social value; the necessity of their assistance in acclimatizing

> white people to the intertropical zone; the desirability of diluting them or compensating for them through a surplus of the white population, which would take on the leadership of the country: that is why the problem of Black people is presented in Brazil in terms of its rigorously practical nature.[25]

Even the evidence of the time of the Egyptian civilization and its contributions to humanity's cultural patrimony is not able to reprimand Rodrigues's spirit. He explains the phenomenon of the separation of Egypt from the rest of Africa in this way:

> In fact, the first differentiation one must make among the Africans who came to Brazil is a distinction between true Blacks and the Hamitic peoples who, though more or less Black, are in fact but a branch of the white race, whose great capacity for civilization is attested by the ancient cultures of Egypt, Abyssinia, etc.[26]

Consequently, true Black people are incapable of civilization and, if there was civilization in Africa, it cannot be attributed to Black peoples but rather is credited to a branch of the white race. The apparatus of raciality, thus, demarcates and distributes good and bad in a Manichean way among the races. Such a concept seeks to encompass all Black African or diasporic experience and relativize diasporic experience, as contrasted with the irremovable principles that affirm Africans and their descendants' chronic incapacity for civilization, their status as minors, and thus their need for guardianship. Therefore, Rodrigues would say:

> Appreciating the progress achieved by Black North Americans in the thirty years that have elapsed since their liberation, Mandarini [*sic*: Gennaro Mondaini], an author frankly favorable to Blacks, states: "[. . .] Though the Blacks of America outwardly seem to have progressed, though they have assimilated the forms of civil life, nonetheless, in the depths of their souls, they are still children; they have gone very little beyond the childhood stage of humanity in which their co-brothers in Africa are found."[27]

The cultural demoralization of the Other simultaneously accomplishes the exaltation of the Self and the negation of the Other. Hence the stereotype of "true" Black people: happy, joking, childlike, impulsive, fun-loving, etc.; *real* Black people! Destined to entertain white people. A model that many people, seeking acceptability, reproduce. Rodrigues continues to cite Mondaini:

> Stanley wrote of them in the *Times*: "In order to rule them, and to keep one's life among them, it is needful resolutely to regard them as children who require, indeed, different methods of rule from English or American citizens, but who must be ruled in precisely the same spirit, with the same absence of caprice and anger, the same essential respect to our fellow-men." "All travellers are agreed in saying," writes Letourneau, "that the majority of the black races in Africa may be compared to our young European children: *they have all the lightheadedness, the capriciousness, the want of prudence, the volatility, the same quick and confined intelligence, as a child.*"[28]

Human incompleteness would have the inherent attribute of animalization, which responds more to primordial instincts than to the demands of a rationality that drives action. Thus Rodrigues reiterates Letourneau [and Mondaini]:

> "For the Black from Africa, abandoned to himself and living according to his own nature, his dominant impulses come less from his brain than from his belly." To pass from such a phase of development to the one that characterizes modern civil nations is certainly not feasible in a triennium of civil life, but rather will require centuries and centuries for social endowments, which Afro-Americans acquire through intimate contact with whites, transmitted from generation to generation, to become characteristic of the Black race in America. On the scale of civilization, Afro-Americans still occupy one of the bottom rungs, the Anglo-Saxon race one of the top, if not the top: Americans have full consciousness of this fact and cannot resolve to treat such inferior people as equals, just as an adult does not treat a child as an equal, nor do the better classes do so with the lesser ones.[29]

As for Kant and Hegel, for Rodrigues the absence of or difficulty with self-control remains a distinctive trait of Black people compared to white people. There is a specific method in Rodrigues's cases for "leading them" and "living among them" that involves the understanding that Black people have a characteristic lightheadedness, capriciousness, impulsivity, volatility, a both quick and limited intelligence, which marks their incapacity to reach the status of moral subject. Ari Lima endorses this understanding of Rodrigues when he states that:

> Nina Rodrigues sees no possible way for this race to compensate for its inferiority and bestiality besides moral guardianship, intellectual guidance, surveillance, and control of cultural and behavioral patterns. Despite Rodrigues's intellectual value and his relevance for the

construction of a field of study, it is this evolutionist and racist substrate that informs anthropology about Black people in Brazil.[30]

Júlio Mesquita Filho[31] is one among the many available examples of Brazil's intelligentsia's adherence to European racialism and its political project for Black people. According to Mesquita Filho:

> The doors of the slave quarters opened in [18]88,[32] allowing the dozens and dozens and dozens of thousands of men who came from Africa to be transformed into citizens and to infiltrate São Paulo's fragile collective organism, where they would not only delay, but virtually impede our cultural development.[33]

It is necessary to contain and administer this "infiltration." Mesquita Filho speaks at a time when figures such as Luiz Gama, the Rebouças brothers, Teodoro Sampaio, Machado de Assis, Juliano Moreira, Mário de Andrade, Cruz e Sousa, and Lima Barreto already existed – exemplary Black figures in letters and sciences.[34] These Black figures were proof that education could lead Black people to take on the responsibilities that their new citizenship required. Black people were here, acclimated and acculturated; they had already shown talent for arts and sciences, but continued to be disadvantaged by the argument about their "chronic incapacity for civilization."

Mesquita Filho does not refrain from expressing what is, from his point of view, an essential reservation about the quality of desirable migratory flows to his country: "The contribution of Black Americans is not desirable for Brazil's racial melting pot. A Black contingent at this moment would be more detrimental than useful to the civilizing work to which we are committed."[35]

As a counterexample, in his assessment of the stream of European immigrants he would make statements that refer us to the complicity that the racial contract promotes, as Charles W. Mills describes. According to Mesquita Filho, "A great stream of immigrants would invade our territories, enabling a boom in coffee cultivation in São Paulo, as well as the beginnings of what would be, fifty and sixty years later, the powerful industrial park that today makes us so proud."[36]

Over time, epistemicide made sure that the graph of education, disaggregated by color, displayed two parallel lines that showed no possibility of intersecting in the future. What one sees during the post-abolition period is the constitution of a consistent and permanent pattern of inequality between Black and white people for eighty years of the twentieth century: "Documents from educational authorities during the 1930s, when Brazilian schools began to welcome a significant number of the children of immigrants, exhibit warnings referring to 'racial cysts,' attributing to schools the principal responsibility for 'nationalizing the immigrant.'"[37]

The adoption of the obligatory use of the Portuguese language in all schools was the chosen instrument for this end. There was a double strategy: the nationalization of immigrants and the denationalization of Black people.

## The Mechanisms of Hierarchization: There Was (Not) a School in the Middle of the Road

> Those who regularly attended school had a mother and father. I remained unable to attend. One day I discovered that the Freemasons had formed a group of schools throughout the city for children who could not pay. I was able to get into one of these and started to learn a little more. Until school was over. Later I went to do a literacy course created by an abbot of the São Paulo Monastery, on Florêncio de Abreu Street. The school was for day laborers. But, since no one knew if I was or wasn't one (I never was), I was able to enter. I learned a little more. Nonetheless, I never was able to learn enough to say I knew how to read and write.[38]
>
> José Correia Leite

The above epigraph summarizes the fundamental dimensions of epistemicide: access; that is, the guarantee of providing opportunities in public spaces and the guarantee of actual conditions that allow the Black population to benefit from them. The testimony of José Correia Leite, one of the most honorable Black activists in the post-abolition period, editor of the newspaper *Clarim da Alvorada*, and a member of the Frente Negra Brasileira (Black Brazilian Front),[39] is brought up here in order to demonstrate how the process of exclusion from schools continued to operate even after abolition, promoting epistemicide and constituting the apparatus of raciality.

The elder militant's words describing the education system in the 1920s resonate with the results of contemporary studies on the difficulties that Black students face accessing school, staying in school, and completing their education. In this respect, in one of his studies, Ricardo Henriques concludes:

> despite improvements in Black and white people's average levels of education over the course of the century, the pattern of discrimination, that is, the difference between white and Black people's education, remains stable across generations. Among adults, we see that, unlike their white contemporaries, Black children, parents, and grandparents experience the same educational differences throughout the entire twentieth century.[40]

When what is at stake is assuring privileges and a hierarchized social structure according to racial and class parameters, controlling access to education is extremely important, since education is part of the set of social opportunities that lead to equity and social justice. And because it was intended to be hierarchized, we cannot affirm that education is based on equity and social justice.

As a result, we are dealing with a strategic and fundamental element, education, within the architecture of the apparatus of raciality. As Foucault declares, analyzing the effects of power that a particular domain institutes renders an understanding of the apparatus's functionality more accessible. In the case of epistemicide as a sub-apparatus of the apparatus of raciality, it is the racial inequalities naturalized in education that arise as the effects of power. According to Henriques,

> The naturalization of inequality stems from historical and institutional origins, linked, among other phenomena, to slavery and its late, passive, and paternalist abolition, and also to the corporativist character of a considerable part of the Republican period. Since inequality became a natural experience, however, it does not appear in the eyes of Brazilian society as artifice. The naturalization of inequality in turn engenders in Brazilian society theoretical, ideological, and political resistance to identifying or combating inequality as a public policy priority [. . .] inequality and racism are denied in everyday life.[41]

Now, by considering the educational inequalities that exist at present, we can target them for future transformation or change. However, even a superficial look at educational policy, or, rather, at the way policies of access to and distribution of educational opportunities were carried out, leads us to deduce that they intentionally aim to guarantee hierarchical social patterns dictated by the apparatus of raciality. In addition, they thus define who would take on the social burden that would result, in accordance with the idea of the cultural inferiority of African people and their descendants, as well as the process of primitivization to which they were subject – thus condemning them to underdevelopment.

A preliminary overview of the magnitude of these inequalities is provided in the document *Desenvolvimento com justiça social: Esboço de uma agenda integrada para o Brasil* (Development with Social Justice: Outline of an Integrated Agenda for Brazil), which we cite here at length:

> The white population accounts for close to 54% of Brazilians, while the Black population accounts for 45%. Nevertheless, an examination of the racial makeup of poverty reveals that the 53 million people in poverty and 22 million in extreme poverty are not democratically distributed as far as race goes. Black people represent 45% of the Brazilian population but close to 63% of the population in poverty and 70% of the population in extreme poverty. White people, in turn, are 54% of the total population but only 36% of those in poverty and 30% of those in extreme poverty. Indicators of income distribution also reveal a strong racial bias against the Afrodescendant population. Thus, beyond the unacceptable level of poverty in Brazil, this reveals that there is an enormous overrepresentation of poverty among Black Brazilians. Poverty in Brazil has a color. Poverty in Brazil is Black. [. . .] Educational indicators, in turn, confirm the intensity and the structural character of Brazil's pattern of racial discrimination. Currently, twenty-five-year-old white youths have 2.3 more years of education than Black youths of the same age. Nevertheless, despite the fact that both white and Black educational attainment has continually grown throughout the [twentieth] century, this difference of 2.3 years of education between white and Black youths of the same age remains the same among the parents and grandparents of these youths. The pattern of racial discrimination, manifest in the different educational attainment between white and Black people, is not only significantly high, considering the average levels of educational attainment across Brazilian adults, but, most importantly, it is perversely stable across generations.[42]

Since for subaltern classes education is avowedly the most effective and dependable instrument of social ascent in Brazil, the control and distribution of educational opportunities are instituting a racially hierarchical social order. This way of administering educational opportunities allowed the promotion of (racial) exclusion of Black people and the (social) promotion of white people from subaltern classes, consolidating, over time, the whitening of power and income and the depoliticization of the racial problem, thus preventing it from evolving into an open conflict.

Since poverty has been racialized to the point of turning Black people into "a kind of ontological symbol of the economically and politically subaltern classes,"[43] educational data disaggregated by color demonstrate that Black people have lower educational attainment than white people with similar socioeconomic origins, and that by the end of the 1990s white people were seven times more likely than Black people to finish university. Data from the IBGE[44] confirm these ethno-racial inequalities: Black people have fewer years of education than white people. In the fourteen- to fifteen-year-old age group, the Black illiteracy level is 12% higher than the white illiteracy level. The structural elements of this finding were the variables of color, race, and ethnicity, which guarantee the social subalternity of Black people in accordance with a national project whose fundamental aspiration is to develop the best of our European heritage.

The epistemicide is carried out through multiple actions that are linked together in a feedback loop, connected as much with access to and the ability to stay in the educational system as with the denigration of Black students' cognitive capacity. Racial exclusion by controlling access to, success in, and the ability to stay in the system shows up in such a way that any time access to education is democratized, the apparatus of raciality is rearticulated and produces shifts that update this exclusion.

As I understand it, at the beginning of the Republic, control over who would have access to public school was set in motion for that purpose. Afterward, the instrument became control over who would have access to quality schools. The decline of public school coincides with the social assertion of a white middle class that can pay for quality education. It is also the moment of a process of differentiating this white middle class from the popular classes that were clearly Black. This sends us back to Charles W. Mills's argument about the racial contract, as we have seen.

The data presented by Ricardo Henriques on the inequalities present between Black and white children and their educational trajectories anticipate a future that awaits them in adulthood, in terms of social subalternity.

## The Mechanisms of Normalization of Inferiority and Superiority

A paradigmatic example of the mechanisms of racial domination present in the school apparatus is included in a study by Eliane Cavalleiro in her book *Do silêncio do lar ao silêncio escolar: Racismo, preconceito e discriminação na educação infantil* (From

Silence in the Home to Silence in School: Racism, Prejudice, and Discrimination in Early Childhood Education).[45] She illustrates the operation of one of the most effective tactics of racism's domination in Brazil, which is the silence about or silencing of the existence of the problem of racial discrimination. The author especially reveals how this tactic is inscribed in the relationship of racial domination, used by each of the two poles of this relationship with different strategic objectives, which we will demonstrate and examine here.

This silence also manifests in the relationship between student and teacher, in the administration of the school apparatus, in the attitudes of white and Black students' parents, and in the discourse of pride in racial relations in Brazil that is present in teaching materials, accompanied by a portrayal of human superiority. Silence has as its byproduct a kind of schizophrenia or supposition of paranoia for Black students, since they experience and feel a problem that no one recognizes.

In addition, relational pairs we have already identified intensify in the student–teacher relationship – student–teacher, ignorant–erudite, etc. – which are defined by a "natural" moral debasement that their socially devalued color imposes on Black students from the outset. Thus, the school apparatus is one among other operators of domination and of the "manufacture of subjects" – subjects with a sense of superiority and inferiority. Sovereign subjects and dominated ones. The souls of the masters and the souls of the slaves.

> These negative stereotypes reinforce and perpetuate students' low performance, in many cases leading the students to internalize a negative self-image. In a study on the behavior of elementary teachers in Rio de Janeiro, [Azoilda Loretto] Trindade examined how schools discriminate. She found teachers who described Black children as suffering from "cultural deprivation," "lack of food," "linguistic deficiency" and "emotional neediness." [. . .] In another study on teachers, students, and textbooks, Vera Figueira also points out that negative stereotypes are consistently linked to Black people – by teachers, pedagogical texts, and other students. Trindade summarizes: [. . .] "The children are symbolically massacred, because the students, especially our Black students, study in public schools that create in them a feeling of inferiority and lack of belonging to our society, making social mobility difficult for them and crystalizing, naturalizing, inequality."[46]

In *Socialização e relações sociais: Um estudo de família negra em Campinas* (Socialization and Social Relations: A Study of a Black Family in Campinas), Irene Maria F. Barbosa states that school "is often the arena for the first and decisive interracial tensions suffered by Black children."[47]

Studies point to the persistence of a pessimistic imaginary among teachers about the educability of Black people. It is as if the old construction of Black people as incapable of knowledge still resonates. Rebecca Reichmann states:

> Teachers appear to unconsciously bolster the process of social exclusion. Teachers' expectations affect children's self-esteem, whether positively or negatively. Thus the racial prejudice that contributes to teachers' low expectations can threaten the development of a child's emotional and cognitive health. In our study completed in Maranhão in 1994, an exasperated elementary teacher said in an interview that with these children the best you can do is manage to get them to class, if only once in a while, to learn some addition and to write their names.[48]

Elsewhere, studies seek to clarify how the racist attitudes Black children face daily in school impact their self-esteem, and, consequently, the development of their capacity to learn. In a classroom study in Campinas, Reichmann observed that

> students called a young Black child "monkey," "ugly," "*preta*," "darky," and "stinky." The child remained ambivalent as far as her self-identification, identifying herself as *morena*.[49] This difficulty in defining her own racial identity can be extremely negative for the development of the child, because it impedes the expression of emotions and interferes with motivation, affecting her academic performance.[50]

Various authors have demonstrated that changes have been made to children's literature in response to criticism of the stereotyped images of Black people, and especially how their families, social ties, etc., were generally represented. However, it has yet to be confirmed how much these changes have actually altered the impression of social subalternization.

## Aporias of the Black Intellectual: Abductions and Rescues

The remarkable poem that we present at the end of this chapter will precisely describe the process of the colonizer's "whitening" through a colonial educational system. Even when Black people master the paradigms of Western reason, they are subject to epistemicide through the declaration of Black people's innate cognitive incapacity, through the absence of an alternative to this hegemonic epistemological field, through the acculturation promoted by the paradigms of hegemonic reason, and through the dismissal of other forms of knowledge.

There is a paradox about the very question of what is the universal that we bring to academic reflection and that is present today in discussions across the globe. Black people who achieve excellence in any area of knowledge embody this paradox, because their lives and their stories express resistance to the stigmas that distance them from intellectual and academic life. They declare: "We can think as well as or better than you."

The exclusion from school that is commonly reported in studies about race and education, especially in primary education, assumes new configurations when Black people enter higher education, at which point a tumultuous scholarly trajectory and a cumulative insecurity about their own intellectual capacity dramatically confront each other. As bell hooks notes, an anti-intellectual attitude defensively emerges as a tactic to avoid confirming the self-fulfilling prophecy. In this context, hooks signals the strategic function that intellectual work plays in challenging the predictions that exclude Black people from intellectual activity. According to her, "intellectual work is a necessary part of liberation struggle, central to the efforts of all oppressed and/or exploited people who would move from object to subject, who would decolonize and liberate their minds."[51]

Yet, once the subjectivity produced in Black people by the apparatus of raciality is marked by internalizing insecurity about their academic capabilities, as expected, an attitude of contempt emerges, which has a paralyzing effect on their academic progress in intellectual pursuits. Analyzing the attitudes of some of her students, hooks writes:

> Many of the Black female students I encounter are uncertain about intellectual work. I am awed by the depths of anti-intellectualism they are assaulted by and internalize. Many of them express contempt for intellectual work because they do not see it as having a meaningful connection to "real life" or the realm of concrete existence. Others who are interested in pursuing intellectual work are assailed by doubt because they do not feel there are Black female role models and mentors or they feel the individual Black female intellectuals they encounter do not receive rewards and recognition for their work.[52]

And hooks synthesizes the binds that limit Black women's intellectual possibilities: "It is the sexist/racist Western conception of who and what an intellectual is that rules out the possibility that Black women will come to mind as representatives of intellectual vocation."[53]

This contempt for intellectual life reflects an internalization of the idea of being out of place: as though to assume the attitude of the sly fox before the grapes that continually move out of reach and, with disdain, declare, "They are too green." As though to assume this attitude to assuage the feeling of inadequacy, of not belonging in a space where almost the only access granted to us is as the objects of study by those who are gifted, by nature, with the capacity to "know" and especially to explain. As hooks says: "Such representations impressed on everyone's consciousness the notion that Black women were all body and no mind."[54]

bell hooks observes that the way in which established portrayals of Black people in the sphere of knowledge play out in the university arena impacts their academic choices, in agreement with Cornel West's words in "The Dilemma of the Black Intellectual":

> There is always the need to assert and defend the humanity of Black people, including their ability and capacity to reason logically, think coherently, and write lucidly. The weight of this inescapable burden for Black students in the White academy has often determined the content and character of Black intellectual activity.[55]

This is related to the historical distancing of Black people from this area in the educational process. In any case, Black intellectuals who seek academic recognition risk distancing themselves from a larger Black public: "Choosing to write in a traditional academic style may lead to isolation. And even if one writes along the lines of accepted academic style there is no guarantee that one's work will be respected."[56]

hooks draws on herself and her own academic trajectory to understand and explain the hardships experienced by Black people, especially Black women, in achieving the condition of knowing subjects:

> When I published my first collection of essays, *Talking Back*, I was surprised by the many letters I received from Black women discussing the essay which focused on the difficulties I faced as a graduate student. Stories of persecution by professors, peers, and professional colleagues

> poured in. Accounts of Black females being interrogated by those seeking to ferret out whether the individual was capable of completing work, of thinking logically, of writing coherently were a norm. These forms of harassment often undermine Black women's capacity to convey skill and intellectual ability.[57]

Employing these strategies of denial, doubt, and making Black people feel unwelcome reiterates to them the idea that they do not belong in the university, that they are "out of place" there. It is an invitation to give up and an incentive to academic failure, as hooks shows:

> Given the lack of sustained public affirmation and support for Black females choosing intellectual vocations, when confronting such work in isolation, in private spaces, it is not surprising that individual Black women may find themselves overwhelmed by doubts, that such spaces may intensify fears of lack, fears that one's ideas could not possibly be worthy of a hearing. Black women must re-vision notions of intellectual work that enable us to embrace a concern with a life of the mind and the welfare of community.[58]

As a form of resistance to isolation and negation, hooks cites West's proposal of a combat strategy that articulates the individual production of knowledge with community struggles and a strategy of making intellectuals visible in the public sphere:[59] "Instead of the solitary hero, embattled exile, and isolated genius – the intellectual as star, celebrity, commodity – this model privileges collective intellectual work that contributes to communal resistance and struggle."[60]

Despite the difficulties imposed by the very dynamic of university institutions, we add the need for Black people to constitute their own institutional spaces that they can reference and that support their trajectory: "Concurrently, academic competitiveness militates against the formation of Black intellectual communities that cross institutions and disciplines. Such communities emerge from the resistance efforts of Black women and men who recognize that we strengthen our positions by supporting one another."[61]

Subjects and subjected knowledge emerge from West's reflection as elements that carry a specific form of intellectual insurgency able to criticize and displace the hegemonic discourses that reiterate established power and knowledge, as well as the subjection they produce. Thus:

> "The major priority of Black intellectuals should be the creation or reactivation of institutional networks that promote high-quality critical habits primarily for the purpose of Black insurgency." [. . .] Asserting that "the central task of postmodern Black intellectuals is to stimulate, hasten, and enable alternative perceptions and practices by dislodging prevailing discourses and powers," West offers a paradigm that allows for an emphasis on ending sexism and sexist oppression as a necessary pre-condition for Black intellectual insurgency.[62]

Educating Black researchers in the traditional canons of academic tradition ensures the non-insurgent, and especially non-communal, character of their production, in opposition to West's aspiration. Frequently, the subordinate, manufactured Black intellectual becomes a critical delegitimating agent of activist practice. Instead of "dislodging discourses," there are Black intellectuals who legitimize white knowledge about Black people, racial relations, etc. They are used, consequently, to confirm "dominant powers." Meanwhile, insurgents suffer academic isolation, since the apparatus of raciality continues to function, but they can find motivation and endorsement from an audience outside of the academy:

> In fact, when we do insurgent intellectual work that speaks to a diverse audience, to masses of people with different class, race, or educational backgrounds, we become part of communities of resistance, coalitions that are not conventional [. . .] the affirmation that has come to me from individuals and locations that are on the margins strengthens and inspires me.[63]

It is true that to seek endorsement from those outside the community to which one supposedly belongs and from which one should receive recognition does not alter or overcome the obstacles that impede the actual inclusion of Black people in academia. If intellectual survival in other spheres of social life assures the endurance of Black intellectuals, it does not guarantee they will overcome the factors that promote their debilitation within academic institutions. This despair is expressed in the insurgent alternative turned "inward," in which Black intellectuals recognize their validation in the closed loop of their production about their community:

> The predicament of the Black intellectual need not be grim and dismal. Despite the pervasive racism of American society and anti-intellectualism of the Black Community, critical space and insurgent activity can be expanded. This expansion will occur more readily when Black

> intellectuals take a more candid look at themselves, the historical and social forces that shape them, and the limited though significant resources of the community from whence they come.[64]

hooks shows us the consequences of denying the authority of the speech of Black intellectuals that occurs in academic institutional dynamics, leading many "brilliant young scholars" to give up intellectual work because they feel scorned in the academy and devalued outside of it.[65]

On this evidence, hooks reiterates West's position regarding the importance of Black people creating "escape routes" from the apparatus and the mechanisms that disqualify subjects who, as Foucault describes, are "speaking subject[s], discursive subject[s], subject[s] of experience and knowledge,"[66] but who are minimized in these processes. We need strategies that allow our merit to be evaluated not by "structures, institutions, and individuals who do not believe in our capacity to learn."[67] Thus the fundamental importance of alternative spaces of validation:

> It is impossible for Black female intellectuals to blossom if we do not have a core belief in ourselves, in the value of our work, and a corresponding affirmation from the world around us that can sustain and nurture. Often we cannot look to traditional places for recognition of our value; we bear the responsibility for seeking out and even creating different locations.[68]

Among the difficulties and challenges that appear for Black people who enter the university are the accumulation of the mass of determinations that accompany them in any scholarly trajectory, in whatever refers to the conflict of raciality/knowledge and power. It is in post-secondary education that this conflict reaches a privileged sphere, where the potentiality of Black people for scholarly knowledge is constructed and reconstructed, denied or affirmed.[69] Far from signifying that they have overcome stigmas and stereotypes, entering the university is the moment of Black people's final confrontation, in the field of knowledge, with the mechanisms that have shadowed them throughout their scholarly trajectory. The whiteness of knowledge, the self-fulfilling prophecy, the exclusive authority of white speech – all these ghosts have to be faced without mediation, in the name of what Foucault called the "insurrection of knowledges."[70]

*I was six when*
*Mama was careless*
*she sent me to school*
*alone*
*five days a week*

*One day I was*
*kidnapped by a band*
*of Western philosophers*
*armed with glossy-pictured*
*textbooks and*
*registered reputations,*
*"Holders of BA*
*and MA degrees"*

*I was held*
*in a classroom*
*guarded by Churchill and Garibaldi*
*pinned up on one wall*
*and*
*Hitler and Mao dictating*
*from the other*
*Guevara pointed a revolution*
*at my brains*
*from his "Guerrilla Warfare"*

*Each three-month term*
*they sent threats to*
*my Mama and Papa*

*Mama and Papa loved*
*their son and*
*paid ransom fees*
*each time*
*Mama and Papa grew*
*poorer and poorer*
*and my kidnappers grew*
*richer and richer*
*I grew whiter and whiter*

*On my release*
*fifteen years before*
*I was handed*
*(among loud applause*
*from fellow victims)*
*a piece of paper*
*to decorate my walls*
*certifying my release.*[71]

# 4
# Prohibitions

## Prohibitions of the Subject: Black People Are Not

There are multiple prohibitions unleashed by the apparatus of raciality. Black people are prohibited from being human beings, from being subjects: legal, moral, political, and knowing subjects. Prohibition generates procedures of exclusion, which are present in discourse as well as in the social practices derived from the inscription of individuals and groups in the ambit of abnormality, in the sphere of non-being, nature, and unreason.[1] Prohibitions are allied, after all, with the formation of a certain social imaginary that naturalizes Black people's inferiority.

In *A invenção do ser negro: Um percurso das ideias que naturalizaram a inferioridade dos negros* (The Invention of the Black Being: A Journey Through the Ideas that Naturalized the Inferiority of Black People), Gislene Aparecida dos Santos analyzes representations of Black people that circulate in the West, as well as the strangeness of blackness, which designates exoticism – presented as threatening and fascinating – as the way to symbolize Black/African people.

Racism is sustained in the terrifying imaginary Europeans constructed about Africans and Africa, which, as Santos shows, is described as a "land of sin and immorality that produces corrupt men; peoples from torrid climates with hot blood and abnormal passions who only know how to fornicate and drink."[2] The identification of the Black body as bearer of evil, to use a Foucauldian expression, is noted in opposition to the white body, bearer of the highest human attributes. The polarity established between the colors of black and white results, according to Santos, in a black and African aesthetic.

It is quite appropriate to assume that racist ideology has fed on aesthetic values formed around Black people and the fascination and mystery that Africa and its inhabitants have inspired, transforming difference and mystery into monstrosity and abnormality.[3]

As I understand it, such an aesthetic can be perceived through Foucault's categories of the monstrous and the abnormal. They reveal the cultural constructions that subjugate the Black body beyond the scientific invalidation of the concept of race – which is undertaken in the contemporary moment through advances in genetics – and which further determine Black people's cultural immobility, which leads to their persistent social condemnation. We must not forget, as Santos warns, however, that the discourses prior to slavery as well as those constructed under the aegis of scientific racism remain part of the social imaginary around Black people.

## The Monster

In the construction of the Other as threat and danger, prohibition means denying the Other admission to full humanity and promoting their displacement to an intermediate territory between full humanity and animality, inscribing them, in Foucault's terms, in the grid of intelligibility of the monster. The monster is,

> so to speak, the spontaneous, brutal, but consequently natural form of the unnatural. It is the magnifying model, the form of every possible little irregularity exhibited by the games of nature. In this sense we can say that the monster is the major model of every little deviation. It is the principle of intelligibility of all the forms that circulate as the small change of abnormality.[4]

It is in this grid of intelligibility that Black people are understood in nineteenth-century racialism and remain deeply embedded in people's conscience: as an intermediary between human and animal, the manifestation of human incompleteness.

In fact, the sexual monster is invariably associated with the figure of the "*negão*." Indeed, in the social imaginary, the majority of Black people are "*negrões*,"[5] whatever size they may be. In his article "Vera, Clara do Anjos, Iládio,"[6] Joel Rufino analyzes a passage from *Dão-lalalão* by João Guimarães Rosa, describing the force of this imaginary about Black people through the character of Iládio, and the way it offers a form of punishment:[7]

> Soropita shacked up with Doralda, a whore from Montes Claros, in the sticks of Gerais he lived there in a haze of pleasure and security. Once, returning home, he comes upon a band of cowboys, headed by his old friend Deraldo. He's happy. Among the band, however, was the Black Iládio: his presence set off Soropita's insecurity and then panic. He had delusions that the Black had possessed his woman, had reveled in her white flesh, had thrust his deformed and dirty member into her grotto of Venus. A dirty mule, since she was called White Girl, he suspected that the scandal was public.[8]

For Rufino, "we have in this magnificent story a synopsis of what Black people mean to white people – filth-lust and danger. In sexual situations, Black people appear as white people's subconscious."[9] Rufino asks the reader how this story gets resolved. And he himself responds: "through submission,"[10] since Iládio says, asking for forgiveness, "I'm dead, I'm dead, Boss Surupira, but I'm begging you not to kill me, by the mother of God, angel of God, don't kill me . . . I didn't do anything! I didn't do anything! . . . have mercy . . . have mercy. . ."[11]

In *Preto e branco: A importância da cor da pele* (Black and White: The Importance of Skin Color), Marco Frenette describes the stereotype of the Black rapist and how it is consistent with the imaginary of Black women's sexuality, shaped by a mixture of strangeness, irrationality, hypocrisy, and the reiteration of established stereotypes, among which is the stereotype of savage Black sexuality. Frenette describes the sensations that stem from unequal relations between white men and Black women, shot through with peculiarity in which

> what is reinforced is the impression that what is happening is not an exchange of love and pleasure between equals: the white man feels as though he were on an adventure with a female being of another species. It is as though he were practicing a higher degree of zoophilia; having relations with an extraterrestrial; intimate contact with the imponderable.[12]

## The Individual to Be Corrected

In his genealogy of abnormality and the abnormal individual, Foucault inscribes the figure of the "individual to be corrected."[13] This individual does not appear, like the case of the monster, as an exception or a strange spectacle, since "the individual to be corrected is an everyday phenomenon. He is so much an everyday phenomenon that – and this is his first paradox – he is, so to speak, typically regular in his irregularity."[14] Thus, in the register of the "individual to be corrected," another form of subjectification emerges, one that is imposed on Black people from the imaginary constructed about difference, in which irregularity becomes their regularity.

Considering the social disposability that characterizes Black people's situation in the post-abolition period, founded in the conviction that they do not have the aptitude for disciplinary society, Black beings appear as inherently incorrigible. This condition determines the forms of control and punishment that are exercised upon them, as well as the state of permanent suspicion in which they will be socially perceived; the forms of normalization that will correspond to them stem from suspicion and incorrigibility.

Prohibition becomes possible by constructing individuals or collectivities with regard to whom there is a generalized and "profound conviction" that they are guilty,[15] a figure of the juridical field that for Foucault "authorizes conviction without proof,"[16] but which also allows acquittal without the proof of the absence of a crime. The figure of "profound conviction" slips from the juridical field to the cultural and social ones as permission for all those who hold the authority to speak, an authority derived from belonging to institutions entitled to pronounce the truth about an object or anything else. It is this quality that spreads out to the rest of the racially hegemonic group, like a contagion derived from belonging to the raciality considered superior and which bears the greater talent for thinking, judging, and executing justice.

This is what authorizes any white person to feel themselves a specialist in Black people and in racial relations, as well as to be free to vocalize whatever would be better, or appropriate, for Black people, making explicit "the effects of truth that may be produced in discourse by the subject who is supposed to know."[17] This occurs even if it consists of a discourse that, as Foucault says, is "statutory and discredited."[18] In the case of Black people, color operates as a metaphor for an original crime of which color is a kind of proof, the mark or sign that justifies this presumption of guilt. For Foucault, "one is not suspected with impunity":[19] that is, the guilt that is presumed a priori due to color unfolds in a priori, preventative, and educational punishment. Suspicion transforms the social scene for Black people like a kind of virtual panopticon[20] since, for Foucault, in panopticism, "the supervision of individuals is carried out not at the level of what one does but of what one is, not at the level of what one does but of what one might do."[21] Thus, the social scene itself is where surveillance and punishment are carried out as techniques of racial control. As Frenette declares,

> For all forms of discrimination, there are moments of truce and some chance for conversation. But for Black people, there is no rest. To be Black is to permanently live in a hostile reality. [. . .] That is why, regardless of the spiritual or intellectual road that Black people decide to take, they need to keep in mind a fact completely banal in its essence, but completely crucial in its consequences: the existence of white skin to the detriment of Black skin. It is an absurd and cruel circumstance that the nebulous measure of all things exists in the gaze of the other.[22]

As a result, the punishable matter is Black raciality itself. Black people's infractions are an expected and encouraged consequence of the substance of the crime, which is blackness. This is why children in primary education demonstrate discriminatory reactions and behaviors they have learned from adults. Among the various situations that Eliane Cavalleiro describes among her observations of everyday activities in a municipal school in São Paulo is the following scene: a white child suggests to a Black child that he take home a car abandoned in the sandbox because, as he says, "Blacks have to steal."[23]

Foucault demonstrates that psychiatric discourse in criminal matters produces the figure who will be incriminated by means of *doubling*, which permits

> the offense, as defined by the law, to be doubled with a whole series of other things that are not the offense itself but a series of forms of conduct, of ways of being that are, of course, presented in the discourse of the psychiatric expert as the cause, origin, motivation, and starting point of the offense.[24]

These procedures are present in the juridical sphere in the sentences handed down to Black and white defendants, as Sérgio

Adorno has demonstrated in his study on the topic. They are procedures that are so refined that, as Adorno points out, there is a process of whitening of the defendant during the case if it is trending toward acquittal. According to Adorno,

> there is a phenomenon that we observe that is the color "dance" in these cases. Many times individuals begin as "*pardos*"[25] and end up "Black," or begin as "white" and end up "Black." There is a phenomenon that I have more or less characterized as the "browning of the population." "White" people tend to turn into "Black" people and "Black" people many times tend to "lighten" themselves, according to the outcome of the case. Obviously, these methodological issues are quite thorny. Many of them we have been able to resolve with relative success while others remain unresolved.[26]

However, beyond the legal sphere, other multiple doublings are prosecuted insofar as raciality becomes a crime inscribed on the skin of the subject: animality, promiscuous sexuality, cognitive incapacity, ugliness, violence, and death. Each doubling corresponds to specific forms of prohibition, punishment, and subjectification in different dimensions of social life. The pole of the raciality of the elect corresponds to its opposites, in terms of doubling and subjectification.

According to Foucault, on juridical/psychological matters, "it is not the legality of the proof, its conformity to the law, that makes it a proof: it is its demonstrability."[27] In the context organized by the apparatus of raciality, this rule will also manifest: Black and white people should demonstrate in their existence what is attributed to their respective racialities, making the production of these realities imperative for the legitimation of social hierarchies, knowledge, and power that raciality engenders.

## The Negation of "I's"

In *Preto e branco*, Marco Frenette unveils the entanglements of the everyday production and reproduction of racism in schools, the family, the media, in all of Brazilian society. He reveals our best-kept secret in all its nuances: the way in which white superiority and Black inferiority are constructed, what these constructions are for, and especially how to conceal them, since, according to Frenette,

It was an obscene relief to look at our white skins, which we saw as informal future passports to the good things in the world. It was a restrained happiness not to be Black. [. . .] We always liked to have a *pretinho*[28] close by in order to feel that we were better than him.[29]

He continues:

While I was still a child, I was taught to praise the monotony of whiteness, while I confused dark skin with the absence of dignity or courage. In my years as a young child, long before I reached an age when I could glimpse the possibilities of reason, I was encouraged to use my color as a crutch to establish myself as a person. [. . .] And one of the most pernicious things I was taught in my basic racism course was to maintain a physical and spiritual distance from black skin, since with the slightest touch I could be the victim of a fantastic fellowship that would change me forever. I would become one of them, I was told.[30]

The author also demonstrates limit-situations of the loss of humanity and the self-flagellation to which Black people, destroyed by an inferiority complex, are driven. To wit, Frenette presents the shocking testimony of a Black man, Daniel Pontes Ribeiro, a civil construction worker, who came to Frenette as the then-editor of the magazine *Caros Amigos* (Dear Friends) to show him his writing and seek his help publishing it. Daniel Pontes's writing repeats the same note over again, as the following passage shows:

Daniel Pontes Ribeiro declares that the Black race is a plague. A damn plague. Blacks are total shit. Black men and women have to be exterminated. Black men hate Black women. Black men prefer white women. All white women are married to apes. Black men prefer white women because white women are more beautiful than Black women. White women have good hair. White women have noble faces. White women have thin lips and noses. White women smell good, like perfume. White women smell like orange blossoms and white jasmine and medicinal eucalyptus. Black women stink like shit. Black Brazilian women are more than ugly, they have animalistic features.[31]

In view of the dramatic nature of this testimony, Frenette concludes this episode of the book with the following:

If Ezra Pound said that the poet is the antennae of the race, we say, then, that the antipoetic and painfully sensitive antennae of this civil construction worker captured all the moral, emotional, and sexual

> misery that the racial question comprises. As an involuntary depository of a shameful collective unconscious, Daniel produced the strange documentation of the psychic perturbations that any Black man gifted with a minimal amount of sensibility suffers, whether he is an intellectual or a manual laborer.[32]

Regarding subjects' psychic reality, the denigration that raciality undertakes transforms Black people's blackness into the essence of the "Black subject," a subject in quotation marks, to the extent that this denigration results in the very negation of the condition of subject. Conversely, whiteness has at its disposal a plurality of I's that comprise the subject.

As we have already noted regarding Heidegger's ontic, the apparatus of raciality produces the denigration and/or negation of I's in human relations. Human diversity and the multiplicity of identities that span individuals with their different characteristics – profession, gender, class, etc. – disappear when the Black factor comes into play. Blackness comes before personhood, blackness comes before individuality, blackness comes before profession, blackness comes before gender, blackness comes before university degrees, blackness comes before wealth. All these dimensions of Black individuals have to be redeemed a posteriori, that is, after verification, as befits those who are a priori suspect. And even after this verification, Black individuals will be submitted to different tests to prove that they are something besides Black. This is why Frenette says that to be Black is to never be able to rest: because Black people as portrayed, as constructed in discursive practice, freeze the latent I's within their bodies, and make them dormant, anemic; they transform them into unrealizable impulses, given the tyranny of the "Black people" attached to them. In contrast, when faced with a white person, we don't know a priori whom we have before us.

Whiteness doesn't need to be affirmed, because affirmation from a place of privilege would mean breaking the pact of silence about the racial hegemony produced by whiteness. As Liv Sovik points out,

> being white in Brazil is to have relatively light skin, which functions as a kind of silent visual ticket to enter places with restricted access. The problem of white people comes up today because Black cultural and political activism and official statistics tell us that Brazil is not just a country of mixed-race people, but of *negros* and *pardos* on one side, and of white people on the other.[33]

Black people's defensive attitudes arise from this perception of the visual password that whiteness carries with it, such as those attitudes relayed by Moema de Poli Teixeira in her studies and which demonstrate the implicit requirement that white people endorse Black people in all social situations. Consider the author's example (my emphasis): "One of the ways to get a *badge* is to be, for example, in the company of a white person [. . .] *this badge is the Black person's passport to social coexistence.*"[34]

## Moral Assassination

One of the effects of controlling social mobility as a form of prohibition against those who are racially subalternized is a certain specific social attitude held by the racially hegemonic group about those Black people who escape the mechanisms of vigilance and enter into the private spheres of whiteness. Milton Santos's testimony delivers a verdict:

> From the beginning of economic history, Black work has been essential to the wellbeing of the dominant classes, giving it a central role in the creation and perpetuation of a conservative and unequal ethic. Crystalized interests produced deep-rooted slave-owning convictions and maintain the stereotypes that go beyond the borders of the symbolic to impact all other aspects of social relations. That is why, perhaps ironically, Black people's slightest social ascent has always given way to veiled or overt expressions of resentment (paradoxically against the victims).[35]

Resentment of Black people who escape vigilance and manage to avoid prohibitions gives rise to new forms of racial restriction by demonstrating the inadequacy of those who have broken through the barriers. The moral assassination of Black people who enter into the private spaces of the racially hegemonic is one demonstration of the resentment that Santos identifies. Consider the emblematic case of the singer Wilson Simonal, who died in 2000, in which Santos's phrasing reverberates.[36] Nelson Motta explains how Simonal was condemned to ostracization by a baseless accusation that resulted from resentment: "Envy and resentment are the weapons that Brazilians wield with exceptional deftness and hostility. Simonal paid the price."[37] In my article "Meu irmão, meu limoeiro" (My Brother, My Lemon Tree),[38] I described Simonal's significance in the 1960s and 1970s:

> He was the enchanted prince of the Black youths of my generation. Gorgeous, charming, irreverent, and dignified. Never a hint of the subservience that was expected of Black people. It seemed as though his trajectory for success was as infinite as his talent and his capacity to rally and delight the crowds with his songs. His memorable rendition of "Meu limão, meu limoeiro" (My Lemon, My Lemon Tree), which electrified the entire Maracanãzinho stadium when he conducted an orchestra of 50,000 voices with all the swing that God and the Orixás gave him, was something unforgettable. Black Simonal was amazing![39]

However, the prince suddenly turned into a frog, accused of the most serious act that someone could commit at that time: that of being a *dedo-duro* (informer),[40] in the service of the military dictatorship. Then the unthinkable happened. In those times of unrelenting ideological policing, mere suspicion was enough to destroy someone's life. In 1972, Simonal was accused by the newspaper *O Pasquim* (The Lampoon) of being a collaborator with the regime, and thereafter his moral assassination was irreversible. The music star was thrown into isolation, he lost contracts, he was treated like he had a contagious disease, and, finally, he died. Eventually, something that we Black people already knew, but which we had no means at that time of denouncing, was revealed to the public. Less-than-noble feelings far from the revolutionary ethic that reigned at the time played a part in how his martyrdom took place. As I have said on a different occasion, ideological policing was fertile ground for the expression of unspoken feelings: envy, resentment, racism, and many others that haunt celebrities, especially if they are Black.

In 2003, the board of the Ordem dos Advogados do Brasil (OAB, Brazilian Bar Association) found Simonal innocent of the accusation of having been an informer during the military regime, and the official pronouncement of his innocence threw some of the affair's main characters back into the public eye. According to Ziraldo,[41] who at that time was part of *O Pasquim*, "he was a fool; he thought he was the king of the castle, poor thing. And he was. He was snobby, intolerable. He died of grief; no one deserves what he suffered."[42] In the article "O julgamento de Simonal" (Simonal's Trial), Pedro Alexandre Sanches says that "the antipathy against Simonal came from before. In July 1969, the leftist weekly *O Pasquim* published a cover interview with the headline 'Não sou racista' (I Am Not Racist) in which it indicted Simonal with questions about racism and the fact that he ate caviar and had a butler." He was made an example of and punished for his insolence, and his moral assassination was nothing other than the start of putting him back in his rightful place.

Caetano Veloso[43] said the following about the case: "soldiers interrogated me for six hours and they gave me the names of artists who were helping them denounce others, etc. There were various names. [. . .] Simonal's name was among them. [. . .] It seemed like they were using an easy name to make it seem believable."[44] Now, what made the accusation against Simonal believable is the fact that he was Black. As long as he enjoyed the indulgences and applause of the white world, he seemed untouchable. But then he became the target of intense hostility, of a thirst for destruction and an intolerance out of proportion to the supposed "error" he had committed, especially in comparison to the major crimes and offenses committed by white people that were tolerated and covered up.

Jaguar[45] stands out among the *O Pasquim* group responsible for the libel that was challenged by the new information that the OAB brought to light. He had already obliquely confessed to "having helped to destroy a singer's career," and when faced with the new evidence, he stated his position: "I started it. He was understood to be a *dedo-duro*. I don't have any regrets."[46]

Ironically, in 1967, Simonal, together with Ronaldo Bôscoli, composed the anti-racist song "Tributo a Martin Luther King" (Tribute to Martin Luther King), in which he said the following:

*Yes, I am a Black man of color.*
*My brother of my same color.*
*What I'm asking is for you to fight, fight some more.*
*The fight isn't over yet.*
*For every Black man who goes*
*another Black man will come.*
*To fight with blood or not*
*You can also fight with song, brother.*
*Hear my voice, oh! Yes. Fight for us.*
*The great Black struggle is a struggle for peace.*
*The great Black struggle so we will all be equal.*
*So we will all be equal.*

# Part II
## Resistances

# Prologue

For Foucault, all apparatuses of power produce their own resistances. Afrodescendants' attempts at social affirmation take place on the level of ideas, individual behaviors, and political action through a wide range of attitudes, varying between opposite poles. There could be, on the one hand, depoliticized – but neither innocuous nor inconsequential – forms of opportunism or collusion with the discourses and practices historically constructed around racial relations in Brazil. On the other hand, this affirmation is also expressed through the constitution of collective subjects divided among different political perspectives and parties, which articulate different projects of inclusion for Afrodescendants in Brazilian society. Thus, Black resistance, as a manifestation of the effects of power produced by the apparatus of raciality, is situated in the same realm as the notion of resistance in Foucault's philosophy of apparatuses. For him,

> there is no single locus of great Refusal, no soul of revolt, source of all rebellions, or pure law of the revolutionary. Instead there is a plurality of resistances, each of them a special case: resistances that are possible, necessary, improbable; others that are spontaneous, savage, solitary, concerted, rampant, or violent; still others that are quick to compromise, interested, or sacrificial; by definition, they can only exist in the strategic field of power relations.[1]

We have seen how the post-abolition period in Brazil configured an apparatus of raciality charged with establishing a new social configuration of the national modernization project that the emerging Republic pursued. We likewise have seen that this apparatus of raciality, like any apparatus of power in Foucault's conceptualization, is supported by apparatuses constructed at other historical moments, according to other objectives and strategies, but always appropriated and given new meaning with each new historical configuration. In this sense, the apparatus of raciality benefits from the representations of Black people produced before and during the colonial period, which informed the constitution of masters and slaves, articulating them and assigning them new meaning in the light of the racist ideology in effect during the nineteenth century, which Hannah Arendt analyzes in *The Origins of Totalitarianism*.[2] In Brazil, the supposed and enshrined inferiority of some and the superiority of others are what defines the new social hierarchies that would emerge in the post-abolition period, as an answer to the diversification of the social structure that the Republic, the abolition of slave labor, and the establishment of political liberalism imposed on the nation.

However, it is also obvious that the apparatus of raciality is above all constituted by a contract between white people, founded in complicity about the social subordination and/or elimination of Black people and non-white people in general, whether in Brazil or the wider world. This is a dynamic driven by the articulation of disciplinary techniques derived from the apparatus of raciality and from elimination, both informed by biopower.

This is the context in which Black resistance arises. If, as Foucault declares, all power has opposing resistance, this resistance comes about, first of all, in strategies of physical survival, since the angel of death that is the biopower of racism imposes upon the dominated raciality the very act of staying alive as the first act of resistance. Staying alive: Black people will face the challenges of maintaining their physical health and of preserving their cognitive capacity, in order to understand and develop a critical view of the processes of racial exclusion to which they are subject and to find the paths to individual and collective emancipation. Few people are capable of completing this journey or of traversing this difficult path: to physically survive, to liberate reason held hostage, to establish a break with the captive condition of the discourses of racial domination. The condition of social marginalization and ignorance to which the majority is subject tends to be maintained in the struggle for the basic reproduction of life and attention to basic necessities, in which food security is a daily challenge.

In Part II of this book, we will not deal with the different modalities of Black resistance that have manifested historically, as other authors, such as Marco Antônio Cardoso, do.[3] We do, however, learn about them through the voice of several subjects who embody an ancestral memory with their lives, the tortuous process of identity construction, the confrontation with racism and discrimination, individually becoming conscious of the political and collective dimension of this process, the construction of critique and autonomy of action and thought about the effects of power and knowledge produced by the apparatus.

These subjects are also, from Foucault's perspective, the expression of subjugated, buried, or subjected knowledge, despite the individual success that each one has attained, but they remain in the minority in the areas of discourse and political action regarding raciality in Brazil. They are witnesses and, at the same time, insurgent voices against subordination, epistemicide, and other "cides" to which Blackness in Brazil finds itself subject.

They do not exhaust the many forms of resistance, combat, and racial affirmation in Brazilian society. They lend themselves to illustrating the consequences that the apparatus of raciality/biopower produces, according to the relations of force that sustain it, considering that where power exists, resistance exists. We intentionally chose two Black people with light skin and two with dark skin, bearing in mind the historical urgency that at a particular moment promoted the whitening of Brazilian society in order to indicate subjects whom the apparatus shapes in terms of their resistance. Since reason is held hostage, we could say that they represent "captives" who have escaped from the apparatus. In each of them can be found strategies for struggle and the construction of knowledge/power.

We introduce witnesses into this book who are at once survivors of the strategies of biopower, of the apparatus's technologies of subordinate integration, and survivors of epistemicide's tactics of holding reason hostage. They are among those who escaped the apparatus of raciality's and biopower's control and achieved autonomy of action and thought in terms of the modes of subjectification imposed by the apparatus. They are subjects produced by the power/knowledge dynamic of resistance. In the search for autonomy before the apparatus and as a process of permanent defiance, they construct an ethic that is renewed in collective action and the identification of care of the self with care of others.

The choice of these people is of particular interest for this work because of their synthesis of the articulation of an individual trajectory of mobility and success with the conditions of collective subjects of an emancipation struggle. This choice consists in the search to overcome the mechanisms of the apparatus of raciality that allows a mobility that is individual, minority, and subordinate, but which opposes the collective mobility of Black people as a group. The constitution of the Black political subject is one of the greatest prohibitions imposed on Black people, as well as the phenomenon that would collectively promote that sector of society. The life trajectories traced here threaten the processes of cooptation and negation of the Black raciality available to Black people in Brazilian society, in which the individual project, the acritical admission of meritocracy, the surrender to individualism, and the rhetoric of personal will for the majority that "hasn't yet arrived" reiterate the idea of the lack of will, of selfishness, of self-indulgence. The price demanded and paid by these "winners" is to corroborate the incompetence of the others. In many cases, the possibility or beckon of individual mobility is also an invitation to reject the collective memory of historical exclusion, of racial belonging. Thus, what motivates us to include these witnesses here is what they reveal as strategies of resistance and rupture with the apparatus of raciality's various strategies of subordination and biopower's strategies of survival.

The challenge of working with testimonies, for me, fundamentally resides in not falling into the kind of analysis that the work itself strives to critique. That is, the challenge of not turning insurgent Black intellectuals into mere primary sources for research, abandoning and even rejecting their status as authorities on their own self-knowledge.[4] In this sense, our intent was to treat them with the respect they merit and recognize the status that they have earned and which represents them, and thus, in the context of this book, to treat them as the bearers of the authority to speak on the topic on which we are proposing to work.

In addition to being subjects of knowledge about racial relations, they are victims of the processes of subalternization present in racial relations. Arnaldo Xavier, for example, embodies survival of the "let die" engendered by biopower at the time of his testimony. Finally, they are still insurgent witnesses to this entire process of subjection and death. How should I handle them?

I found answers to this methodological question in theories of testimony, in particular those that emerge from a subjective point of view and tend to prioritize victims' perspectives, such as the one developed by Márcio Seligmann-Silva.[5] Seligmann-Silva describes two approaches, the principal concepts of testimony in the German and the Latin American traditions. According to him, the former is strongly influenced by memories of World War II, and the latter is linked to a larger array of historical experiences that range from the memories of the Latin American military dictatorships to social movements' struggle for land and for citizenship rights based on gender and race/ethnicity. In the German tradition, Seligmann-Silva highlights the importance of North American theorists' contributions to the debate, who, according to him, represent "a kind of 'historical turn' in the context of so-called poststructuralism, in the framework of history as a trauma that complicates the notion of 'historical fact' and impedes its innocent and positivist definition."[6]

For Seligmann-Silva, the characteristics of testimonial discourse are: the event; the person who witnesses it; the testimony; the scene of the testimony; and the testimonial literature. The author identifies as a distinctive characteristic of the German tradition the fact that the event took place in a central location, understood as something radically unique since "the intensity of the event left profound marks on its survivors and their contemporaries, marks that impede a 'cold' or 'disinterested' relationship to it."[7]

In the Latin American tradition, Seligmann-Silva identifies the predominance of counter-history in the historical record, since the witness in this situation should "present proof of another point of view that differs from official history [. . .] what is emphasized is the continuity of oppression and its omnipresence on the 'Latin American continent.'"[8]

In the German tradition, Seligmann-Silva points out, the person who testifies is considered as much a survivor as a *testis*: "a third party who would be summoned before a tribunal to give their version of the 'facts'"[9] in the place of those who succumbed to the catastrophe. *Testis* is the predominant form in the Latin American tradition, according to Seligmann-Silva, in which what stands out is the witness's collective being, either emphasizing the "description of the exemplary nature of the 'hero' [or] finding a voice for the 'subaltern.'"[10]

In the German tradition, the testimony would be literalized and fragmented. In addition, in the Latin American tradition, it would be presented as realistic, factual, and as a rule anchored in orality since it was coming from populations who did not write, for whom a scholar would function as mediator/compiler. In both cases, the scene of the testimony is the courtroom.

In our witnesses, the characteristics that Seligmann-Silva assigns to both traditions are imbricated. Our witnesses are first of all survivors of a radically unique event, which was the enslavement of their African ancestors, the effects of which persist in their memory, their bodies, their lives, and the history of their country. They are also the bearers of a counter-history in which subjectification, stigmas, and stereotypes promoted by slavery and by the subsequent processes of racial exclusion are re-signified and displaced. They are *testis* of those who succumbed to the slave trade, to enslavement – and who were or are silenced by an unfinished abolition – and have only been seen by others in their compiled mass, ironically or with perplexity. They are the survivors of disciplinary powers and biopower that subjugate and exterminate their raciality during the post-abolition period.

Finally, from a Foucauldian point of view, they are the result of multiple situations of subjectification and transitory constitution of subjects. They are Black, *mulato*, *pardo*, Afrodescendants; professors, doctors, lawyers; feminist and anti-racist activists; writers, either full-fledged intellectuals or insurgent and/or subalternized intellectuals. They are the bearers, heralds, and architects of an emancipation struggle. They are also prisoners of the correlations of contradictory forces that slice up the spaces for activism, and the hegemonic powers instituted by the apparatus, and, as a result, they are dominated by the hegemonic raciality. They are subjects and objects of a civilizing process that has raciality as a distinguishing factor for individuals and collectives as one of its fundamental features. And it is crisscrossing all these "places" that they speak of here. Who are they? Paraphrasing Conceição Aparecida de Jesus, they are people who have "Zumbi's[11] revolutionary commitment, understood as a shrewd awareness of filiation and belonging,"[12] making itself present in their life trajectories.

The criteria for selecting witnesses were that they be mature people (all under the age of age sixty when they testified),[13] with reasonably established life trajectories and persistent lifelong practices of confronting discriminatory practices that reflected some of the concepts and strategies for struggle used by contemporary Black resistance. Each witness was asked to provide us with two hours of testimony. This period was divided into four topics: family history; educational trajectory; professional choices and activist activity; and the place of education in their lives and in their political activism. Each testimony was taken, recorded, and transcribed, and underwent a first round of revision, by me.

This first revision was sent back to the authors so they could give their consent for us to use it and so they could also revise or edit it as they wished. Since we were dealing with Black leaders, with a prominent place in the movement and thus on the national stage, we understood that it was necessary for them to be completely comfortable with the publication of their testimony as the subject of philosophical reflection. Upon returning the material, the authors had edited two of the testimonies in such a way that the original spoken versions were transformed, losing much of the feeling they contained at the time they were recorded. In the other case, the spoken version was not edited, but we considered what the author removed to be important for what this study hoped to demonstrate. This required us to negotiate with each of them, in order to restore to the edited transcripts moments in which colloquial speech had a greater power of demonstration than the written word and in the case in which the author had made cuts.

In all these cases, the negotiation was successful and the testimonies that follow are the result of this process. I asked each of them to write a short profile of themselves and to give me a photo of their choice. As one can see, the photos reveal the fortunate results of the elixir of life that they certainly have used throughout their lifetimes.[14] Finally, since from a Foucauldian perspective resistance is a structural dimension of the apparatus, the subjects whom we empanel here as witnesses to demonstrate this resistance constitute a structural part of the architecture of this study. As such, each one has a specific chapter which forms an integral part of the corpus. Finally, in what follows, we present biographical information for an initial introduction so that we know who they are. (We have decided to maintain the biographies as they appeared in my 2005 PhD dissertation, which was the origin of this book, without updates.)

Edson Cardoso, historical activist with the Movimento Negro Brasileiro (Brazilian Black Movement). His activism has always been linked to the dissemination of information, and to political education and coordination. He defines himself as an activist who fundamentally mobilizes people and creates publicity for the fight against racism and racial inequality. He was a member of the National Executive Commission of the MNU (Movimento Negro Unificado; Unified Black Movement) from 1979 to 1985, when he edited the newspaper *Jornal do MNU* (Journal of the MNU). For twelve years, he served as a legislative assistant in the House and the Senate, contributing to the institutionalization of the fight against racism in the National Congress, through almost two hundred statements, projects, and reports. He was the coordinator of the Comissão do Negro do Partido dos Trabalhadores no Distrito Federal (Black People's Commission of the Workers' Party of the Federal District) (1984–7), when he edited the newspaper *Raça e Classe* (Race and Class). He headed up the organization of the I Encontro Nacional dos Negros do PT (First Black People's Meeting of the Worker's Party) in 1987, the Marcha Zumbi dos Palmares, pela cidadania e pela vida (Zumbi dos Palmares March for Civil Rights and Life) in 1995, and the negotiations that created the Organizing Committee which promoted the Brazilian Black Movement's participation in the World Conference Against Racism (Durban, South Africa, 2001). He holds a master's in Social Communication from the University of Brasília. At present, in addition to editing the newspaper *Ìrohìn*, he devotes himself to mobilizing entities across the country for the Marcha Zumbi dos Palmares + 10, which is planned for November 16, 2005. In memory of the march that took place in 1995, this one updates the Brazilian Black Movement's program of demands. He is married to Regina Adami, who is also an activist with the Black Movement, and has two daughters, Inaê and Tana. He is the author of *Bruxas, espíritos e outros bichos* (Witches, Spirits, and Other Creatures) (1992) and *Ubá* (1999), as well as articles in newspapers and journals on topics involving race.

Sônia Maria Pereira Nascimento is a lawyer who specializes in family law as well as human, women's, and Black rights, capacities she draws on for her political activism as an attorney and trainer of civil rights agents. She was president of Geledés – Instituto da Mulher Negra (Geledés – Black Women's Institute) for two terms. She was the executive coordinator of that institute and coordinator of the programs Atendimento Jurídico às Mulheres em Situação de Violência Doméstica e Sexual (Legal Services for Women in Situations of Domestic and Sexual Violence) and Promotoras Legais Populares (PLPS, Public Prosecutors). She was a member of the Conselho Estadual da Condição Feminina (State Council on the Condition of Women), a member of the non-governmental agency Elas por Elas na Política (Women for Women in Politics), and representative of that same organization in the Movimento Nacional de Direitos Humanos (National Movement for Human Rights). She is still an active member of the Ordem dos Advogados do Brasil – Secção São Paulo (OAB, Brazilian Bar Association – São Paulo section), where she was a member of the executive board of the Comissão da Mulher Advogada (Women Lawyers' Commission) and of the Comissão da Defesa dos Direitos do Consumidor

(Consumer Rights Defense Commission), and coordinator of the subcommission on combating discrimination in consumer relations. She developed projects aimed at military police training on human rights together with the Military Police of São Paulo. Sônia Nascimento is a practicing Catholic, devoted to Our Lady of Aparecida, and an active member of her religious community, where she works in pastoral health. She is also a classical singer.

Fátima Oliveira is a doctor, feminist, and anti-racist activist, and specialist author in the areas of reproductive rights and the health of Black populations, as well as a pioneer in the study of genetics and bioethics from a feminist and anti-racist perspective. She is the author of various books such as *Engenharia genética: O sétimo dia da criação* (Genetic Engineering: The Seventh Day of Creation) (1995) and *Bioética: Uma face da cidadania* (Bioethics: A Facet of Citizenship) (2004), a book that functions as a bioethical reflection on the condition of women on the topics of reproductive rights, population policies, etc. She has also published *Oficinas mulher negra e saúde* (Black Women and Health Workshops) (1998), *Transgenêticos: O direito de saber e a liberdade de escolher* (Transgenetics: The Right to Know and the Freedom to Choose) (2001), *O "estado da arte" da Reprodução Humana Assistida* (The "State of the Field" of Assisted Human Reproduction) (2002), *Clonagem e manipulação genética humana: Mitos, realidade, perspectivas e delírios* (Cloning and Human Gene Manipulation: Myths, Reality, Perspectives, and Fantasies) (2002),[15] and *Saúde da população negra no Brasil* (The Black Population's Health in Brazil) (2002).[16] She is currently the executive secretary of the Rede Nacional Feminista de Saúde, Direitos Sexuais e Direitos Reprodutivos (National Feminist Health, Sexual Rights, and Reproductive Rights Network), one of the most important feminist entities in Brazil and Latin America. She is a member of the Communist Party of Brazil (PCdoB) and a columnist for the newspaper *O Tempo* (The Times) of Belo Horizonte (Minas Gerais).

Arnaldo Xavier, poet. He was a member of the Cineclub Glauber Rocha (Glauber Rocha Film Club) and of the Grupo Levante (Stand Up Group) in Campina Grande, one of the founders of Pindahyba Editions, a poets' cooperative. He was the author of the *Manual de sobrevivência do negro brasileiro* (Black Brazilians' Survival Manual) (with Maurício Pestana, 1993), *A rosa de recvsa* (Rose of Refusal) (poems, 1978), *Terramara* (with Cuti and Marian Alves, 1988), and contributions to a diverse array of Brazilian poetry anthologies: *Antologia da Nova Poesia Brasileira* (Anthology of New Brazilian

Poetry) (1992), *Antologia da Poesia Negra Brasileira* (Anthology of Black Brazilian Poetry) (1993), various editions of *Cadernos Negros* (Black Notebooks), *Doc(k)s-Poésies et expressions d'avant-garde en Amérique Latine* (Doc(k)s- Poetry and Avant-garde Expression in Latin America) (France, 1976), and *Schwarze Poesie* (Black Poetry) (Germany, 1992). Arnaldo Xavier died on January 26, 2004. He is included among the witnesses of this work in memoriam. This is my homage to a partner, trusted friend, and comrade of three decades who was with me for a good part of the development of this work, sharing anxieties, discoveries, and paradoxes. But keeping in mind that Arnaldo Xavier's testimony was not collected in the same way as the others, his will not be used for analysis, but as a testimony of an insurgent Black life that I had the privilege of sharing.

# 5
# Edson Cardoso

It was a disagreement that revealed a Freudian slip, perhaps weighted with symbolism. He was supposed to be in São Paulo on November 25[1] for a 5:00 p.m. talk with the youth of the Geração XXI (Generation XXI) project, an affirmative action project developed through a partnership between the BankBoston Foundation and Geledés – Instituto da Mulher Negra (Geledés – Black Women's Institute). In deference to me, he had agreed to travel the night before to grant me an interview. We arranged everything by phone; I was supposed to meet him in the hotel where he was staying the night of the 24th. However, for some strange reason, my brain registered the date of our meeting as the 25th.

*Source:* From Edson Cardoso's personal archive.

He is serious and somewhat ceremonious in his gestures and attitude. He carries himself in a proud and dignified manner when discussing the racial question. Sometimes irritable and with a nervous temperament, he is rigidly principled and intransigent in his devotion to the racial cause. He is our noblest knight. He is patient with neophytes and intransigent with the elders who stray. At 9:00 a.m. on the 25th he called me, with that light exasperation in his voice that I knew so well, demanding I explain my error, one of those that, I know, he considers unforgivable for responsible activists. Caught by surprise by such irresponsibility, I offered an extravagant apology and asked for his forgiveness, and then asked him to come to my house to do the interview. Disappointed but still loyal, he came.

He arrived at 9:45, with his serious manner, formal greeting, no room for mundane niceties. I was still embarrassed and didn't know for sure what to do to cheer him up and mitigate the bad impression. We had met fifteen years before the interview, and at that point we had been speaking weekly for five years. Our intimacy was one of comrades in the struggle, in which there was only room for analysis and evaluation of the ways forward, the Black Movement's rights and wrongs, of the racial question's continuity and change throughout time, of the challenges that persisted as political work for our generation, which was growing older every day.

The interview would show me how little I knew about this elder activist, about his family, his dreams and loves, despite so many conversations that had unfolded over the years. But on that occasion, I also rediscovered why he had been for so long our noblest knight.

Roseli Fischmann had prepared me for how a person's most important experiences emerge in semi-open interviews like the one I planned and in the life history methodology. And I came across unexpected pain in my old friend, the familiar pain of color, and in this case of light skin color. It was painful to live through him the suffering that we also caused for my sister Solange, guilty of having the lightest skin color of my parents' seven children. It was illuminating for my own life story: like Edson Cardoso, I also had a family member linked to the graphic arts. I am the granddaughter of Gabriel, a printer, a proud light-skinned *mulato*, who in Campinas in the 1920s dared to send his daughters to private school, as happened with my mother and her sisters for six years, until he died.

I offered him [Edson] the interview questions. He was quietly surprised by the idea that he would be the title and content of one of the chapters. He read them carefully and said with his always noble air, "We can begin." As I had expected, I was more nervous than he was. There is always something solemn in his figure that has to do with the seriousness of the racial question for an elder activist. Then he began:

Look: I think that what I can say about my life story are rationalizations I've developed that stem from what I do as an activist, valorizing certain aspects to the detriment of others. I don't know if everyone does this, and sometimes I don't know if it's as authentic as an interview about a life history should ideally be, but I would say that I was born to a family in which my father was the son of a Portuguese father and a Black mother, though this Black mother was not his wife, that is, he didn't have a wife, he wasn't married, he had two children with a Black woman, he had a family structure, so to say, with some property and died very young, when he was thirty-six years old. And those two children would have no link to this white family. My granny Julieta would take up with other Black men, so I had uncles, my father's half-brothers who shared a mother with him, and who had different skin color from my father. My father had light skin and kinky hair like my other uncle, his brother with the same father. I think my father harbored great bitterness over this, over his white family's rejection of him, a family with which he had no significant relationship. My father married my mother, who was a Black woman. The children were divided: of their six children, three or four had the darker skin of my mother's side, and at least two had lighter skin. I was the second child, my older brother, a year and a bit older than me, was born with fairly dark skin, like my mother, while I was born with lighter skin, like my father.

So, during my childhood – and I think that this is perhaps the first thing about race in my life, and it was at home – my parents saw me as the white one in the family. But the pronunciation of *branco* (white) wasn't just like that. It was *brrrranco*, with an emphasis on the "r," as though to emphasize that I wasn't quite white how others meant it, but anyway, that I was the white one of the family. And during my childhood, there were frequent allusions to me having been found in the trashcan since I had a different skin color from my other siblings, and it was more pronounced for me because I had the lightest skin. And I don't know if it carried weight for me, but the fact is that I connected with my mother differently from my siblings. I don't know if it has some Oedipal trace; I also thought my mother was a very pretty woman, but I connected with her in a way that my siblings perhaps have not, out of fear that she wasn't really my mother, that this wasn't really my family, but the fact is that it affected me somehow. So, as incredible as it may seem, of all my brothers, I'm the only one who engages in activism on race, and I think that these things in some way weighed on who I am, on what I do. But, nonetheless, I would say that there was a moment during my adolescence, also linked to a love interest, that I think was very special. That is, we were raised in a Black environment because on our street in Salvador, Santo Amaro, that was Recôncavo, in Santo Amaro,[2] everyone was Black. And so in a way we had a very distinct consciousness of which group we belonged to.

Once, in Feira de Santana,[3] when I was fourteen, I had an experience that I never forgot, which I think was very important to my consciousness. There was a girl, I was just finishing *ginásio*, I was between *ginásio* and *científico*, I was fifteen, which was the first year of *colégio*.[4] And there was a girl maybe twelve to fifteen who I thought was very pretty; she was from a different family in that city, they were of German origin, though she didn't have blonde hair, she had kind of brown hair, and I thought she was very pretty, I would go to her door, she would be at the window, I would look at her, I'd come back, look at her, I'd follow her around at school, the kind of thing we did at that age. I was fourteen or fifteen and once we were playing ball somewhere where her class was going to have physical education and I thought that was the day when I would finally say something to her, talk to her. And then, at the end, when the afternoon was almost over, around 5:30 or 6, she left with a group heading toward the avenue and I called out to her and said that I wanted to talk to her, that I had something important to tell her. We had never spoken before. My world was somewhat different from hers, I was two or three years older, and she was in her own world. I told her I wanted to go out with her, directly, just like that. And she said to me: "No, I won't go out with you, because you're Black." And she went on to meet her friends, who were waiting for her. I was left standing there, and went home late that afternoon, my mother asking me wasn't I going to take a bath, and I said no. Something happened there, I never insisted again or anything, but something happened to me at fourteen or fifteen that could seem strange: I was always aware that that's how things were, but on what level of awareness was that such a defining moment? One thing was, let's say, if we have to know something, and I did know, there is a way of knowing that I found out then and there, not just that I was Black, but that this fact was extremely problematic for me, that it was an impediment. Knowing is one thing, but it hadn't come up for me like that, that it was actually a problem. It did that day. And it really affected me, it affected me a lot, I always had a very agitated, nervous sensibility, so it marked my life. I never forgot that day, it really affected me.

Well, my brother's death in a car accident was also a defining experience, my brother died in January of [19]68, a very turbulent year, he died at the beginning of the year, and my shock at my brother's death, speaking about it now with people like you who are somewhat familiar with my personal world in Salvador, my family, you have no idea what it was like to lose my brother when I was eighteen years old, it was brutal for me. Some people think I went crazy. I didn't think so, and I still don't think so today. It was simply unacceptable to me. He was there, he had just had a birthday a week before, he had turned twenty, healthy, in his own style, how could he die in such a stupid way? For me it was a defining moment, it caused a great outrage in my life, in a year in which there was great outrage, but my personal outrage was so brutal. So you have an idea, I was someone who wore my brother's clothes, I was someone who would visit the cemetery alone late at night, I was someone who began to create poetry, who began to write. It was a very brutal shock for me, and without a doubt there was something in the society I was living in that I couldn't accept. So, together with my brother's death, which I couldn't accept, I rejected how things were more generally, and that year I start at the Colégio da Bahia to do high school and I start to read leftist things; I join a reading group linked to Ação Popular[5] and start gaining awareness of how society functions. I begin to channel a little of my outrage toward the fight against the military dictatorship, toward protest. But something in me that caught the attention of my colleagues was something they said was a personal problem: how can someone be so outraged with something that was inevitable? And I didn't think it was like that; it was indeed something that deeply marked my youth that would leave me quite alone, quite outraged, and I spent this period of my life very alone. And I think then I wrote a poem on the topic in [19]70 that started to illuminate for me the difference between being on the left and the racial question. There was a police chief in Salvador named Gutemberg who clamped down on anything that was known at the time as "hippie." So long-haired hippies, people are already starting to talk openly about potheads, there's brutal repression from the military in general, but this police chief from Salvador has a special role. And so, I was reading an article in the newspaper that talked about his brutality, he was saying how he didn't like people with long hair and especially Black people. When I read that, I remember that I wrote a poem for Police Chief Gutemberg.

I'm trying to recover flashes of what I think was forming my racial conscience.

Then I write a poem in which I try to use the elements of denial of identity that were familiar, which were: you need to iron your hair straight, you need to put a clothespin on your nose to make it narrower. Anyway, in the poem there was a little program of what you should do, but you can't be out on the street with your hair like that, you deserve a very special kind of crackdown. I might have it [the poem], yes. And the poem ended like this: that they had to use boiling water on their skin to lighten it; they're subversives.

Well, on to when I met Roberto. Roberto was someone in the group, the reading group linked to Ação Popular, and who wasn't a high-school student. He was Black and he wasn't doing high school, high school was interrupted for him. I didn't understand why, so he was what, then? He was nothing. He was someone who had studied, school had been interrupted, and here was a guy who was part of the reading group. Well, I start going to the public library with him, where I met Luiz Orlando,[6] and then a group of Black people got together, young people with no money, not even to buy a book, to buy anything, and we stayed there at the library. It's there with Roberto that I got the first inkling that beyond the left's concern with change, there was the topic of race. He's died, he was a good friend of Luiz Orlando's and he was the person who gave me books, and so those were the first ones, the first inkling that I would have of the idea that there was even literature, authors. He's the first person who talked to me about the existence of Abdias Nascimento,[7] that kind of thing. That was 1969, when I got these inklings. So I finished high school, but I didn't take the *vestibular*.[8] Look, I was a problematic person when I finished high school. The repression of AI-5[9] came down, my third year was in a very oppressed school. I was strongly disillusioned with everything during that period. My mother pressuring me, I took the *vestibular* for a technical school and I was accepted to "Bridges and Roads," but when the time came to start, to enroll, a job came up and then I took the job, which was being a salesperson for a lab.

And then I started to work. I had the chance to have some money, I made a good salary, and I would read a lot. I wasn't in university, but I was reading a lot. And I decided to leave, I always had a desire to leave, to go, leave, see other places. I went to Rio de Janeiro, alone, without knowing anyone. It was an interesting experience for me, because the effort to be in a city alone, without knowing anyone, looking for a job, it was a very hard experience for me, to see doors shut for incomprehensible reasons, because I felt I was qualified for that job. Everything was very complicated in Rio de Janeiro, but the cultural experience was very rich. The first place I went was the National Library; I had a library card, I got a card, I would look for a job until a certain time, and then I would stay at the library until it closed. I remember that at that time I read all the Dostoevsky they had in the National Library; I went to the theater, to see plays, to see Fernanda Montenegro, she was in *The Investigation* by Peter Weiss. So I was also getting to know a more cultural side that was important for me, as I was looking for a job. Well, my money ran out, then I returned to Salvador, I took the *vestibular*, I got into the Federal University of Bahia (UFBA), and I was interested in literature, writing poetry and reading lots of novels, reading a lot. I studied literature, and there I would have my first contact with a Black group, because those friends, Luiz Orlando, Roberto, are with a group at the ICBA,[10] and they invited me to join them. I had gotten a group of students from the university together and I was participating in the political struggle in the university. I ended up as president of the Student Association, so I told them that I wouldn't have enough time, that I had a lot going on, because they wanted me to be in charge of the literature for the group – now I would say that it wasn't at all about how much time I had, but that it wasn't the right time. But I remember my excitement at sitting there in the white chairs of the ICBA, sitting with a group of Black people, of whom two have died: Manuel, who later became an educator and died, and Roberto. This was in 1974, sitting with a key group that declared itself a Black organization.

It was my first experience and I didn't stay; I went back to university things. There I was dating a lot, which I had done little of up to then. It was a period when I had a good reputation in the department, I was a good student, I was politically active, so I had a lot of girlfriends at the time. It was a majority woman school, so it was a time when I was in the middle of things, and I was also working, I was doing proofreading for the newspaper *A Tribuna da Bahia* (The Bahia Tribune) at night, so I was doing school, working, serving in the Student Association, it was crazy, but it was a wonderful time for me. It was perhaps the happiest time in my youth. I was feeling recognized and everything.

But in the group I'd gotten together there was a preference for Black people. It's funny that today, looking back, among the group

I was the one who saw the difficulties that we Black people had in comparison to the others who were studying at the university. There was a difference: I myself was working at night in order to be able to go to university. There was a difference in how we were treated. I'd had something that the others hadn't had. They hadn't come from good schools, they hadn't done the reading I had, they were, let's say, very behind in comparison to the others. They were – I'm remembering here two people specifically – they were people who made a great effort to keep up with classes, not just because they had outside needs, but because they didn't have my background. My father was important in all this, because my father worked in printing, he made a career as a printer, he became the manager of the shop. And I think that on account of my father's family history, he didn't want to be a worker like the others. This was something very clear in his relationship with the neighbors, with everything.

My father was someone, so you have an idea, who read two newspapers. My father bought books, there was a bookshelf with books in my house. So, if there is one thing that my father valued, it was reading, and in our house, we could say that our habit of reading came from my father. It was something that teachers would come over to the house and "Bah! So many books!" They were kept in the living room, a big bookshelf, full of books. So I can tell you that before I was fourteen years old I had read everything that Jorge Amado[11] had ever published, we had it all in my house. So we would grab things and sit there, reading, looking for smutty passages, that kind of thing, but we were there with a book in our hands, reading. So, when I go to study literature, I already have the habit of reading that had largely come from my father. Even today, it's impossible for me to travel and not stop by the airport bookstore to buy a book, to not be reading on the plane, in the hotel, reading for me is something that I'm used to and I could see it was something the others didn't have.

I grew up in a family with a strong mother and father, we were poor from a material point of view, but with a family in which the children were going to graduate, no child was going to work before they turned eighteen, there was a whole ritual to anticipate the future. My brother's death caused a lot of turmoil, he was older, he was someone who was very intelligent, it was going to cause a lot of turmoil for everyone. But there was a path to growth laid out through studying, my father really valued learning a lot. My father died when he was eighty-two years old, a man who had only finished elementary school, but in conversation, speaking, my father was extremely informed about what was happening. If you wanted to see my father happy at Christmastime, you gave him a book. He even began to ask for them because he kept track of what was coming out, he subscribed to *Veja*,[12] magazines, "Don't you have over there in Brasília this thing that came out with whoever?" Because he wanted to take a look, he was always like that. That made reading very important for me. I think the focus on reading, on studying, it comes from my father. Now, beyond the family part, there was a tradition among printers in relation to the other workers, the other classes. People who worked in printing always liked to say that they were something else. It wasn't the same, dealing with paper, with books, it wasn't the same as a bricklayer, not at all. That is, they always established a difference, so my father liked to say that he knew the authors, that people came there, that they gave him books, the authors of published books. Because my father worked at the Benedictine printers, which always had a great intellectual tradition, it's an Order with an intellectual tradition. So my father ended up in a place where he would make a career, where there was a large library, which is in São Bento, and the priests valued those who read and those who studied.

So my father is there alongside Dom Jerônimo[13] and I don't know who else and my father is valuing this reading thing even more. So in the story of his life, class, the place where he went to work, the sum of all of it led him to value reading. The habit of reading the newspaper, the habit of reading magazines, and books, my father passed it on to all of us. Today, when I see my two girls, one who I think is already like that, she feels strange without a newspaper, at fifteen, because for her it's becoming a habit to read the newspaper every day. But you see for the majority of Black families, access to culture is exclusively through network TV. There is no other means, there's no theater, no cinema, no books, no newspaper, nothing. Just network TV, which antagonizes Black people in every way. Right, they don't have anything, and we had access to other forms, and that's very important for a critical consciousness, without a doubt.

Well, so it wasn't the right time. I show up to this group and, yes, I was different and it wasn't because of money: our families were equal in economic and financial terms. Our relationship was a kind of leadership that I had in the process, the capacity to dare, to say: we are going to take on the Student Association, put an end to the garbage that is the student union, clean, paint, add a ping-pong table, get a newspaper subscription for the student union, do something different, extend our horizons. Anyway, I was seen as a leader, someone who could make these things happen. So what would happen, poetry had seduced me such that I had already written a poetry chapbook, and I thought that to improve my poetry I needed life experience, to live more intensely, the desire to leave again kept growing, to leave and try things. I edited a very modest poetry chapbook with ten poems and I sold it. With the money I earned selling this chapbook, I left Salvador. Since I really enjoyed Spanish, I took three semesters of Spanish. I thought I would go to Argentina, to Uruguay, so I went straight to Porto Alegre, also without knowing anyone, just as I had gone to Rio, I went to Porto Alegre with my poems.

In Porto Alegre, I would have, indeed, my most defining experience. In Porto Alegre, I looked for work wearing a jacket and tie, and I didn't find anything, and I even wrote poetry about it. The racial contrast in Porto Alegre is very different from Salvador. In Porto Alegre, it was becoming clear to me, shall we say, that the barrier was in fact racial. Perhaps my own thinking had matured, but the fact is that Porto Alegre would be the place where I'd work as an assistant bricklayer – note that I had four years of university – assistant bricklayer, loader in a Transdroga[14] depot, I'd work as a polishing assistant. I was a good student, I wrote well, I had finally published my chapbook – and I would work. I'd strip off the jacket and tie, if I wanted to stay, and I would work doing things that I never in my life thought I'd do. And I was working hard. In Salvador, I had worked for a newspaper, I'd been a lab salesman, and I'd taught a few classes. I was on a certain level, but in Porto Alegre I was demoted to the "place for Blacks," so to say, and I was coming from the land of the "Black university graduate," Salvador, where during slavery in the medical school we not only had Black students, but Black professors, in the middle of slavery. It is different to leave Salvador and go to Porto Alegre. The tradition of a Black middle class that dates from the time of slavery is real. Edvaldo Brito[15] isn't an exception in the twentieth century. There were people like Edvaldo Brito in the nineteenth century but they were exceptions. Few, but they did exist. You have a tradition, you have Black doctors, you have engineers. Edison and Nelson Carneiro's[16] father was a professor in the Polytechnical School. And the sons got law degrees. So in Salvador there is a rather deceptive middle ground because of this world of exceptions. And in Porto Alegre things are very different.

Arriving from Salvador, with my physical appearance, what happened had to happen. Well, the fact is that I went to the library, my reading thing, and the library was open on Sundays. And sometimes on Saturdays I worked until six at night, but on Sundays I went to the library in Porto Alegre, and at the library I come across an announcement: a group of young writers from Porto Alegre was meeting at the Culture Club. I went one evening and I took my poetry chapbook with me and I then met people who were writing, like me, and there I would become a part of a group that was galled Grupo Korpo Insano (Insane Body Group) and we prepared an anthology for the 1977 Porto Alegre Book Fair. There I would get to know the city's more middle-class world. I shocked them, with the kind of work I did, my isolation in Porto Alegre, since I wasn't someone involved with drugs, with anything. They were confused by my poetry, which was all written in Porto Alegre, which I published there, linked to the values of a different life that wasn't theirs. But I would say that what I was looking for was just that. Well, from Porto Alegre to Brasília I was romantically involved with a girl from Rio Grande do Sul, someone much older than my twenty-seven years: she was forty-five. I was deeply involved romantically, and after a few girlfriends and such it was my first long-term relationship with a woman, a serious one. She was someone who had a very special understanding of my blackness, in a way – she died last year at seventy-two years old – she even encouraged me in it. I remember very well her calling my attention to the formation of the MNU[17] in 1978. So it was curious, because she was not a Black woman, she was from the border, with a racially mixed background, but she was white from Brazilian society's point of view, but let's say, a Southerner like Brizola,[18] a real traditional guy. Her father was from a very traditional border family, Santana do Livramento, and he was the editor of *Plateia* (Audience), a newspaper from there. She only finished high school, but she was a person who read, read poetry, and I met her because of a poem of hers that I was supposed to read in a recital. We were introduced to each other there and immediately had a great connection. We talked about poetry and she loved Bahia. So conversation ebbed and flowed, we had a very strong personal and physical connection, it was very intense, our relationship was very intense for several years.

After meeting one of her daughters, who lived in Brasília, I moved there; otherwise Brasília would not have ever been on my radar, it hadn't been until then. Look at what fate had in store for me. When I arrived in Brasília, I would work doing lots of different things, but I resumed something positive that Brasília would offer, which were my studies. Since I was already studying, I took another *vestibular* for the University of Brasília and sent for my things from Salvador. I figured that in the worst-case scenario, I could graduate in three semesters, but I had to work.

So I went to work for a printer, I worked at a bookstore checkout counter, and afterwards I went to work for the magazine of the CNPQ (Conselho Nacional de Desenvolvimento Científico e Tecnológico; National Council for Scientific and Technological Development). It was there that I met Elmodad, who saw my interest in racial issues, because at that time I was reading quite a bit about the racial question, and she told me that she would introduce me to some people. So in 1980 she introduced me to the MNU folks in Brasília. I would go to the meetings still without thinking that this was something I would dedicate my life to, but look, I was already thirty. There was nothing in me, up to that age, nothing that told me to. I had, of course, an inclination toward literature, I was going to teach, I liked to speak, be a critic, but nothing that said I would join the Black Movement. And there I went to a meeting, I went to two, they wanted me to speak, to give a speech, and me not taking any of this seriously, until at one meeting two new people came in, and someone had to say something to them, so I signed up and I spoke. If you were to ask me what I spoke about, I don't know: the fact is I said something. When the meeting finished (the MNU didn't have its own headquarters; the meetings were in what we called the Santa Clara pharmacy loft, it was a little shop above a pharmacy), Jacira asked me to stay, there was a bar next door, did I want to have a beer so the two of us could talk a little? When we began to talk she told me: "Do you have any idea of how important you are to other people?" She asked me directly. And the penny dropped right then and there. That's how it is, perhaps many people wouldn't have noticed it, they wouldn't realize how important they are to others. I don't know what happened during that meeting that she thought she had to say that to me. She said: "You should think about this a bit." Ok, well, after that conversation, I went home and felt like a different person, because of the importance I had for others. From there it grew, my involvement didn't just expand but also gained intensity: it was what I did all day, I'm someone who would do it every day and I continue to this day.

So that's how it was, you know, something suppressed and at a certain moment, ta-da, it was never-ending. And it was there that I would really understand myself, my life began to make sense, and I looked back, things were going a certain way, but everything, everything, made sense to me. But that's how it goes, it's going, and someone grabs me and shakes me like that and asks "Do you realize?" I was going along, but I didn't think I was in charge, I was there and all, I was plugged in to the topic, to the subject, but I wasn't. . . So it started, and it started in a very special way, and, let's say, that feeling of a full cup, of plenitude. The racial question would give me, I think, what not even sexual pleasure, which is something very intense, gave me, the feeling of finding myself. I completely understood myself from that moment. If I look at the Edson from before, as much as people might say that I could have been interesting at some time, but nothing was interesting and I wasn't even interested in myself, as this peace came over me. Things rounded out and what would happen? Look at this sign. There I found Black women, I began to see people, I began to see everything differently, and inevitably things calmed down.

When I got married, I was by then attentive, participating, smelling, grasping, everything changed, meaning changed. It's something that comes back and it was very important. Because of my background, I was always very patient with others who didn't take on responsibility, because I know that everyone takes their own time for decisions. Now, the decision I'm referring to is irreversible, it means an everyday commitment, in your job, where you study, where you teach. Everything becomes how you live, your house, your intimate relationships, it's a totality and this urge. So I was doing what had to be done. In activism, I look at myself honestly, an activist in the very definition of the word, I think I'm a person who actually activates, who makes things happen, and from there on what happens is this: I don't stop, I feel like someone who wants to do even more, because I think there's more to do.

I'm very interested in questions of identity. I think if you sit down to lay things out you see the violence that was slavery, which is something always viewed by white people. We have very few accounts of what it was like . . . for us, here in Brazil, I don't mean that's how it should be, but in the larger bibliography. For us, very few accounts remain of what it means to plunge into an enslavement that will deny the values of culture, humanity. What does this actually mean? How far does this go? What damage does it do, that you can deny everything, and everything about an individual? It's not just cultural values, manners, practices, deny them as part of humanity. What does this mean? I have to extract something from this object, because I want an object to which I can deny anything, I want to extract productivity from it. Those who talk about it are white historians, always speaking in a way that doesn't reach me.

The anguish we see in Cruz e Sousa[19] is, perhaps, for example in literature, in poetry, also, what gets closest to what could be a soul convulsed by this denial, you see? That is, someone who, within slavery, wants to affirm his refined sensibility as a poet and present himself in the language of the Other as though it were his own language. A refinement of expression that he wants to affirm, and the Other insists on seeing him exclusively as yet another Black person. The image of being enclosed that he used in one of his poems is perhaps the image that comes closest to this idea – especially because it comes from a Black person. An image that wants to affirm his values and his integrity. It's perhaps the most legitimate image of the process, the walls that are erected and that close in around you. I think the way that he puts it, perhaps he has the sensibility that comes closest to telling us what it has meant to be in this situation. The fact is that such a systematic and constant and lasting negation that is so, so continuous, we don't know how it affected those who still had the memory of their history, and how it would affect those who had lost such memory, because one thing is the impact of those who could remember, of those who could recover, and the impact on those who no longer even had this memory. What is this process? That is, the individual doesn't know anything about where they came from; they don't know anything about the values of their civilization or culture and they are systematically negated through every means, in every aspect.

Now, I think that no instrument exists with which we can understand in terms of psychology, medicine, in sum, all that we can understand about a person, all the channels of knowledge that a human being has constructed, no one has seriously applied themselves in a country like Brazil to examine the significance of all this on people.

So, the first thing that I want to draw attention to is: what do we need to recover? I insist on the question of identity because what comes to my attention is that the relationship of domination is created through this negation: I affirm myself as superior and master through this negative that is you. And isn't that how it is? If so, what's essential is here in this relationship. That is why Black and indigenous people have a status that is differentiated from others, and since they are the dominated group, it's clear that this is part of the very nature of domination, but also a component that can be reduced to a banal formula, which is the negation of the identity of the Other, of the values of their culture and humanity, or whatever it may be. Whatever may be the other mechanism of economic domination, all the other elements that are part of domination. There is something here that was understood at the moment of justification in order to keep things as they are.

I think, then, that the first thing needed to change things is to breathe into people a perception of a historical trajectory. Look at this: there was a letter in the [newspaper] *Folha* [*de São Paulo*] yesterday or the day before from a woman asking why people would want to know the history of Africa. She even thinks it would be better not to know it, because people are going to discover that it is in no way as idyllic as they think. When people speak of recuperating history, they think we're talking about recuperating a history from the point of view of good people versus bad. But that's not at all what we are talking about. What we are talking about is the following: we managed to take a historical episode that historians considered minor out of their hands, which was the case of Palmares.[20] In thirty years, a single historical episode produced the effect that you now see. Now, when people talk about history, they're speaking of a collection of episodes, of processes, of possibilities that they generate, because a single episode generated the most important civic holiday in the country,[21] it generated a revolution in people's minds, it forced institutions, mothers' clubs, associations, unions, the Supreme Court, in some way to open up to a true reflection about racial inequalities, or not, a single episode that people recuperated from official historiography. Imagine now how many other events exist and what kinds of effects they could produce.

So there's something fundamental in the fight against domination: it's this recovery of a specific trajectory, a discourse of identity. What one can do in this area is fundamental. The slides that I brought, that I won't be able to show, include an engraving from the nineteenth century in which a Black youth appears next to a young chimpanzee and a young orangutan. The caption asks us to note the extreme similarity among the types. Then I move on to an image from the 1970s taken from the magazine *Machete* in which Hoechst had a two-page advertisement with a series of photos of the same Black woman trying to pronounce the word Hoechst and it says above: "Our secretary is a genius; after fifteen days she managed to pronounce the name of our business." So the Black secretary appears with her mouth twisted this way and that, desperate. In fifteen days, the genius learned to pronounce the name of the business. So I go from the monkey thing to this one, and then to an image of the Santa Marta drug store for Mother's

Day in 2004 in which a Black woman is looking at a Black child, a positive image, and then I show an image of Lux soap, then an image of a Black woman, an African, as a Nobel Prize winner. Look carefully, from animal to Nobel laureate, so to say, in sequence. Since they're young, my idea was to bring this to them so they could see the following: this only happened because of our efforts, that is fundamental. If anyone thinks that it is mere change on the level of representation, I say: that's where the problem is, racism is on the level of representation. If you manage to produce a positive image, you are directly combating racism, whether or not material living conditions have changed. So the struggle over images is a fundamental struggle. Let me say this: I am concerned with this recuperation of identity and history, I am concerned with this thing on the level of representation, which I consider fundamental, that is, altering and forcing a reflection on finding another way for us to represent ourselves.

Another plan that I think is fundamental is to be able to recognize ourselves in the Other, that is, the politics would happen that moment when human beings sit down together and recognize each other. So we have to get to a moment of recognizing each other sitting together and making a decision that doesn't need to be a consensus, but, as the left used to say, mostly consensual, and go out to do something related to the decision that the group made. We Black people, we're far from this plan and I can't see that far, [a point] unrelated to this problem of representation, of domination, and of racism. That is, what keeps us from sitting down together is the difficulty in recognizing ourselves as such; it's the difficulty of overcoming a portrayal that we have of ourselves, an extremely negative one. So everything that we do in this direction is extremely political because it is going to contribute to this moment of recognition, of consensus, of a basic agenda and collective action of the collective subject that we want to create. It's going to be difficult to create a collective subject if I see myself in a negative way in relation to others; there is no way to form a collective subject at all. It's complicated. It has to happen through the recognition of the Other. We act collectively because we recognize ourselves as such. I think these things are related, so to speak.

This would be my priority action plan, that is, I work on the history thing, on the things that I publish, I work on this question of image, of representation. I already set myself to analyzing C&A's[22] advertising in a book, because I think this is a very important thing and I work with the plan of constructing this moment when we can sit down together and make a decision about our survival as a group, about our interests as a group and act, that is, do politics. These are my priority action areas. I see these things as related. I don't think we have gotten to the full extent of the damage that's being done to subjectivity in all its aspects. We still need to dive deeply into this, without victimization, but this damage has a lot to do with our difficulty in constructing a collective subject, without a doubt. Another aspect that I think is important to highlight is that the Other who dominates is conscious that domination is perpetuated through this fragmentation, this negation. I consider Brazilian society's greatest prohibition to be on Black people getting together as such; there's a panic that has run through all of society for centuries. It has nothing to do with Haiti. It starts before, it runs through the entire colonial period, the whole period of slavery, up through modernity. Political parties, unions, business associations, have the same panic of Black people meeting, whether to build a family, a house, on a street corner, or whether it's a group of muggers.

Be that as it may, it's extremely threatening to the unconscious, to subjectivity, to all aspects of Brazilian society, for Black people to get together. It seems that something absolutely threatening to the Order will take place, and I think they're right. But that's the principal prohibition; this dimension of racism that we need to highlight, that racism has various dimensions, it has this dimension of subalternization, of oppression, of the exploitation of work, the exploitation of women, of housing, of the sanitation of the water you drink, of murder. It has various dimensions. But it has the dimension of denying you the ability to get together with others to combat it. And this is a special dimension. People underestimate this dimension. Racism, to function, throws you in that neighborhood, but it impedes you from reacting to that situation, in that neighborhood, as a Black person. This is a central dimension of racism. It's remarkable, moreover, how some Black people linked to political parties say that white people can participate. I was in a meeting in Porto Alegre a few days ago and various Black people made a point of reinforcing in their speeches that white people could participate. Can you imagine a meeting of white people in which white people were constantly asking "Where are the Black people?" But now that Black people are going to get together to protest, white people have to participate.

It's remarkable how people whose center of political action is in the unions, in the party, in other places, make a point, in their words, of highlighting that white people have to participate and can participate. We want to mobilize Black people, and you're coming to me with white people have to participate? That's their problem, it's not our problem, but these guys bring it to us as though it were our problem. They're linked to a center that has already said no to Black people getting together. Mobilization just of Black people can't happen. You see: this accusation of racialization of public space is hilarious, because white people accuse us of racializing public space when we make proposals based on racial identity, as if the public space where they are weren't already racialized. It's naturalized, I guess. We show up, and then "It's dirty!" This business of race, you made it dirty. So I don't know . . . It makes you want to demand: we, those people, you know who you are, we wanted to demand something: to find out how to participate. We don't know how to say this in a way that doesn't upset you, but we want to participate. How can we speak like this? Do you authorize us to? That's what they want. How can we speak like this, that we don't want to be where we are, and we want to be where you are? Can you tell me a legitimate way to say that? They say: "Come on, let's have a seminar, let's make a decision, so you stay there and we'll get together with Yvonne Maggie,[23] we'll get whoever together . . ." So they see how it's done. Because, when we say "we Black people," it can't be. You can say, "Ok, so I'm going to get rid of all the Black people, you talk to those people, got it?" Because, how are we going to say "we Brazilians," "we the people of Brazil," how can people say that? That's what they want, for us to ask for authorization to say how we make demands, because what's wrong is how we're making demands. "That way isn't polite, it's not appropriate and will make things worse . . ." But will it make things worse? Because that dimension is the one that has more weight in Brazilian society, more structure, more of everything that Brazilian society has. Because you see that the error the SEPPIR (Secretaria Nacional de Políticas de Promoção da Igualdade; Special Secretariat for Policies to Promote Racial Equality) commits is to presuppose that there was a mode of production in Brazil based on the exploitation of the Roma; presuppose that being homosexual obligated the guy to plant sugarcane; that some guy's mobility disability or any other difficulty meant he had to work planting coffee.

I'm trying to say the following, this prohibition reaches the following point: there can't be a Bureau of Black People, there just can't. So since there can't, Roma, Jewish people, Palestinians, are invented. Invented in what sense? Invented because I am placing them in a dimension in which historically they didn't exist. That's it. Discrimination against the Roma is adequately addressed by the anti-discrimination legislation that already exists in Brazil. Our demands aren't. Our demands have to do with the structure of Brazilian society, from the beginning of its colonization. Our demands put into question the way we live and how we're here, how we distribute revenue, power, wealth. The demand of the Roma is "Don't bother me!" "Don't interfere with my group!" "Leave my group alone!" The demands of Black people are not the same. The demands of homosexuals are "We want to live as we are, as homosexuals." That's all they're saying. But our demands are not the same. We want to determine what Brazil will be like. That's the difference. We want a reckoning with that history. We were linked, always, as we have always been, to the center of things. Because they want to, they want to push us, it's a way of pushing us to the side. No, we want to remain in the center, we came already in the center.

The racial dimension was always central, that is, there is no way to think about a historical trajectory of that length through Brazil without associating one group's declaration of supremacy over the others with all the values of colonial domination. That is, that fact was always implicit in everything. Implicit and explicit. If you look at concrete situations, things were even said in the most banal everyday situations. During my childhood in Salvador, I even caught expressions like "white people's street" and "white people's house." That is, housing identified with a racial group. That's it. By looking at the house, what condition it's in, the conditions of the place: it's a "white people's street." That's profound, you see? You just see the space and you can already tell that that space is white people's . . . "Eh, he's working in a white person's house!" These were common expressions in the [19]50s, "He's working for a white person!" That's how it was.

So it was very clear for our Black world: here one racial group dominates the other. The division is perfectly clean in Brazil. If you pick up the literature that was written in the [19]20s, it's very revealing, in my view, of this debate in a very intense way: that is, we had begun a new century, we had a Republic, and we had to define the Republic even from the point of view of race, and what was in the world. We need to better situate Nazism in all this. That's why I say: there is an emblematic level, which is *O Presidente negro* (The Black President) by Monteiro Lobato,[24] in which this discussion is clear. What would be Brazil's future with this Black population? Look at the example of the United States: in what way, how are we going to do this? If you pick up *Retrato do Brasil* (Portrait of Brazil), by Paulo Prado,[25] another intellectual from São Paulo from the same time, doing the same analysis, he would say in his book that except for the possibility of a laboratory solution – notice how things were in the air – the solution was really whitening,[26] and he was saying that some people already looked white in the 1920s, as a result of miscegenation. At the time, people used the world "Aryanization." Monteiro Lobato had already brought up the laboratory solution: the increasing demographic of the Black population is such that whitening can't solve it, so the solution has to come from a laboratory. That's where the solution is found, which is called the final solution. That's why I say: if you translated Monteiro Lobato into German and brought in an actor to perform it in that tone that Hitler used to make his speeches in his films, some moments would be identical.

What I'm trying to say is that Monteiro Lobato's book is Nazi *avant la lettre*, before Nazism took shape as an ideology. The ideas that were part of Nazism were out in the world, circulating. They had the right situation to follow through, but they weren't the Germans' ideas. In Germany, the perfect conditions were found, but in Brazil they are in *O Presidente negro*, where even the phrase "the final solution" is used, still in the [19]20s. And it was in the [19]20s that he, Monteiro Lobato, would say the following: that the solution is sterilization of the Black population, that not one more would be born. So yes, there we have a solution. The intellectual Paulo Prado is thinking of whitening and says that the proof of the success of whitening is that some people already look white by the end of the [19]20s, that with just a little more the problem would disappear. But Monteiro Lobato prefers sterilization, a laboratory solution. Nazism would use the laboratory in a remarkable way, that is, it was a leader in using science to find the means of exterminating undesired populations.

Luis Fernando Verissimo has a book about the opponent, the thumb.[27] In his five-fingers series, the opponent would be considered the finger of civilization. If human beings didn't have this fifth finger, they wouldn't be able to grab anything; they can because of this one here. He came up with the following situation: a scientist is going to do a study, there is an organization that controls the world, white people win everything, the majority of the world is not white, and white people are very worried about it. The scientist for this group is going to do a study of monkeys in Africa. He starts from a hypothesis: that there is a genetic anomaly in white people that protects them from the thing that he is going to create and, as a result, white people would be immune to it. He creates something that will destroy non-white people, except white people also begin to be affected, and the virus spreads around the world. We're now at the beginning of another century and people continue to think it's possible to create racist means of demographic control of the non-white population in a laboratory.

The play *Anjo negro* (Black Angel) by Nelson Rodrigues is from 1946. In the play, a white woman reproduces with a Black man and has Black children, and she kills them all because they shouldn't even be born. João Ubaldo Ribeiro, at the end of the (twentieth) century, wrote the novel *Feitiços na Ilha do Pavão* (The Sorcery of Peacock Island) (1997), in which he imagines a time machine from the future where there is room for miscegenation, but not for Black people; Black people are placed in a *quilombo*[28] and the *quilombo* is the expression of racism. To go to the *quilombo* is to be racist; affirming one's Black identity is to be racist. They are the worst characters in the book. There is only room for miscegenation with Black women, who will have the future; they are a machine who also project the future. So what I always say when I'm working with students, when we work on these three texts that span the entire twentieth century, and take up three intellectuals with the stature of Monteiro Lobato, Nelson Rodrigues, and Ubaldo Ribeiro, considered the greatest of the twentieth century in Brazil, this is what all three think: there will be no Black people in the future. So the racial dimension is inherent in concerns, if you will, about the country's future.

I think that if we go in the dimension of population control, the forms of control of the Black population in Brazil go to the extreme of extermination. We haven't sat down to calculate it, but when we do we'll be terrified, even just taking into account statistics from newspapers. If you take thirty years, the number of Black people killed in Brazil over three decades is so large that it represents a form of control that surpasses all logic, because when you say "social control," you want to keep a population under control, but the way you choose, the preferred way, is their death.

So let's say: I kill in various ways, but preferably the guy identified as reactive, who would be the young man most predisposed to action, to reaction, at the age of rebellion, to the possibility of confrontation . . . control is "that one can't go on living," that's what control is. He can't go on living, and that's brutal, of course. If you consider these images in an ideological, literary, poetic superstructure, you'll see that in fact that's how it is. And in the physical world, things happen that way but much more brutally. There's a text by Caetano[29] that I want to use in the Salvador course that it's worthwhile for you to listen to.

Another thing that plays out is the process of rereading the past, which is also a form of control. Whatever I say about the past, that it wasn't as terrible as you say, works to delegitimate your possibilities of organizing in the present. So while you fight for Palmares, there is a whole set of new authors writing historiography who always look for a way to legitimate compromise in the past, to see a somewhat softened slavery. Then Caetano reaches the point, in "Noites do Norte" (Northern Nights), of bringing Zumbi together with Joaquim Nabuco, which is as far as a person can go.[30] But he has some opening lines about slavery that you won't believe. There are five or six sentences where he talks about it. You wouldn't believe that someone could refer to the enslavement of human beings in this way: to speak in this way, a way of construing the past was constructed that could only have the goal of delegitimating any action in the present that has a historical figure at its core. Monteiro Lobato's book disappears; his is not a book to be debated, it's not a book to be discussed, it's not a book to be cited, it disappears, and you, at the same time, are trying to make all forms of oppression disappear.

So I have various forms of control: I have this control over representation; I have this control that goes as far as extermination; I have the control of turning history on its head and distorting it – they're various forms of disappearance. I didn't bring up the editorial in the journal *Raça* (Race), we can see the results in our people's discourse. The editorial has two expressions that I separated out, where the writer says that we should react, that it's our time to fight without violence, and further on that we should work within the law. And you sit there asking how someone, the target of so much violence, is so worried about a non-violent reaction, and how someone who had no hand in writing laws, all laws that were written to benefit those who are already there, is so concerned with acting within the law. Who is she trying to keep from upsetting? She is forced to admit that something is underway in Brazilian society, that Black people are pressuring for civil, political, and economic rights, etc., etc. She has to admit that her magazine in some way wants to get closer to this discourse, but at the same time she is afraid that it will get out of control. But whose? Her control? She should say: "Great, we're going to break the law." It's a curious thing to examine the effects of all this on Black people's discourse, which is wonderful, the guy showing up and being openly scared, like SEPPIR. I mean, the editorial of *Raça* magazine is SEPPIR, it's the same terror, it's the same fear of taking responsibility, it's the same thing. A fear of taking responsibility for any proposal that doesn't have the seal of approval and acceptance by white people. We are dependents in Brazilian society, we're being controlled, and all our actions either have white people's consent or they can't take place.

Candomblé[31] in Bahia stopped needing a license only in the 70s, the 1970s, the twentieth century. This is not just a detail. You have to consider that Candomblé in Bahia has something specific that it doesn't have anywhere else in Brazil; there is a reality of historical authenticity in Bahia that is undeniable. This thing about Xangô is really intriguing to me, this choice, this presence of Xangô behind the *terreiros* in Bahia.[32] As the guarantor of the perpetuation of the collective, at a time when slavery put it at risk, he is the entity who is most frequently referenced. Now, a place like that, in which religion is so open to resistance that it wasn't dominated, controlled, that was a space where, in fact, white people did not enter, white people didn't authorize it. That's what I'm trying to tell you: in a place where they didn't have control, they said: "We can't let this shit take place." As long as it wasn't full of Jorge Amados, and I don't know who else, it couldn't be free. It was only freed when they said: "We are the twelve *ogãs*[33] there, you can allow it . . . because in the end, in the end, that's it, we vouch for it!"

This is what I think: in some ways, the game was more honest in the pre-Republican period.[34] I was reading a little about the Rebouças[35] in a history magazine and understanding better the loopholes they were able to take advantage of. In Bahia, in 1823, there was a battle to kick the Portuguese out. Brazil got its independence in 1822, but in Bahia they were even reinforcing the troops. So they had to mobilize a lot of people to expel the Portuguese. Some free *pardo* and Black people already mobilized were also involved in the fight because it was an opportunity, and people were being called up to participate. The Rebouças took the opportunity.

After the expulsion of the Portuguese, one of the brothers would go to France to study; he returned with a degree in medicine, and would teach in the Medical School in Bahia. The other began to practice law, he studied and publicly recognized his right to practice without a degree from the Law School. He practiced law, he took a position against the Malê Revolt,[36] and evidently there was a loophole, there was a context there, he had a position in the system, he was elected as a representative, and as a representative he sought to operate within legislation's loopholes. His work as a representative was extremely positive, and his children would also go on to study in France. His nephews, Antônio's sons, came back to create the Engineering School in Rio.

Lima Barreto[37] is the Black intellectual who perhaps best exhibits this. He says that the Republic is not good for Black people. He says: "My father had a job during the monarchy and afterwards they had him taking care of an insane asylum, and he went crazy, and I had to leave Engineering School in order to support my family . . ." and then he went crazy too. He is a person who it's worthwhile to pick up, because he has read, in his research, he can find other things, but that's a topic that is worth researching by itself, this confrontation, that opportunities existed under the Empire that the Republic made more difficult.

The first ones to come into the Republic were stigmatized, even one who I'm interested in studying, who is Manoel da Motta.[38] He would suffer from problems at the beginning of the Republic when he was elected as a federal representative. I'm not so much interested in the figure of Motta, I already have all his speeches. My interest is in the Black Movement's reactions to the obstacles that were placed to prevent him from taking office. Do you have any idea? He goes to Pelotas at the invitation of the Black Movement to a meeting that includes the participation of three hundred people. Pelotas had two newspapers, it had various agencies. I thought to myself: I've done so many events, putting on events is so difficult, how is it that someone could have an event at the beginning of the last century to support a Black representative and bring three hundred people together? There are things that history doesn't register, but in November 2005 I'm not going to do anything, I already know, but I want to, because something's sticking in my head, I keep tracing it, there's something, something big. There was a protest in Brazil completely by Black people.

There's an education that I don't want, it's not an education that serves my people. What do I have to do? Say how education should be. Have an institution that from its very origins opposes what's already there. It might be quite small, but one that isn't the education we're offering. What's the problem we have in Brazil? It's that for us, education is always their school, it's the school that's already there, it's never like this: we are educating how we want our children to be educated. Our institutional weakness in this sense – is not institutional in the sense of government, parliament. No. It's that we don't have institutions, the ones we have are weak. In the

United States, what they did was like this: no, we educate our own pastors, excuse us, we are going to train our own, we aren't going to learn in their school how they speak to Black people, no. We are going to teach. We don't invest, when we criticize education, we talk about public schools, but we never talk about what we're doing. I think that every initiative we have in this direction is for education. Where do I want to go with the newspaper? It's ridiculous to keep thinking, for example, that if I were talking to an idealized American that I have here in my head and complaining to him, like I complain in the editorial of this issue, about how the newspapers don't publish the President of the Supreme Court's speech that was in favor of Black people, he would say: "But Edson, why didn't white newspapers, white people's newspapers, publish something that's in favor of Black people? Do you want to explain it to me? Because I don't understand what expectation you have, after 516 years. How is it that you don't have your own newspaper?" There is something that is linked to us not having political autonomy, we don't have autonomy.

Look, it's not just political organization, it's any other form of organization. Even if we are incredibly unified as a people, we don't say, "Ok, I'm going to found my newspaper." Because if you aren't capable of doing that, we won't be capable of doing anything. That's what's revolutionary in Frei Davi.[39] I'm saying: that prep course that the Black Movement started – I was in the IAPI,[40] the IAPI has a church, in São Paulo parish, a young Black priest, Father Gabriel, they run a pre-*vestibular* prep course there. I was talking to Seu[41] Aluísio, who's a retiree of Petrobras,[42] and he said that he managed to educate all four of his children. This was before the speech. There I heard him speak and all and he pointed out to me: my girl is doing her master's and my boy too, he's teaching in the prep course. At one point, I said: Seu Aluísio didn't just figure out how to educate his children, he educated his children because they are already at university and they came back here, so that others can have the opportunity to increase their chances of getting in, he taught his children well. Look at what's happening! This indeed is giving an answer, it's not just having a quota, it's saying, "I'm going to teach a Portuguese language class for you." This is what we need to build, that is, not the possibility of this idea, because they have it there already, because it's a majority Black neighborhood, the people are from the neighborhood, they identify with the church, with a Black priest, and they feel like they're part of a collective. It's not the fragmentation that Brasília has. No, in my city, everyone knows who Seu Aluísio is.

If it's education you're talking about, it's an education for which we have to construct parameters, references, and practices. There's another education that we want to ensure. I think there are both things: I confess that I am more interested in this other one than in changing things over there, even though I am over there, but all the institutions needed to do what Father Gabriel is doing, that is, have a school, train them, show them how to do it. That's my concern about Ìrohìn.[43] Let me put it this way: we have to train people, if not, we won't make it.

Now the difficulties with education in general are the result of the panic that they have about anything that could possibly reinforce the Black population's identity. It changes the relationship of domination. So that can't happen. There is the law no. 10.639[44] that means the following: some Brazilians don't have a right to the past. So I say: cultural rights are part of human rights. It's an aggression against people's human rights not to allow them to have access to the past. Now, those whom I don't want to have access to the past are exactly the people whose access to the past would change the relationship of domination that I want to perpetuate. Saying this in a very simplified way, it works like this: "For what past, if the past as you understand it reinforces claims for reparations? I'm going to have to multiply Zumbi for you. I won't do it. Isn't the history of Palmares enough?" because evidently the past will bring with it a much broader, very different reflection of the process, right? If Black people were responsible for it? It's a lie, it's idiocy, it's a discussion I don't want to be involved in. It's evident that many Black people participated in the process, if not it couldn't have happened, but that's not what this is about. When you say that Jews collaborated with Nazism, you would never say, not even to yourself, that Jewish people weren't victims of Nazism. Stop it.

It's not the fact that Black people participated, that they were accomplices, that they benefited from the enslavement of people; that's not why Black people's demands regarding slavery have no legitimacy. That's pure idiocy, it's an ideological thing, it's an ideological condition, I don't let myself waste time on it. But the truth is that I feel that people needed to separate one from the other: education on one side and comprehension on the other.

Italians demanded dual citizenship because of a historical process, or, rather, the declaration of an Italian-Brazilian identity comes to be through history. Thus without history there is no way to declare it. When I say I am a son, a grandson, I am appealing to history, to historical documents, to assert and claim dual citizenship. So the declaration of identity is made in history, there's no way for me to say I'm Italian-Brazilian just because I feel like it, because I think I am. It's in history. In our case, if it's impossible to make these declarations individually, which they can do, the recuperation of a collective identity would happen through an apprehension of history. One thing is to apprehend a family history to benefit the individual. That would be impossible for us, but we can apprehend a collective history.

Now, when someone says that, they don't mean Black identity. That's not the question. It's not: "Learn what from Africa?"; that's just a detour from the debate. But, people, no, what you want me to say is that in Africa there's nothing to learn, you want me to say that there can be no Black identity. So you have to understand the difference between two concepts: diversity and pluralism, that the problem of diversity in Brazil is that we didn't do anything to make it happen, it's a historical fact and the result of a historical process, from which we must recognize that Brazil has great diversity. The problem is in the political response that I give to a diversity framework. There's where the problem begins, because racism hierarchizes diversity. So I can never guarantee pluralism because, for me, one is worth more than the other. I'll give the example that I give to the kids. You're going to make an ad with four people. If you want to respond to the existing diversity in our country, you'll say that you want to guarantee a pluralism of representation of this diversity in the ad, and you'll go and do it. But if you hierarchize diversity based on racism, you'll say that everyone has to have light skin and straight hair, because if not the product will be tainted, it won't stick, it won't work. So our problem is in valorizing identity, recognizing that no, it died . . . diversity has to do with what history is, it's there, for Black, indigenous, Arabic people, Italian-Brazilians.

So we have to talk about reparations, put some bacon in the beans, it's no longer who controls it. Like the police commander in the March of [19]95 who called the other one over and said, "He's the one to talk to for whatever you need, you report to him, he's in charge." I said: "God Almighty, help me out, me in charge of those crowds? No, I'm not in charge." [*Laughs.*] Gosh, it's scary, it's scary that you don't want to know who's coming, putting mothers whose children were murdered first, and look, I'm going to fight to create the thing of mothers of murdered Black children, you'll see. Do you think I'm going to kill people, who aren't people without families, who don't lose something? What are you talking about? My brother wasn't murdered, he died in an accident and I saw how it changed my mother's life, my family's life. Imagine a mother who loses a child to murder, a worker. One thing is to think, "This person doesn't exist for Brazilian society." "Wow, you're going to throw out an Afro-Brazilian priestess?" What a march, eh, Sueli? The march appears on the horizon and with a huge political power.

Well, what was the commitment that I took on? I took my family on, I sat down at the table, and I told them: "I'm going to dedicate myself to this. It could result in various outcomes, everything could be glorious and come out well, or it could all go down in flames, betrayals, and things that I'll have to pay dearly for." I know I'll pay dearly, but there's no turning back for me.

Ah! That's a little frightening because of how seriously I explain things. I could try to be a little lighter in my explanations, but there's no way. It's how I tell it, if it's real.

The murder of people is real. If the statistics about Black people's situation are real, we have to have a way of responding accordingly, at least by mobilizing people. I mean, if we can't even do that, between the two, one, either the statistics, that a Black woman earns a third of what a white man earns, if that's real, Black women need to go out into the street and say they won't tolerate it, or we have to end up accepting it. So it seems to me that what's at stake here is the very existence of a movement that measures up to the reality of exclusion, of oppression that you live with. We need to broaden our theoretical approach. We haven't created parameters with the necessary conceptual depth, etc., etc., to drive a leap of that magnitude. Ok. However, it seems to me that we can't, therefore, hesitate in deepening our experience of struggling to organize. Listen, it's not by sitting down in academe, through research, that I'm going to achieve this broadening. That's not how it is. This broadening is also the result of deepening the struggle and its capacity for organization. So, if I refuse to get into that situation, I refuse to have an experience that will be necessary for that leap. So, I am always postponing that possibility, and it's precisely by postponing that possibility that theory isn't being developed.

It's not by sitting down and reflecting. You have to sit and reflect but also deepen a practice of struggle, deepen your organizing. We aren't in a condition to say to ourselves: Edson, go to Teresina, Teresina has a large Black population, people don't have a lawyer, they are suffering humiliations, as they told me in a meeting. How can someone be humiliated like that and look at you and say: "We can't do anything because here there's no lawyer who will take on our cause, we have no Black lawyers and we are in this situation." And there's no organization to say, "Edson, go to Teresina, and you'll stay there for two years." We don't have the organizing experience in which we've attempted these possibilities. How can I quit without having tried? You can't do that; it's deepening the experience of struggle and organization. How can I have a country with a population that ignores the experiences that Black people have had in the world? Mind you, even in the struggle against oppression, that we already talked about. I remember I discussed this with you before, like this: all white experience is universal, and Black experience doesn't even rise to the level of local. How could what happened in the United States have happened, this concerns me, the boycott of 1955–6, the year-long bus boycott, in a city deep in the South of the United States. I refuse to take the bus and come across a little old lady walking and say, "I'm walking for my children's future, I'm walking for our future." This is a page in history that elevates a human being of any color, but I can't study it in school because that's a Black thing. If it were a white thing, it would be required curriculum and there'd already be white people specializing in it, thinking that the French Revolution was blah, blah, even a pain in the ass. Now, Mandela's experience isn't universal, it's not to be found in school.

So, when we want content, we want to talk about that too. We want to talk about bringing Black experiences to school in the same way that white experiences are there and are universal; they can serve as the measure of human actions. What Mandela did could only be done because he was imprisoned; he could criticize apartheid in a doctoral dissertation from university in London. After he graduated, he went to London. London wanted him to come, he arrived and wrote a dissertation and "Gosh! How brilliant that guy's dissertation is." But it's different for someone to come and say, "No, I'm going to speak up for myself" and speak up as he did against apartheid. So the March is our prison, it's the equivalent of the experience that we need to speak up about as he did.

Ah! I confess that I don't know much about the Frente Negra Brasileira (Brazilian Black Front).[45] I think that I wouldn't know how to analyze it. It's a weakness of mine. They say there were 200,000 members in Brazil at that time. Sometimes I say, I almost say: it didn't lead to anything. But is it true that it didn't lead to anything? Could it be that this thing that is spread around the entire country is the result of that process, that outlook, that it catches like that? Human effort always results in something. I think we still underestimate a mobilization of 200,000 people. I think that we are the result here of that process of the Black Front, the way that we are found across the whole country, it's very possible that they have a lot to do with all that. You can't erase the experience of 200,000 people in history. I'm telling you: you can't take the MNU and say that the MNU came to nothing. Today the MNU is nothing, but it led to a lot.

The Black Front has to have produced a consciousness at an important moment in the country that allowed things to happen. I think that an impact study needs to be done and it hasn't been; there needs to be an intellectual to think it through. So, I don't know why it didn't continue, but an analysis is needed. I once heard a speech of yours, many years ago, in Brasília, in a class, you were saying that we don't draw from our most recent experiences, nor from long past ones, nor from the experiences of others. In the end, we're still shallow. One of the reasons for this need for deepening is limited study, little knowledge of our memories, of the struggle. That's part of the process of education. You need to broaden these experiences, transmit these experiences. We don't know anything about Haiti, for example. We are very ignorant of processes which if we understood them would strengthen our possibilities for action. This intellectual ignorance is revealed in our intellectual poverty as a movement, it's true. We need to do something about it, it's urgent. We need to develop education and people who can recuperate these possibilities. There's no doubt, that's a part of broadening, it's a requirement.

The other one is experience. There's a Portuguese poet who spoke of a knowledge that distinguished him from others, because his knowledge was gained by experience.[46] And there is a know-how that this knowledge doesn't offer, which is the one built through experience. I think that we need two things, we need to do this overview, this reflection, we need theoretical progress, like you did with your dissertation. Compel us to think about concepts and everything else. We need this, to see other experiences that could contribute. So we have to reexamine our organizations' practices, the little appreciation, the little reading that happens.

It's . . . it's an impression that isn't mine, to start with. The first person who I saw point in that direction was Doudou Diène.[47] I cried a lot that day. I think that there has to be an explanation that isn't the traditional one, a more historical explanation, a more general one. The crossing of Black with white, ideologically, yields white. It's not about biology; that is, a crossing with white yields white because they're trying to stamp out a Black majority. So, a crossing with white is white. A Black majority crossed with white, the result is white. The idea is to put an end to Black people. And it was always like that, it was always understood like that, so much so that I always point out that in *Anjo negro* it's surprising that a woman considers the children she has with a Black man as Black, that they can't be born because of it, because they're Black and the meaning that was always imposed on Brazilian society was that of whitening. If you take up Caio Prado Júnior, Gilberto Freyre,[48] those authors of great works of economics, sociology, and such, it's quite probable that in all of them, an unquestionable truth is that of the whitening of Brazilian society. It appears as dogma at the core of social sciences in Brazil.

The whitening of Brazilian society is considered the obvious of the obvious. So you get to the end of the last century and at the beginning of this one and you get the IBGE[49] social indicators from 2003, which came out in 2004. There, something that I had already said in a magazine the year before is that the published indicators include an increase in the number of Black people, resulting in great measure from the work done by Black-identified associations and organizations. So the IBGE observes movement in the opposite direction, and that's still without affirmative action. That is, Brazilian society made a pivot, and what a pivot. This is ideological, one has to understand. Because nothing happened from a demographic point of view; on the contrary, the loss of Black people through murder, sterilization, isn't part of this domain, it's in a situation of extraordinary oppression of the Black population, the loss of births, of murders. Brazilian society made a pivot in the ideological domain. It was going in one direction and then suddenly . . . how could this happen, that after a history of whitening it suddenly goes in the direction of blackening?

Affirmative action comes along and accelerates this effect inasmuch as people are applying for the benefits based on a Black identity. So you're going in one direction, ah! Look at me coming along saying to people: in the short term this isn't good because it's going to affect Black people actually getting the benefits because, let's say, neo-Black people end up taking the place of the Black people who were already there. Ok, in the short term, but look at the medium and long term, look at what society is being shaped in the future. Ten white people lean against a wall. None is the same as the others and we live with this perfectly well and we say:

Brazilian society is majority white. Well then, we are going toward a majority Black society, in which we'll put ten Black people against the wall and none of them is like the others, and we'll say: "No, Brazil is a Black society, that's how it is." Look, our generation is responsible for this inversion, not that we did it by ourselves, but it was principally our generation that brought about this pivot. For all of Brazil's intelligentsia, it looked like this: obviously, Brazilian society is whitening. And meanwhile, it's shifting.

So I think if this is possible, what else isn't possible?

# 6
# Sônia Maria Pereira Nascimento

*Source:* From Sônia Maria Pereira Nascimento's personal archive.

I met her in 1971 when, having passed the state public clerical exam, we took up our positions in the Treasury Bureau, in the recently created microfilm department. It was then housed in a very modern room for the time, all glass walls, where for eight hours or more, interrupted only for lunch, we ran modern microfilm machines. Every day we competed for who would have the better output. On average, each machine processed around 16,000 documents per day. Sônia always won; she was faster. And also charming, good-humored, and charismatic. Ever since, I've called her the "queen of spring" and "Pollyanna," because she invariably tries to respond to life with positivity and to others with tolerance and generosity. She is a sincerely devoted and practicing Christian. She has a fault, which I call "Mother Theresa of Calcutta": she's always available to help anyone and to forgive. I was always envious of her, a "positive" envy, as we used to tease. She is tall, and I am short. She has prominently Black features, a plump mouth, pronounced cheekbones, a wide and open smile. Me, totally the opposite. She walked down the hallways of the Treasury Bureau like a Queen Nzinga.[1] Red dress, colorful scarves around her neck, very short hair with an audacious cut for the time. She had a refined air. And her voice? Deep, warm. And her smile? Full. Everyone turned to look when she went by. She became the leader, the boss of our division. She managed conflicts among the clerks, she negotiated with the higher-ups. She listened to everyone's complaints. The bosses trusted her.

Those were long and happy years, despite the discrimination that we experienced. Many times, because the new organization in which we worked was more modern and better equipped, it caused jealousy in the division where we were housed. We were eight Black woman clerks, except for a single blonde one. Our glass-walled room was secretly called "planet of the apes." We suffered. Sônia knew how to handle those situations. Furious, I easily provoked the ire of our bosses and coworkers. It was a hellish trek to go from Vila Bonilha, where I lived, to the Clóvis Bevilácqua Square, where I got off my bus, the Penha–Lapa line, overcrowded with people, breaking down along the way, the suffocating heat spoiling my lunch I'd prepared the day before (which I would eat regardless). And, worse, my timecard would be marked late and accordingly all the docked pay that would come at the end of the month. No, that didn't happen, because Sônia was always there, before anyone else, irregularly punching the cards of everyone who still hadn't arrived and convincing the bosses to keep what they saw – or what they were tipped off to by other clerks – a secret.

It was many years before we would work together again, until after much insistence I convinced her to come be part of Geledés – Instituto da Mulher Negra (Geledés – Black Women's Institute. Since she is a queen and was born to reign, she was elected president of Geledés twice.

Throughout all those years, I imagined that I knew everything about her. How wrong I was. This interview showed me unsuspected suffering that my friend had lived through. The pride and dignity that surrounded her, inherited from her extraordinary mother, never allowed her to be anything but a beautiful, charismatic woman in our presence, with a wide smile and a special way of "taking things in her stride," and, like a good Pollyanna, to always find a positive aspect of everything, even when the sky was falling on our heads.

In this testimony,[2] out of the love, friendship, and trust that I am proud to have earned, she allowed me to penetrate dimensions of her soul that retain the indelible mark of the pain of color that I, pathetically, had supposed hurt her less.

The nickname of "Pollyanna" was more an expression of my limitations in understanding her way of managing the pains and afflictions of blackness with dignity and without self-pity. Thank you, Sônia, for the way that you honor us and yourself.

I was born in December, on the 6th, in São Paulo, the capital city, in the neighborhood of Itaquera, known at the time as Itaquera do Campo, the daughter of Zilda Gama Pereira Nascimento and Benedito Mineiro Nascimento. She was a maid; he was a laborer, a truck driver, who worked in the Municipal Market. My mother, a warrior, a woman who wanted to be a teacher, the daughter of Castorino Alves de Alencar Pereira, a native of Florianópolis, who knows why he ended up in those lands, in Ijaci – a settlement of the city of Lavras, Minas Gerais, a learned man, a spiritualist, he grew crops. The only person in the region who knew how to read, he became the local teacher; he had many students and he always told my mother that she would take his place and would be a great teacher. He created Ijaci's first spiritualist center. On a return trip to Lavras, my mother received the articles of incorporation of the spiritualist center, drawn up by my grandfather. He was my mother's idol, she was always by his side, inspiring jealousy and desperation in my grandmother, Maria Augusta Alves de Alencar Pereira, a Catholic who didn't let any of her eight children (João Batista, Marta Augusta, Zilda Gama, Jequi Solimões, Ynah Augusta, Emílio Luiz, Joana D'arc, and Áurea Celeste, each two years apart) get to know any religion but her own.

Her dream of being a teacher began to fade when she was eight years old and in third grade, and my mother lost her father in a truck accident. Her older siblings went to work in other cities and my grandmother needed someone to take care of the children so she could also go to work, so she took my mother out of school. Since she wanted to study so badly, to be a teacher, her godmother, whose husband had a pharmacy, understood the difficult situation my family was dealing with, and promised to take the child [to live with her] so she could finish school. She was almost ten years old.

In that house, her godmother put a stool in front of the stove and taught her to cook and do all the domestic tasks, so she never went to school again. Since she was very sharp, she was also called on to help in the pharmacy; her godfather was excited about her interest and taught her much about the profession, saying that later she could study to be a pharmacist. Since studying was all she wanted and there she wouldn't have an opportunity to do so, when she was fifteen she went to Rio de Janeiro, where her sister Marta worked, who arranged for her to work in a family's house. She didn't stay very long because the man of the house frequently harassed her, until one day the woman left and he tried to grab her. She ran to the bathroom until the woman came back home, told her what had happened, and got a slap to the face because, as the woman screamed at her, her husband would never even look at a Black girl like her.

She returned to São Paulo, arranged a job in another family's house, "good people." The house was "hers," which means she did all the housework and took care of three children; the oldest was her age, the second two years younger, and the third five years younger, [who would become] my godmother. She brought two of her siblings to São Paulo, arranged jobs for them to help their mother in Minas. She stayed there until she got married, when she was twenty. My father worked a lot, he wanted to give the family what he never had. Two years later, when he was twenty-four, he died of TB, tuberculosis – the stigma of the disease was such that you couldn't even say its name. I recently found out the truth, because we were told that his death had happened in a car accident; [she] invented it so we wouldn't suffer discrimination because of the disease.

A widow, with two daughters, me and my sister Suely, exactly a year and ten days younger than me, she went back to my godmother's house, where she stayed for just a short while because another maid had already taken her place. Without the means to support herself or us, she had to resort to Social Services to get food assistance. For her it was a great humiliation. Once she had a job, she returned to Social Services the following month, stood in line, and, with great pride, let them know that she had not come to request help but rather to return her card because she had gotten a job.

She went to work in a boarding house whose owner accepted her with two children and treated us very well. As a cook, she made lunch and dinner for more than twenty people, took care of everything, went to the market and shopped at the store. The house also had a maid who went out dancing with the owner and, since she knew some of her secrets, had certain privileges; she was white. For no reason, the owner, who was "good people," began to pick on my mother for just about anything, until one day she humiliated her for not cleaning the house to the point that she responded that she was not a maid but a cook, and that she should speak to the person tasked with cleaning. She got the following response: "The person here who has two daughters is you, not her." My mother, who was finishing making lunch, turned off the stove, went to her room, put our clothes in a bag, and left; she didn't know where to go, and just stayed there on the sidewalk, crying. The owner apologized and implored her to forget everything and come back to finish lunch. She said she forgave her, but she wasn't coming back because she still had two daughters and she was paying dearly as a result. She went to my uncle's house, who was already married and lived with his mother-in-law. She worked in other families' houses, so she couldn't take her daughters with her and her sister Áurea, fifteen, who had come from Minas to work. She needed to find a place where they could stay together. She told us that she scraped some money together, went to Aparecida do Norte,[3] and in front of Our Lady of Aparecida she prayed and begged: "O Mother, your son carried my husband away and I cannot manage to raise my daughters alone, I come before you to ask for your help and protection to care for, educate, and help my daughters graduate . . .," thus dedicating us to Our Lady of Aparecida. She said that while she was praying, she began to feel strength and courage, and she returned home willing to face whatever came.

She got a job working for a lawyer, who directed her to Social Services to send us to board at the Baronesa de Limeira childcare center. She took us and handed us over to a nun. When the nun opened the door to take us inside, my mother snatched us from her arms and ran away. She returned to Social Services to try to get a job that would let us stay together; everyone already knew about her escape. A spot opened up in a childcare center where she could work and live with us. It was in Angélica Avenue, no. 842, Santa Cecília neighborhood, it was called the São José da Santa Casa de Misericórdia Home of São Paulo. It was an enormous two-story house, with bedrooms, a dining room, an office, a living room, a linen room, a pantry, a kitchen, a storage room, a laundry room, classrooms, a hall, and an enormous yard. She went to work as a cook; there were other professionals who did the laundry and the ironing, a nanny, a manager and a director. She was always very grateful for the opportunity, we were three and four years old. In that school, I did everything. I wanted to stay there because we were together and we could eat, study, and graduate. There were times when the director ended up leaving my mother responsible for close to eighty people, between children, adolescents and youths; if something happened to them, she would blame my mother, and not the manager or the nanny. She said that all the children were very attached to my mother and that the manager, the women who did the laundry and ironing were sickly – and the magic words: "They don't have daughters here." If anyone was sick, she had to run to Santa Casa for first aid, bring the doctor, make an appointment. She was also the one the girls talked to, sought advice from, would ask about things, confided in, they called her "mother" and she was mother to everyone there, making the director jealous. Some girls who were pregnant also went there, those whose families didn't want "society" to find out; they stayed and my mother took care of the girls, she indulged them because they were pregnant, they needed special treatment, she accompanied them to the hospital, and when the babies were born, she was the person who took them to the adoptive family. Everyone was white; my mother really suffered.

There were also the girls who were adopted and later returned; they came back in a terrible state, some of them depressed, my mother took care of them, she also gave them special treatment. When the employees were sick, also special treatment. I wanted to be like her, do everything she did, be good and generous. All of us, when we got hurt, ran to her. She would kiss us and, presto, the injury was healed. With the other girls, she would put them on her lap, snuggle and kiss them; my sister complained and she said that we had a mother, and they didn't. My sister said that she wanted us to have our own house so we wouldn't have to share with anyone. I liked the Home a lot, despite the racist hostility to our things: like samba, samba schools, physical features, kinky hair, Macumba,[4] lots of prejudice with everything, but I didn't realize why I wanted to be white. There was a Black woman who was always asking for food and clothes, she was "Maria the Beggar," a nickname the director gave her; we wanted to die of shame. Black children, with the exception of Inês, who was very intelligent, smart-mouthed, and two twins, Virgínia and Verônica, who stayed there until they were ten, the daughter of a very pretty and intelligent maid, and us, no other Black child went to school. They went to a family home or to boarding school.

I was a tomboy and a rascal. I was frequently punished by my mother, but the vast majority of the time it was because of the director and a manager; they exaggerated the stories of what I did and even invented situations that I wasn't part of. My mother spanked me and cried, sometimes more than I did. I was punished and cried and then would stop to console her. A minute afterwards, I was smiling and playing with her, so she wouldn't think she had hurt me. I remember that I would say to her, "Don't worry, silly, it didn't hurt." And she would say: "Did you see they were talking about you?" or "Did you see what you did?" I had a big mouth, and sometimes I talked back. She would humiliate us [*she cries at this point*] . . . my mother and the two of us, and she said it was so I would learn.

The Santa Casa had many benefactors and many donated to the Home and on holidays we would go to some of these people's houses to work and keep the children company; it was quite fun for me, I enjoyed it, we weren't treated like maids, we ate at the table, we were the girls from the São José Home. The older ones would even travel with them and so would get to see other states. On my mother's vacations, for two weeks, we would travel to Aparecida do Norte or to the house of my father's cousin, who had five children, or to my uncle Jequi's, who lived in his own house and had a daughter, and a few times to Santos, because we got an "invitation" from one of these benefactors; it was a couple of "good people" with a couple of children who had an apartment there and would take us, my mother would pay in domestic service. It was bliss, to stay with our family and have our mother all to ourselves.

We were adults when, during our conversations, she told us about many other situations that had taken place at the Home. She didn't let us know so we wouldn't want to leave that place, the place that had welcomed us so thoroughly, where we could study, eat, and that had such a formational role for us. You see, we went to the Municipal Theater, I was five when I went for the first time to see a children's ballet; the brother of the director was a city councilor and would send invitations to the Sunday matinee. My mother understood that we should experience it to say if we liked it or not. When I went, I loved it, even today I still know a little and I really like classical music.

Since everything comes to an end, the São José Home also came to an end, it closed its doors, the Santa Casa went through hard times, and so we went from a house with twenty-five rooms to a room in a boarding house, which also belonged to the Santa Casa, where two beds fit and we were three people, we slept across, we adolescents died of shame in that house, because of our classmates. And my mother would say: "You go talk to your classmates, those who come and come again are your friends." We had to start over, and from then on it would be on our own, we had practically nothing. Just my mother working directly in the Santa Casa, earning practically nothing. We would leave school and we'd eat lunch in the Santa Casa. We were fourteen, fifteen years old and we were finishing *ginásio*.[5] Later, Ling [her sister] got a teaching internship at the church we attended, and I went to a little shop; I only stayed a short time because I had to dedicate myself to my studies, it was an obsession for my mother, school and our own house. She would say that she couldn't leave us a house, but she was preparing us so we could get one.

Afterwards, we worked in other places, with some of those benefactors. When I was eighteen, I went to work for the Santa Casa as a secretary and Ling went to the Pestalozzi Society of São Paulo to teach gifted children. The president of this school was a friend of one of the benefactors of the São José Home, Mrs. Maria Aparecida Barbosa, a psychologist who really respected my mom and liked us. Now, our life's dream was to have a house, the three of us were working, it was enough to pay rent. Soon, a "beloved" ex-manager of the Home bought a house and was going to vacate the one she was renting; she asked us if we were interested and, moreover, she wanted everything new for the new house, so she left "ours" practically set up. It was in a little complex, at 342 Fradique Coutinho Street, no. 6, in Pinheiros. To us it was a palace. In the complex there were innumerable houses, with independent entrances with gates and everything. Ours was down below; those things that the Portuguese built, there was a house above, below, even lower, even higher, in front, in back, on the sides. It was our palace. We had a place to live like a normal family, bring relatives over, they could sleep in our house. A dream. One of our "sisters," Pedrina, came with us.

The house itself was like this: one of the girls from the Home, Olga, had married José, the "adoptive brother" of the director, and both of them were always over and on one of these visits he said: "Mother, we bought a house, it's in a residential complex that's being built on the Raposo Tavares highway; on one side will be basic houses and on the other, where we're going to live, the houses will be larger for more senior employees." Mom asked how they had managed it; he refused to answer and didn't offer any more information. That stuck with us, having your own house. My mother started telling us to pray because if it was the will of God and Our Lady of Aparecida, we would also have our house in that place. A few days later, Bia appeared at our house, the son of the person who ironed in the São José Home. She told him about José's visit and about the complex in Raposo Tavares. He knew about it, and had even already registered. He told us it was a group of cooperatives, INOCOOP – Instituto de Orientação às Cooperativas (Institute for Orienting Cooperatives) – and the superintendent was Mr. Zezé, the brother of the director, the one who had been the city councilor. He provided all the information, his address and phone number, so we could talk to him. He was a person with a big heart and he had respect and affection for us at the Home. We always worked for his electoral campaigns distributing pamphlets and, even when the Home closed, we never stopped visiting the director and her family. I don't have to tell you that the following day, my mother called him, and to her great surprise he said:

> Mother, you don't have a house? You rent? The first person who I asked Maria Olímpia about was you and she said you didn't need one! For the love of God, Mother, come over here tomorrow, we're going to talk, there's a waiver, bring your documents. It's just that the people have been paying a deposit for almost four years, it's not a lot, but you'll have to get the money, if not all at once, in two or three installments, maximum, and leave the rest to me.

Once a week, my mother cooked for Mrs. Aparecida Barbosa, the psychologist, and that day told her about the house and Mr. Zezé's proposal. She told her that she didn't have the money or a way to get it. She was our guarantor for the house where we lived. She listened and said, "Mother, I'm going to get you that money, and you can pay me however you can." She went to talk to Mr. Zezé and closed the deal; the only thing he asked was that we never abandon Maria Olímpia.

The house couldn't be in her name because her salary was less than the minimum necessary for registration. As soon as possible, I put it in her name, it was her house. Look, the houses were distributed by drawing, but even today I don't buy it, because the location of our house was one of the best: it's exactly in the middle of the complex, in the fourth lane, you go up Raposo Tavares or down Corifeu de Azevedo Marques Avenue, it's the same distance. It's a house in the middle of the first block, with four rooms, a living room, a bedroom, a kitchen, and a bathroom, a staircase of just three steps to access the house. The corner houses had three or four bedrooms and the ones in front of ours had two and you could build a garage and on top to expand the living room. We talked to him, and he responded:

> Mother, it's better to stay with this small house; there's space and you can add on to it, the payment is low and the girls might get married and you can still afford it by yourself. And what's more, you're going to get older and you won't be able to be going up and down the stairs. You're not at the beginning of the street, which attracts thieves, because this is going to improve and draw attention.

Look, wasn't this a blessing? Wasn't it handpicked? So, we went on paying and two years later I went to get the keys without my mother and sister knowing. When I arrived and showed the keys to them, we hugged each other and cried a lot, because the thing she wanted most was to have a house and she prayed for it every night.

Can you believe that the day of the move, it slipped my mind, I didn't manage to do it, I didn't help with anything, I who had taken part in the whole process because it was in my name, I was part of the cooperative, I had to attend meetings, it was intense. The day of the move, I went to visit a cousin in the hospital whose whole body was burned. I really regret it. And so we went to return the keys to the owner. Once, my mother went to complain about him to the police station, because he tried to raise the rent more than was allowed. He was called in, he was a little angry; he liked her a lot, but he took advantage of the tenants. Imagine with us, just women! But after that he never made another false step with us. We handed over the keys, and he said: "Dona Zilda, I'm very sad to lose a tenant like you, who was never late with the rent." My mother never made a single payment or installment late, she said we Black people only had our name as a guarantee. And he continued: "But on the other hand, I'm happy because you're leaving here for your own house." He came to see our house. It was crazy. We moved into "our mansion" on May 4, 1974. When I arrived, we hugged each other and cried a lot. First things first: arrange a place for Our Lady of Aparecida, then everything else.

My Aunt Áurea became a widow at thirty-five years old and with eight children. My mother roared at her with each pregnancy and afterwards said: "Ah! They're already here, now it's time to turn the page." She was her sister and goddaughter. Some of my cousins went to *colégio*,[6] they stayed with us on weekends. They'd leave school and stay here at home, when they finished school they returned home. The baby of the family left home to get married in 1997.

When she retired, my mother returned to her studies; school had changed. Now she's studying, and enjoys school so much that she does her housework quicker and around 3:30 p.m. does her homework, then she lies down to rest, prays the chaplet and goes to school. She goes by herself.

Lately, we've seen her crying because, if you can believe it, she thinks that she gave us too much responsibility by taking care of other people, that we didn't have time to get married. Could it be? And I say: "Do you think that if we wanted to get married, we'd call you?" I raise my hands to heaven for not having gotten married, for being able to be in my safe haven, my mother is my safe haven, my sister, my house, it's bliss.

Look, if she hasn't heard from me all day, she calls and leaves a message on my cell phone: "Sônia Maria, it's your mother. I want to know where you are; I'm letting you know that you have a family." Thank God that we are this woman's daughters. I was very ashamed, because I thought that I hadn't done anything to pay her back for all the sacrifice. There's something that's really nice: she never presented her life to us as something full of sacrifice, suffering, or anything like that. On the contrary, she talks all the time about how Ling left from the Tietê waterfront, caught the bus, would go to Campinas to go to school, and return home. Really, afterwards she ended up living there, her studies became full time; it was during the time when you suggested I work for the subway to help increase our income, to support her. When she finished her studies, she went back to work and helped me put myself through university. She passed that on to us. That we should help others because we always had someone who helped us, teach because we always had someone who taught us, give others a chance because we had many. You have to pass it on, have to spread it.

There was no room for a man in this orchestra; he would break up our harmony. This figure, father and mother, man and woman, for me it was all her. After my father, my mother never dated; she was brave, authoritarian, sweet, and independent. My aunts and uncles, all of us, we were scared to death. I never heard my relatives speak about someone interested in her, and look how pretty she was and . . . sweet. But imagine taking on her siblings, daughters, biological or not, nieces and nephews. It was impossible even to flirt, and what man would put up with all that?

My mother really wanted to study, she was fixated on studying, she always demanded that we put a university diploma in her hands. She always demanded it, she examined our notebooks, quizzed us every day, demanded the multiplication table be ready on the tip of our tongue. She said that she was scorching her belly on the boss's stove so we wouldn't have to do so, it was up to us to study. Study well so that we wouldn't have to depend on anyone, except our own effort. We had to take what was ours. Perhaps she couldn't give us much, a house, for example, but she wanted to give us the circumstances that would allow us to buy one. As children from the São José Home, we had scholarships for elementary school at the Casa Pia São Vicente de Paulo Day School, run by Vicentian nuns; it's still there today in Alameda Barros, in the Santa Cecília neighborhood, a very good school. Afterwards, Nossa Senhora da Glória Seminary, on Nazaré Avenue, today the School of Music and Art of the UNESP (State University of São Paulo), in the Ipiranga neighborhood, and every success, passing grade, promotion, my mother said: "You aren't doing anything more than your duty, we are survivors, our ancestors, who suffered terribly, came on horrible ships and survived so we could be successful here." And she always absolutely required that we study. She put great effort into the schools; she would ingratiate herself with the nuns, bringing them coconut candy, chocolates, and other things, all because she thought it would help us be accepted. And she always told us that they were in the right: "The nuns are always right." We were never in the right when they would call to complain. Until one day one of the nuns gave me a warning and told my mother that I was arrogant and had my nose in the air, and to my astonishment, she replied: "But do you want me to cut off the tip of my own daughter's nose?" I couldn't believe it, I was so happy because it was the first time in my life that she had acknowledged that I was in the right; the first time that she hadn't said that the nuns were right and I was wrong. The two of us really celebrated, we laughed all the way home, slapping each other on the butt, I kissed her face, and from that day on she never again said that only others were in the right and we weren't. When some complaint came down, we would sit down, discuss, and she would say, "I want to trust you, tell me exactly what happened, the truth, and I'll trust you." So this school experience was a very good one, my mother against the nuns.

*Ginásio*, while Ling and some others went to the Colégio São José, which belonged to the Santa Casa, the girls experienced discrimination there; my sister wanted to study education, but the girls from the São José Home who were poor had to study to be secretaries.[7] But she wanted to be a teacher, imagine what it would mean to my mother to have a daughter who was a teacher, it was the only thing she wanted to be; she wanted to study education, and the nuns insisted on the secretary course. My mother went, discussed, asked, implored, and they agreed, but said that she wouldn't be able to teach because no one would hire a Black teacher. She got an internship, and at the end of the final year, she was already teaching. She was sixteen. All of this outraged her. I, on the other hand, always kind of took it in stride, because when they decided to say something with some racial connotation, I would say: "You're not offending me. I am in fact Black, what else are you going to say?" I repeated my mother's words when we would complain about someone offending us by calling us "little Black girls." She would show us a mirror and say: "It's what are you, you are in fact Black, and so what?"

I did my fifth year at Godofredo Furtado, in Pinheiros, a state *colégio*, but I couldn't adapt, since I was used to going to school with nuns, with good organization, discipline, and classrooms that weren't very full. I went to Nossa Senhora da Glória Seminary, a *colégio* run by Josephine nuns, the same congregation as the Santa Casa one and the Colégio São José, a highly sought-after state school because it also had vocational training, like sewing, embroidery, cooking, home economics, and other subjects.

Except mathematics, which I failed in my last year, I was a good student in all the other subjects. I really liked history, English, and Portuguese. A Black teacher joined us, Dr. Clélia, the only one in the school, who was an advocate. I'd always been a leader, and she liked that about me, and practically adopted us, the two Black students in the class, Zélia and me. She would say: "They'll do anything to keep you from making it, but don't get discouraged, we're in it together, we're going to fight and we'll make it together." She encouraged us a lot, I think that's why I didn't know whether there was racism there, because I didn't feel it. There were many Black students, but the majority of them were boarders. There were few of us, the Black day students. She made me her assistant, I was the class representative, I began to study much more, she was our Portuguese professor. She frequently gave pop quizzes and I always had the lesson prepared; I knew everything and she was proud of me. She encouraged us a lot, but also asked a lot of the two of us. She would say that we had to know what it meant to be a leader, it was to be first, speak up, study, because we were Black girls and the world [*she laughs*] was conspiring against us. We needed to repay her for that, so in Portuguese class we were always the top students in the class.

But in that sense our education from the São José Home contributed quite a lot, except in math and geography, I would spend time with the older girls while they studied, and so I learned a lot with them, how to speak Portuguese correctly, basic knowledge of English and French, the location of Brazilian states, Latin American and European countries and their capitals, and especially history, which I really enjoyed. In the vocational training, I really liked sewing; I made a number of projects and I still have my notebook with notes.

In the last year of *ginásio* I wanted to be a nun, but in *colégio* a nun by the name of Umbelina arrived, who had worked with indigenous people in the Amazon. She was socially conscious and criticized the comforts of the nuns who taught in the Seminary and said that if she was going to live a life like that, she would serve God better through the sacrament of marriage. That was all it took for me to never think about the topic again.

After I finished *ginásio*, I went to try to study accounting at the Frederico Ozanan School, a private school. After a year, with great difficulty because I detested math, inputs and outputs, assets and liabilities, I went on to be a *colégio* student; I returned to classical public school, at night, in Macedo Soares, over there in Barra Funda. The principal was interesting, but the teachers didn't care as much about the students as in religious schools, and the discrimination was more explicit. I had just three classmates I was friendly with, and they were white, there weren't many Black students; we avoided each other. Me, because they were the prototype of everything bad that I had always heard said in the Home about Black people. They were at the bottom of the class, they talked back, they didn't do their schoolwork, and they avoided me, I believe, because I acted like a "white girl." At the end of my second year, I went with the three classmates and some of the other students to do *colégio* equivalency class in Rio Grande do Sul; my mother almost died because I only had a year left and this business of *colégio* equivalency wasn't serious. I saw an opportunity to travel with classmates and I went. We did well in the subjects we took. When we arrived, we realized that the *colégio* equivalency exam would be given in the same school. I took it, and I passed. I went to do the prep course for the *vestibular*.[8]

To get into USP (University of São Paulo), I did the Objetivo School's prep course, on Paulista Ave., I won a scholarship; I was already working at the Bureau of the Treasury. There I studied a lot, I wanted to go to university. Though I really liked courtroom films and books, and my teachers told me that I should take the *vestibular* for law because I was ready to study at USP, I said that I wanted to take social sciences, influenced by the political times we were living in, by Inês, one of the "sisters" that I very much admired and who was a sociologist. She studied at the Maria Antônia, she was a friend of Zé Dirceu, Aloysio Ferreira, and the whole gang, she worked at the Treasury Bureau with Travassos's[9] mother (an icon in the fight against the dictatorship, sought by the police), and in the São José Home the director talked about politics a lot, her brother was a city councilor, some of the older girls, like Inês, even dared to argue with her, everyone read a lot there, the *Estadão*[10] every day. But the real reason that I didn't study law is that I didn't think it was for me. Study law, at USP, at the Law School on the São Francisco Square? It wasn't for me, I thought, I could never be a lawyer. Because I'm Black. I didn't have much confidence, despite all my mother's effort. She was a confident woman, and she always tried to spread it to us, but I didn't have confidence in myself, but my mother, I felt, wanted me to go to law school [*she cries*]. I also thought I should study law, because when I turned fifteen I won a little trip and I went to the Court of Justice to hear a verdict; there was a police officer there, I screwed up my face to say that I was eighteen. At the end the jurors were leaving, and I asked the officer: "What are they going to do now?" The officer said: "Don't come down here with that face, you aren't eighteen."[11] He gave every indication that I could be there, but at a certain moment I thought I couldn't do it, and it was the thing I most wanted in the world [*crying*].

I have been to more than three hundred trials in my life. At the beginning, I would try to hide, but I thought all that wasn't for me; how many times did I end up crying, watching the trial, asking, "Why can't it be for me? Why can't I do that?" [*crying*]. So I started at USP, in social sciences, and I tried to be satisfied.

I bought new clothes for the first day of class. The first and second days I didn't understand anything; the third day, I worked up my courage and after José de Souza Martins's class, I got together with my classmates from the Objetivo who were in the course and we went to talk to him to ask him make things a little easier, to start at a more basic level so we could understand, because we were new students and we couldn't understand anything. He looked us up and down, which crushed us, and said that we were the ones who needed to study to be successful, that in case we didn't know where we were, this was a university. We took it hard, we were a group of three students, no one finished, one went over to education, one left for London, and me.

The first year was just awful, awful, because I didn't understand anything, I didn't know how to ask for help, but I still tried to talk to my professors, very few of them paid any attention to me; I thought that I just had to try harder. I experienced discrimination there. There was a boy who had been to prison and came back, Mantovani, he was way ahead of me, he lived in the same residential complex as me, and we became friends, we studied together, we discussed a lot, I began to understand. When I had anthropology class and we discussed Black people, I couldn't see myself in that discussion, for me the discussion didn't consider actual Black people, I didn't see myself, I didn't identify with those studies, they discussed Black people in such a folkloric way, at that time it was folkloric, but one day I gathered the courage to stand up and say, "It's nothing like that, that's not my life, we have lives." They got rid of me, they ridiculed me and I left school. But the studies were based on the work of a white authority on Black people. My sense was that he had never interviewed a Black person. I gave up once and for all, perhaps I didn't know much about my own identity, my race, my community – but they didn't either.

There was a lot of contempt too. Check this out: imagine, in the bygone years of 1974–5, I had a white classmate who invited us to her house. She was from the student association, she participated in councils, and when we arrived there was a Black maid dressed in a black uniform, with a little white apron and a little white cap, and she would call the worker with a little bell under the table that she'd ring with her feet. The woman would come and remain standing at her side awaiting the revolutionary's orders. It looked like a scene from a soap opera set in the era of slavery. Revolting!

Another thing: I bought new clothes for the first day of class at USP, and when I got there, and everyone there with their ripped clothes, and me with my new clothes, that's how it started [*laughing*], terrible [*laughing*], my experience was awful. I had a friend, Nancy, who told me that she worked for a multinational, she was an executive secretary, she wore a skirt and jacket and high heels to work, but outside of work she'd go home and dress like a hippie to go to class; she wasn't brave enough to go dressed like a secretary, we'd die of laughter. We ran into each other years later at the courthouse and again at the Federal Court; she had also gone to law school.

The last one: we were in a classroom and a strike committee came by saying there would be a work stoppage, classes would be canceled in solidarity with the workers imprisoned in I don't remember what country (classes would be canceled for the most incredible reasons). We were supposed to have exams the following Saturday and we couldn't have class because of other work stoppages. So I said to the professor: "They already know everything when they come into class, they've done high-level debate, and we're stuck here looking at each other without understanding absolutely anything," so I suggested that the professor continue with class outside the classroom far away for us, the new students, who didn't know anything. She agreed. We were having class, and the strike committee came by saying that we were crossing picket lines and harming those who went to the assembly, and cursed at us. I was the only Black person, and so imagine, the only face they remembered was mine. I was stigmatized, some of the students stopped talking to me. That was violence, an aggression. After that I found it outrageous and I was brave enough to show up to a June Festival they organized, with singers and guitar players performing, and at the end I went to greet the musicians and one of the students who was on the strike committee came up to us and said they shouldn't greet me because I was a "a scab, a sellout," and what's more, he said what he could and shouldn't say. Today I have my doubts; I don't think that the reason was that I hadn't gone to the assembly or that I crossed picket lines, because I didn't, but it was actually the racial issue: how could we be there and not obey?

Rafael (an activist in the Black Movement) passed by, and Márcio Damásio (also an activist in the Black movement) too. By then, I was desperate; I went to talk to them, I asked Márcio for help, and he said, "Unfortunately, I can't do anything, because I think the same thing as them. We have to stick together." I don't know if Márcio finished university, because he was also very angry. It was very hard for me and the time came when I thought: "What am I doing here?", that's enough, it wasn't the place for me. Today I imagine what the students who arrive under quotas must feel like, with all this ill will from the majority of professors.

Some ten years after I left university, I ran into the son-of-a-bitch from the strike committee, who recognized me and came over to apologize, saying he was very young at the time. And I told him I knew he was young, but why had he done that to me? And he shut up. It was great, it soothed my soul.

My mother! She was very happy. I had done, like I said, the Objetivo course, and Ling did pre-med, she was so proud of our accomplishments that she even subscribed to the magazine *Veja*, because one of Ling's teachers had said that it would be interesting for the *vestibular*; yet again, she went all in. There was more: when we finished *ginásio*, she said, "And now I want *colégio*." When we finished *colégio*: "Now university!" When I was working at the Santa Casa, she wanted me to take the public service exam, it offered security. I started as a clerk at the Treasury, and her: "Are you going to stay in this job forever?" And that's how it went until our retirement. When we got the results, she just said that she was very proud, and she was, you could see so much happiness in her eyes, lots of congratulations, hugs, and she told everyone about it. She continued to visit the homes of a number of ex-employers, and one of them had a daughter my age, but I had gotten into USP to study social sciences, Ling to PUC-Campinas (Pontifical Catholic University-Campinas) for physical therapy [*laughter*], and the daughter of the employer didn't go to university. She asked: "How is she going to pay for it?" My mother responded: "She's a teacher, she teaches in the morning at the Pestalozzi Society and in the afternoon she goes to Campinas." She told the neighbors, the word spread, and she just laughed like crazy. We lived on Fradique Coutinho and everyone ended up finding out that we had gotten into university, everyone knew in the Santa Casa too. That's when she had hell to pay, because her main boss reacted terribly and some of her coworkers began to ignore her. People were contemptuous; a cook has two daughters in university, one at USP and one at PUC? She made special food for patients, doctors, and employees who had problems ingesting salt, she made it with lots of care, these doctors and employeess came to congratulate her, and the news spread. The boss changed her assignment, he gave her something much more difficult that had her going up and down stairs many times every day and out of contact with the doctors and employees. It was a habit among some of her coworkers, those who finished earlier, to help the others so that everyone could leave together, and some of them stopped helping; it was shocking. They were white employees, the majority of them, there were one or two Black ones as well, and the main boss was Japanese.

Well, how did law end up entering my life? I left USP; at that time I was already working in the courthouse as an official of the court. There was a director there, more specifically the 3rd District Court of Pinheiros, he was a bad, racist person. One day we had quite an ugly argument, the first one of my life. I thought that I needed to do something to get out of there, it was December 29. I arrived home, I looked via telephone for a university that still had admissions open; there was just one where admissions would close the next day and it was in Mogi das Cruzes, so I went there and applied. I only told [my mother] when I got the decision and I was accepted; she went out telling the whole world, and I told her not to because Mogi wasn't a big-name university, and for someone who had studied at USP, there was a lot of discrimination, and I thought that it wasn't a school that I should feel proud of, "don't tell anyone." Look at me, again. Imagine, my mother had been so happy I had started at USP, but when I started studying law, when I felt her accomplishment right there, it seemed like she said, "Now can I relax?" I stayed for three years at USP, but I never did the third year, because I was stuck in starting, stopping; I stopped twice, I never finished the third year and only got that far because I pushed so hard.

In law, it was terrible because it was a no-name school, far away, and its reputation wasn't the best. Since I already worked at the courthouse, I had some knowledge of legal matters. I was elected the representative of the class, and since I had a bald style, they called me Piná, like the *passista* from the samba school Beija-Flor de Nilópolis, from Rio de Janeiro.[12] I felt super, I was with my people. At the end of the year, I felt I wanted to try for USP, but then I told myself, "I won't, it's not for me." And thinking of those people, it was like a nightmare. I won't say that I don't regret it; obviously if I'd gone there I would have a diploma from USP, it makes all the difference. But I have colleagues who are great who also went to Mogi. But I confess the thing about "there I'm a friend of the king's";[13] there I was the representative of the class, I was well regarded. I was afraid of being discriminated against again; I won't deny it, I was afraid.

What difference does a diploma from USP make? The status of having gone to USP, maybe I would have learned more, had more confidence, the relationships, the professors, in the end, the Arcadas.[14] It's also a symbolic thing, to study where Castro Alves[15] and so many other figures from our history studied, it would be fabulous. But, the truth is, you really learn by practicing. Ok, I didn't go there, I didn't go, but that doesn't make me less of a lawyer. But with my self-esteem so low, I went to do the Damásio course, the prep course for the exam. When they asked me which exam I was going to take, I said I was only there to review, that I wasn't going to take any exam. They said: "But why not take advantage of being here and prepare for an exam?" I said no because I wasn't prepared. "But this is a prep course!" Me boycotting, always thinking it wasn't for me, I couldn't. I talked to the white students; I never had a Black classmate at the Damásio.

The Damásio was a prep course for the exam for legal careers. An exam appeared for a Judicial Appraiser official in the Federal Court, and at the same time for a district attorney. A colleague from the court and I decided to take them: I wanted the federal official, it was very good; she wanted district attorney. Ok, we studied the whole year, the two of us, at her house. It turns out that both exams were scheduled for the same day. We decided on the federal official so that later we could better prepare for the next district attorney exam. There were more than 3,000 signed up and ninety openings; she was accepted in fifty-fifth and me in sixty-fifth place. We never thought about another exam. I retired from that job.

Thank God, I don't have anything to complain about: I have a salary and good health insurance. You're right in talking through this whole rigmarole. I was going through life saying that at this age I hadn't done anything in my life, and talking with a client some time ago who was talking about her husband, she said, "Dr. Sônia, he is forty-three years old and he hasn't built anything in his life. At forty, we're already halfway to the end; you have to already be stable, already be thinking about retirement, you have to already have been to university." She went on talking and I hung up, my thoughts were racing: it's true, at forty years old, forty-five, you already have or should have all of this, and I do! I didn't hear anything else she said, I began to realize all the things I had achieved. Today that's how I see my life: there are still things left to achieve, many of them, but I have already achieved many more.

But I retired after twenty-seven years of service because of Geledés. Remember that the legal staff was leaving and you needed a lawyer? I was involved in activities from the beginning, but when I joined the organization, we worked so much, all of us, it was a revolution in my life, to be there, an integral time in the pioneering organization of stark raving mad Black women. Geledés's power, the example of the organization, the intense activities that we carried out were daunting for the time. The achievements, the events, the level of the talks, the first health event when we brought in the president of the Center for Black Women's Wellness from Atlanta, when Harlem Désir and Bryan Stevenson came, the participation in the Rio Eco-92 conference, one of ours in a conference panel at the Women's Tent, up there next to the officer.[16] Participation in all the conferences: 1993 in Vienna, through Deise; 1994 in Cairo, with Edna; 1995, Niza in Beijing; 1995,[17] the whole organization in Brasília for the Zumbi dos Palmares March, and us running the event. There I was at home, among my own, that was my place.

I'm finally a Black woman who has the courage to put a ring on her finger, enter a courtroom and expect to be treated well, because I never had an ounce of confidence in my legal practice, so I let a lot of things go. I'm going to tell you something: my mother, when I graduated, said: "I'm going to give you a ring." And me: "Don't do that, how silly, a lawyer ring." Even though I had my diploma in hand, I thought: if she wants to give it to me, I should accept. So I said to her: "My God, of course I want it, if you want to give it to me, you can!" She opened her closet and took out the ring that she had bought at the beginning of the year and paid in ten installments; the ring was in her closet, and she gave me the ring.

I never wore it because I thought that I wasn't a good lawyer, and now I'm going to wear the ring, and now I speak up; I've had the experience of entering in a courtroom and the judge not looking me in the face, leaving and feeling like nothing, and today I only speak if he's looking me in the face. I went to do a divorce, I was in braids, the judge didn't look at me, he just stared at my braids and said to the couple: "If you need anything come talk to me." Look, it was an uncontested divorce. If you need anything come talk to me [*she emphasizes*], I said: "Talk to you, your honor?" Judge: "Yes, talk to me, whatever doubts you may have, talk to me, have you seen what's written here?" [Sônia]: "Of course, each of us has a copy, Judge." Then, the judge says: "Oh, good! But you know perfectly well what you're doing here, you got instructions about it? If not, talk to me, right now or later, if you have any doubts, come talk to me." Just leaving me there like that, and me thinking: what could it be that he wants to do? So I said: "But say what, your honor?" Then the client says: "I don't understand, because she's my lawyer, we've been friends for more than twenty years!" Judge: "Ah! So you know what's written here?" Client: "I do, she's my friend, more than my lawyer, she's my friend." Judge: "But still, I'm telling you, if any doubts remain, talk to me."

At that moment, Dr. Catani enters the room, a retired district attorney, who's renowned in family law. When he saw me, he said: "I can't believe it, my God, you're here?" "Look," he said to the judge, "careful, because this one here is something else at family law, be careful with her . . ." It was, God, imagine, I'm not all that, but that's what he said. And the judge: "Really? Ok, then."

So then he started to look at me, but I couldn't manage to do or say anything else, I could barely sign the record of the hearing, it was awful. We left the room, he called out to me and I stopped with my back turned, thinking, "I'm not going to look." He called to me again louder this time, saying, “Hey, Dr. Sônia.” So I turned, he got up, with Catani right there, and came to shake hands; I extended my hand, but I wanted to slap him in the face. I dragged myself away, holding on to the client until the elevator; when the elevator door opened below, I broke down into tears. He broke me, and I keep thinking the following: I’m an activist, but no one expects something like that, no one’s prepared, I could only think about getting out of there. I arrived home later that night, talked about it and prayed, and, boom, now I had to try to forget it. The next night I went to the Baha’i meeting, for the Institute for Healing Racism, and we began to talk about discrimination and someone said, “No, it’s not that bad! Racism exists, but it’s not all these other things too.” I lost it, I started to shout, “Watch it, racism doesn’t exist for you, but I’ve even thought about killing myself and you all come to talk to me about kindness, sickness, we’re going to pray for a cure, is that it?” Another time I also lost my mind because people want to minimize racism, it was in the Public District Attorney course at the OAB–SP[18] where you went to talk about racism, prejudice, and racial discrimination, and a student said that racism doesn’t exist, that she had freckles on her nose, that she was also discriminated against, and when I went to tell her about what had happened to me in the courtroom, I lost it.

Now I’m a little better, but I went through many other similar things, with judges too, looking me in the face and thinking that I’m the defendant: “Sit over there!” before I sit down on the attorney’s side, then him saying he’s sorry. Now I stop, I stop and look at him. “I don’t sit there, what is that?” But it’s hard to be humiliated in a courtroom. At the courthouse, at the Banespa[19] branch inside the courthouse, there was a large sign that said: “Attorneys Only.” I was in line, it was my turn, the teller asked, “Are you an attorney?” I turned toward the sign and said, “I do know how to read, at least.” She was super awkward, she apologized and said, “Do you know what happens?” I responded, “I’ve known what happens for many years.” I did stints at the COJE – Centro de Orientação Jurídica e Encaminhamento da Mulher (Women’s Center for Legal Advice and Referrals), with the District Attorney. There was a secretary at the door who would say, “Now you can go in and speak to the attorney.” People would come in and say, “Where’s the lawyer?” Sometimes I would even stand up to look around the room: “There’s no one else here, it’s just me!” Once a young woman said, “Then I’ll come back tomorrow.” She left the room, except that the next day it would be me again, so I said to her, "You can wait for another attorney to come." No one came, I let her sit there, in the end, "Do you want to come back tomorrow?" "No, I'll talk to you, are you a lawyer?" And you just swallow it, because if you don't, you spend your whole day fighting and being stressed.

It reminded me of genocide, it made me remember Érica's case: Érica was forced to listen to a professor who studied the Jewish Holocaust, and as he delved in, he claimed that what Black people went through during slavery was Disneyland next to what Jewish people suffered in the Holocaust. Yes, it happened in a classroom in the University of São Francisco law school, the one in Pari Park. She began to tremble, she burst into tears, got up and left. He thought he hadn't said anything wrong, the problem was in her head and not his.

Going back to the courtroom, listen to what Margareth, a Black lawyer, did. The judge said to a girl, pretty, blonde, the victim of a mugging where the defendant was Black: "But these Blacks are worse every day." And my Black attorney colleague said: "Ah! Your honor, did you hear what you just said?" He responded: "Ah, Counselor, pardon me, I didn't realize what I was saying, pardon me." So the white court reporter buried her head in the computer, the victim too, she turned completely red, dying of fear for what could happen; the judge realized, and ended the victim's statement. Next he called the defendant, but she didn't want to be in the same room as the accused. When he arrived, the defendant asked: "So, ma'am, am I going to stay in jail?" She said: "I think so, because you had the bad luck of ending up before a judge who said that we Black people are worse every day." And the judge apologized to her. I guess what he was trying to say was maybe that Black people are mugging people more and more boldly, who knows?

Back to Margareth: they were in the deputy's office and the client was offering some clarification. The deputy wanted to force the woman to say that she had had an abortion, and the Black attorney said: "This is sickening, you are forcing her to admit to something that she didn't do." Do you know what the deputy did? She expelled the attorney from the room. She, Margareth, didn't reveal that the attorney was her husband. She [the deputy] went into another little room and talking to someone there, said: "That's a *preto*[20] for you." When the time came to leave, Margareth arrested her, the deputy: "Well, you just committed a crime, there are plenty of witnesses, I'm arresting you." Lawyers don't do this, but after the prosecutor's course she took, no one could get past her.

The deputy began to cry and apologized and said: "It's fine, just about my colleague; I can't say he doesn't represent you. I'll release him, but you'll have to answer to the representatives of the OAB." That's how it is; people think that they can do what they want with Black people. It wasn't long before two investigators appeared to pick up the lawyer; they wanted to take him in, they showed up saying, "Where's the so-called lawyer?" Margareth said: "That so-called lawyer is my husband, and he was expelled from the room by that deputy who said 'that's a *preto* for you.'" Detail: the two investigators were Black, they said right in front of her: "She said that?" "Ask everyone here." They said: "Ah! Leave it be," and they left. They can count on this complicity, because in the past this didn't exist. She said: "You want to take the lawyer in; they didn't obey her." You see? They think she can say anything, every white person thinks they can say anything, and they continue to think so in 2004, in December, they think they can. Some of them are careful because maybe they've already had to respond to some lawsuit; if not, they think they can, it's enough just to be Black, because it's not written on their faces, lawyer, dentist, that's why a young Black dentist was killed, you see?[21] It's not written, but he's a *preto*, period.

SOS Racismo[22] was a learning process. An important service that initially aimed to discuss with the judiciary the treatment given to crimes of racism and those motivated by race, to demonstrate through the actions proposed in favor of the victims of racism and racial discrimination that the judiciary had no answer for this kind of crime – which, thanks to the Federal Constitution of 1988, which declares its disavowal of racism, was no longer a misdemeanor but rather a serious crime, not subject to bail. However, due to lack of knowledge or lack of will, judges haven't wanted to wade into this debate. It was well known, the discussion was already taking place in society, it had lots of visibility, mainly the first lawsuits. Thanks to the people who came before me, Arruda, Sérgio, Leila, Mariza, Isabel, and the intern at the time, Diógenes, they managed to make the service so well known that we had a huge number of cases. People sought Geledés whether for cases of discrimination or not. The impression people had was that we were their private lawyers, they felt at home, they brought their friends, acquaintances, and cases – and what cases – they almost turned the service into a Black PAJ (Procuradoria de Assistência Judiciária; Legal Prosecutorial Assistance). We had to rigorously control it.

The media sought Geledés for information, cases, victims. With the soap opera *Pátria minha* (My Country), for which we took Rede Globo to court, the repercussions were enormous.[23] All of us at Geledés were in some news outlet or another to talk about the soap opera and the legal case. We were interviewed by all types of newspapers and magazines, some weeklies; I talked to a Japanese newspaper, and you to a Norwegian one. In São Paulo, all the major newspapers commented on it and they covered it almost every day. A US consul said it was a battle between David and Goliath, TV Globo and Geledés. We were threatened too, by skinheads. The Federal Police came, all the social movement organizations, political and religious ones.

When I took it on, I didn't imagine the scale of the problem, of the drama. At the beginning it was very painful, I cried with many of the victims. One of them was devastated; she had experienced discrimination from the police, from her neighbor, and her son too, and she would say:

> Do to me what you want, but not to my son. I never talked to my son about this, I always said don't go near it, but when he did, he ended up in jail, he was held responsible because the cause of the violence was never investigated. No one required it be investigated, because it was always with a white person; white people are always right.

It was very painful; this woman was unemployed, desperate. She saw a sign announcing a job opening; when she arrived they told her that it had been filled. She sent a white person in and they asked for her documents; the job existed, she was passed over because of the color of her skin. In the hospital, a white patient, the nursing assistant came over and he said: "I don't want to be treated by a Black nurse." This was in a public hospital, where we're still the majority. Do you think you can? These were the kinds of cases that we, Maria Sylvia, Diógenes, and I, heard at SOS Racismo. The victim wanted to take the defendant to court, the executioner; the vast majority didn't want to hear anything about compensation, they said they weren't looking for money, that "I don't want to dip into anyone's wallet, I want her to respond to the suit so she never does this again and she learns to respect Black people, or at least not to be sued again." There was so much pain: in school, teachers who discriminated against the students, who discriminated against the parents of the students, the way they treated students. The students went to their parents to complain, the parents complained to the school and they were also discriminated against, dismissed.

We had a case in which the mother said that a teacher wanted her son to leave the school, and the teacher didn't want that student in her class and everything that was said about slaves she exaggerated: she said that all Black people were slaves, that those who came here were already slaves and had to be slaves because they were so docile. She exaggerated the charge of docility, of laziness; she said that many times slaves had to be beaten, she said, "Blacks have to be beaten to make them work." This upset the child, and since the mother had been talking about it with him, the child got up and said it was all a lie. He began to argue with the teacher, and was expelled from the classroom. In the principal's office, the teacher invented some other thing for the principal, that is, the child suffered a series of aggressions. He didn't want to go to school anymore and the mother, worried, asked him why and he ended up telling her. The mother was thinking he was going to school, but he'd go up to the door and then leave again, stay in the street until school was over, so the mother was called in because he was missing class, but the damn teacher didn't mention what she was doing with the boy.

There were other cases such as customers confused with thieves in stores where the person was blocked from leaving. No alarm sounded, but security suspected that they had stolen from the store and ushered them to the security room, dumped their bag on the floor, and not finding anything, apologized and sent them away. It happened in the Zêlo store on Vinte e Cinco de Março Street. The young woman came in, she had a sealed bag in her hands, with a towel that she had bought in the store next door, looked around, and since she didn't find what she was looking for, was leaving the store when security took her to the little room, opened her sealed bag, saw the towel, gave it to the salesperson to see where she had stolen it from, except they didn't have that kind of towel in the Zêlo store, and do you know what he did? He threw the towel at her and said, "So get out of here, bitch!" And he punched her in the face and threw her out of the store. Can you believe it? She fell down, someone stopped to help her and said: "Let's go to the police." There were some police officers passing through a little square close by, when they were notified, went to the store, where, of course, they denied it; the police officers asked if she wanted to do anything, but they were already saying that they were from the store and she was alone, so to think about it carefully. She left it at that. So she took a taxi to leave and told the driver and he told her to go to the police station, since they should sue the store. They went, the deputy sent an investigator with her, and at the store they told another story. The police officers were passing by, she pointed them out and they were called in and confirmed that they'd been called, but that she had refused to go to the police station, and the taxi driver also told the investigator that the same thing had happened to a lot of people and that's why he had taken her to the police station to see if they could put a stop to it. The investigator asked if there had been a fight in the store, and they said there hadn't. "So why does she have this bruise?" he asked. Well, Zêlo was prosecuted and sentenced to pay a fine. They always think they can do it; she's Black, so they can.

They defended themselves by saying that it wasn't the store's security guard, except when the police were called, the store manager and the security guard were found talking inside the store, and the manager was giving him orders; they said that someone had informed him that she was stealing. And, if the security guard wasn't from the store, what was he doing inside the store, in the security room? There was no way to get out of it; they paid the fine.

Another case was that of a Black woman who ran a rotisserie in an upper-middle-class neighborhood. The white woman went to buy one of her products, didn't like it, and began to insult her with dirty *preta*, that it wasn't a place for *pretos*. The woman, of course, wanted to get rid of the Black woman.

That was also the case in a condominium: we received a complaint from a sixty-year-old woman who was discriminated against in her own apartment in the condo building where she lived; a new manager came in and posted on her door that monkeys couldn't live in the building. She was offended and didn't understand what was happening, because she worked in the Federal Congress, in Brasília, and only came here on weekends. She went to talk to Delfim Netto,[24] whom she had worked with, and he asked her if she was the only Black woman living in the building. She was shocked, because until then she didn't know she was Black, so she asked him, "but what Black woman?" He responded: "Whoever, Black men, Black women, are there other Black people in the building?" She didn't answer, she went to talk to Bernando Cabral,[25] whom she knew very well. And Bernardo Cabral asked her the same question. She almost went crazy and almost drove us crazy when she came to us, asking us what all that was about, what were they doing to her. Without knowing, we asked her the same question. So she said she didn't know she was Black, no one had ever told her such a thing. And this whole time the manager was "harrassing her." It was true that she had some relatives who were a little darker and she occasionally had them over, but she wasn't, and now the manager wanted her out because monkeys would be able to visit the condo building. This woman was really going crazy. Afterwards we returned her documents to her, first because I wanted us to go to her house to speak with her and to show the manager that Black lawyers existed, and second because the "white" woman wasn't sure whether she'd be successful with the case if she was accompanied by Black lawyers. She went nuts over being called Black, she didn't know she was Black, and she was suffering discrimination at sixty. And the woman said she really wanted to clean up the condo building, she didn't want Black people there, it's so common, Black people of a little wealthier class living in some luxury condo being attacked, to make them leave.

There was the case of dona Aldair, in a condo in Jandira in which we suggested repossession, because she left due to pressure from the other residents, because she was Black. Eventually she ended up leaving. The process was so violent that her daughter didn't want to go back under any circumstances; she wanted to live somewhere more modest.

These kinds of cases were very common. This one wasn't our case, Dr. Nadir Campos, the son of a famous criminal attorney from the region of Marília, a university professor there, he thought that racism didn't exist, it was a social, not a racial, issue, because he had certainly never felt or perceived racial discrimination until the day that he, a Black prosecutor, married to a white woman, had his light-skinned daughter discriminated against by the manager in the same way as the other cases. They wanted to kick the child out of the playground where she was playing; the manager thought she was dealing with a relative of some doorman, and kicked them out very rudely. So now the issue wasn't social anymore, he felt it in his skin, because he had status, power, and perhaps even more money than the manager, but the manager was a different color than him, she was white. He filed a racism suit against her, and, reportedly, it was denied. Months later, on May 13, there was an event at the Jabaquara Courthouse to celebrate the date.[26] On the panel were Dr. Eunice Prudente, the USP law professor; Maria da Penha Guimarães, president of Conad – the OAB–SP Commission on Black and Anti-Discrimination Issues; Vicentinho, the federal representative; Colonel Vitória; Dr. Nadir, the organizer of the event; and me. The audience was packed with clerks, prosecutors, and judges, and, to everyone's shock, he [Dr. Nadir] began to say that Brazil was racist, São Paulo society was racist, the Public Prosecutor's Office was racist. Ever since the aggression his daughter had suffered, he finally understood that racism exists, that it's cruel and it isn't just in some Black people's heads; he was shaken and became an "activist." The vast majority of people, after a situation like that, exhibit a desire to contribute to the cause, they want to do something, because they had never imagined that it existed and they don't believe it could happen to anyone, and especially to them, of all people.

I usually say: "Wait, your day will come," because sooner or later, kind of like adoption, someone will break the news. The cases I know of are varied, beginning with the sister of one of our colleagues. The family was dark-skinned, and she was a little lighter, she was the white one of the family, considered white, and one day, when she was fourteen or fifteen, they were crossing Consolação Street in front of a car that was speeding, and the driver shouted the fateful phrase: "Just like a Black woman!" She and the whole street heard that she was Black; she almost had to be carried home. Black families have the habit of telling the lightest child that they're white, the white one of the family. The day comes, she was fourteen and the other woman was sixty. Some find out due to love and others due to pain. The majority is with lots of pain. I am sure that many know that it exists but to avoid suffering, it's better to try to free yourself of it. Do you remember the 138 colors on the 1980 census? Unless you say, "I have light skin, why deal with all this? It won't happen to me." Except our society makes you question if you know who you are, if you're Black, and to be Black is to be inferior, so it makes you question if you know you're inferior. That's why, in my view, the issue of quotas in universities and in the labor market will be much more difficult here than in other countries. We are colonized and we want to be part of the First World, and that's something that astonishes me, if a Black person is American or European, just those from the First World, they are no longer Black, they become "my American, or English, or French, or German, or Belgian friend," especially if they have an accent, even better . . .

Or, a more recent case that happened in July 2004, in the São Matheus Hospital. A hospital employee brought her mother-in-law to the doctor. When she was seen, she saw that it was a Black doctor. She closed the door and refused to enter; he noticed and the attendants as well, and they went to speak to the doctor so he would go to the police station. He didn't want to; he stayed there almost an hour astonished, without seeing anyone, it was his first time, a completely foreign situation for him. They went to ask her why she had done that and she replied without the slightest embarrassment that they would go to another doctor, because they'd told her that at that hospital she could only be seen by that doctor, and she left. She didn't know him because she didn't work in first aid, she didn't know the doctor at all, not to say that it doesn't matter if the doctor is good or not; he was Black, period. She's our student in the Promotoras Legais Populares (PLPS, Women Public Prosecutors) course. She doesn't know that I know, all the assignments that have to do with racial issues, I give to her; she doesn't know I know but we'll discuss it.

I love this project of Promotoras Legais Populares. It's for access to citizenship and incorporating new concepts of equality and respect, where women are as important as men in their human, social, political, and economic value.

These women are going to go out and act in and for the community, becoming leaders for referrals, advice, and promoting the instrumental role of law in women's lives, in their everyday lives. Right now we're giving this course in the São Mateus General Hospital, in the São Mateus neighborhood, for fifty hospital employees, leaders chosen from among 150 people who were interested. We have class every Saturday from 9 to 1. You can see the change in the students in every class.

In the OAB PLPS course, different students sign up for political parties and in the city's periphery they look for organizations that they can join, they're in Consegs – Conselhos de Segurança da Comunidade (Community Safety Councils) – or in the Conselhos Gestores de Saúde (Health Management Boards) and they're already giving talks about what they learned in the course. They'll be ready to respond to and lead on the wide range of cases of racism that take place with the Black population in the region.

Look, here in the capital, for whoever was part of this process since 1992, I should say that it's gotten better, the judiciary has given more effective responses and sometimes is getting ahead of problems. A judge, after hearing a victim's statement, said that they were dealing with paragraph 3 of Article 140 [of the Brazilian Penal Code] and a fine was appropriate;[27] he even prejudged and with no restraint, without beating around the bush, treating the case like any other crime and no more than before, and after reading the charges, took on an attitude as if to say, "Counselor, please spare me" or "I have other things to do and you're going to waste my time with these little things?" One of them even said so in my presence, the victim's, the aggressor's, and his lawyer's, without the slightest bit of restraint, he berated us, claiming that we could resolve all this without going to court. At that time, I only heard this once, at a hearing in Guarulhos, in a school discrimination suit. The teacher coordinator suffered an aggression from a student with all the other students there and the judge began to discuss the issue of race, saying about racial discrimination that you can kill a person when you discriminate. Completely flabbergasted, I thought, "God exists! Who is this man?" He was Jewish and had experienced discrimination as a child.

Today things are going more in the civil direction; we've gotten compensation, it takes longer, but the law regarding reparations in cases of moral damage is easier. The Federal Constitution deals with the question of human dignity. A finding we're working on, because human dignity encompasses almost everything. There is the understanding that racism violates that article of the Constitution.

There is still a lot to improve, there is still so much to do before we can let our guard down, retire; the racism cases are still being filed, but fewer than in the last decade. Small progress. I believe that the enormous visibility that the topic has had in the media, NGOs, political correctness, discussions of diversity, etc. . . . they've called attention to the topic, and you can't ignore it anymore or deal with it in just any old way. I'm pleased with the actions of young people today, they're more attentive to current problems. My only fear is the precedent of arrest first and investigate later or someone else. Which I think is dangerous, and which I hope is a media thing and the enormous media exposure, because not all humans resist their fifteen minutes of fame, as Andy Warhol said. They can investigate, the 1988 constitution gave them independence and authorization to investigate; they end up resolving more cases than the police themselves. And what's more, they aren't afraid, they go straight to the top, they denounce Febem (State Foundation for the Wellbeing of Minors),[28] they denounce police officers, businesspeople, politicians. Sometimes they are the voice of those who don't have a voice, like in the case of Bar Bodega. All Black people, accused by the police officers rushing to find some guilty party for a crime committed in Jardins, the Public Prosecutor filed the case, the kids were released and the police are now standing trial for the atrocities they committed against the boys. I keep imagining that one day we'll have them on our side, voices crying out against racism in Brazilian society. Is it a dream? I don't know . . .

Yes, Alexandre de Moraes, in his book about constitutional law,[29] explains it as being a spiritual and moral value inherent in a person that manifests in the conscious and responsible self-determination of one's own life and which brings with it a presumption of respect on the part of all other people, constituted in the minimum that all legal statutes should insure, such that only in exceptional cases can the exercise of fundamental rights be limited, but always without compromising the necessary respect that all people merit as human beings. It requires that individuals respect the dignity of their fellow persons just as the Federal Constitution requires that they respect it as such. And, also, that this conception of fundamental duty is summed up in three principles of Roman law: to live honestly, to harm no one, and to give to each what is owed. Pretty neat, right?

These are different times, Brazilian society has undergone a certain maturation, there are external demands that are forcing change – globalization, the internet – that make information available about what's happening in the whole world at the exact time when it's taking place, access to everything is instantaneous. There's no censorship, there are no secrets, there are no states, there's no more privacy, there is a giant market, and as a result, things are opening, opening is being encouraged, whatever is necessary, reducing corruption, putting an end to small-minded mentalities, to *coronelismo*,[30] to slave labor – ultimately, there's a new world order. There are countless examples in countries that had to adapt their policies given this new order. Look at the new Europe, Iraq and the whole region: if they're not of interest to the markets, they'll suffer harsh retaliation.

The Brazilian people have slowly been discovering that they have rights and that these rights aren't being respected and they're blowing the whistle. In this sense, everyone, whether authorities or not, is being watched and compelled to act. The Public Prosecutor is held to that standard.

There's an air of citizenship, slight, but powerful experiences, people are getting to know their rights, and an example of this is the Consumer Protection Code, the Child and Youth Statute, the special courts are citizenship institutes, but there is still a long road ahead.

What you say is good, "consumer, yes, citizen, no." It's still the market, everything is the market, everything is consumption. Look at China – a dictatorship, and it had to open up to the market, and the question of human rights takes a backseat because of the market. And in this context, we, we Black people, are also being looked at with lots of interest, after all we are 75 million people who aren't even being considered, and now we're being seen by the market as 75 million possible consumers. From there to becoming citizens is something else. They should think "we should proceed very carefully" because giving power to people who have gone through what they went through, coming here in the conditions in which they came, suffering what they suffered, going through what they went through and still go through, if they obtain more space, they'll want to share power, and that's out of the question.

We knew we were Black women and it was necessary for us to visit our own spaces, period. We began to visit the Aristocrata Clube, a club for Black people that wasn't activist, it just had cultural activities, two or three times per year, read about the Black Panthers, Angela Davis, Martin Luther King. Here in Brazil, we got to know Eduardo de Oliveira e Oliveira and Dr. Iracema [de Almeida]; we began to participate in meetings with the members of the GTPLUN, Dr. Iracema's group.[31] But activism came later, after I met you at the Treasury Bureau. Whenever there was a break, that was the only thing you talked about. We just wanted to read the magazines *Cláudia* or *Nova*, *Realidade*, or talk about our families, boyfriends, other small talk – and you were just Black people, Black people, Black people, help! Ok, the invitations to meetings began, and then to participate in the Núcleo de Mulheres Negras do Conselho Estadual da Condição Feminina (Black Women's Branch of the State Council on the Condition of Women), the Coletivo das Mulheres Negras (Black Women's Collective), and from then on I began my activism in the Black Movement.

Later, the meetings at Edna's house, where Geledés – Instituto da Mulher Negra was born, I was very honored by the invitation. Now it's my family that says that I only talk about Black people, Black women. I inherited it from you.

Later there was another space that I really wanted to get to know, that I liked but that people always spoke poorly of, which were the samba schools, because it was a Black thing, but once we left the Home, we began to attend the parades in the avenue because my mother really liked them. So much that I cheer for Camisa Verde, it was the first school that I saw in my life and I loved it, so much that I became a fan. But I always thought about how they achieved so much order and discipline and we didn't know how to do anything. I loved it, because the history of Brazil is the history of samba; they performed what they were singing and I went crazy. Once I got a high grade on a test because of a samba storyline, the one about "the month of October in Belém of Pará" that was the Círio de Nazaré festival. I knew the samba and on the avenue had watched a "piece" on the festival. So, some time later, I sought out a wing of subway employees, whose head was part of the association. Once

I went to a costume selection meeting for the costumes that we, everyone in the wing and relatives and friends, would make every weekend from December on. The seriousness and dedication were amazing. Today, they get more money, they've fallen into the hands of white people and TV, so-called globalization; it reaches the whole world, so they're not so interested in Brazilian history. The sambas are always the same, the costumes are always the same, if you've seen one you've seen them all; I can't take anymore how they put an end to our things.

I went out in 1982, 1983, and 1984. When we gathered, all the schools were together, and when they called a school to enter, everyone hugged each other and wished each other luck, and when they called yours, the president would ask us to think about the school's flag, about the work each one of us had put in and how the success of the school was in our hands. There was a single cry: if you were drunk you were removed, you had to go in clean. In there, there was only happiness, you didn't need to keep your eye on the jurors; what was important was to enjoy the benefit of our three months of work.

Now Carnaval is for tourists. There was a time when Black people would form the blocks in the street, the police would arrive and everyone would take off running. There were parade marshals, my uncle was a Camisa Verde parade marshal at the time. According to him, who still had to run from the police, now that there's more money coming in, it's been recognized as something important for Brazil, Black people are no longer in charge of the schools and often not even in the schools. We'll shortly lose our Church of the Blacks of Paissandu.[32]

Like any Black child, I wore braids, and for her to let me comb my own hair – since she pulled a lot and it hurt – she would say: "If you want your hair to be like Olguinha's, we have to comb it, you can't cry." She had indigenous hair, very straight. I let myself be braided but I thought all that suffering would be worth it, in my head it wouldn't be just hair, we would be white, and time went by and that didn't happen and I would ask, "Why, God, if I did everything right?" [*laughs*]. I had to get something out of it. Time went by and nothing [*laughs*], nothing changed, there was some problem [*laughs*]. I always liked being a girl, I like being a woman, and I remember that I got two books from my mother, by the Father Michel Quoist: *O diário de Ana Maria* (Ana Maria's Diary) and *O diário de Dany* (Dany's Diary). Ana Maria's was for adolescents, and it was an introduction to girls' sexuality that taught about the process of menstruation, ovulation, etc. . . . Mom said what she could for the time, but she instructed me to read it and I really liked to know what was going on in our bodies, and when I felt bad cramps I knew what was happening, and remarkably: I was proud. And the other book was about boys.

Seriously now, despite everything, I was always a very proud Black woman and I liked and wanted to be loved. Now, a Black woman as a political being was because of Geledés, because of the need to occupy spaces, leadership, etc.

I was quite a tomboy and I got interested in dating a little later; I liked to flirt with the boys only at dances, I never wanted to get married. Actual dating happened a little later, with a Black boy, and my first kiss was not at all pleasant. It was awful, he stuck his tongue in my mouth, I was horrified, I shoved him away [*laughs*]. I was worried because everyone had said that kissing was so nice, I thought I'd turn into a woman of easy virtue [*laughs*], so "I'd do it with everyone." I began to come on to him everywhere, I'd meet the guy and sometimes I'd get in the car, not to go to a motel, but to kiss, I like kissing, caresses, and touch. Afterwards he would make a date for another day and never show; it was always white men. Until I met our friend's brother and during one of our periods of break up, get back together, I went to do the prep course for the *vestibular*. When I left USP and met a professor and began to go out with him, it was Joel Rufino,[33] then I got back together with our friend's brother and you know the rest.

I never received a marriage proposal nor [asked] to live with any of the few Black men I dated. I also didn't want to get married, to depend on anyone else. I was harassed, but not by Black men. Like I said, I liked it, I threw myself into this game of seduction, at the Treasury Bureau. I took care of myself and I got myself ready to walk by and see men turning to look at me. I was desired and I liked it, pretending I didn't notice anything, look how terrible . . . [*laughs*]. I began to read Marina Colasanti[34] and came to my senses. I still don't want to get married, but now I'm more open to dialogue. Someone to go out with, have a conversation . . . I'm a difficult person, very independent, and at this age . . . But who knows what's ahead, right?

I don't deny that it's occurred to me to run for office, in the São José Home. As I told you, the brother of the director was a city councilor, we discussed politics a lot, we read a lot, and even the *Estadão* every day, the city councilor came by a few times to talk about politics, and I was little and was completely fascinated. He was from Jânio's party – we were all *janistas* in the Home – and I remember my mother's arguments with my father's cousin who was a die-hard *adhemarista*.[35] My mother said Adhemar was a thief and would end up emptying the city's coffers; he snapped back that Jânio was crazy and a liar because he was never going to sweep out anything and the broom was just a way to deceive the public. I loved it. Later, when Adalberto and Theodosina[36] declared their candidacies, since they were Black I went to look for *santinhos*[37] of them, and without them knowing I handed them out to the family, in services, and I campaigned for them. She said there had to be Black people there. We were very involved in the campaigns of Helio Santos and Chico Whitaker,[38] and he didn't want to hear a thing about being reelected because, even though he was from the PT,[39] what he saw and was required to do didn't motivate him to return to that legislature. The city councilors had signed a legal raise, but because of the economic situation at the time it was immoral and he opposed it, including in the newspapers, and as a result suffered a boycott by all the other city councilors, the right wing of the PT, that was the most radical of the parties, it was a sign. So, I think that it's not for me because I don't have the stomach to put up with the deals that are made to serve certain interests. I don't know, life is long, and no one knows about tomorrow. But I won't deny it: I really like politics, but . . .

# 7
# Fátima Oliveira[1]

*Source:* From the Oliveira family's personal archive.

She fascinates me. She is a doctor, a smoker, and an adamant carnivore. The mother of three biological children and one adopted one – the son of a brother who lost his wife in childbirth – and a girl who was given to her at eleven years old, who has given her the grandchildren that she pampers and proudly spoils. She works like a dog because she says that she has a reputation for laziness in her family, and since she actually thinks that it's the truth, she does everything extremely promptly so she can be free later. It's a lie. She raised five children between being widowed and a second marriage. She is on call every week, she travels throughout the country and the entire world representing the Rede Feminista de Saúde (Feminist Health Network). She's the author of four books, the last one a novel about abortion in relationships between women and priests. She is still one of the few Black women who have a weekly column in a major press outlet.

She writes an opinion column in the Belo Horizonte newspaper *O Tempo* (The Times). A traveling salesperson, she lived in Imperatriz and São Luiz do Maranhão, in São Paulo, and settled, who knows for how long, in Belo Horizonte.

She joined the Communist Party of Brazil (PCdoB) at sixteen years of age. She is still a member and one of its most valuable intellectuals. It's a party notorious for its centralism and the discipline it demands of its members, but she is the one who heedlessly and irreverently denounces in her articles those whom she calls the "neoliberals" of the PT and her own PCdoB. Even I, someone who keeps proclaiming independence and autonomy as far as political parties go, haven't been able to go that far in my public protests.

She also has enough self-esteem to make any Argentine jealous. A rare thing among Black people, women, and people from the Northeast of Brazil, and she is all three at once, though she might consider herself or be considered "*morena escura*," dark brown, within Brazilian racial categories. She has absolute confidence in the knowledge that she carries, matched by her conviction in defending her positions in public arenas. She dialogues with areas of science in which women and Black people think they don't belong. She introduced the topics of bioethics and genetic engineering as part of the feminist and anti-racist agendas. She is a pioneering interlocutor, critic, and convenor of the debate with the scientific community from an ethical perspective.

I met her through feminist activism. For years, I had reservations about her party affiliation. I was seduced by her independence, courage, and capacity to think and act on behalf of the causes that we embraced. She has many adversaries and sometimes she borrows trouble. She's a boss; she's Fátima Oliveira! Look:

I was born in Graça Aranha, in the middle of the *sertão*[2] of Maranhão, a small city with just 2,000 voters. At the time, it was a village called Palestina. I'm the first woman doctor born there and also the first elementary school teacher. I'm from a family of rural smallholders. My father was a merchant and my grandfather owned a butcher shop and a small farm.

Since I was the first granddaughter and due to a tradition in my family, when I was going to be born, my mother went to my grandmother's house – my mother was an only child and lived in another village – and stayed there for a year. Afterwards, Dad decided to settle in Graça Aranha; however, when they moved to their own house, the story is that I stayed living with my Grandma.

My grandparents were my grandparents and my godparents. My parents' house wasn't painted, it was just made of bricks. They say that when I woke up I would cry a lot because I missed the walls, there with just the brick. So, I stayed in Grandma's house. I grew up there and called Mom and Dad by their names. Grandma, I called her Mother, and my grandfather "Paivelho" (Oldfather). After me, Mom had six more children. There are three women and four men among us. Dad died when I was ten. Mom ended up a widow at twenty-five and with seven children! The year after my dad's death, 1964, I went to study in another city.

This wasn't in a region with large estates, that is, there weren't "landowners." My grandfather had cattle. But the cattle owners had their ranches, where they raised their cattle in fences. My grandfather's farm was almost in the city. We could walk from there to the house in ten minutes. It was a ranch. He had the cattle, a cowboy.

In this city, the women made a living by breaking open babassu nuts; the men created plots wherever they wanted, wherever they thought was best. My grandfather would say that he had moved there because he had been born and grown up in "lands of landowners" and he wanted to live free. So he chose to live in a place where there were no "landowners." Graça Aranha was a region of vacant lands, that is, lands without owners, they belonged to the Union. The economic base was babassu nuts; small-time merchants. The lands there were vacant, and the people who raised cattle fenced the land just enough to have their own ranches. There weren't large rural properties. This was very interesting. Now it's not like that anymore. Entire villages, historic places, with more than a thousand inhabitants, today are fenced in. They've turned back into "lands of landowners."

I went to live in Imperatriz because my family of origin lived there. My grandfather left Graça Aranha around 1972. When I took the *vestibular*,[3] he was already living in Imperatriz. My first husband was the son of people who also had plots of land, of rural smallholders, and he wanted to get involved in farming. He had a family inheritance that was enough to get started. We went to Imperatriz, and he bought land and was a farmer all those years. It's an inheritance that he left for the children: a farm that is called Fazenda Santa Rita de Cássia, on the Arapari Ridge, a region that's five hundred kilometers from Imperatriz. It's funny that he didn't much like cattle, he was more of a farmer. He was a big rice planter and raised Mangalarga horses.[4] He died on that farm in a horse accident.

We have a great connection with horses. All my children have horses. I had one when I was a child. Just like my grandfather always branded a calf for every grandchild that was born. That way each of us had a certain amount of cattle. Any that descended from that calf that we got when we were born was branded with our name. It's a nice memory . . .

Today I still have my "branding iron," made by my grandfather, with the letters MF, Maria de Fátima. The calf that I got the day I was born was branded with it. I still remember her. She had reddish brown hair with a white spot on her forehead. I forget her name, but I know she was very grumpy when she had a calf and she was difficult to milk. When we were kids, my siblings and I, we had the habit of going to the corral early in the morning to drink fresh milk. And sometimes I would whine that I only wanted to drink milk from my cow. Sometimes the cowboy, his name was Dé – he was my grandfather's cowboy his whole life and I'm the godmother of one of his children – couldn't lasso the cow to milk her and I started to cry. One day he lost his patience with me after trying to lasso the cow several times to help me, and said, "Drink from any other one, girl, this cow is bold and cheeky like her owner." It stuck with me. When someone wanted to make me angry, they'd say that I was grumpy like my cow.

When I became a widow, in 1986, I was thirty-two years old and had five children: Maria, Débora, Lívia, Gabriel, and Artur. I had three children and adopted Artur and Maria. So my oldest, Maria, and youngest, Artur, are adopted. Artur is my nephew, he's the son of one of my brothers, whose mother died in childbirth. I became a widow with the five children. It was difficult. But after eight months of widowhood, I got married again. I always say that I got married quickly because the first loon who wanted to marry me, I accepted. I thought I'd never get married again. My grandfather said I was such a poor thing, that with so many children I'd never find another man who wanted to marry me, he was sorry for me because I was so young to end up without a husband. Well, I found one. And quickly.

I got married for the first time in 1975, in my third year of medical school. The second time was in 1987. My husband lived in São Luís, so I went back to São Luís, where I stayed for another year before moving to Belo Horizonte in 1988.

I have Maria, who was adopted, she came to live with me before Débora – my first biological daughter – was born. Maria was given me by my first "sick person," a man I took care of when I was still a medical student, who was the first sick person for whom I was responsible. He was hospitalized for two months, so he was a patient I attended to every day, until his discharge. I'd even go on Sundays to the hospital to make a visit: examine him, see test results, and prescribe medicines. One day he asked:

> Would you want to raise a child, Dr. Fátima? To keep you company because your husband works so far away. I have a lot of nieces who are very poor, girls who need to study and who can keep you company. I have a cousin who has many children, and the way we can help is to find a good family to raise one of the girls, to send her to school.

I told my husband about it, who said, "Tell him to bring her because she'll keep you company." But I didn't tell Mr. José either yes or no. But on the day of his discharge, he asked for my address and asked: "Can I bring the girl to you?" And I said yes.

That's how it went. I didn't even know who this girl was. When she arrived at my house, it was Good Friday of 1976, I was sleeping after lunch when the bell rang. I went to open the door, it was Mr. José with the little girl. She was eleven, very thin, with a little green dress, flip-flops, and a newspaper wrapped around a few clothes. He handed the girl over with her birth certificate and everything. But he said, "Her father and mother didn't come because they didn't have the money for two round-trip tickets."

My husband paid for his and the girl's tickets and gave him some more money for when the father or mother wanted to come see her. After he left, my husband cried, because he never thought someone would just hand a child over to someone else that way. But they did.

Maria didn't know how to eat rice because she was from a region of Baixada Maranhense, Anajatuba, where the basic food is breaded fish. She had never brushed her teeth; she didn't know how to read; she didn't know almost anything. We couldn't enroll her in school because no one would accept her, since she didn't learn how to read until she was eleven. So we hired a private teacher to teach her how to read.

I had to fire three maids because of Maria. Until recently I didn't buy flour for my house because of her. The only way I found to have her learn to eat rice was by not having flour at home. But two of the maids secretly bought flour for her!

When I was without a maid, I went to the university and took Maria with me. Some of the professors objected. But I brought her because I didn't have anyone to leave her with. One day I left her alone for an afternoon and she stuck a hairclip in the electrical socket! When I arrived, she said completely innocently: "Auntie, if you put your finger here in the little hole it makes you shiver." I wanted to die . . .

She was extremely lazy about studying. It was a problem. She didn't like to, but I insisted that she had to study, at least up to high school, which she finished with great difficulty. When she was sixteen or seventeen, she went to work in a women's clothing store, a boutique, with my sister. She would study in the morning and go to the store in the afternoon. The next year, she began to study at night, and would stay in the store the whole day. She learned about business, which is how she makes a living now. She did well. Today she lives in Rio de Janeiro and has two children, Lucas and Luana, who are my grandchildren you saw today at home, they're here on vacation.

My father was the son of Portuguese parents. He was white. My grandfather, my dad's father, Odílio Pereira de Oliveira, was white with green eyes. Dad was the son of my grandfather's first wife, there are two brothers, Gildino, my father, and Juarez, my uncle. Their mother died when they were children, and my grandfather gave them to Mãe Jesus – a sister of my dad's mother.

Dad met his father the day I met him too! Dad started to socialize with his father just a year before he died, in 1963, because after my grandfather gave Dad and his brother to his sister-in-law, Mãe Jesus, he married another woman and never went to see them again for over thirty years. And he didn't live far away. Mãe Jesus raised those two boys like her own, together with her own children. I don't remember how many, there were a lot of them. Dad considered her his mother and while he was alive he was in charge of her and her husband's livelihood.

My mom's family is all Black and lives in a place that's called Belém dos Pretos (Bethlehem of the Blacks) – which is their land, but it's not exactly a *quilombo*[5] – my grandma's mother bought it, so it's been theirs for many, many years, more than a century, I think. It's in the town of Colinas, Maranhão, and I went there many times before my great-grandmother died, at the beginning of the 1960s. The only ones who don't live there are Grandma and Uncle Luiz, who is Grandma's brother, who for many, many years has been a cowboy on my children's farm in Imperatriz.

Paivelho thought that education was very important, that those of us who were Black, who were poor, it was through education that we were going to become important, because according to him, money could run out, but no one could take knowledge away from us. So my grandfather made a great effort on behalf of all the grandchildren.

My grandfather's family was all Black. He's the son of a cowboy who worked for Gonçalo Moreira Lima – who was a state representative for Maranhão for more than thirty years. My grandfather and his brothers and sisters, there were a lot of them, were born on Gonçalo Moreira Lima's lands, on the Fazenda Serra Negra, the town of Colinas.

My grandfather was the only one of Bodô the cowboy's children to leave the region, but he had a lifelong friendship with Seu[6] Sales – the representative Moreira Lima. They were friends, and he and his campaign in Graça Aranha always trusted my grandfather. Moreira Lima, who stayed at our house during his electoral campaigns, was the representative who boosted the candidacy of José Sarney for governor of Maranhão. And when I say "boost," I mean it literally, since Moreira Lima, besides, was a very rich man who could contribute money to Sarney's campaign. Sarney's runner-up was the representative's son-in-law. I don't remember what party he was in, but I know that he spent twenty-eight years among the opposition until José Sarney's election as governor.

Dona Lili, Seu Sales's wife, whenever she referred to my grandfather said: "Of old Bodô's children, Braulino was always the one who was most stuck up. He left good old Serra Negra with us and went to take care of his own life."

There was one of my grandfather's brothers who she really liked, but she hated that he had joined the "rebels" and, according to her, turned into a bandit. His name was Cornélio. We never met him. He was Paivelho's brother who joined the Coluna Prestes[7] and never let his family know. Dona Lili recounts that Cornélio didn't allow Fazenda Serra Negra to be "invaded" by the Coluna Prestes, nor for the farm's business to be plundered – it was with words like that, "invasion" and "plunder," that she referred to the Coluna Prestes – but that Cornélio went to the Serra Negra farmhouse to tell her and Seu Sales that the Coluna wouldn't touch Serra Negra. My grandfather said very little about the subject, just that his brother Cornélio turned into a follower of Captain Prestes and "fell into God's wide world," and never contacted the family again.

But it was because of my grandfather's friendship with representative Moreira Lima that I became a friend of the family too. When I started medical school, I went to live in their house, where their daughter Zuzu Brito also lived – she was a businessperson and ex-director of the Business School at UEMA (State University of Maranhão), with her five children: the twins Ana Thereza and Silvana Thereza, Leila Thereza, Djalma Filho, and Luís Eugênio. For many years, in exchange for living there, I helped Leila and Luís Eugênio with their "homework."

Their house was called the Serra Negra Mansion, with a plaque and everything at the entrance to the enormous garden in front. There was a marvelous library with, I think, the only collection of the newspaper *A Pacotilha*,[8] from the time of the Empire. There was a pilgrimage of Brazilianists lining up to see *A Pacotilha*, which is a treasure, beautifully bound, and it was fully microfilmed. In general they spoke to Seu Sales, who was an intellectual and read a lot, or to me, because I was the only person he allowed to touch the library, since he said that I knew how to treat that treasure. But he was so proud of his library, which he said was the most important personal library of Maranhão, and one day he asked me if I could take care of it because the maids were ruining his books. So I began to take care of it.

Once a week, I would tidy the library, and the children, especially Djalma Filho, who today is a prosecutor for the State of Maranhão, loved to leaf through *A Pacotilha* and took advantage of the chance to do it whenever I was in the library. In every issue of *A Pacotilha* there were many announcements of "fugitive Blacks." In all of them, the owner advertised a reward. He would read them out loud and he always commented, "Do you see, Auntie, if you'd been born then you wouldn't be here all *porloche* (fancy, proud) studying medicine. You could be one of these fugitive slaves, with how ornery you are." I remember that we read a lot of these announcements. There are issues of *A Pacotilha* with whole pages of them.

I still have a deep friendship with this family until today. My children call her Aunt Zuzu. When I arrive in São Luís, her children stay because of me. When Débora was studying in Australia, she sent a postcard to Aunt Zuzu. On the phone, she told me, "You're more like me than my own daughters. Only your daughter would send me a postcard from Australia, only your daughter. That's good upbringing, my child!"

I have a sister who died. There are seven of us. Mom ended up a widow at twenty-five years old with seven children. But my youngest sister died, I think a year after Dad.

My grandfather gave all of my siblings an equal chance to study. The difference is that very early on I went to a boarding school. My grandfather moved to Imperatriz because in Graça Aranha there was no *ginásio*[9] and he wanted all his grandchildren to go to school.

After I was born, my grandmother had one more child, so I have an uncle who's younger than me, the same age as my second brother, so my grandfather kept his son, me, and all the grandchildren in school. Before moving to Imperatriz, he rented a house in São Luís for all of us, with Mom there keeping track of everyone, in a rented house in the center of the city. That is, so that all of us could study in good schools, Mom had to stop working. She handled my father's business for some years, but with this decision of my grandfather's, that everyone had to study, she had to close her small business; it was declining a lot anyway, it wasn't sufficient to support the family.

In Imperatriz he [Paivelho] could buy land for his crops, his cattle, have things close by and have everyone live in the city where there were good schools. Mom also sold her house and bought another one in Imperatriz. But he also started a small business in Imperatriz. It was purchasing beans, corn, etc. That is, it was a little wholesaler of these things. That's how he made his living: from his plot and his little business; the one who took care of it was my uncle, who was already a young man and a good businessperson.

Among my siblings, two didn't finish high school: Juarez and Zezinho. Júlia went to university for geography, but she's also a merchant, like some of my other siblings. We're a family of merchants. Everyone gets involved in business, except me. But I was also the owner of a store when I lived in Imperatriz. Júlia's first business, which was a boutique, was a joint venture between us. It's called Xikita Bakana. She did the work and I set up the store; I made the initial purchase in cash. I gave her 50% of the store. It was a beautiful store. It was there that Maria learned to work. When I got married for the second time, in 1987, I moved to São Luís and sold my share to her.

I kept the store for six years. I had a ritual every day: I'd leave the hospital at 6 in the evening, I'd go by the store to close up the cash register; I'd go by my grandparents' house; I'd only get home in time for *Jornal Nacional*.[10] Every day I'd go to my grandparents' house. I'd arrive, and the two of them would be sitting in chairs out front. Sometimes I'd eat dinner with them. My husband didn't understand it. He said I had a fixation with my grandparents.

I moved to Minas Gerais because my second husband was a miner who landed in Maranhão at the time of the dictatorship; he was persecuted by the dictatorship. Here he studied economics, was a leader in the student movement, but he had to go underground; he was convicted by the dictatorship at least three times. After amnesty, he stayed in Maranhão for a while, but decided to return to Minas. That is, I came to Minas as my husband's trailing spouse! We arrived here in February 1988. In January 1992, we moved to the city of São Paulo, where I lived until December 1995, because since mid-June 1991, he'd been transferred to São Paulo.

I remember when I went to school for the first time. I loved books, messing with papers and playing school. Dad was a man who read a lot, since he was a child. Before I knew how to read I remember how I loved to page through the magazines *O Cruzeiro* (The Cross), *Seleções* (Selections), and the *Almanaque do Pensamento* (Almanac of Thought). Dad was an excellent storyteller. At that time, the age for a child to go to school was seven. I saw my older friends going to school and I cried. I wanted to go any way I could.

There was a rural school in the city that was called the Humberto de Campos Rural School. But there weren't even always teachers in that school, because it was up to the political boss of the place to pay a teacher for the rural school. When I was six, a teacher came who set up a private school. It was Teacher Izídio. It was a school in a stable and the students brought their own chairs. The classes were all together.

One day Teacher Izídio was going to school and I was sitting on the sidewalk of our house with my grandfather, and I asked him to call the teacher over to ask if he would take me at the school. I was six. My grandfather called him over and said: "This girl is crazy for school. She's only six. Will you take her at your school?" He said: "You can send her." I remember that my grandfather asked him how much it was. When he heard the answer he stuck his hand in his pocket and said: "I'll pay for three months." And he paid, right there on the sidewalk. The next day, I went to school, carrying my chair.

I learned to read very quickly. Before I turned seven, I had learned to read the ABC reader, the primer, and I'd read the book for the first elementary year. It was a book called *Vamos estudar* (Let's Study), by the publisher Agir. I remember the stories in that book to this day. At any rate, in a year at Teacher Izídio's school I learned to read and write. From then on I loved to read and recite poetry. I quickly memorized all the ones I liked. Then there was nothing else in the first year to read, so I went on to the second year. This was all in one year of school.

That was when the teacher Maria do Carmo arrived. She wasn't a trained teacher [who'd studied education], she was a kind of rural teacher. That teacher lived in the house of the area's political boss, next to our house. So, the elementary school, the Humberto de Campos School, reopened after many years without a teacher. The new teacher reclassified the students who came from Teacher Izídio's school. There I was sent back from the second year to the first, because of my age. I studied the first, second, and third years in the Humberto de Campos Rural School.

When I was nine, I got a Singer sewing machine from my father. Did I already mention that he sold sewing machines in his warehouse? Mom is an excellent sewer, but Dad detested that she sewed. However, she was very stubborn and kept making clothes. When he complained that she never left her machine, she said that she was making clothes for Grandma and for us, that it was absurd for her to sew so well and not be able to sew for her family. She also did gorgeous machine embroidery. She was a famed sewing teacher, so at home there were always two or three machines going, since she taught a lot of people. I always had beautiful clothes. I was raised wearing a new dress every Sunday during my childhood. When I was an adolescent, when I went back to school, I'd bring a new dress for each Sunday.

When I was a child, I loved to play around with Mom's sewing machine to sew doll clothes. Whenever a broken needle appeared, it was a sure sign that I'd been there. One day Dad decided that I should have my own machine, since I liked to play around with Mom's. It was a Singer machine, white, set in a yellowish wood table, the latest model that had just come out. However, I never learned to make clothes. I learned to embroider by machine very well. I know all the stitches. I have some bedding that I embroidered when I was ten, Richelieu embroidery. I like sewing machines; I don't have one now, but I remember that when I was already married I bought one. I don't know what I did with it. I think I gave it away when I moved from São Luís to Belo Horizonte. I like embroidery. It takes my mind off things.

In the town of Colinas there was a very famous school, still called the Colinense School today – that was Father Macedo's school, where all the rich people in the region of Médio Sertão sent their children. It was the only city that had a *ginásio*, *científico* (science school), and *magistério* (normal school – teacher training).[11] There was also a system of scholarships for people who couldn't afford it, but I don't know how it worked. But I think it was with money raised by the church in the Our Lady of the Conception festival, the patron saint of the city. I think on December 8. It's a very famous festival in the region; it lasts almost a week.

My family always attended the festival. I remember that when I was in *ginásio*, I won an ox in a raffle at the church festival and Paivelho immediately said that he was going to donate the ox back to the church, to have another raffle to benefit the school. I was so angry I almost died. I even cried. When we got home, he branded a bull calf for me, saying that we didn't need the raffle ox from the church, we could give it back to the church to help the others, the poor. He was a very, very interesting person of extraordinary principles.

The Colinense School was a religious school, Catholic, which benefited from significant international support, I think German. It was a beautiful school, coed, that had students from many other cities. There was a dorm for girls and another for boys; it wasn't called a dorm, it was called the Student House – where the girls lived and where the dining hall was. The boys slept in another house, but they ate with us, from breakfast on. It was a magnificent dining hall, in a marvelous old house.

That school was very expensive, it was all private, it was a first-world school. Every family in the region dreamed of being able to send their children to the Colinense School. It gave you a certain status. Father Macedo, who was the priest who baptized me, was a friend of my family's. When we arrived there, he remembered our parents, from the day he baptized us. Whenever he ran into me, he'd run his hand over my head and say: "Fátima is small and isn't going to grow because she only drinks well water." A reference to the fact that there was no river in Graça Aranha. He was a very progressive man for the time.

I went to Colinas for fourth grade, when I was ten. There I studied in the João Pessoa Elementary School and I spent the entire year studying for the admissions exam to *ginásio*, a kind of *vestibular*, in the Colinense School. They could administer the exam to children who were finishing fourth grade and those who were wrapping up fifth grade. If we were in fourth grade and we passed the admissions exam, we'd go directly to *ginásio*, without needing to go to fifth grade. I took it and passed. I started *ginásio* when I was eleven.

I studied at the Colinense School until the third year of *ginásio*. For the fourth and last year of *ginásio*, I moved to the capital of Maranhão, São Luís, where I did the last year of *ginásio* at the Luiz Viana Municipal School and after that started teacher training, at that time called Normal School, at the Education Institute. Both public schools.

Telling these stories, I figure that the type of school that the Colinense School was [is one that] I could never afford for my children, even being a doctor. I can't say how my grandfather paid for all of it.

I went to medical school without ever having to work. I was always just a student. A family of smallholders, small-time merchants, always paying for the places where I moved to study. I can't imagine today how much money it cost, how it worked, because I could never provide for a daughter, even one, in the conditions in which I went to school. Especially since my grandfather was illiterate, my grandmother was illiterate, my mother only finished third grade and my father also.

I think that money had a different value then, although my grandfather was a man of means. In that poor and miserable little city, he was a man of means, since he owned his own house, his cattle, he owned the city's butcher shop, he ran a purchasing warehouse (rice, beans, corn, and cotton), he was the chief of police. Ah! The police chiefs were named by the political bosses.

My father had a store that we called a warehouse, where he sold safes, bicycles, sewing machines, beds, Cimo[12] furniture (beds, tables, chairs, desks, etc.). He was a city councilor twice. He was a man with a very promising life, but he died when he was thirty-three. He owned a very nice house. He also had two other businesses: one for animal hides (goat, sheep, margay), and he was a *cachaça*[13] wholesaler, that is, he was a "vat owner." In our house there was a "vat room." He bought *cachaça* from artisanal producers, since in our city there was a significant number of sugarcane plantations and small sugar mills.

My father's level of culture was impressive. And he wrote very well. Some time ago I found the books for his warehouse, written by him, in my mother's house. Pages and pages without a single error in his Portuguese. I remember lots of this kind of thing, a person who always had magazines and was always reading. Since he traveled a lot for business, he bought these magazines that I was talking about and when he finished reading them he'd say: "Fátima, you can take this magazine, I've already read it." I was always known for liking to read a lot, so much that my father would read magazines and then give them to me. And I was still very little.

I remember the last time that I was with him. We were very close. Dad would say that when he was a child he would cry with happiness when he found something to read, because he didn't have things to read. That's why I think he understood my taste for reading. The last time I was with him was the day Kennedy died. I've already written a piece about this. On the radio *Voz do Brasil* (Voice of Brazil) came on.[14] I came running into the living room of his house: "Gildino, I'm going to take my first communion. Are you going to buy my silver chaplet and my missal with the mother-of-pearl cover?" I would take my first communion on November 30, 1963. To which he replied: "Write it down on a piece of paper and sit down here with me. Don't talk, because they killed President Kennedy." And I stayed seated at his side listening to the news of Kennedy's assassination. My father died three days later on a trip he made to the city of Caxias, where he dealt in hides; he died in a car accident while he was returning home. When he arrived already dead, he was dressed in beige linen pants and a white, long-sleeved linen shirt (Dad only wore linen clothes). People who knew him say that he was always dressed very elegantly: he was very distinguished. And my godmother Margarida says that none of us take after Dad, that "he was a man who worked a lot, but was always dressed to the nines, in linen. He liked to dress in luxury." In his shirt pocket were my missal with the mother-of-pearl cover and my silver chaplet, and with them the little paper where I'd written down what I was asking for. It's a very strong memory, because I was the one who took the chaplet and missal out of Dad's pocket.

In 1964, my grandfather said I wouldn't go to those "pathetic little schools" there, since I had already learned everything that could be taught there. I was very studious, so I would go to Colinas, to the "priest's school." The first year I went to live in dona Necy's boarding house. I was the only little girl in the girls' boarding house. I was in fourth grade. There was an unforgettable conversation between my grandfather and the owner of the boarding house. He asked her: "Here there's breakfast, lunch and dinner, it's not a snack, right? Because my daughter eats dinner. If there's no proper dinner, you can charge me more and make dinner for her, because she was raised eating dinner."

For a year, in the morning I would go to elementary school and in the afternoon I'd go to the Colinense School, for the admissions exam classes. Once I got into *ginásio*, I'd have the right to live in the Colinense School dorm.

Another interesting thing about my grandfather is that he thought that women needed to study and graduate. He'd say that I would be a teacher, because a woman who had a profession wouldn't put up with a man's abuse. His whole life he wanted me to become a teacher. But Grandma, on the contrary, would say that "he sent his daughters to school so that they wouldn't marry the bumpkins from around there, so they'd marry a different kind of people. That was the goal of all the sacrifice." Ever since I was little I'd heard and knew about this opinion from my grandmother. For her what a young lady needed was to arrange a good marriage, and this business of studying was to "pass the time." That is, wait for a good husband.

But I knew I wanted to be a doctor, since I was very small. I really liked science. At the Colinense there was everything you could imagine that sparked your curiosity: a science classroom, a language classroom, a geography classroom. I learned to handle a microscope the first year of *ginásio*. In the science classroom, there were even fetuses of various sizes under the microscope that we learned to handle. These are the things, especially my enjoyment of science, that stand out the most about my life in school.

I also remember how I was impacted by the theory of evolution. There were two or three pages on the theory of evolution in my science textbook and I thought it was wonderful. When the teacher taught the class I already knew everything, because I had read a lot about it in other books in the school library. Understanding it was fascinating. The theory of evolution always moved me a lot.

From then on, I understood that the existence of the world was not the work of God. It was all stimulating to me. Since then, I've studied and read everything about evolution. So it's not by chance that genetics became a hobby of mine and it's also not by chance that the theory of evolution makes up two chapters of my first book, *Engenharia genética: O sétimo dia da criação* (Genetic Engineering: The Seventh Day of Creation). And I really enjoyed writing those chapters, because the theory of evolution is the greatest intellectual revolution of our times; it's there that science and religion are definitively separated.

Once a week, it was mandatory for all classes to meet in the science classroom, where the objective was to do experiments; learn to handle test tubes, microscopes, etc. Everything necessary for research.

At that time there was also a library with 10,000 books. It was beautiful, with all the luxuries you could imagine. Every week all the classes would go to the library for two hours. They called it reading class – it was so that we could learn to use the library: find and handle the books; stay silent, etc. I loved it. I read so, so much. I learned to read by making notecards, a practice that I continued for years on end, until after university. Everything I read, I'd make notes, which is a very important methodology; afterwards I slowly lost the habit.

When I arrived at university, the thing that most left an impression on me was that 90% of the class had never seen a microscope. And these were medical students. I knew how to use a microscope, the lenses, everything. With the difference that at the university there were both manual and electric microscopes. Since I handled the manual one well, the histology professor inquired: "Where did you learn to work with a microscope?" I replied: "I've been working with a microscope since I was a child." He said I was lying. I insisted that I was not, and told him where I'd studied. Using the microscope is one of my most pleasant memories that I have of my time as a student.

When I was in the last year of teacher training, I went to study in the *vestibular* prep course for medicine. My grandmother thought it was absurd for me to want to be a doctor. She argued that I had studied too much and that being a teacher was good enough, that I was inventing things to study so much that she would die without seeing me become a doctor; that with all this I was going to end up an "old maid," etc. And to have a daughter who's an "old maid" is a disgrace; it means that she hadn't found a husband, that no one wanted her.

She thought that if you studied too much you wouldn't get a husband. But whenever I said I wanted to be a doctor, my grandfather would say that I could, but when I tried to do scientific training [instead of teacher training] he wouldn't let me. It was a big fight, but he stayed firm: "No, you have to have a profession." It's true, whoever does *científico*, and he knew this, would finish without having a profession. He always said that I needed to be a teacher and afterwards I could study whatever I wanted, that while he was alive he'd guarantee it. So, I did the teacher training. But I didn't even go to my own graduation party, because I didn't want to be a teacher. The first time I took the *vestibular*, I didn't pass. In the *magistério* at that time there was no math, physics, chemistry, or biology. So, to study teacher training and then take the *vestibular* for medicine puts you at a disadvantage.

I graduated with a medical degree in 1978, when I was twenty-four. In a city like São Luís de Maranhão, in the 1970s, if you pass the *vestibular* for medicine, whoever you are, you become a little like "God" for your family and social circles. Across the university, a medical student is very prestigious, and therefore seen differently. Medical school is quite cruel, because it's the only major in which you have classes in the morning and the afternoon for all six years. In my time, there were even classes on Saturdays, all day; it's not possible to work while you're a medical student. It wasn't until the fifth year that I didn't have class on Saturdays. You have very little time to study, just at night. Even at a public school, it's very expensive because of the books. You don't study medicine without books, which demands a certain financial condition, a privileged condition, starting with good nutrition, a series of things to endure the pace of things.

The sixth year of medical school is a year when you have practically no theoretical classes. It's your intern year, when you stay in the hospital the whole time, in various areas, from first aid to intensive care. In São Luís there was the Dutra Hospital, which today is a university hospital, but at that time it was the INPS (Instituto Nacional de Previdência Social; National Social Pension Institute), which was attached to the Federal University of Maranhão and received ten sixth-year students annually, on a competitive basis. I entered the competition and was one of the ten students in the Dutra Hospital in 1978. We received minimal monthly salaries as interns. It was the first money I earned in my life. I really valued having my own money for the first time. I learned to handle money as a small child.

Ever since I learned to read and write, I wrote down everything in my grandfather's warehouse; as I mentioned, he had a butcher shop, a little cattle ranch, and had his own plots of rice, corn, and beans, and was a buyer of "*legume na folha*" (crops on paper). That meant the following: in cities in the interior, people with more property, who have money, earn a lot of money in a way that exploits others. Look: people need to plant their plot and need money to do so, so they go to those who have money and sell "*legume na folha*," that is, a hypothetical crop of rice, beans, corn, etc. That is, they go plant the crop, but the buyer of the "crops on paper," as was the case of my grandfather, fronts them the money. The seller ends up in debt, with a firm date to deliver the crop after the harvest. If they don't deliver the product on the agreed-upon date, the account begins to accumulate interest upon interest.

For example, I sell some sixty sacks of "rice on paper." Obviously the money that the guy fronts is a lower amount than if I showed up with the rice ready to sell; there's a market price in the region to buy "on paper." The buyer of the "crops on paper" also runs some risks. He uses his cash, as my grandfather said: "clean and dry money," but runs the risk of never seeing his money again. So there was a notebook where these purchases of "crops on paper" were written down and another with the butcher shop accounts. After I learned to write, I wasn't even seven, my grandfather would say: "Fátima, grab the notebook with 'purchases on paper.'" So I'd grab the notebook, because before there was a young man that he would pay to do this, but he didn't know how to write or read . . . after I learned to read and write, at seven, I took care of the two notebooks. He would do these purchases of "crops on paper" on Sundays, market days, then he'd open the office. There was a room in my grandfather's house, an actual shop with a table, chair, everything. People would arrive, he'd negotiate, I'd write it down in the notebook. There were promissory notes, I knew about promissory notes since I was small, that I would fill it out and if the person didn't know how to sign their name they'd put their finger on a little pad with ink . . . everything duly witnessed. The witnesses to the deal, they did have to know how to sign their names.

I remember that my handwriting was nice and that Dad, who in the beginning would correct everything I wrote in the notebooks, would say to my grandfather: "Seu Braulino, she already knows what to do, she knows to put the right amount of money down. She can help you now. Don't worry." So, on Sundays, I'd spend the whole day working with my grandfather on it. As a result, I knew a lot about how businesses work and the value of money from very early on.

When I went to study in Colinas, for school breaks, I'd come home. Grandma would say that I had a whole week to sleep as I liked. That is, to wake up whenever. After a week, I'd adjust to the rhythm of the house. Which meant taking on running the household. Those are very pleasant memories, returning home from school. The day that I'd arrive from Colinas, there'd be a whole procession of visits. Almost the whole city would come, adults and children. Or at least relatives and the whole neighborhood. Grandma would make lots of sweets, which were served at every visit. It was a ritual. A week before my arrival, she'd make sweets, various kinds to serve during the visits, which would last almost a week.

After a week for sleeping, school break was for three months at the end of the year. I began to take care of the household. That is, I needed to get up every day to make breakfast. A whole bunch of things, starting with corn and rice *cuscuz* . . .[15] A huge job. I'd put the rice and corn in to soak at night. Early in the morning, I'd grind the rice and corn, one at a time, to make the *cuscuz* meal. Grandma took many years to accept that the corn or rice meal "ground in a grinder" was also good, because she didn't like them. They had to be ground with a mortar and pestle!

Coffee was also an endless drama. Grandma's coffee had to be fresh. For her, fresh coffee meant grinding the roasted coffee when it was ready to be made . . . We roasted the coffee at home. We had a coffee roaster. My job was: make breakfast for everyone. There was a girl who worked in Grandma's house, but I was the one who had to make it during school breaks. If it was time to work in the fields (the vegetable plots were close by), I could be making food for twenty, up to twenty-five fieldworkers (from eleven on up). I didn't just make it, I would take breakfast to the workers in the fields.

It was really a brutal contradiction, because I studied in a very fancy school and then during school breaks I was thrown into housework. But Grandma would say that "if you don't know how to do it, you don't know how to order someone else to," and that if I didn't know how to do "everything," how was I going to take care of a house, unless I was going to be one of those idiots that maids hoodwink . . .

Her logic was that I needed to know how to do everything that there was to learn about being in charge and being a lady of the house. Today I see that it really was training in how to be in charge, because in our house there were always lots of adult women: the cook, Albertina, who lived with us for many years; Aunt Custódia, who stayed there for years, in addition to some relative or other of my grandfather's who was always studying, or learning sewing from my mom, or sent there because of some boyfriend the family didn't approve of (it was a habit to send young women to a relative's house to get them away from "boyfriends with no future").

During school breaks, in the afternoon, after I made all those meals and took them to the fields, I'd go out to collect from the people who owed my grandfather money. That was interesting. Thus, a week after my arrival, he'd sit down on the sidewalk and say: "Grab the notebook for the butcher shop and the one for the 'crops on paper' and a sheet of writing paper."

With his utensils in his hands, he'd begin: "Whatshisname hasn't paid. Write him down." We made a list of people who owed him money, from the butcher shop and the "crops on paper." I had a bike that I got from my grandfather. It was a "girl's bike," the kind without a top tube. I got that bike before my father died. I remember him saying that my grandfather spoiled me.

So I'd collect from the people who owed my grandfather money while we lived in Graça Aranha, that is, until I was almost eighteen.

I'd do it with this ritual: I'd arrive home for break and after a week take charge of everything. Once I was in possession of the list of people, from Monday to Saturday, I'd go out on my bike to collect money. In the early evening, he and I would sit down in the living room, in some lazy chairs, some people call them lounge chairs, and I'd account for the day's collections. I'd settle the money, or the excuses and extensions of deadlines for payment. If I didn't receive enough one day, he'd squabble, he'd say I wasn't demanding payment right, I don't know what else . . . that way, with so many people owing him money, how could he afford my school? So I had a strong enough motivation to be a relentless bill collector. My studies depended directly on the money that I was able to collect from my grandfather's debtors!

I was a respected and insistent bill collector. Today I can see that I was really aggressive. There were people who would pay my grandfather when my break was approaching because they knew I was coming. They'd say: "I'm going to pay soon because that cheeky girl of Braulino's is about to arrive." When I arrived at the houses, lots of people would hide, but I'd stay there waiting, and I'd collect. Once my grandfather showed up with a [truck]load of rice at the doors of the house, at the storeroom door. He got a pile of stuff out of the truck, from radios to old pots and pans. I asked Grandpa what all that was. He said that a man had owed my grandfather for a long time without paying, so he went to his house and took everything he could find; he said that since the man didn't have money or product to pay with, my grandfather could take everything he possessed in that house.

I was so horrified that I couldn't even speak, since I was in a school where we discussed politics, that kind of thing, poor people's difficulties and suffering, how rich people exploited them, and in that situation, my grandfather was indeed considered a rich man, next to so much misery . . . I went to my room and cried myself to sleep.

I also remember a big fight that I had with my grandfather. I think it was the first time that we had a real fight; arguing, yes, we argued a lot, but they weren't fights, but he said that I talked back, that I couldn't hear anything and keep quiet. But he liked that I was like that. He would even tell other people that I was no fool. He even thought that I should be a lawyer because I talked back and wasn't foolish; that it was nonsense that I wanted to be a doctor – he was the only person who didn't think it was nice that I wanted to be a doctor – he said that I had to be a lawyer because I liked to debate so much. It was interesting and I still remember him saying: "You really like to debate. If you were a lawyer, you'd be a great lawyer. One of the good ones."

Going back to the serious fight with my grandfather. There was a young man who owed my grandfather money and I went to collect it. When I arrived at his house, he decided to speak in a friendly way with me; he invited me to sit down, which in general the people who owe money wouldn't do. He said that his wife was sick. There were a bunch of snot-nosed kids around, with protruding bellies and covered with sores . . . a poor house, really poor, almost without anything. He added that he'd lost his plot in the last harvest, since the cattle belonging to I don't know whom came into the field and ate everything. So he'd lost the harvest and couldn't pay. His wife was still sick and he couldn't clear any ground and he was "working as a day laborer" (in other people's fields) and all the money he could save up was for treatment for his wife. I looked over in the corner of the house and there was a woman lying in a hammock, who was just skin and bones . . . incredible poverty . . . the fire in the woodstove was out, a clear sign that no food had been prepared that day.

Though I felt pity, I didn't give up: "And when will you be able to pay, set a deadline. You tell me, and I'll give it to you." I also had the authority to extend deadlines and negotiate with the debtors. But he told me he didn't know. I was tough: "Look, I'm here to collect, you've owed us for a long time. I have a promissory note you signed. So you have to set a deadline to pay because my grandfather will want to know, etc."

I left that house without getting anything. Not even a possible timeframe for receipt of the account. But this case was one that pained me because I already had a fairly acute political conscience. When I got home, when the time came to settle the day's collections, I asked my grandfather why he didn't dispense with that account, because that man didn't owe much; that he was a good payer, that he'd been paying down the account for some time, and if I wasn't mistaken, it was the first time he hadn't paid a little toward his account.

My grandfather turned toward me, he said a bunch of things, but above all he said that at that rate of taking pity on whoever owed him, I'd have to stop washing my hair with shampoo, and looking me in the eyes, he said: "You know how to make lye soap, don't you? You're going to have to use your know-how." At that time we made soap at home, various kinds: white – from coconut milk, from ox tallow, etc. We didn't buy almost anything. They were things women did, so I also learned to make soap. But I didn't like to make soap, in fact I hated it, since it took a whole day to make it. I was allergic to the smell of lye. I'd sneeze the whole day, my eyes would swell, my nose would run . . .

My grandfather would always proudly say that I was a "fine businesswoman." That is, that I knew how to do business and he trusted my judgement. If one of the customers said that they'd settled something with me, he'd say: "In that case if she gave you her word, it's settled. She knows how to do business. And around here if you agree with her you agree with me. It's the same thing."

I was familiar with all his business. So much so that when Grandma wanted to travel – she loved to travel to Teresina, the capital of Piauí – she always said it was for her or us, me or her son, to see the doctor or go to the dentist. As a matter of fact, once a year I'd go to the "eye doctor" since I've worn glasses ever since I was thirteen. I would go so often that I still remember his name, Dr. Evaldo.

But actually, what she really liked was to go shopping in the capital. She also loved to buy jewelry, things with gold and pearls, for her and for me. And when my grandfather said that she was spending too much, she said that every young lady had her "little gold things" and that she wasn't going to raise me any differently. But before getting ready for any of her trips, she would always ask me how my grandfather was doing for money. That happened before she started a bakery.

Grandma had a bakery for four years. She was very skilled, the bakers suffered at her hands, since she quickly learned everything about making bread and she always found some flaw whenever a loaf didn't come out perfectly. After the bakery she was even more powerful, because she had her own money and she did what she wanted with it, without consulting or asking my grandfather. At that time, whenever my grandfather gave me the money for my expenses, when the time came for me to go back to school, she'd call me to her room and say: "This is mine, for whatever you might need." It wasn't a lot, but it was a little more money, and it wasn't "marked," that is, for a particular purpose, but I don't think I ever bought anything else for myself with that money besides books and more books . . .

When I turned eighteen, my grandfather went to São Luís so I could open a bank account. It was at the Banco Real. I still remember him today talking with the manager and saying that he could "deal with" whatever I needed, if he needed to one day. I don't know how, but he was introduced to that manager by someone; at the time the manager said "Seu Braulino, you can open the account for the two of you, it's safer." My grandfather said:

> The one who needs an account is her. She's the one who knows how to read, she has a little money, she lives in the city, in someone else's house, and she doesn't have anywhere to keep her little money that I give her. I've never needed a bank until today, sir. I don't need to deal with bank money, just with my own money.

I had a boundless sense of autonomy. I was the only one who arrived at the boarding school with the money to pay for the whole semester of school. The one who paid was me. There was no bank or post office in my city, so when I went back to school my grandfather handed over the money for the semester. I even took the semester's money to the woman who washed my clothes. Yes, I paid to have my clothes washed; she came to my dorm twice a week to get my clothes. She washed and ironed. So all this cost money. And that's why Grandma and Paivelho would always tell my husbands that "our daughter was well brought up. She always had everything and never had to do rough work. Just study. She's a fine young lady."

Though I was the youngest, I was the only one in the Student House who handled my own money. The parents left the money with the dorm director, dona Stela, Stela Rosa e Silva, who was a Black teacher. She taught at the Colinense School, but she directed the Student House. Once she asked me: "Your parents don't give you money?" I told her: "They do, but I'm the one who holds onto it!" I paid her the monthly fees. I always thought she was very annoyed at how much autonomy I had.

Since I always had money, I sometimes loaned it to my colleagues. And that gave me a lot of power. My whole life, my grandfather gave me money to buy a snack – it was money that I kept separate, it was to buy a snack at school every day. He kept track. But I never ate snacks, or very rarely, because I'd buy magazines, books, with that money. I never learned to snack, even today I don't snack, I just eat breakfast, lunch, and dinner. Up until I finished teacher training I had money to buy snacks, for every class day. It was enough for a soda and a pastry.

I began my collective activism as part of the student council starting at the Colinense School, where we got a very important political education, not just through the student council, but through an activity that was called a study series, which was a week of debates about a particular topic, whose speakers were always very important names in education, politics, and intellectual life.

I remember a study series about cooperativism that was wonderful. The whole school came to a halt for the study series, it was a historical event at the Colinense, not to mention that at least a month before, the school bubbled with research and preparation. Another memorable thing were the science fairs, which took place every year. Obviously I participated in all of them, including when I was already studying in São Luís, where there were also science fairs, in each school and then citywide.

The Colinense School had a very strong student movement and a student council that not only engaged in politics, but was also very involved in cultural demonstrations. Every Saturday, the whole afternoon, school stopped and you had to stay at school for the student organization's activities, which were cultural activities, like reciting poetry, putting on plays, etc. This happened class by class, weekly, with a schedule and everything. I was the class representative in the student council for the three years I studied at the Colinense.

The first year I was in school in São Luís, I didn't get involved in the student council, but the next year I was the person who set the opposition ticket. That was when I was good friends with Father Rogério Dubois, a French priest who taught religion class in the school. He was the parish priest in the Fátima neighborhood, a working-class neighborhood, and he always had a strong working-class movement and was a stronghold of the JOC – Juventude Operária Católica (Young Christian Workers).[16] I was in the JOC. I got very close to Father Rogério as well because at that time I spoke a little French and read it very well.

In the middle of my first year of teacher training, I decided to live in the Fátima neighborhood, because of this work with the church and the JOC. I didn't leave the Fátima neighborhood until the last year of teacher training, when I was getting ready for university, since after being in education classes all day, I'd go to prep class for the *vestibular* at night, which was downtown. The decision to leave the Fátima neighborhood was more my grandfather than me. Very slyly, he told me that I needed to live downtown because it would be tiring to continue living in the neighborhood. I told the JOC about my grandfather's worries, and in a formal meeting, we determined that it would indeed be better for me to move and dedicate myself more to school that year. Years later I found out that some friends had warned him that I was going around with "communist priests and nuns" from the Fátima church and I could be sent to jail.

After I moved to the neighborhood at sixteen, the parish nuns began to establish the Pastoral da Mulher Marginalizada (Marginalized Women's Ministry), which at that time was called Ninho (nest), created by Bishop Fragoso, a progressive bishop in the Northeast who is the uncle of Jô Moraes, state representative of the Communist Party of Brazil (PCdoB) here in Minas Gerais. These nuns were followers of Bishop Fragoso. What was the work? It was supporting women who were sex workers: find out their needs and their children's needs; get their children in school; doctor's appointments and medicine when they got sick and even food when they couldn't work. Many of them had a lot of children.

For around two years, in addition to the nuns, it was just me and Lurdinha, another young person from the neighborhood who got interested in the work. It was these nuns who gave me the first things that I read about the situation of women. Once I was at the university, I'd always come back to the neighborhood because I continued to arrange doctor's appointments for those women. So, me getting into medical school was very good for the Pastoral da Mulher Marginalizada, since I got to know the clinics better, and as a medical student, I had good access to health services and even to the University Hospital. By International Women's Year, 1975, I already knew the situation of women very well.

When I was still in *colégio*, I had my first contacts with the PCdoB. I was still an adolescent. For a long time, many years, I was friends with a boy named Sérgio Braga, who was an economics student, and just a decade later I found out that he was the president of the party in Maranhão during the time when I met him. So, at the time when I was doing the second and third years of *magistério*, we would meet on Sunday evenings after Mass. He was never my boyfriend. We were friends. I had my boyfriends and he had his girlfriends, but it was very funny because both his girlfriends and my boyfriends were very jealous. But it was through Sérgio that I found out about the Araguaia Guerrilla,[17] for example.

What did I do with Sérgio? We carried out important work in the School for the Blind in Maranhão. Sérgio was friends with a young blind guy, Pedro, who was married to Glória – the director and founder of the School for the Blind, ESCEMA, and who was blind and Black, from Rio de Janeiro. Pedro, her husband, was a social sciences student in Rio de Janeiro, but after getting married he was studying something else in Maranhão that wasn't exactly social sciences, which they didn't have at the UFMA (Federal University of Maranhão). On Saturdays and Sundays Sérgio and I would read to Pedro. Not always schoolbooks. Many, many times we'd read books by Che Guevara, Régis Debray, I remember very well. Ah! We also read *Geografia da fome* (Geography of Hunger) by Josué de Castro.[18] Sometimes other people showed up. It was a "party meeting," except I didn't know it. It was the time of the dictatorship; they were killing people.

In reality, the meetings at ESCEMA were something of a PCdoB cell. People of historical significance in the Maranhão PCdoB of the time came through there. Glória was someone who was above all suspicion, because she and the School for the Blind were protected by Dr. Antônio Dino, who was José Sarney's vice-governor when he was governor. Dr. Dino was governor of Maranhão for two years, when José Sarney was elected senator. So our unit was above all suspicion.

At school, I was always involved in many things at once. I was in the JOC, Pastoral da Mulher Marginalizada, this work with ESCEMA, which took me many years to understand its significance.

In Imperatriz, in the [19]80s, I participated in a project with women that was very interesting in two aspects. A more general one, with people in the health arena, but directed to poor populations, whose focus was women, and the other, more directed toward the organization of women.

The first one was the Barco de Saúde (Health Boat) – a boat with health professionals, doctors, pharmacists, biochemists. The project was conceived by the ophthalmologist Lindalva Amorim, from Maranhão, born in Imperatriz, who was a PDT candidate for constitutional representative.[19] It was a boat that traveled the river regions of the Tocantins River with doctors with various specialties, holding appointments, with biochemists and lab technicians to do fecal exams, urine exams. This boat project lasted for two years.

It was a project that a lot of people supported. I never traveled with the boat, since besides my job as a doctor from Monday to Friday, I did a twenty-four-hour shift from Saturday to Sunday in rotation; I had five children; I worked an average of sixty hours each week; I was the Director of the Medical Association of Imperatriz; and I directed the largest hospital in Maranhão's interior, a women's enterprise: five women partners and one male one. But I was a person who arranged money for work on the boat; I participated in all the preparatory meetings and the ones that evaluated the boat's missions; I arranged medicines, etc. The Barco de Saúde was explicitly political work, though it appeared to solely offer aid, since it traveled the river regions, offering medical and dental care, doing simple lab tests and distributing medicines through medical appointments, every two months. I remember that during all the boat missions there were childbirths.

Some women from the Barco de Saúde group began to get together separately to reflect more on the woman question, especially about domestic violence. We discovered the Conselho Nacional dos Direitos da Mulher (National Council for Women's Rights); the Conferência Nacional Saúde e Direitos da Mulher (National Health and Women's Rights Conference) [which took place in Brasília from October 10 to 13, 1986]; and the pre-Constitution process of 1988.

Together with Lindalva Amorim, we organized the whole process of women's debate about the Constitution in Imperatriz. Including when the Conselho Nacional dos Direitos da Mulher (CNDM) was founded, in 1985, we brought the lawyer Comba Marques Couto to Imperatriz, who at that time I think was part of the CNDM Team of Experts. Anyway, she was there on behalf of the CNDM. When Comba was in Imperatriz, it was just after my husband had died. We organized one of those Women and Representatives meetings in the Medical Association. I was the founder of the Medical Association of Imperatriz, and the whole time I lived there I was on the board of directors. It was the first time that the Medical Association loaned out their space for something that wasn't by doctors. We managed to fit three hundred women from Imperatriz and the surrounding areas in the meeting.

Afterwards, we created the Women's Union of Imperatriz, which didn't last for too long after I went to live in São Luís, but before, I held an important event on Women and Representatives, in the pre-election period, also at the Medical Association of Imperatriz.

One of the most important political actions we undertook during that time was to prevent Dr. Elsimar Coutinho[20] from giving a lecture at the Imperatriz Medical Conference in 1986. We relied on the support of PDT city councilors and a state representative from the PCdoB in publicizing a motion repudiating Elsimar Coutinho, who, when he found out about the document after we sent it to him by telex, declined the invitation.

In São Luís, in 1987, I participated in the Women's Union of São Luís, during which time I met the members of the Mãe Andreza Group of Black Women. Accordingly, I resumed closer contact with the Black Movement through Mãe Andreza, and, obviously, thorugh Luizão.

So I was already participating in all the Black women's movements from 1987 on, the period when Black women began organizing on a national scale with greater visibility.

When I arrived in Belo Horizonte, in February 1988, after a week I went to a meeting of the Movimento Popular da Mulher (Popular Women's Movement), the MPM. They were preparing for that year's International Women's Day. On March 8, 1988, I already knew almost everyone in the movement in Belo Horizonte. I arrived during a very intense period of meetings, the mobilization for the Constitutional Congress. So all that process that I'd done in Maranhão, participating in so many "women's" and "constitutional" things, gave me a foundation, here in Minas, for joining the national process. Afterwards came the State Constitution, the City Charter for Belo Horizonte . . . I was elected president of the Popular Women's Movement in 1989, after I'd been here a year.

That's how I became the first Black woman to direct a feminist organization in this country. When I went to São Paulo in January 1992, I still had a year left of my term in the Popular Women's Movement. In São Paulo, I joined the Popular Women's Union of the State of São Paulo (UPMESP). I already knew you and some others from Geledés, Lucinha, for example, ever since the First Black Women's Conference, which took place in Valença, Rio de Janeiro. Since I was in Minas, I participated in all the mobilization for the First Black Women's Conference, and also in the first meeting that discussed the creation of a Feminist Health Network, under a tree, during the 11th National Feminist Conference in Caldas Novas, Goiás, 1991.

In 1992, in São Paulo, I joined the Rede Feminista de Saúde (Feminist Health Network). I worked hard to build it, having been on the Comissão de Ciência, Tecnologia e Ética (Science, Technology, and Ethics Commission) and part of the organizing committee of the 8° Encontro Internacional Mulher e Saúde (8th International Women and Health Conference) (1997). Back in Belo Horizonte, in 1996, I coordinated the Minas Gerais Regional Feminist Health Network until May 2002. Since 1996, I've been part of the leadership of the Network, I'm on the board of directors. In the 7th Network Conference, in Caeté, here in Minas, in 2002, I was elected executive secretary for a term of four years.

There were just three Black people in a class of sixty students in the medical school. It was me, Bentevi, and Quelita – she was a girl from the Baptist Church, from a middle-class family of public servants in São Luís, who studied her whole life in the Baptist School, a school that never had fewer than ten students in the medical school. Bentevi, also an evangelical, had also studied at public school. And I came from public school. Those are the backgrounds of the three Black students.

An understanding of the racial issue appeared in my life with Luizão, my professor in medical school. But as far as perceiving racism, I think that when you don't have an awareness of racism, you don't notice it. It's an exercise that I still do today to remember situations of racism that I experienced, especially because from very early I was in majority-white environments, hegemonically white, beginning with the Colinense School, which at the time was a model school for Maranhão, considered one of the best schools in Maranhão of all time. And it was a private school.

The truth is, as a Black woman, I had the privilege of having my grandparents in a good economic situation; and of being that girl who famously liked to study, and they could fund this family eccentricity. I was always very studious, an excellent student, the kind who stands out. Being an excellent student confers many privileges, whatever color you are. First, because fellow students end up close to you because they're sucking up. I always had the best notebooks, because I was famous for copying down even the teacher's sighs. I was one of those students who people would come over to your house to copy your notebooks, because they were always more complete. I was very dedicated to studying.

So, this position of good student, of outstanding student, is one that creates lots of jealousy, but people also have to respect you a lot, even the teachers. So perhaps that helped me to not notice, to not suffer so much. Perhaps. That's the idea I have right now, but I'm also not sure!

The truth is, my awareness of serious racism appeared after I became a doctor, especially when people were surprised to see me; when they asked me when the doctor would arrive. In general, I've never looked like a doctor, even now. There's a stereotype. In the popular imagination, doctors are white! In Maranhão, I wasn't seen as or taken for someone who's *preta*, or *negra*, but as *morena*.[21] But, even there, a doctor is white.

I think that conversations with Luizão really touched me because we always were closer to Grandma's family, which is all Black. Dad's family was one that could be considered generally white, as my grandmother said, a family of people who'd been "*descascada*" (peeled), which is to say that they weren't Black.

The situations of racism that I remember experiencing during my childhood, that I was aware of – I'm not saying that I didn't face racism before – was Grandma saying that my godmother Zuleide, a neighbor, was jealous of me in school because I was learning to read quickly, before her daughters, who were around my age. Those girls were all white.

About being the first Black executive secretary of the Feminist Health Network, I have an increasingly mercilessly critical view of that experience, because it's a very difficult one. These labels of being the first one at this, the first one at that, they're heavy burdens. But they also always have to be remembered, because they demonstrate the road that a Black woman traveled, and a door that was opened, at great cost and with lots of sweat. For example, I discovered that I was the first Black woman to organize a debate on feminism in Latin America when I granted an interview to the Coalition. I am the first Black woman to reach the executive secretaryship of the Feminist Health Network. I'm the first Black woman to direct a feminist institution in Brazil. I was the president of the Popular Women's Movement in Belo Horizonte, Minas Gerais. I also don't remember any other Black woman directing a feminist institution in Brazil after me. I'm referring to feminist organizations besides those created by Black women. I'm the first Black woman to form part of the Board of Directors of the RSMLAC (Rede de Saúde das Mulheres Latino-Americanas e do Caribe; Latin American and Caribbean Women's Health Network), and note that the RSMLAC turned twenty in 2005.

The RSMLAC has carried out very important work in Latin America and the Caribbean, but there are few Black women in it. There were few Black women in the Feminist Health Network. Mazé, Maria José de Oliveira Araújo, always had a very critical view about that: the Feminist Health Network having such a white profile.

The concern for the incorporation and presence of Black women in the Feminist Health Network was such that during Mazé's term in office, an Advisory Council for Black Women's Affairs was created to supplement the work of the Board of Directors. I was elected to this council in a National Conference of the Network in Pirinópolis, Goiás, in 1996. During Mazé's term in office, the *Jornal da Rede* (Network Journal) was also developed, a special journal about Black women's health. Though it was published under the subsequent administration, it's a project marked by Mazé, someone who has a deep awareness of the everyday necessity of fighting racism.

Her administration in the Technical Area of Women's Health in the Health Ministry leaves no doubt.

I work on issues that are novel and obviously are very difficult for people who don't have a solid scientific background to tackle. Because both the Black population's health and this part of genetics, bioethics, a bioethical look at genetics, new areas of genetics, require a very solid knowledge of genetics, basic and solid, because whoever doesn't have that knowledge can't speculate, they can't carry out philosophical and political analyses of these issues. What I offer that's new is a feminist and anti-racist point of view about all these "new things" in biosciences and in the establishment of this new field of aid, research, and study, which is the Black population's health.

I think the originality of what I do and what I publish is my capacity to take a speculative and reflexive look at these issues, from a solid theoretical base. Thus, the field of the Black population's health without a solid base in genetics, with a fatalistic vision, with a vision that indicates that genetics are destiny, there's no way to explain how to guarantee the rights of women, the rights of Black people, or health assistance or a field of research that respects the Black population.

Without such prerequisites it's very difficult, because the field of the Black population's health is the only area of research and study that I know of that was established in Brazil outside of academia, as the work of many hands and many heads. Universities are having to drink from our fountain, a fountain created by social activism, to work with the health of the Black population. That is, not only do policy makers drink from this fountain, but universities as well. No one systematized this in Brazil before I did, unfortunately. So my theoretical production is the key reference for whoever wants to do work in this area. It's a fountain whose origins are undeniably in activism, since though I'm a recognized intellectual, I'm not a university professor, because I never wanted to be. I always chose to do other things, but, paradoxically, what I do most of these days is teach classes, give lectures, conferences, etc.

Since 1996 I've worked in the Clinical Hospital of the UFMG (Federal University of Minas Gerais), and whenever positions open for clinical medicine professors, colleagues ask me why I don't try to become a professor. And they're surprised when I say that I've never wanted to be a professor. For me, taking that path would distance me from my way of doing activism, how I do it and how I like to do it. Being a professor would tie me to a single place full time. I always thought that if I were a university professor I could never do the things I do, in the way I want, need, and like to, whether in feminism, the Black Movement, or bioethics. I navigate well among these three areas and I take care to have a consistent and significant political and theoretical presence.

I always say that all my theoretical production in the area of the Black population's health I owe to Elza Berquó, because before meeting her I hadn't written anything about the Black population's health. So I didn't understand that what I knew, especially in genetics, contributed a lot to establishing the field. And why do I say that I owe this to Elza Berquó? I knew her from various Brazilian feminist occasions. One of the ones I remember well was a big debate about abortion in the National Congress that was put on by the National Women's Health Council. Another one was pre-Cairo,[22] I was still living in Belo Horizonte, and I'd read a lot of Elza Berquó, and I liked her a lot because she was the one writing about and arguing against forced sterilization and everything else. When I moved to São Paulo, I went to a seminar, I think around August or September 1992, on behalf of the City of São Paulo's Women's Coordinator during Luiza Erundina's government.[23] I think it was in the Parlatino,[24] it was a seminar on public policy in different areas. That day I met Joel Rufino, who gave a terrible speech, we even fought during the debate.

I was representing the Women's Coordinator to speak about public health policy. I remember well that I prepared for a week. In 1992 the terminology of "public policy" hadn't been popularized. So it was during Luiza Erundina's administration that this terminology was used more frequently. Joel Rufino went to challenge my talk in which I had worked on the necessity of the intersection of race/ethnicity and gender, which was not easy to express at that time.

Vera Cristina de Souza was there, she was a fellowship recipient in Cebrap (Brazilian Center for Analysis and Planning), in the Reproductive Health Program for the Black Population, whom I didn't know. At the end of the event, she came to talk to me. She introduced herself saying that she was a Cebrap fellow and that in March 1993 the program would hold a seminar on the Black population's health, and that she wanted my contact information to invite me.

The following year, there was an event at the Conselho Estadual da Condição Feminina (State Council on the Condition of Women), in preparation for March 8 that year, and I ran into her again, when she took the opportunity to tell me "look, the seminar will be in a week." I went to Social vs. Biological. It was the first seminar that the program was holding and there was a big theoretical problem about health to resolve: whether the Black population's health determiners were social or biological. At that time the program had already carried out a large study on sterilization.

Among those present, beyond the fellows, I remember well Luiza Bairros, Edna Roland, Damiana, Isabel Cruz, among others. All the comments that I made at that seminar went against a direction in which the seminar was going that I thought was terrible, which was a biological and fatalist perspective. I remember that one of the people, almost at the end of the seminar, said something like: "Right, well, we have to concede, there's no way around it, there are some things that are our own problem and we have to concede that." So as to say "biology is indeed destiny!"

I asked to speak again and said that the seminar was taking the path of genetic fatalism, which I refused to accept. Then everyone wanted to know what this genetic fatalism was, which is a philosophical concept, a vision of the world that believes that genes define everything and everything will be this way or that because it's written in genes. I always say that genetic fatalism exists for species: cats give birth to cats, rats give birth to rats, women give birth to humans. So genetic fatalism for species exists, because no one has ever seen a woman giving birth to a puppy, but for other things, there are interactions. However, the seminar arrived at that conceptualization of genetic fatalism because it was looking for a way out – which was working on things more as social problems, as primary determiners in the process of health/sickness.

I understood that people couldn't embrace that way out, because human beings are also governed by biological laws, but that's not genetic fatalism, there are biological laws from which we can't escape because we are also governed by them. But it's not necessary to have genetic fatalism to respect and recognize biological laws. They were looking for a way out, because the only possible conclusion for the group that was there, which was a progressive and anti-racist group, was to slide over to the social side, but I also saw that as a great prejudice against us. Another doctor present was Dr. Marco Antônio Zago, the big star of the seminar, to whom we're indebted for huge contributions, a partner who does everything he can do for the Black population's health. We learned quite a bit with Zago because it was there that he presented, for the first time that I saw, a map of the principal diseases that target the Black population. That is, this map that we have today of the Black population's diseases was designed by Zago, though it's very focused on sickle-cell anemia.

When the seminar ended, Elza Berquó invited me to go to Cebrap afterwards to chat, because she had been very impressed by the things I'd said with such conviction and she wanted to clarify some matters, since my insistence during the seminar had inspired her to talk more about the topic. Some time afterwards I went to Cebrap and we chatted again. At the end she said: "You've left me with some doubts. There's only one thing to do. We're going to research, we'll discuss this. Would you agree to organize a seminar about the issues you've brought up?" I said I would. I worked to put on that seminar for three months. I had discussions with geneticists from across Brazil. I invited Frota, Osvaldo Frota-Pessoa, who was the only Brazilian geneticist who participated in composing UNESCO's Declaration on Race and Racial Prejudice, and is one of the first geneticists in Brazil. I invited all the big geneticists in Brazil. Many declined because for them genetics didn't have anything to do with race, and according to a great many of them, what I intended to delve into in the seminar had already been resolved long ago. Why take up an outdated debate? That was partly the issue.

We held the event, which was called Alcances e Limites da Predisposição Biológica (Capacity and Limits of Biological Predisposition). There's a Cebrap publication by that name. This seminar is a landmark in the establishment of the field of the Black population's health and its proceedings are published in *Cadernos Cebrap 2: Alcances e limites da predisposição biológica* (Cebrap Notebooks 2: Capacity and Limits of Biological Predisposition, July 1994).

And what is the capacity and what are the limits of biological predispositions? Life is more holistic than many people assume. There is biological predisposition, interaction with the environment, dietary habits, culture, customs, etc. And all of this forms a whole. You can have a predisposition toward some diseases, but healthy habits can keep them from developing, for example. That is, dietary habits, other cultural contexts, can keep you from becoming sick. I know it's difficult for people to understand this: if race doesn't exist, how can we speak of biological predisposition?

Biological predisposition is something you're "born with." The large human population groups are from different regions, with different interactions between environment and biology, with different ways of life depending on climate, etc. So, the origins of the large human population groups, which are thousands of years of environmental interactions, give determined characteristics; it's not just pure biology, the interaction goes way back. Why do African populations have kinky hair and wide nostrils? They are human adaptations to their surroundings, to the climate, skin color, melanin. We are born with a set of things that present as biological predispositions, but which result from other interactions with biology. Biological predisposition is that which "you're born with a probability of."

This "predisposition to" only comes to pass in particular conditions favorable to their development, but it's possible that in unfavorable conditions they never appear or cause harm. The problem is that there are geneticists who don't know that. They know all about genetics, but they don't consider expanding their reasoning to encompass a more holistic perspective, since in general they're very fatalist.

Are eugenicists fatalist? Yes, they're fatalist. Eugenicists have such conviction that they want to eliminate everything that they believe isn't normal, everything that they don't consider standard. The concept of normalcy brings us to many political and ideological misuses, because normal is a subjective and cultural concept. Thus, they consider a standard that diverges from the standard to be sick or not normal. For example, there are cultures in which all the children who are born with some "genetic defect," for example Down Syndrome, are considered as gods. But there are other cultures that kill these children in the search for the idea of perfection, for who knows what. . .

The stuff of genetics is very complicated, but it shouldn't be since genetics itself is quite simple and there is nothing about it that corroborates racism, eugenics, but it's the interpretations that produce this misuse, it's the interpretations that different actors give according to political interests. I've written a lot about this, about political and ideological misuse of genetics.

I'm not advocating for scientific neutrality. I'm talking about facts proven through genetics, genetic laws that don't authorize any of this, but it's the perspective we take on them that makes racist interpretations possible. As of today, there is nothing, nothing, all the theoretical inquiry and all the analysis that we can do of basic laws, of new discoveries, none of them make discriminatory connotations possible according to genetics. What we don't have is neutrality of interpretation, in use, but as far as basic laws; as far as discoveries, no. I challenge anyone to take anything from genetics that confirms racist or eugenicist theses.

That's why I say that people have to have mastery of these basic issues, because if there is one thing that's constantly recycled it's scientific racism. I think today that my great interest in genetics always had a lot to do with the racial question. It wasn't explicit in the beginning, but I always understood that a new field was being created in the area of genetics, which was genetic engineering, and that it could have disastrous political consequences from the point of view of discrimination.

The first article I wrote about the topic was "Engenharia genética e socialismo" (Genetic Engineering and Socialism). I entered this article in a forum of preparatory debates for the 9th National Conference of the PCdoB, which took place in 1992.

In the PCdoB, they do something very interesting: before each conference, a debate forum is set up, which circulates for four or six months before the conference, in which anyone who's a member of the party can enter up to three articles about any topic, of up to fifty lines. I wrote the article I mentioned, keeping in mind that a new field was being created to which communists needed to pay a lot of attention, given that in Friedrich Engels's *Dialectics of Nature* the international communist movement had reflected more about these things, about the science of nature. The last major theoretical contribution about these scientific discoveries in the field of Marxist theoretical inquiry is Engels's book, which is a book that I love, and at that time, I had substantial command of its contents.

I must have written the article around October or November 1991. At the time, I'd already read June Goodfield's *Playing God: Genetic Engineering and the Manipulation of Life*, which is a super interesting book, a critical analysis by a feminist of these "new things" of the biosciences. Since I read a lot, I already had a lot of knowledge in the area. At the time I was already worried about those things.

In the debate forum, I wrote "Genetic Engineering and Socialism," keeping in mind that a new field was being created, with the business of DNA and such, with genetic engineering, and that communists should be worried about this, and a made a reference to the fact that this had been a dormant debate in the international communist movement ever since *Dialectics of Nature*.

When the debate forum ended, the party conference took place, and Rogélio Lustosa – who was a colleague I liked a lot, he's since died, he was the editor of the journal *Princípios* (Principles/ Beginnings), which is the theoretical journal of the PcdoB – put in the work of combing through the articles from the debate forum that he considered most interesting and stimulating and that inspired the most letters that came to the forum – because people also responded with letters, which were also published – and proposed to the authors that they write articles about those topics. So I received an invitation to write an article that expanded on the little fifty-line article.

I wrote it. It was a huge article; I think I wrote some thirty pages in order to submit the article, which is called "A vida é uma molécula de DNA manipulável" (Life is a Manipulable DNA Molecule). I like it, I think it's a fine article. It's in the journal *Princípios*, no. 26, pp. 48–56, August–October 1992.

The article is written in a style designed for wide appeal. Because of the the soap opera that Fábio Júnior[25] was working on at the time, women would drink tea made from the plant he peed on . . . the plant was an aphrodisiac and gave the women the sensation that they were having sex with him. It was madness across the city. Practically all the women were customers of the tea from that plant. I wrote in the article that it would only be possible through genetic engineering . . . In the article there's a survey of government investment in that area.

Tereza Verardo, the author of a book with Moderna, *Aborto: Direito ou crime?* (Abortion: A Right or a Crime?), was on the Woman's Council, and was extremely enthusiastic about the article. I really harmonized with her in the work of the Council. Tereza took my article to the editor of Moderna's Coleção Polêmica (Polemics Collection), to José Carlos Castro, who called to invite me to Moderna. I didn't know that Tereza had spoken with him. After hemming and hawing, I agreed to talk. It took a while for me to agree to write a book on the topic, despite his insistence, saying something like:

> Look, your article really impacted me, the way you write. Here at Polêmica we have a project for a science book for the general public on this topic and we've never found anyone to write it, because people who understand the topic, they're all professors and they don't want to write for regular people, they only write for their peers.

It was a huge challenge, because the book had to pass through the sieve of the owner of the press, who was a biologist, [José Mariano] Amabis, and Zé [José] Carlos was risking giving a book to an unknown writer. He was insistent: "In the three years that we've had this project, you're the only one about whom I said, after I read your article, this is the woman who will write our book. . ."

I thanked him, said that I didn't have time to write, that I was very busy . . . He didn't give up. That is, I'm a writer today because Zé Carlos was so insistent with me. Rogério Lustosa too, he was tough when he said:

> Do you realize what São Paulo could offer you as a person with this book? How many millions of people get a deal like that in São Paulo? I think that as a communist you don't have the right to refuse! Do you know how many communists in this country have written for a major press? You don't know because there aren't any. And on a topic on which you have a very interesting theoretical reflection. Fátima, this is urgent. When you begin the book you'll write more and more and more and more and more things. . .

I don't like to say how long it took me to write the book, because I don't even believe that I wrote it so quickly. The whole book was written on a typewriter, because I didn't have a computer, I had an Olivetti typewriter. All, all, all of it. Zé Carlos was the one who sent it to be typed at Moderna, which is something they don't do for anyone. And the book was a success. I have great fondness for Zé Carlos because if it weren't for him I might never have become a writer.

About my relationship with my peers? I think that I was received well. My name is well known in bioethics, as a thought-provoking thinker, as a person who established a new current in bioethics, a feminist and anti-racist perspective, since all my work in bioethics has that tendency. As such, the great mark I've made on bioethics is having established that line of thought.

My books are very successful, in terms of sales and political repercussions. When I show up at bioethics conferences, generally a lot of people come up to me and many say, with pleasure: "The first bioethics book I read was yours." Both *Engenharia genética: O sétimo dia da criação* and *Bioética: Uma face da cidadania* (Bioethics: A Facet of Citizenship) were published by Moderna.

Anyway, they're books that can be classified as popular science. But they address very specialized topics that only those who are interested in buy. If you assume that every book is read by three or four people, minimum, each book has probably been read by lots of people. *Engenharia genética* has sold 42,000 copies; if it's been read by four people per copy, it's reached around 168,000 readers; and *Bioética*, which sold 24,000 copies, would have been read by close to 96,000 people. Anyway, this should have some importance and have a positive resonance in the struggle against racism.

This is all very gratifying and interesting to me, personally, because my books should make some contribution to our struggles, feminist and anti-racist ones. So I'm very at ease saying that I don't need to write anything else about the Black population's health, feminism, bioethics, since from the point of view of someone who, as an intellectual, is aware that they should make political contributions, I think that I've made mine. I am very at ease with my life, because I managed to theorize; I had the courage to write what I think, to state my differences and opinions on controversies with self-confidence. I contributed to opening, establishing, and consolidating new fields.

There is a field opened by many hands and neurons in the academic sphere, in the sphere of bioethics, a trail that many people can follow. I am extremely satisfied with my life. Very satisfied. Very, very. I think that for what I could contribute, the theoretical strength that I had, that I had the intellectual foundation for, I am aware that I've done it. That's that.

I think the things that I helped to open up and construct, that I helped to think through, the things that I've had the opportunity to publish in these fields, are undeniable and respected references. They're things that people in academia can't deny, can't write without mentioning, without citing. I receive an enormous number of master's theses, doctoral dissertations, that people send me, in which things I've said, produced, are cited.

Recently, I received a doctoral dissertation from a Mackenzie professor,[26] he sent it to me on a disk, and it's super interesting, it's about bioethical consciousness in secondary education, designed for teacher education. It's a super interesting dissertation, in which the whole vein of his work departs from ideas that I developed, or just emphasized, in *Bioética: Uma face da cidadania*, for example, that there is a moral obligation for governments to help overcome technoscientific illiteracy. I talk about this in *Engenharia genética*.

The establishment of bioethics brings up something very important, which is to take back power from scientific corporations. That is, up until bioethics was established as a field of inquiry and political action, scientists only paid attention to what their peers were doing. Bioethics takes this power away from them. From scientists to doctors, today everyone has to account for what they're doing to society. The ethical standards in research aim to guarantee citizenship. Consequently, bioethics, without a doubt, is a facet of citizenship. It's about a field of human rights that is becoming increasingly more necessary and indispensable.

Insofar as genetics advances, as racist concepts try to hijack new knowledge, new reflections, bioethics appears as a field and says: "That's not how it is! You can't do that!" It's bioethics that can make concrete the maxim that says "Just because you can do something doesn't mean you should." The limits of science. Bioethics is interesting also because of that.

Of all these new things, there's nothing more important for the Black Movement than bioethics, because we don't manage to enter into their spaces. Bioethics is still an eminently masculine and white field. Though there are many, many women in bioethics, we don't hold the power in bioethics. Few women produce; the women who teach classes and coordinate them; or who write and publish and gain visibility. No, there are a lot of people in this field. Many feminists, the majority affiliated with the Feminist Health Network, a few rare Black women who are in this field, almost all of them brought in by me. When I lived in São Paulo, you remember that I put all these people up in my house for bioethics events. I arranged free registration for the conferences and all possible facilities.

What I hope for from all this effort is that more Black women, more feminists, take over these places, these spaces. So we are in these spaces to guarantee women's and Black people's human rights. With the objective of preventing theses from prospering that give support to new eugenicist, racist perspectives, yes, yes, yes. I don't have the least doubt that that's the objective. Disasters are possible in this area. I don't know exactly, but I can guess with very little chance that I'm wrong. Take, for example, the Declaration of Helsinki, the primary reference for ethical standards in research, which is the declaration of the world's medical organizations for research; it's revised basically every five or ten years. The last revision was in 2002;[27] it was an open fight between doctors from poor countries and doctors from rich countries. All countries should have ethical standards for research, and not all of them do.

In Brazil we do. I was the only Black woman and the only feminist in that group, which was what guaranteed the color question would appear in national studies. But the reference standard, the Declaration of Helsinki by the World Medical Association, began the process of revision in 2002. We managed to have a good debate. As a representative of Brazil, Professor Dirceu Bartolomeu Greco, from Belo Horizonte, from the UFMG, appeared for the last meeting of the World Medical Association.

The focus of the controversy in the revision process was in points 29 and 30 of the Declaration of Helsinki, which say in general terms that a new drug can only be used in a comparative trial with a placebo if there is no other effective medicine for the disease for which it's being studied [29]; and if at the end of a study, every volunteer, independent of their place of origin and economic condition, should have access to the best medical treatment used in the study, to those discovered in the study or those that the study helped to discover or prove [30].

The principal and most persistent opponents of these two propositions are the two principal organs of health research of the United States government, the Food and Drug Administration (FDA) and the National Institutes of Health (NIH), and the pharmaceutical industry as a block. But since 1999, the American Medical Association had sent a proposed modification to the World Medical Association's annual assembly. Up to now they haven't been successful, that is, they haven't managed to change the content of items 29 and 30, but they have achieved some flexibility, which has greatly altered the responsibilities of researchers and research funders. In addition to which they have sponsored a world campaign to make the Declaration of Helsinki obsolete, which is a hypocritical position.

Greco brought up Brazil's position: we didn't accept the increased flexibility for ethical standards in research in Africa. Why in Africa, specifically in Africa? Because doctors from the North, basically from rich countries, wanted the Helsinki norms to be more flexible so that they wouldn't be obligated to do research on HIV/AIDS in African countries and then pay for the treatment. Because the Helsinki standards take the position that if you deprive a population involved in a study of new medicines, the study is obligated to pay for that treatment – if the medicine is effective for that population. That's how it was since the first version of the Declaration of Helsinki in 1962, and no one dared to question it.

So, something that's in the Declaration of Helsinki is the law for the whole world. For two years it was a titanic fight because they wanted to guarantee that this would not be obligatory in order to do AIDS research in Africa and they wanted the Declaration of Helsinki to say that they'd give the person the same treatment given any other person in their country . . . That is, whatever was available in their country. In the country of origin of the subject of the study. So it was subtle . . . no treatment . . . and if that study indicated an effective treatment, they wouldn't be obligated to give that treatment to the country where they did the study. What the Declaration of Helsinki says is more or less the following: "If you do a study in a place and the person has a disease and the medicine was effective for it, you have to complete the treatment and leave the person with the best treatment that exists at that moment." And they wanted to change it to the best treatment already available in that country . . . And we from Brazil resisted, it was Brazil that supported that, it was the Brazilian bioethicists who handled this in the international sphere. And we won, a position together with the National Health Board, the Federal Medical Council, the Brazilian Medical Association, and the Brazilian Society for Bioethics. We kept the original . . . Any inattention . . .[28]

This change would cause incalculable damage to humanity. And with the blessing of ethics. It became a fight between poor countries and rich countries. And lots of African doctors defending it. Because they're the African elite, the guys who receive money for studies, who want the money to enrich themselves in Africa. We can't harbor any doubt that the displacement of studies from rich countries to poor countries reveals that they are looking for poor regions because of the lower legal and ethical rigor, which allows them to evade ethical research standards. This can also highlight a marked class and racial prejudice. As we saw, the call to racial eugenics has not only been a prerogative of German Nazis. As [Joaquim Antônio César] Mota has declared with rigor and propriety in *A criança como sujeito de experimentação científica: Uma análise histórica dos aspectos éticos* (Children as Subjects of Scientific Experimentation: A Historical Analysis of Ethical Aspects),[29] half a century after Nuremberg, an experiment with children was carried out by British scientists in Sierra Leone, in as cruel a way as in the Nazi extermination camps.

# 8
# Arnaldo Xavier, the Poet (in Memoriam)

*Source:* From Roseli da Cruz Nascimento's personal archive.

Arnaldo Xavier passed away in January of 2005, a few months before I concluded the doctoral dissertation that gave rise to this book. He was my principal interlocutor. I thought I wouldn't manage to finish without him, but I decided to finish for him. In his book *Contramão* (Wrong Way), he introduces himself as follows:

> I was born (Campina Grande, Paraíba, 11-19-1948) the wrong way, with my feet first, almost killing my mother Esmeraldina, two moons before the healers and midwives had predicted, in the shade of a forest of weeds. My father, Maneh Peh de Phumo, was one of the biggest "legal" dealers in the land. In the air there was still the smell of World War II gunpowder; on heads scorching haloes of *Cangaço*, *coronelismo*, *voto de cabresto*, sick *bacharelismo*, of snakes dragged by feet in the deep glens of secular *latifúndios*,[1] of agonizing oligarchies; of populism, of racial discrimination and mysticism. Scorpio. Christian via a baptismal font full of amoebas by some vicar or other. Son of Ossanha

> in the mysteries of babalorixá Amoya's African conches.[2] Materialist, thank god.
>
> Poetry being born hungry and thirsty. From one side a paternal concern for teaching me to read so I could read *cordéis*[3] to the neighborhood without a pot to piss in; from the other the need to speak and do things – since surrendered is the tongue of the cowardly poet/ who boastingly says/ that there is nothing to say/ and nothing to do. Face to face the lack of information and the search for a form of expression before the Brazilian cultural panacea: 22/45/concretus/bossa nova/street guitars/praxus/arena/opinion/young guard/poem processus/tropicalismus and other -us and -isms. While I felt on my skin the problems of floods, lulls, seasonal epidemics, peasants cravenly murdered, invasions of markets by starving *sertanejo*[4] populations, the "core" of the UNE[5] three boys from São Paulo were raising indicators of the directions of Brazilian poetry. Vinicius de Moraes and Co. spoke of little boats and sunny mornings in Copacabana and ice-cold beers. Ferreira Goulart wrote concrete poetry because there was no *Dancin' Days*[6] at the time. Me too. And I continue going the wrong way. With poem/ process[7] as an aesthetic/political process. With Wlademir Dias Pino. With Moacir Cirne. With Hugo Mund Jr. With Ezio Pires. With José N. Pinto. With Aderaldo Tavares. With William J. D. Araujo. With Carlos Aranha. The wrong way with Chicos Pinto y Buarque. With Cae-gilcapinantowuatomzéduprat. With Mário Chamie, Virgílio A. C. Mattos, Sílvio Spada, Raimundo Caruso, Paulo Nassar, Mário de Oliveira, Domingos Pellegrini Jr., Reinol Atem. The wrong way with Zécelsoglauberrocha-ruiguerra. The wrong way with Alcides Neves.[8]
>
> Most effectively going the wrong way with my irreverent partners and constant quarrels with Aristides Klafke in *Pablo*,[9] *Vidaliberdade* (Lifeliberty),[10] *ventonovo* (newwind),[11] *Cara a cara* (Face to Face).[12] So I continue despite the traffic and the snares. Making poetry into an act of love and courage.[13]

That's how he lived. Refusing easy acclaim, innocuous dialogue, the subjectification proposed by racism and its multiple forms of discrimination. Irreverent, he exceeded the life expectancy of his generation of *nordestinos*,[14] which was less than forty years, as well as the beckon of a secure career as business manager. He traded it for poetry, his life's purpose. His mission was to contradict, his resistance that was possible against the seduction of literary or political cooptation; his exercise of liberty.

He detested philosophers ever since he found out that Plato expelled them from the Republic, which also earned him suspicion of the Republic itself. And with him I also came to mistrust both when the topic was us, Black people. He had a special appreciation for Luiz Gama, the Black abolitionist with whom he identified in his irreverence and mordacity; whose emblematic text "Bodarrada" he loved.[15] He also loved [João da] Cruz e Sousa and all the "damned" Symbolists to which he was heir. He received recognition from the concretists, which he also disdained. He had as a poetic project the ontological re-creation of Black people as a form of liberating Black poetry from the shackles and laments of slavery which he considered constant in Black Brazilian poetry. He insisted that we're merely living new forms of slavery, that is, that it never ended for us. He considered with caution, or, rather, with refined disdain, what we considered our social movement's small victories. At those moments he recalled someone whom he revered: the elder [José] Correia Leite, a militant activist in the Frente Negra Brasileira (Black Brazilian Front), who often accused the majority of Black militant activists of his time of being "Blacks with no backbone," in whom he saw the same phenomenon. He was my brother, my bosom buddy, my confidant for more than three decades. That's why he volunteered to be my sparring partner, a generous interlocutor in the creation of the dissertation that gave rise to this book. We were both betrayed by his heart, which wore out before we did. He wanted to see the dissertation finished, the result of the voluntary masochism to which he exposed himself by obligating himself, through me, to penetrate the thought of a French man with whom he sometimes felt intimate because of how obvious some of his statements were, for him at least, and with which his poetry unknowingly dialogued. He insisted that all the songs will be remade the day that we no longer fight against the "enemy to whom we belong." In this sense he knew all of Foucault without ever having read him. He knew the enemy and denounced our belonging to them. *A rosa da recusa* (The Rose of Refusal), the title of his first book, designated the refusal to belong to the apparatus that he fought against. He refused to perform compliant criticism and facile applause, flattery. He loved words more than any of his wives and he died embracing them, challenging them, re-creating them, inventing them, and reinventing their meanings with all of his *axébedoria*.[16] He used to say he was "greatest poet that God *creole*"[17] and that "Black people defy the Greeks."

He loved modernism and Mário Andrade for his modernity. He hated them for their betrayal of the race. Instead of *tupi or not tupi*, he coined *ori or not ori*![18] He had extraordinary confidence in the knowledge that he always pursued and, as would be expected, a mistrust of the rules of academia to obtain it. And intolerance

1888
1888
1888
1888
1888
1888 1888 1888 1888 1888 1888 1888
1888 1888 1888 1888 1888 1888 1888
1888
1888
1888
1888
1888
1888
1888
1888
1888
1888
1888
1888

"Sem título" (Untitled), poem by Arnaldo Xavier, extract from *Schwarze Poesie – Poesia Negra – Afrobrasilianische Dichtung der Gegenwart*, edited by Moema Parente Augel, Editions Dia, 1988, p. 157. Reprinted in *Direitos humanos no cotidiano: Manual*, Sistema Nacional de Direitos Humanos/Universidad de São Paulo/UNESCO, 1998.

for the ignorance sustained by the laziness around reading and studying of which he accused our people. He was a pain in the ass! He would say, in the best *nordestina* tradition, that "affection from a donkey is expressed in kicks." It's unnecessary to say that I was the donkey in our relationship and our affection was expressed *in kicks*! In place of the dialectic, he coined *diaxética*. He said, "I'm not ugly or handsome, I challenge things!" He challenged things, in poetry, in short stories, in music, in life. Like Foucault, he knew that the escape route for a mode of subjectification, free of the infernal network of the apparatus, was in aesthetics and he created and carried it out! Since everything was material for creation, he played with Foucault like he did with all ideas and all words.

# Part III

## Education and Care of the Self

# Prologue

The concept of epistemicide allows us to understand that the negative identity attributed to the Other implies a repeated claim about their incapacity to elevate themselves to the condition of knowing subject in terms validated by the West and, therefore, to be bearers of relevant knowledge from that tradition's point of view. Such a negative identity impacts the Other through the internalization of this negative image and impels them to the self-fulfilling prophecy that guarantees stigmatization, leading them to self-negation or even to adherence and submission to the values of the dominant culture. In this sense, epistemicide is constituted as part of the apparatus of raciality, which unfolds in the ambit of subjectivity, in Boaventura de Sousa Santos's terms,[1] once the epistemological conflict unfolds into a psychological conflict. The result is a fragmented subjectivity, constructed in the junction of a cultural inheritance shattered by colonial violence and the imposition of Western values, via acculturation, that makes it difficult to collectively engineer the conditions that lead to overcoming stigmas and recuperating full humanity. As Fábio Wanderley Reis states:

> Without a doubt, culture is the crystallization, so to speak, of traces or dispositions of our collective psychology, which can refer to race as well as any other aspect of the collective. In the sense that is relevant here, however, culture certainly is not *reduced* to dispositions of collective psychology related to race. Furthermore, a crucial part of the problem in question has to do with the fact that, in the present case, it is the very

> psychological dispositions related to race that spill over into a negative identity and into self-esteem.[2]

When applied to the field of education, epistemicide allows us to analyze the Other as a non-being of knowledge and wisdom, and their nexuses with the context of Western modernity in its intersection with the colonial experiment that continues to unfold until the present in the field of knowledge, as an instrument of the West's cultural and racial affirmation. The denial of the Other as a knowing subject is expressed in policies in which access to knowledge is denied or limited, and which as a rule impose a social destiny separate from intellectual activities. They are politics that promote a self-fulfilling and legitimating prophecy of an essentialized intellectual inferiority and which decree the death of identity as a condition of overcoming stigma, condemning their survivors to a minority and subordinate social integration.

In Part III, I seek to trace some reflections that originate in the witnesses' statements, which unveil in their lives that which the everyday dialectic has constructed, with warrior-like vigor, in the framework of the apparatus of raciality. While school offers multiple forms of subordination, subjectification, and negation, it's from the strength of self-esteem; recognition of one's own capacity for autonomy; examples within the family and the rare Black professionals with whom one interacted during childhood, adolescence, and youth; as well as the triumph of collective memory – it is from these elements that the sap of resistance is extracted. Nevertheless, synthesis will only take place through the collective, where care of the self and care of the other are merged together in the search for emancipation.

# 9

# Education

## Negation and Affirmation

### Education and Negation

One of the most burning issues that involves Black people and education concerns the processes of exclusion of Black people from school that are reflected in dropout indicators, especially for Black boys and youths. From Foucault's perspective, the essential function of school is not to exclude, but rather to fix, since it is an apparatus of normalization. Something specific happens with respect to Black people: in addition to being normalized, they are expelled or excluded from school. The dropout rates confirm this exclusion and indicate the difficulty that some Black students have in adjusting to the norms regarding their raciality that are imposed in school. They are students who experience veiled or explicit doubts about their educability; they are subject to racial subordination imposed by didactic tools, which shape their identity in school spaces; they are always suffering racial humiliations, frequent signs of sociability in scholarly spaces, to which the teachers react with impotence or indifference, as Eliane Cavalleiro's study shows.[1] Dropping out of school or a negative performance in school could reflect the "incorrigible" condition of Black students, in the sense that they don't have the resources, particularly the emotional ones, to comply with the processes of fixing and subjection present there.

Here is an important indication of the relevance of developing an understanding of the apparatus of raciality in its strategic articulations with epistemicide. When articulated with epistemicide, the apparatus seems to be explicitly realized in education, and thus it is relevant to extricate from the testimonies an understanding of how our witnesses navigated these issues in their scholarly trajectories.

With his personal experience, Edson Cardoso exposes the processes of racial socialization that in many cases makes the family fulfill a perverse and disruptive role in the formation of racial identity: educating in a way contrary to racial belonging, introjecting chromatic differences imposed by the political agreement of miscegenation of racial non-fixing as a dimension of racial domination. The family appears as one of the first settings in which one experiences the pain of color, in his case a lighter color than the family collective. Thus he describes the way in which he was seen racially within his family:[2] "*It was* brrrranco, *with an emphasis on the 'r,' as though to emphasize that I wasn't quite white how others meant it, but anyway, that I was the white one of the family.*" And, paradoxically, or indeed by the force of this familial denial of racial belonging, he would be the only member of his family, according to him, to engage in "*activism on race, so I think that these things in some way weighed on who I am, on what I do.*"

Among the experiences of negation that build subjectivity from a young age, Edson relates how the affective domain can be the one that creates the psychological scar in which affective rejection (founded in racial and class difference, which intersect) arises from contact with the Other, the hegemonic I. Coincidentally, it's school that emerges as the setting for the first social experiences of racial negation.

Thus Edson tells us: "*There was a girl, I was just finishing* ginásio, *I was between* ginásio *and* científico, *I was fifteen, which was the first year of* colégio *[. . .] she was from a different family.*" The girl's consciousness of not belonging to the universe where she was, white in majority-Black territory, combined with her obvious consciousness of the incommunicability of those two universes, makes her decree: "*No, I won't go out with you, because you're Black.*" It's a moment of knowledge, of being, and of power. The way of knowing that results from lived experience is that of annulment: "you are Black, so you can't," but it has the pretension of existing, of being a possibility for the racially hegemonic being. The unease that derives from family racial ambiguities disappears completely, broadening Edson's understanding of the social significance of his blackness. He explains the importance of that revelation in the following way:

> *One thing was, let's say, if we have to know something, and I did know, there is a way of knowing that I found out then and there, not just that I was Black, but that this fact was extremely problematic for me, that it was an impediment. [. . .] it marked my life. I never forgot that day, it really affected me.*

The articulation of affective content with political content is also revealed in the references to the "years of lead,"[3] which, in addition to the known violations, would bring for many Black people particular forms of violence through the articulation among the ways in which they were politically repressed, ideologically patrolled, and socially represented. Edson signals one of these dimensions that, perversely, Sônia Nascimento would also experience from a different angle, as we will see.[4] He recounts:

> *The repression of AI-5 came down, my third year was in a very oppressed school. I was strongly disillusioned with everything during that period. My mother pressuring me, I took the* vestibular *for a technical school and I was accepted to "Bridges and Roads," but when the time came to start, to enroll, a job came up and then I took the job, which was being a salesperson for a lab.*

The first contacts with repressive and corrective institutions of those who are a priori suspects follow family and school experiences, comprising a specific element within the apparatus of raciality, and transmitting a certain type of teaching:

> *There was a police chief in Salvador named Gutemberg who clamped down on anything that was known at the time as "hippie." [. . .] And so, I was reading an article in the newspaper that talked about his brutality, he was saying how he didn't like people with long hair and especially Black people.*

This results in another kind of understanding: not just that being Black is an impediment to many things in life, but also that there's a way of being Black that can be bearable for white people. A poem that Edson recalls in his testimony results from this lesson, through which he identifies the processes of self-negation that the dominant raciality demands from Black people for social coexistence:

> *you need to iron your hair straight, you need to put a clothespin on your nose to make it narrower. Anyway, in the poem there was a little program of what you should do, but you can't be out on the street with*

> *your hair like that, you deserve a very special kind of crackdown. [. . .] And the poem ended like this: that they had to use boiling water on their skin to lighten it; they're subversives.*

This is the formula in which the idea of epistemicide is presented in Edson's thought:

> *what comes to my attention is that the relationship of domination is created through this negation: I affirm myself as superior and master through this negative that is you. And isn't that how it is? If so, what is essential is here in this relationship. That is why Black and indigenous people have a status that is differentiated from others, and since they are the dominated group it's clear that this is within the very nature of domination, but also a component that can be reduced to a banal formula, which is the negation of the identity of the Other, of the values of their culture and humanity, or whatever it may be. Whatever may be the other mechanism of economic domination, all the other elements that are part of domination. There is something here that was understood at the moment of justification in order to keep things as they are.*

The negation of Black identity – which miscegenation operates to accomplish – implies, in the political sphere, depriving Black people of the condition of participant in an interest group in which they will be recognized: it's a strategy of control and annulation of the political subject. It is in relation to these harms that education in school and the family in general disregards, silences, denies, allowing its perpetuation and compromising the autonomy of Black people. As Edson says:

> *I don't think we have gotten to the full extent of the damage that's being done to subjectivity in all its aspects. We still need to dive deeply into this, without victimization, but this damage has a lot to do with our difficulty in constructing a collective subject, without a doubt. Another aspect that I think is important to highlight is that the Other who dominates is conscious that domination is perpetuated through this fragmentation, this negation. I consider Brazilian society's greatest prohibition to be on Black people getting together as such; there's a panic that has run through all of society for centuries.*

The witnesses' accounts indicate school as a space of negation of the subject, of permanent processes that constitute the forms of social reproduction of Black people as intellectually inferior, one of the dimensions of epistemicide. Edson testifies to the material and cultural indigence that is prescribed by being confined to poverty, an expression of Black people's social exclusion:

> *But in the group I'd gotten together there was a preference for Black people. It's funny that today, looking back, among the group I was the one who saw the difficulties that we Black people had in comparison to the others who were studying at the university. There was a difference: I myself was working at night in order to be able to go to university. There was a difference in how we were treated. I'd had something that the others hadn't had. They hadn't come from good schools, they hadn't done the reading I had, they were, let's say, very behind in comparison to the others. They were – I'm remembering here two people specifically – they were people who made a great effort to keep up with classes.*

Educational content joins with material conditions to impede the acquisition of a cultural repertoire. For Edson, among the content that is not learned in school and that collaborates with the processes of negation via omission are the examples of the struggle for Black emancipation as a liberatory cultural heritage. That is, the historicity of the political processes dictated by raciality, which could be utilized on behalf of emancipatory struggles, constitute knowledge that is entombed by the racially hegemonic group. This group presents itself to students as the wielders of universal experiences. Consequently, Edson asks himself: "*How can I have a country with a population that ignores the experiences that Black people have had in the world? Mind you, even in the struggle against oppression [. . .].*" Referring to Nelson Mandela and his historic defense made in the suit the apartheid system brought against him, Edson recalls that Mandela's experience is not considered universal, and thus it does not make it into schools like the French Revolution does.

When Edson signals another heroic moment in Black people's struggles in the world, he recalls the bus boycott led by Martin Luther King, Jr. against segregated white and black seats, which lasted 368 days, culminating in the revocation of the legal acts that allowed this form of segregation. The decision of the American Supreme Court was released on December 20, 1956. African Americans' acts of resistance for civil rights followed – demonstrations and protests against segregation at lunch counters; Freedom Day; the March on Washington; the Voter Registration Drive, etc. – which dismantled the American system of racial segregation and gave King worldwide recognition that culminated in the Nobel Peace Prize in 1964. These are different moments in the emancipatory struggle. Edson asks:

> *How could what happened in the United States have happened, this concerns me, the boycott of 1955–6, the year-long bus boycott, in a city deep in the South of the United States. I refuse to take the bus and come across a little old lady walking and say, "I'm walking for my children's future, I'm walking for our future." This is a page in history that elevates a human being of any color, but I can't study it in school because that's a Black thing. If it were a white thing, it would be required curriculum and there'd already be white people specializing in it, thinking that the French Revolution was blah, blah, even a pain in the ass. Now, Mandela's experience isn't universal, it's not to be found in school.*

This criticism gives rise to the political-pedagogical perspective that should inform a plural and democratic school: "*So, when we want content, we want to talk about that too. We want to talk about bringing Black experiences to school in the same way that white experiences are there and are universal; they can serve as the measure of human actions.*"

What we have here is a refusal to include extant and recognized knowledge about the fight against racism, privileging knowledge produced from a disciplinary and normalizing standpoint:

> *So while you fight for Palmares, there is a whole set of new authors writing historiography who always look for a way to legitimate compromise in the past, to see a somewhat softened slavery. [. . .] that could only have the goal of delegitimating any action in the present that has a historical figure at its core. Monteiro Lobato's book disappears; his is not a book to be debated, it's not a book to be discussed, it's not a book to be cited, it disappears, and you, at the same time, are trying to make all forms of oppression disappear.*

These are good examples of the difficulties in implementing law 10.639 from January 9, 2003, which altered law 9394 of December 20, 1996 (Lei de Diretrizes e Bases da Educação Nacional, Law of Directives and Foundations for National Education) instituting Afro-Brazilian History and Culture as an obligatory part of the official educational curriculum. Edson deduces from this difficulty the existence of tactics that perpetuate control over reading the past, and the terms of domination instituted by hegemonic forms of knowledge, negating the potentialities of reading the past from a different standpoint. Resistance results from the fact that, for him,

> *some Brazilians don't have a right to the past. So I say: cultural rights are part of human rights. It's an aggression against people's human*

*rights not to allow them to have access to the past. Now, those whom I don't want to have access to the past are exactly the people whose access to the past would change the relationship of domination that I want to perpetuate.*

Sônia Nascimento shows how the efforts to bestow confidence on Black people always bump up against reality, in which barriers are raised, specifically weakening one's energy and confidence, and producing an anemic will. Frequently, the efforts of Black parents to keep their children from adopting an attitude of victimization toward life as a result of racism and discrimination relativize the extent of the problem and minimize something that unintentionally produces a sensation of schizophrenia. This is especially the case in children who live in educational spaces, where they experience brutal violence because of their color and don't receive an indignant reaction from their parents proportional to the harm that they feel has been done to them. Many times, this attitude on the part of Black parents also reflects their own inability to deal with the problem, and reflects all the concessions that they've had to make in order to assure the minimal dignity that they are able to offer their families. As Sônia says:

*But the real reason that I didn't study law is that I didn't think it was for me. Study law, at USP, at the Law School on the São Francisco Square? It wasn't for me, I thought, I could never be a lawyer. Because I'm Black. I didn't have much confidence, despite all my mother's effort. She was a confident woman, and she always tried to spread it to us, but I didn't have confidence in myself [. . .].*

It's important to note how the apparatus manages to clearly demarcate where Black people's place is and is not. And it does so by introjecting that certainty: "*At the end of the year, I felt I wanted to try USP, but then I told myself, 'I won't, it's not for me.'*"

The administration of wishes and hopes based on the prohibitions that raciality imposes appears in Sônia's testimony in the same direction that Edson signals. She returns to the idea that being Black hampers "certain things"; in this case, entering the Law School on the São Francisco Square. Deep down, she knew that she could, but she gave up, in exchange for what she considered possible, though insufficient in her estimation. Thus she tells us:

*I have been to more than three hundred trials in my life. At the beginning, I would try to hide, but I thought all that wasn't for me; how*

> *many times did I end up crying, watching the trial, asking, "Why can't it be for me? Why can't I do that?"* [crying]. *So I started at USP, in social sciences, and I tried to be satisfied.*

These are the processes of *avoidance*[5] through which Black people learn to identify and move in the spaces in which they can be immune to discrimination. That is, a mechanism of behavioral adjustment to racial hostility in order to avoid the correlating discrimination and suffering.

Even when we lower our expectations, however, to paraphrase the popular saying, "*alegria de preto e pobre dura pouco*" (Black and poor people's happiness is short-lived). The experience of starting university is presented as a rite of initiation for the majority of Black students. There is a common precursor. The youths are poor; they study in schools in which they manage to perform well or excellently; people say that they're intelligent; they like to study and they think going to university is the continuation of a natural process. But suddenly everything is denied to them. As Sônia recalls, "*The first year was just awful, awful, because I didn't understand anything, I didn't know how to ask for help, but I still tried to talk to my professors, very few of them paid any attention to me; I thought that I just had to try harder.*"

Everything that comes after is a reiteration of the idea that "you bit off more than you can chew," that "this isn't for you," that "you don't even know how things are." It's what Edson relates about his Black colleagues in the Federal University of Bahia, whose difficulties were the expression of the material and cultural poverty to which they were subject. The university's bait-and-switch is to say "this isn't for you," that your presence could compromise the high quality that's only for those who deserve it, and *you* are keeping them from having it. This is one of the few situations, perhaps the only one, in which Black people represent an impediment to white people. Their penetration of sacrosanct white spaces represents, as Edson says, a cry of "*It's dirty!*," or fears that the level or quality will go down. It's as though white comfort in the university were clouded by the Black presence. Another dimension of this discomfort ends up producing situations in which real Black people are confronted with the virtual Black people of the social sciences and discover their unbearable lightness of being, as Sônia relays:

> *When I had anthropology class and we discussed Black people, I couldn't see myself in that discussion, for me the discussion didn't*

*consider actual Black people, I didn't see myself, I didn't identify with those studies, they discussed Black people in such a folkloric way, at that time it was folkloric, but one day I gathered the courage to stand up and say, "It's nothing like that, that's not my life, we have lives." They got rid of me, they ridiculed me and I left school. But the studies were based on the work of a white authority on Black people. My sense was that he had never interviewed a Black person. I gave up once and for all, perhaps I didn't know much about my own identity, my race, my community – but they didn't either.*

In this sense, the "valid" Black person is the one who's "validated" by science. By science and for it. In a dramatic demonstration of the epistemicidal reach of these practices, Sônia recalls an episode in a classroom contaminated by cruelty against the Black students there:

*it made me remember Érica's case: Érica was forced to listen to a professor who studied the Jewish Holocaust, and as he delved in, he claimed that what Black people went through during slavery was Disneyland next to what Jewish people suffered in the Holocaust. Yes, it happened in a classroom in the University of São Francisco law school, the one in Pari Park. She began to tremble, she burst into tears, got up and left. He thought he hadn't said anything wrong, the problem was in her head and not his.*

This is an interesting counterpoint between what one learns formally in school, in contrast to what Black people can learn in social movements, and the extent of the necessary contest for the truth to which Edson refers. It still highlights the insensibility of the everyday school environment toward the Other's pain. The contest for the historical truth is presented by Edson as an unnegotiable strategy of rupture against the processes of domination:

*When people speak of recuperating history, they think we're talking about recuperating a history from the point of view of good people versus bad. But that's not at all what we are talking about. What we are talking about is the following: we managed to take a historical episode that historians considered minor out of their hands, which was the case of Palmares. In thirty years, a single historical episode produced the effect that you now see.*

Conversely, celebrated authors like Monteiro Lobato remain the benchmark for early childhood education with his dona Benta, the fat Black cook, mocked by white children, in books and outside of them. But there is something larger, more profound, as Edson points out, that is revealed in Lobato's book O *Presidente negro* (The Black President), as a literary metaphor for the will to physically eliminate Black people: that is, biopower. According to Edson:

> *Monteiro Lobato had already brought up the laboratory solution: the increasing demographic of the Black population is such that whitening can't solve it, so the solution has to come from a laboratory. [. . .] What I'm trying to say is that Monteiro Lobato's book is Nazi* avant la lettre, *before Nazism took shape as an ideology. [. . .] it was in the [19]20s that he, Monteiro Lobato, would say the following: that the solution is sterilization of the Black population, that not one more would be born. So yes, there we have a solution. The intellectual Paulo Prado is thinking of whitening and says that the proof of the success of whitening is that some people already look white by the end of the [19]20s, that with just a little more the problem would disappear.*

It is not, therefore, gratuitous that the problem of sterilization both has become one of the Black Brazilian women's movement's fundamental concerns, for the genocidal implications it carries, and, at the same time, is historically hidden by poor and Black populations' different strategies of birth control. A book like O *presidente negro* should be used critically to demonstrate the processes of denial and rejection to which especially Black girls are subject. However, Edson says, the book is hidden. That is, Lobato's racism is "sanitized" by concealing works like this one, though people continue to consume his books freely, books where the social subordination of Black people, especially Black women, is reiterated through "dona Bentas."

By advancing a comprehension of how education interacts with the apparatus of raciality in strategic ways, it is relevant to remember that it will be in work relations that the limits imposed by raciality on educational investments will be experienced.

Edson relates how the processes of rejecting Black identity would be amplified as he migrated to the southeast and south of Brazil. He remembers, reporting the loss of a job opportunity in Rio de Janeiro: "*it was a very hard experience for me, to see doors shut for incomprehensible reasons, because I felt I was qualified for that job.*"

Insofar as Edson became more radically aware and learned more about the degree of negation that raciality imposes, socially normalized Black subalternity, in the way Foucault proposes, would be presented to him as a condition that invalidates or disqualifies formal education. Allocated to a territory in which racial ambiguities lose ground before a whiteness that is not virtual, but settled within parameters of a real Aryanism – he explicitly receives "Black treatment" – Edson says:

> *In Porto Alegre, I would have, indeed, my most defining experience. In Porto Alegre, I looked for work wearing a jacket and tie, and I didn't find anything, and I even wrote poetry about it. The racial contrast in Porto Alegre is very different from Salvador. In Porto Alegre, it was becoming clear to me, shall we say, that the barrier was in fact racial. Perhaps my own thinking had matured, but the fact is that Porto Alegre would be the place where I'd work as an assistant bricklayer – note that I had four years of university – assistant bricklayer, loader in a Transdroga depot, I'd work as a polishing assistant. I was a good student, I wrote well, I had finally published my chapbook – and I would work. I'd strip off the jacket and tie, if I wanted to stay, and I would work doing things that I never in my life thought I'd do.*

Although she offers the caveat that "*as far as perceiving racism, I think that when you don't have an awareness of racism, you don't notice it*," Fátima Oliveira's first experiences dealing with negation with a racist bias would be linked to the exercise of her profession:

> *The truth is, my awareness of serious racism appeared after I became a doctor, especially when people were surprised to see me; when they asked me when the doctor would arrive. In general, I've never looked like a doctor, even now. There's a stereotype. In the popular imagination, doctors are white! In Maranhão, I wasn't seen as or taken for someone who's* preta, *or* negra, *but as* morena. *But, even there, a doctor is white.*

In Sônia's case, practicing law would demonstrate how appropriate her anguish about a legal career was. Her experiences demonstrate the estrangement, denial, and disqualification suffered by Black people who are considered "out of place." Thus a judge feels authorized to deny her the authority of the knowledge necessary to advise her clients:

> *Oh, good! But you know perfectly well what you're doing here, you got instructions about it? If not, talk to me, right now or later, if you have any doubts, come talk to me." Just leaving me there like that, and me thinking: what could it be that he wants to do? So I said: "But say what, your honor?" Then the client says: "I don't understand, because she's my lawyer, we've been friends for more than twenty years!" Judge: "Ah! So you know what's written here?" Client: "I do, she's my friend,*

*more than my lawyer, she's my friend." Judge: "But still, I'm telling you, if any doubts remain, talk to me."*

This demonstrates how the rules sanctioned by the racial contract are only valid between white people, and that a Black person who tries to enter in has to be vouched for by another white person, the only legitimate source that can offer them credibility.

*At that moment, Dr. Catani enters the room, a retired district attorney, who's renowned in family law. When he saw me, he said: "I can't believe it, my God, you're here?" "Look," he said to the judge, "careful, because this one here is something else at family law, be careful with her . . ." It was, God, imagine, I'm not all that, but that's what he said. And the judge: "Really? Ok, then."*

The process of producing intellectual inferiority has its counterpart on the job market in the process of denial that will lead to professional failure. Whoever can endure it survives. Sônia describes the internal devastation that these practices produce:

*I dragged myself away, holding on to the client until the elevator; when the elevator door opened below, I broke down into tears. He broke me, and I keep thinking the following: I'm an activist, but no one expects something like that, no one's prepared, I could only think about getting out of there.*

Ignorance of the everyday mechanisms produced within the apparatus, whereby racism is utilized to discriminate, bring down, devalue, leads to devaluing the pain and suffering to which people are also routinely subject. It also leads to equating racism and the discrimination that it produces with other forms of prejudice.

*Another time I also lost my mind because people want to minimize racism, it was in the Public District Attorney course at the OAB–SP where you went to talk about racism, prejudice, and racial discrimination, and a student said that racism doesn't exist, that she had freckles on her nose, that she was also discriminated against [. . .].*

Any place is an opportunity to say "who you are" and what the social spaces "reserved for you" are as well as to show you that "you might be out of place."

*I did stints at the COJE – Centro de Orientação Jurídica e Encaminhamento da Mulher (Women's Center for Legal Advice and*

*Referrals), with the District Attorney. There was a secretary at the door who would say, "Now you can go in and speak to the attorney." People would come in and say, "Where's the lawyer?" Sometimes I would even stand up to look around the room: "There's no one else here, it's just me!" Once a young woman said, "Then I'll come back tomorrow."*

In short, denial manifests in different forms of control, as Edson points out: "*So I have various forms of control: I have this control over representation; I have this control that goes as far as extermination; I have the control of turning history on its head and distorting it – they're various forms of disappearance.*" Thus, he describes the relationship of the apparatus of raciality to biopower and the production of forms of subjection associated with techniques of extermination mediated by instituted knowledge about raciality.

Faced with situations of denial, whether due to mere social and affective interactions or Black people's submersion in professional responsibilities, what you see is schools' lack of historical preparedness, as well as the lack of preparedness that is regularly produced in them, to deal with racism. It's missing content, approaches that are denied, a future of social interaction and professional success that isn't even presented as possible for children and youths. Simply pure denial in everything.

## Education and Affirmation

The testimonies exhibit creative forms of reappropriation of the aspects of education that allow multiple escapes, in multiple ways, and plural unique means of resistance. However, common elements persist regarding the role of education as an instrument of personal and social affirmation.

It is in this way that the possibility of a future appears in all the testimonies, directly linked to the very possibility of attaining various levels of education. In Edson's trajectory, the possibility of a future appears as a structuring agent of a family project. According to him: "*we were poor from a material point of view, but with a family in which the children were going to graduate, no child was going to work before they turned eighteen, there was a whole ritual to anticipate the future.*"

Finishing post-secondary education is the triumph of this process: "*Look at what fate had in store for me. When I arrived in Brasília, I would work doing lots of different things, but I resumed something positive that Brasília would offer, which were my studies.*"

The positive nature of living in Brasília, a city that had no other interest for Edson, consisted in the possibility of completing his education. There he graduated and completed his master's, also completing, as far as he was concerned, the family project.

Education appears in the testimonies as a good that goes beyond money, since no one can take it away from them. This valorization is, in fact, a lesson learned in the family, in which education and knowledge are presented as possessions. Fátima Oliveira says:

> *Paivelho thought that education was very important, that those of us who were Black, who were poor, it was through education that we were going to become important, because according to him, money could run out, but no one could take knowledge away from us. So my grandfather made a great effort on behalf of all the grandchildren.*

They added a love of reading to the appreciation for education, as well as a love of books and other means of acquiring knowledge and information. Books work as an entry code to access a desired world and longed-for knowledge. This is why the role of reading is portrayed as determining the possibility of resisting the apparatus of raciality and the strategic role of illiteracy in the epistemicide that is introduced into raciality's purview.

All the witnesses accentuate the importance of a habit of reading acquired in their families as distinguishing their performance in school from that of other students. But still, they present it as a habit that they consider a necessity and a pleasure throughout their lives. In fact, the incentive to read and to educate themselves appears not merely as a tool for formal education, but as a way of constructing autonomy of thought and action that they owe more to learning processes outside of school than to formal schooling. It's worth considering that the majority of Black parents, nonetheless, have low levels of educational attainment, which poses a critical question to the current generation: that of the importance of daycare and preschool especially for low-income children.

Studies carried out by the Ipea (Instituto de Pesquisa Econômica Aplicada: Institute for Applied Economic Research) demonstrate that a middle-class child benefits little from daycare during the period up to three years of age because they benefit from their family cultural context. That is, families offer a cultural repertoire that is sufficient for that period of their lives. However, for low-income children, these studies say that daycare provides the cultural resources and socialization that are necessary for their development and of which their families are deprived.[6]

Edson's father and Sônia's breadwinning and head-of-household mother were, thus, key figures in each of their scholarly progress. What emerges in their testimonies is the significant role of their families in their education, in their remaining in school, in encouraging them to achieve the highest levels of education. Edson says:

> *I think the focus on reading, on studying, it comes from my father. [. . .] My father was someone, so you have an idea, who read two newspapers. My father bought books, there was a bookshelf with books in my house. So, if there is one thing that my father valued, it was reading, and in our house, we could say that our habit of reading came from my father. It was something that teachers would come over to the house and "Bah! So many books!" They were kept in the living room, a big bookshelf, full of books. So I can tell you that before I was fourteen years old I had read everything that Jorge Amado had ever published, we had it all in my house.*

The habit is acquired by mimicry, in which the maternal or paternal figures influence reading behavior. Reading shows itself to be an antidote to the apparatus of raciality's tricks. And what is more, it unfolds in the subsequent generation, as Edson describes: "*Today, when I see my two girls, one who I think is already like that, she feels strange without a newspaper, at fifteen, because for her it's becoming a habit to read the newspaper every day.*"

Fátima also testifies in favor of a father who read and explicitly encouraged reading:

> *My father's level of culture was impressive. And he wrote very well. Some time ago I found the books for his warehouse, written by him, in my mother's house. Pages and pages without a single error in his Portuguese. I remember lots of this kind of thing, a person who always had magazines and was always reading. Since he traveled a lot for business, he bought these magazines that I was talking about and when he finished reading them he'd say: "Fátima, you can take this magazine, I've already read it." I was always known for liking to read a lot, so much that my father would read magazines and then give them to me. And I was still very little.*

Books and reading are perceived as educational and as ways to promote autonomy. Sônia exemplifies how much her mother valued her daughters' studies, even to the point of using her meager earnings as a domestic servant to "*[subscribe] to the magazine* Veja, *because one of Ling's teachers had said that it would be interesting for the* vestibular."

Among the unique features of Fátima's life story is recognizing herself, from an early age, as someone who carried knowledge: "*For many years, in exchange for living there, I helped Leila and Luís Eugênio with their 'homework.'*" Her consciousness of the power and distinction that knowledge gave her appeared early as well, as she tells us about the sumptuous library that her grandfather's friend's mansion contained, and where she stayed: "*I was the only person he allowed to touch the library, since he said that I knew how to treat that treasure.*"

Books and libraries have a kind of mystique, as much for Edson as for Fátima. It seems that the library's mystique is the intellectual world, the possibility of acquiring knowledge autonomously, something that has its own strength, a life that can be transmitted just by reaching out a hand. Fátima says:

> *There was a marvelous library with, I think, the only collection of the newspaper* A Pacotilha, *from the time of the Empire. There was a pilgrimage of Brazilianists lining up to see* A Pacotilha, *which is a treasure, beautifully bound, and it was fully microfilmed. In general they spoke to Seu Sales, who was an intellectual and read a lot, or to me, because I was the only person he allowed to touch the library, since he said that I knew how to treat that treasure. But he was so proud of his library, which he said was the most important personal library of Maranhão, and one day he asked me if I could take care of it because the maids were ruining his books. So I began to take care of it.*

Edson also relays a desire for permanent knowledge at his arrival in Rio de Janeiro:

> *The first place I went was the National Library; I had a library card, I got a card, I would look for a job until a certain time, and then I would stay at the library until it closed. I remember that at that time I read all the Dostoevsky they had in the National Library; I went to the theater, to see plays, to see Fernanda Montenegro, she was in* The Investigation *by Peter Weiss. So I was also getting to know a more cultural side that was important for me, as I was looking for a job.*

Black people, who are generally the first, are excessively honored when they make it to some prestigious activity, which is the measure of the exceptional nature of their situation, and which some people misleadingly take as the result of their individual exceptionality. And it appears that this excessive honor reaffirms the impropriety of their presence, just as the legitimacy of their merit is questioned.[7] Fátima states: "*These labels of being the first one at this, the first one at that, they're heavy burdens. But they also always have to be remembered, because they demonstrate the road that a Black woman traveled, and a door that was opened, at great cost and with lots of sweat.*"

The apparatus of raciality, in its epistemicidal dynamic, produces Black people's intellectual inferiority, insinuating the relationship between power and knowledge. Knowledge promotes initiative, autonomy, daring, leadership, while its absence produces intellectual inferiority. At another moment in his testimony, Edson associates a friend's failure to complete levels of formal education with a situation that reduces him to *nothing*[8] in the social context of the university, testifying how he reflected on that colleague with the perspective that he had available to him at that time. Here, Edson demonstrates how the impossibility of accessing the necessary cultural means for an education that allows the development of a critical conscience, of the capacity to dare, to lead, is equivalent to having nothing, or, at least, to not having that on which almost everything depends:

> *But you see for the majority of Black families, access to culture is exclusively through network TV. There is no other means, there's no theater, no cinema, no books, no newspaper, nothing. Just network TV, which antagonizes Black people in every way. Right, they don't have anything, and we had access to other forms, and that's very important for a critical consciousness, without a doubt.*

At the same time, the capacity for leadership, for daring, are perceived as directly linked to educational conditions, resulting from family encouragement, in association with school and other cultural realms. That is, access to paid TV, theater, cinema, books, newspapers, is identified by Edson as promoting self-affirmation and a conscience:

> *Well, so it wasn't the right time. I show up to this group and, yes, I was different and it wasn't because of money: our families were equal in economic and financial terms. Our relationship was a kind of leadership that I had in the process, the capacity to dare, to say: we are going to take on the Student Association, put an end to the garbage that is the student union, clean, paint, add a ping-pong table, get a newspaper*

> *subscription for the student union, do something different, extend our horizons. Anyway, I was seen as a leader, someone who could make these things happen.*

The production of intellectual inferiority still acts as a hindrance to the development of a collective political subject, and the reversal of the situation of cultural insufficiency is positioned as an essential part of the political agenda: "*This intellectual ignorance is revealed in our intellectual poverty as a movement, it's true. We need to do something about it, it's urgent. We need to develop education and people who can recuperate these possibilities. There's no doubt, that's a part of broadening, it's a requirement.*"

In other words, analyzing how intellectual inferiority is produced, it's possible, on the other hand, to produce and recognize intellectual capacity before it's shattered. When such an approach doesn't take place, slavery returns with its radical singularity, destroying values, integrity, and the very humanity of a being. The monopoly of white people's speech about Black people is established in texts, books, or projects, seeking to restore the production of inferiority. But education, by proposing to think the universal, has to face the premise according to which everything that annuls the Black person annuls the white person too, by considering the ethics that should govern every educational act. Without this universal perspective, there is no possible education, as Edson recalls:

> *I'm very interested in questions of identity. I think if you sit down to lay things out you see the violence that was slavery, which is something always viewed by white people. We have very few accounts of what it was like . . . for us, here in Brazil, I don't mean that's how it should be, but in the larger bibliography. For us, very few accounts remain of what it means to plunge into an enslavement that will deny the values of culture, humanity. What does this actually mean? How far does this go? What damage does it do, that you can deny everything, and everything about an individual? It's not just cultural values, manners, practices, deny them as part of humanity. What does this mean? I have to extract something from this object, because I want an object to which I can deny anything, I want to extract productivity from it. Those who talk about it are white historians, always speaking in a way that doesn't reach me.*

The apparatus's completeness appears here, accounting for all dimensions of life. A fundamental dimension is the one that seeks to contain resistance and impede it from reaching the political dimension, which is the condition of transformation of social reality and of racial asymmetry that the apparatus constructs, everything that Black people don't find about themselves in school. The reiteration in schools that "we are all equal, without distinction of any kind," without the requisite analysis tied to historical perspective, hampers Black people's political organization.[9] Black people are dissolved into the "Brazilian people" and their processes of political organization acquire the connotation of social revolt, and thus they must be forcefully contained. Edson makes the following reflection:

> *It seems that something absolutely threatening to the Order will take place, and I think they're right. But that's the principal prohibition; this dimension of racism that we need to highlight, that racism has various dimensions, it has this dimension of subalternization, of oppression, of the exploitation of work, the exploitation of women, of housing, of the sanitation of the water you drink, of murder. It has various dimensions. But it has the dimension of denying you the ability to get together with others to combat it.*

White people's panic at Black people getting together in exclusive groups corresponds to Black people's panic at being accused of "reverse racism," of "divisiveness," of losing their places in unions and parties due to "ethnic radicalism." In some cases, it reveals Black people's insecurity, for professing an idea of class and race allegiance in which political subalternity is currency for negotiation. What is more, it reveals a belief in slow, gradual, and cautious change, that is, without open conflict, and an adherence to a racial contract that despite distributing bits of power, consolidates subalternization. Thus in many cases, we have party and union education operating to produce docile bodies in the political field.[10] Edson testifies:

> *I was in a meeting in Porto Alegre a few days ago and various Black people made a point of reinforcing in their speeches that white people could participate. Can you imagine a meeting of white people in which white people were constantly asking "Where are the Black people?" But now that Black people are going to get together to protest, white people have to participate. It's remarkable how people whose center of political action is in the unions, in the party, in other places, make a point, in their words, of highlighting that white people have to participate and can participate. We want to mobilize Black people, and you're coming to me with white people have to participate? That's their problem, it's not our problem, but these guys bring it to us as though it were our problem.*

The necessity of including white people in Black people's demands stands, for Edson, as a renunciation of the right to political self-determination, as submission to their protection or caution imposed by a fear of their hegemonic condition. Edson's position demarcates a difference between a political perspective centered on racial identity from others shaped by other political/party, ideological, or corporate commitments. There is, as a result, an education to be undertaken that has racial identity as the center of the process of affirmation, in contrast to identities that shatter its aims, imprison, and constantly reimpose negation.

The lack of respect for the right to autonomy appears in the disqualification of forms of struggle. In general, white people take positions on Black people's issues with the attitude that they know what's best for them, dictating the acceptable terms under which Black people should make demands or not. The tacit pact proposed is a simulacrum of political action: "We'll let you play at doing politics, provided that you don't cross any lines." Or: "Provided that it's an exercise attended by white people we trust." And even: "Provided that it doesn't go beyond the boundaries of the simulacrum."

> *You see: this accusation of racialization of public space is hilarious, because white people accuse us of racializing public space when we make proposals based on racial identity, as if the public space where they are weren't already racialized. It's naturalized, I guess. We show up, and then "It's dirty!" This business of race, you made it dirty. So I don't know . . . It makes you want to demand: we, those people, you know who you are, we wanted to demand something: to find out how to participate. We don't know how to say this in a way that doesn't upset you, but we want to participate. How can we speak like this? Do you authorize us to? That's what they want. How can we speak like this, that we don't want to be where we are, and we want to be where you are? Can you tell me a legitimate way to say that? 'They'*[11] *say: "Come on, let's have a seminar, let's make a decision, so you stay there and we'll get together with Yvonne Maggie, we'll get whoever together . . ." So they see how it's done.*

From the perspective of Black activism, for Edson, education is a place that appears as a possibility for broadening our theory, the construction of a conceptual density that allows an expansion of the critical conscience that is realized in emancipatory political action. He uses as an example Nelson Mandela's trajectory.

It is education as an instrument of the emancipation struggle that is constructed with theoretical breadth, conscience, and resistance.

Finally, Edson identifies the ultimate objective of his compromise and the role of the educator in activism around the racial question:

> *Now, the decision I'm referring to is irreversible, it means an everyday commitment, in your job, where you study, where you teach. Everything becomes how you live, your house, your intimate relationships, it's a totality and this urge. So I was doing what had to be done. In activism, I look at myself honestly, an activist in the very definition of the word, I think I'm a person who actually activates, who makes things happen, and from there on what happens is this: I don't stop, I feel like someone who wants to do even more, because I think there's more to do.*

It is precisely this theoretical breadth articulated with an activist practice that Fátima embodies, the permanent relay between theory and practice in a continual feedback process that Foucault discusses.[12]

The search for other modes of subjectification that break with the paradigms instituted by the apparatus of raciality is positioned as a demand for education and for knowledge production. This also highlights the dispute over historical truth as a fundamental battlefield to change the presuppositions of racial domination and make another subjectification viable. The historical redemption of Zumbi dos Palmares recuperated the myth of the hero for Black Brazilians, opposing an official historiography that took for granted that Black people's acclimation to slavery was a natural trait derived from their social institutions. Its symbolic efficacy is expressed in the ever-greater space that celebrations in his honor gain as part of the agenda of the Black movements and the rest of society. A redemption constructed, above all, through the strength of activism, which creates the model of identification that forms an escape route from the apparatus.

# 10

# Education and Care of the Self

For a society that desires to be white and civilized within the parameters of Western culture, the Black body is in and of itself a transgression. The ideal type is, therefore, the Black person with a white soul, that is, a refined Black person, governed by a white alter ego. Undeniably, in every situation of subjection, the oppressor is a constitutive part of the psychology of the oppressed, a truth that Frantz Fanon has exhaustively studied, and whose title for one of his books is self-explanatory: *Black Skin, White Masks*.[1]

The stereotypes associated with Black people are widely known: *Pai Tomás* (Uncle Tom)[2] and *mãe preta* (mammy) (Black people "with white souls," submissive and with a bovine loyalty to their superiors); the *malandro* (trickster/scoundrel) and the *mulata* (cunning Black people, with an exaggerated sexuality and morally flexible or ambiguous); the *menor* (minor)[3] and the *marginal* (delinquent) (expressions that cast the Black person as dangerous, violent, and cutthroat); Black people as entertainment (soccer players, artists, Black people as symbols of racial democracy); Black elites (those who white people say under their breath are "aping" them); the subaltern intellectual; the exception; the activist. Folklorized identity; fixing of identity: these are some of the modes of subjectification made available by the apparatus of raciality. Expectations for moral behavior are constructed with regard to each of them.

Nonetheless, in the area of resistance, there is the possibility of a renewed ethics that revolts against these modes of subjectification and the social mores that correspond to them. At the core of this renewed ethics, a "care of the self" is found, a term I borrow from Foucault, but with a different meaning, since it has to do with the possibility of the construction of collective subjects freed from the processes of subjugation and subalternization.[4] In my definition – formulated from the accounts of Edson Cardoso, Sônia Maria Pereira Nascimento, and Fátima Oliveira – care of the self is realized in care of the other, in the collective search for emancipation.

As Nelson Mandela stated when refusing the apartheid regime's offers of conditional freedom, "the hunger for my own freedom became the greater hunger for the freedom of my people."[5] "The struggle is my life," the title of his book,[6] is, from my point of view, a paradigm of autonomy of the subject that engenders a project of emancipation sustained by a renewed ethics. The construction of this ethics is the final result at which political (and knowing) subjects can arrive from the clashes in which they engaged and continually engage in order to surpass the modes of subjectification produced by the apparatus of raciality and by biopower. In the witnesses' accounts, care of the self is linked to the sense of belonging to a cause and to the role of peers in the construction of a racial consciousness as an instrument of political struggle oriented toward collective emancipation. Peers emerge as the guides through a rite a passage of individual and/or family racial consciousness to a collective consciousness that can mobilize political action. In the case of Edson Cardoso, this awareness first comes through the intervention of a friend who at that time seemed like someone who "was nothing," because he hadn't finished formal schooling. This is how Edson expresses that consciousness he had at the time of education as an element that provides an identity. But it is precisely this "nothing" that will insert it into the racial question, which literature will introduce to him:

> *It's there with Roberto that I got the first inkling that beyond the left's concern with change, there was the topic of race. [. . .] he was the person who gave me books, and so those were the first ones, the first inkling that I would have of the idea that there was even literature, authors. He's the first person who talked to me about the existence of Abdias Nascimento,[7] that kind of thing. That was 1969, when I got these inklings.*

Note that it is in the space of the school, at the university level, that Edson is confronted with the invisibility of a literature produced by Black people about Black people, an expression of the scope of the epistemicide that in Foucault concerns the knowledge buried by the hegemonic knowledge/power. It is likely correct to state that a significant part of the school-age population, and perhaps even of the teaching population in Brazil, finds itself in the same ignorance from which Edson was wrested in 1969.

Edson also points to the excitement of this other kind of encounter, among equals, among peers, who are responsible for marking out their own identity with autonomy and courage within a space in the educational system.[8] It is an encounter that for him has the educational power of demonstrating that raciality offers a real possibility of constituting, beyond the left or together with it, a specific perspective of struggle dedicated to structural change. Edson, however, relays that despite this nascent feeling of belonging, he still wasn't ready for the engagement that was being encouraged, and he didn't stay: "*But I remember my excitement at sitting [. . .] with a key group that declared itself a Black organization. It was my first experience and I didn't stay; I went back to university things.*"

It's important to remember that as a child, when they're asked "What do you want to be when you grow up?" no one thinks of responding something like "I want to be an activist for a social cause" and much less "A Black activist." It is the apparatus that leads us to resist. Edson signals how the process of engagement was slow for him, as it was for the majority of our generation, since it is complicated to transform an individual racial identity into a political consciousness founded in raciality:

> *I would go to the meetings still without thinking that this was something I would dedicate my life to, but look, I was already thirty. There was nothing in me, up to that age, nothing that told me to. I had, of course, an inclination toward literature, I was going to teach, I liked to speak, be a critic, but nothing that said I would join the Black Movement.*

At another moment in his account, Edson articulates the definitive impact on him at the moment of his recognition, of his full admission that he belonged to an identity that had been questioned since childhood. The recognition of a value, of importance, within the very thing that had constituted his first experiences of discrimination, of differentiation. Edson says explicitly: "*my life began to make sense.*" This happens when he's confronted by one of the leaders of the Movimento Negro Unificado (MNU, Unified

Black Movement) about his importance in promoting a racial consciousness in other Black people. As he relates:

> *When we began to talk she told me: "Do you have any idea of how important you are to other people?" She asked me directly. And the penny dropped right then and there. That's how it is, perhaps many people wouldn't have noticed it, they wouldn't realize how important they are to others.*

The inflection point comes, then, from the recognition of the importance that we have to each other and from the recognition that, though we're diverse, we are subject to the apparatus of raciality: this drives our resistance and reorganizes the purpose of our existence. This process is mediated by the contradictions of racial belonging, the identification of the struggle as the only path possible for individual and collective redemption for the oppressed segment, and the recognition that this is not situational but an integral part of life, a necessary condition for *being* and *belonging*, an emancipatory condition of life on the individual and collective planes. That is why it has to be engaged in and reengaged in every day, because the contradictions are present in the everyday of each of us as individuals and together. Racism doesn't rest. That is precisely why the struggle has to be permanent, continual.

> *I was going along, but I didn't think I was in charge, I was there and all, I was plugged in to the topic, to the subject, but I wasn't. . . So it started, and it started in a very special way, and, let's say, that feeling of a full cup, of plenitude. The racial question would give me, I think, what not even sexual pleasure, which is something very intense, gave me, the feeling of finding myself.*

Edson's awareness through the other's recognition teaches him to also recognize the other, his partner, the Black woman, as his counterpart in this universe. Peace and tranquility are also manifest in the possibility of recognition and acceptance of the Black woman, re-signified as a companion in a unique existential condition, an accomplice in the secrets dictated by raciality. The displacement of the gaze trained to desire the hegemonic Other is an adaptation, in Edson, arising from his reconciliation with himself, from his reencounter with his people, from integration among life, desires, and struggle for transformation. Decolonization[9] of the gaze and desire appears to contribute to a process of subjectification divorced from the immediate game of the apparatus: it happens outside of it, in the underground of freedom. In Edson's case, it is in the precarious seat of an almost clandestine Black organization (the MNU) in which he discovers where his real importance resides and for whom: that is, for his own people. It is there that the subject confronts fragmentation and continues in the direction of acquiring a new level of unity, now determined by raciality, a new optics of comprehension of the world (thus Levinas reverberates, for whom "ethics is an optics"[10]). Edson expresses this moment of arrival as follows: "*this peace came over me. [. . .] There I found Black women, I began to see people, I began to see everything differently, and inevitably things calmed down.*"

If, for Edson, recognition appears as a condition of the construction of the collective subject, it is also he who points out the apparatus's tactics that conspire against achieving this other gaze and other optics, as a specific way of doing politics. In his statement, rebuttals of the processes of subjection produced by raciality will appear in the framework of resistance, processes which operate to postpone or annul the emergence of the Black person as a political subject or disqualify their practice. Among them the question of self-recognition, in a collective sense, is presented as a challenge. For Edson,

> *We Black people, we're far from this plan and I can't see that far, [a point] unrelated to this problem of representation, of domination, and of racism. That is, what keeps us from sitting down together is the difficulty in recognizing ourselves as such; it's the difficulty of overcoming a portrayal that we have of ourselves, an extremely negative one. [. . .] We act collectively because we recognize ourselves as such.*

What appears is the internalization of white guardianship as a tactic or precaution, as an involuntary compromise of one's autonomy, or as the expression of cooptation. Just as Foucault describes, the apparatus engenders the forms of resistance[11] such as the reverse of the will to power and here, in our case, of Black raciality: "*It's going to be difficult to create a collective subject if I see myself in a negative way in relation to others; there is no way to form a collective subject at all. It's complicated. It has to happen through the recognition of the Other.*"

Regarding the conditions of possibility for this recognition, Edson states that for Black people they would arise through the institution of an emancipatory education that would deconstitute the knowledge, the images of control that reproduce stigmatization of the Black body and its destiny to be subordinated. That is, the constitution and visibilization of knowledge that we produce about ourselves, countering the knowledge of domination. Thus, for Edson, an emancipatory education is essential, one that articulates the necessary theoretical breakthroughs about processes of subjugation, like the knowledge produced by this experience of subjugation.

> *There's a Portuguese poet who spoke of a knowledge that distinguished him from others, because his knowledge was gained by experience. And there is a know-how that this knowledge doesn't offer, which is the one built through experience. I think that we need two things, we need to do this overview, this reflection, we need theoretical progress [. . .]. Compel us to think about concepts and everything else. We need this, to see other experiences that could contribute. So we have to reexamine our organizations' practices, the little appreciation, the little reading that happens.*

Thus the control of Black people's means to become knowing subjects seems strategic for the permanence of domination. The imbrication between knowledge/power and education, the latter in its role as control and distribution of historical truths, is also present:

> *Now, when people talk about history, they're speaking of a collection of episodes, of processes, of possibilities that they generate, because a single episode generated the most important civic holiday in the country, it generated a revolution in people's minds, it forced institutions, mothers' clubs, associations, unions, the Supreme Court, in some way to open up to a true reflection about racial inequalities, or not, a single episode that people recuperated from official historiography. Imagine now how many other events exist and what kinds of effects they could produce.*

In a social context in which Black people are permanently placed in doubt as knowing subjects, Fátima Oliveira presents herself as a producer of knowledge in scientific areas from which Black people traditionally find themselves omitted. She does it with the conviction and certainty that she is both teaching knowledge producers in the fields of genetics and bioethics, and offering to the public and to social movements (notably those for women and Black people) the tools for monitoring and defending against possible articulations between scientific publications in these fields and the technology of biopower, particularly concerning its eugenicist potential. It is the political subject and the knowing subject who offer to the sciences unknown or sidelined dimensions. Thus, she confronts biopower at one of its sources. Fátima describes her field of theoretical-political intervention this way:

> *I work on issues that are novel and obviously are very difficult for people who don't have a solid scientific background to tackle. Because both the Black population's health and this part of genetics, bioethics, a bioethical look at genetics, new areas of genetics, require a very solid knowledge of genetics, basic and solid, because whoever doesn't have that knowledge can't speculate, they can't carry out philosophical and political analyses of these issues. What I offer that's new is a feminist and anti-racist point of view about all these "new things" in biosciences and in the establishment of this new field of aid, research, and study, which is the Black population's health.*

If Edson well describes the contest for historical truth, we have Fátima highlighting the same contest over scientific truths. In this case, she has been winning, because a field of knowledge has been instituted around the topic of health and the Black population. Regarding the seminar that she organized to discuss the relationship between genetics and Black raciality, she relates:

> *I invited all the big geneticists in Brazil. Many declined because for them genetics didn't have anything to do with race, and according to a great many of them, what I intended to delve into in the seminar had already been resolved long ago. Why take up an outdated debate? That was partly the issue.*

Challenging any fatalist perspective, Fátima peremptorily declares that "*Biological predisposition is that which 'you're born with a probability of.'*" It might come to pass or not.

From her perspective, there are specific dimensions of resistance to the contests and powers involved in the production of knowledge, dimensions that pass through society's appropriation and monitoring. Such contests are informed by an ethics in the service of respect for human dignity. Within these ethics, a strategic element is the displacement of scientists from their "ivory towers" to dialogue and negotiate ethical parameters for research on human subjects with society.

> *The establishment of bioethics brings up something very important, which is to take back power from scientific corporations. That is, up*

*until bioethics was established as a field of inquiry and political action, scientists only paid attention to what their peers were doing. Bioethics takes this power away from them. From scientists to doctors, today everyone has to account for what they're doing to society. The ethical standards in research aim to guarantee citizenship. Consequently, bioethics, without a doubt, is a facet of citizenship. It's about a field of human rights that is becoming increasingly more necessary and indispensable.*

Knowledge/power and social criticism cooperate for Fátima to sustain a position according to which it becomes a moral imperative and a question of the rights of citizens that scientific research be subject to mechanisms of social control.

*Insofar as genetics advances, as racist concepts try to hijack new knowledge, new reflections, bioethics appears as a field and says: "That's not how it is! You can't do that!" It's bioethics that can make concrete the maxim that says "Just because you can do something doesn't mean you should." The limits of science. Bioethics is interesting also because of that.*

From the formation of new technologies of power and their interface with racism and sexism, Fátima, in addition to demarcating the racial and gender hegemonies present in the field of genetic research, alerts us to the strategic possibility that Black activists and women appropriate this knowledge and enter these spaces. She does so by revealing the racist bias with which these new technologies can come to be interpreted: that is, as new possibilities for reprogramming these technologies in the strategies of biopower. Thus there is a growing need to introduce other optics into the field, forged in resistance to racism.

*Of all these new things, there's nothing more important for the Black Movement than bioethics, because we don't manage to enter into their spaces. Bioethics is still an eminently masculine and white field. Though there are many, many women in bioethics, we don't hold the power in bioethics. Few women produce; the women who teach classes and coordinate them; or who write and publish and gain visibility.*

In Fátima's reflection, biopower manifests in all its range as a technology of white supremacy destined primarily to protect its own vitalism. Accomplices in strategies of manipulation of the lives of subjugated peoples appear as well. For Fátima, Foucault's "let live and let die" acquires the following expression, taking as its reference the efforts to revise the Declaration of Helsinki:

> *The focus of the controversy in the revision process was in points 29 and 30 of the Declaration of Helsinki, which say in general terms that a new drug can only be used in a comparative trial with a placebo if there is no other effective medicine for the disease for which it's being studied [29]; and if at the end of a study, every volunteer, independent of their place of origin and economic condition, should have access to the best medical treatment used in the study, to those discovered in the study or those that the study helped to discover or prove [30]. [. . .] Because doctors from the North, basically from rich countries, wanted the Helsinki norms to be more flexible so that they wouldn't be obligated to do research on HIV/AIDS in African countries and then pay for the treatment. Because the Helsinki standards take the position that if you deprive a population involved in a study of new medicines, the study is obligated to pay for that treatment – if the medicine is effective for that population. That's how it was since the first version of the Declaration of Helsinki in 1962, and no one dared to question it.*

The implications among power, knowledge, and resistance are underlined in these strategies, involving scientific research that is frequently, though not only, linked to the university and to the compromises that the university accepts or cannot take on. Thus, Fátima continues:

> *and if that study indicated an effective treatment, they wouldn't be obligated to give that treatment to the country where they did the study. What the Declaration of Helsinki says is more or less the following: "If you do a study in a place and the person has a disease and the medicine was effective for it, you have to complete the treatment and leave the person with the best treatment that exists at that moment." And they wanted to change it to the best treatment already available in that country . . .*

Fátima additionally points to the displacements that she identifies in African scientists who, integrated into the hegemonic logic of scientific production, give up their raciality to belong to a scientific community. They're scientists, but no longer Africans; they only trust their peers. They are just as Charles W. Mills describes the African American philosophers who are indistinguishable from their white peers. Fátima reports: "*Any inattention . . . This change would cause incalculable damage to humanity. And with the blessing of ethics. It became a fight between poor countries and rich countries. And lots of African doctors defending it.*"

Fátima reiterates this reservation alongside Edson, who casts doubt over the German Nazi monopoly on genocidal practices unleashed by biopower by using evidence found in national literature. She identifies these same practices on the concrete level of inequalities among countries and racial groups, which condition scientific perspectives linked to the reproduction of life, and lead to positions like those she describes:

> *We can't harbor any doubt that the displacement of studies from rich countries to poor countries reveals that they are looking for poor regions because of the lower legal and ethical rigor, which allows them to evade ethical research standards. This can also highlight a marked class and racial prejudice. As we saw, the call to racial eugenics has not only been a prerogative of German Nazis.*

Citing a study by Joaquim Antônio Mota, she provides a strong denunciation that is at the same time a convocation to resistance on a national and international scale: "*half a century after Nuremberg, an experiment with children was carried out by British scientists in Sierra Leone, in as cruel a way as in the Nazi extermination camps.*"

Consequently, from Fátima's perspective, the social movement is educational for the scientific sphere, contributing research agendas that emerge from the struggles undertaken against the technologies of biopower. According to her:

> *Universities are having to drink from our fountain, a fountain created by social activism, to work with the health of the Black population. That is, not only do policy makers drink from this fountain, but universities as well. No one systematized this in Brazil before I did, unfortunately. So my theoretical production is the key reference for whoever wants to do work in this area. It's a fountain whose origins are undeniably in activism, since though I'm a recognized intellectual, I'm not a university professor, because I never wanted to be.*

From her process of teaching, education, and activism around issues of genetic engineering, as well as from the conviction that it is necessary to mainstream these topics, Fátima extracts an ethical and pedagogical proposal with clear recommendations to schools, which she lays out in her book *Bioética: Uma face da cidadania* (Bioethics: A Facet of Citizenship):

> A proposal for education in bioethics needs to be examined and debated with society, scientists, and especially teachers and professors. It's

> necessary to foster the debate among teachers and professors to know the degree of worry and comprehension they have of the social, political, and ethical implications of the new knowledge and applications of biology, and if the knowledge transmitted/received is an instrument that is capable, adequate, and sufficient to initiate bioethical reflection.[12]

Edson's testimony clarifies several arguments presented throughout this work about the constitution of resistance before the apparatus of raciality and its complexities in the "seat" of biopower.

It contains aspects that locate the place of the individual in the formation of a collective subject, the target and opponent of their own development and actualization. Edson is the topic of his own political trajectory, and demands the recognition of this collective subject to comprehend the knowledge processed in experience, in struggle, giving political meaning to the very act of knowing.

In this way, the understanding that school should reflect the difficult job of incorporating "Black experience" as a defining element of human actions, as it is in our society, is necessary but, like a suture, also causes pain and suffering. This must happen whether from a political point of view involving representation as the scope of existence, or by recognizing the role that strengthening racial identity plays as the basis for transformation.

Edson points to everything from the discoveries that children and youth can make throughout their trajectory in school, to the importance of appropriating spaces of knowledge formation (among them, the university) as necessary strategies for skirting permanent racial barriers.

Personal suffering and discoveries are immediately put aside in favor of an understanding of a reality in which knowledge through education and knowledge through lived experience come together to form theoretical advances that are fundamental to the constitution of an identity. Moving beyond traditional arguments, this identity is guided by the notion of a historical subject, recognizing and appropriating "*our most recent experiences [. . .] long past ones.*" Edson believes that in strengthening the memory of and experience with the struggle, one can find the experiences with organization that can serve as the measure for human actions that can posit Black experience not just as local experience, but as the basis for worldwide tensions produced in the oppression of Black populations.

As an optimist, Edson also credits the expectation of strengthening political identity (being Black in a white world) to the possibility of forming basic standards for action for the Black population. They would thus defeat internal traps of victimization that lay the foundation for "*the damage that's being done to subjectivity in all its aspects*," as well as become capable of confronting propositions naturalized in public space, accomplishing "*a reckoning with that history.*"

To meet this challenge, Edson understands it to be necessary first to recognize all accumulated efforts and experiences as an educational process, and, afterwards, to focus the historical autonomy of Black experience on achieving political autonomy. Here, community relations appear as the ethos of this survival and should construct parameters, references, and practices for "*another education that we want to ensure.*" For Edson, this is a construction beyond affirmative action, whose nerve centers are policies of quotas. No, for him it's necessary to form bases of support that justify this construction, starting with Black groups; they are necessary for reconstruction over the space of the panic that Brazilian society exhibits about naming Black groups as such, once other groupings of color are lost in socioeconomic indicators, perpetuating relations of domination.

Edson also laments the limits of debates about diversity and pluralism before a racism that hierarchizes them, or even of the law 10.639/03 in its inability to structure changes to the relations of power that the possession of knowledge effects. What is more, historically situating the achievements of these collective subjects allows for the revolutionary act of belief in their transformation. And, by political definition, of their beliefs, the indefatigable expert continues.

Taking up Fátima Oliveira's story, we have the origin of the construction of her trajectory, a Black provider, her grandfather, who announces early on the sense of a communitarian perspective that care of the self would later assume. In the cracks in processes of subjection, he finds the paths to endow himself and his family with the autonomy that the apparatus tries to usurp.

> *My grandfather gave all of my siblings an equal chance to study. [. . .] Before moving to Imperatriz, he rented a house in São Luís for all of us, with Mom there keeping track of everyone, in a rented house in the center of the city. That is, so that all of us could study in good schools, Mom had to stop working. She handled my father's business for some years, but with this decision of my grandfather's, that everyone had to study, she had to close her small business; it was declining a lot anyway, it wasn't sufficient to support the family.*

Coming from a small landowning family, and therefore with a clear awareness of the importance of intellectual formation as an asset for social mobility and recognition, Fátima would be exposed to ideal educational conditions. According to her, "*Once a week, it was mandatory for all classes to meet in the science classroom, where the objective was to do experiments; learn to handle test tubes, microscopes, etc. Everything necessary for research.*"

There is a "magic world" of books available to an active and interested mind, beyond the effective methodologies for absorbing knowledge:

> *At that time there was also a library with 10,000 books. It was beautiful, with all the luxuries you could imagine. Every week all the classes would go to the library for two hours. They called it reading class – it was so that we could learn to use the library: find and handle the books; stay silent, etc.*

Fatima also remembers that study techniques guarantee the best results from the student: "*I learned to read by making notecards, a practice that I continued for years on end, until after university.*"

The distinctively high quality of teaching joined with a family education informed by the perspective that she calls "*training in how to be in charge*" from the point of view of the dominant class:

> *It was really a brutal contradiction, because I studied in a very fancy school and then during school breaks I was thrown into housework. But Grandma would say that "if you don't know how to do it, you don't know how to order someone else to," and that if I didn't know how to do "everything," how was I going to take care of a house, unless I was going to be one of those idiots that maids hoodwink. . .*

The training consisted of very precise techniques in which "knowing how to do" conditions "knowing how to give orders." The transmission of traditional family knowledge takes place through these techniques, knowledge that demonstrates the dignity of work as care of the self and the other:

> *After a week for sleeping, school break was for three months at the end of the year. I began to take care of the household. That is, I needed to get up every day to make breakfast. A whole bunch of things, starting with corn and rice* cuscuz *. . . A huge job. I'd put the rice and corn in to soak at night. Early in the morning, I'd grind the rice and corn, one at a time, to make the* cuscuz *meal. Grandma took many years to accept*

> *that the corn or rice meal "ground in a grinder" was also good, because she didn't like them. They had to be ground with a mortar and pestle!*

Thus, the "training in how to give orders" in Fátima's testimony is similar to what happens with Sônia Nascimento regarding the Black teacher who inspired her leadership potential, pushing her to take on leadership roles in the classroom and the school, because she believed that Black people had to learn to lead. This is contrary to the school instruction described by Foucault in *Discipline and Punish*,[13] which is designed to produce docile bodies. In this case, it's at the hand of a teacher who serves as a model – the only one, yet a model.

The values of the school and larger society therefore confront the communitarian values imposed by family traditions. Family belonging dictates norms and behaviors that relativize the privileges that the school promotes. On the other hand, they enter into conflict with the critical propositions that the school proffers for understanding social reality. Thus, the routine work of ruthlessly collecting from her grandfather's debtors is unveiled in all its social meaning, making explicit to what she owed the special opportunities that she enjoyed. A new awareness follows her grandfather's realism: his ability to maintain those conditions was directly conditioned by his capacity to collect the resources owed by his "crops on paper" debtors. Fátima says: "*So I had a strong enough motivation to be a relentless bill collector. My studies depended directly on the money that I was able to collect from my grandfather's debtors!*"

There is a healthy conflict when what the school teaches a child or a youth contrasts with family practices. Fátima's reaction expresses it clearly:

> *I was so horrified that I couldn't even speak, since I was in a school where we discussed politics, that kind of thing, poor people's difficulties and suffering, how rich people exploited them, and in that situation, my grandfather was indeed considered a rich man, next to so much misery. . . I went to my room and cried myself to sleep.*

Among lessons learned by Fátima outside of school, this new conflict is accompanied by the experience of a paradoxical ethics and a new form of subjection resulting from her social class: that of becoming an agent of oppression as a condition of maintaining her family and individual privileges, which, it seems, would have an impact on her later political choices. Her grandfather's prediction is clear: "*you collect or you won't be able to buy shampoo. Only once you're working.*" And Fátima remembers: "*I was twelve years old.*" She then experienced a feeling of surrender: "*and I continued collecting money by bike until I was fifteen, at which time he moved and no longer bought 'crops on paper' or worked as a butcher.*"[14]

The tight bonds of family values signaled a communitarian sense of existence and a strategy of social ascent – "*That school was very expensive, it was all private, it was a first-world school. Every family in the region dreamed of being able to send their children to the Colinense School. It gave you a certain status*" – and it seemed that this would naturally lead her to a lifestyle significantly different from the one that she pursued.

From the conflicts and contradictions that result from the different educational experiences to which she was exposed, in and outside of school, despite the many opportunities that could have led her to settle into the lifestyle of the dominant classes, Fátima was destined for political activism, where she placed her knowledge and all that she had access to at the service of the causes that she chose.

Her family support, her consistent education, the models of autonomy conveyed in her family, her non-conformity, her willingness to face and question like her grandfather said, the defining encounter with social questions, her party orientation, redefined a family strategy oriented toward social ascent and belonging to the dominant strata of society. She considered family expectations, and she became someone important, like her grandfather wanted. But important for women, for Black people, for socially subjugated groups, transforming care of the self into care of her loved ones, as her grandfather had done. Thus, the path of social mobility, mediated by educational attainment, charts our path to known places, while the other kinds of education that compete with formal education can lead to the re-signification of that very education and steer us to life projects that escape from its hegemonizing power. Academic knowledge, transmitted in school, contains limitations and strengths. If it normalizes – and this is looking at school as an institution – it also offers instruments of liberation to accomplish what we are proposing here. This is not its objective, but it is irrepressible, and becomes involuntary nourishment for resistance.

Fátima illustrates how knowledge can be placed at the disposition of social projects, interestingly having had a familial education in which school was fundamentally at the service of a strategy of individual social mobility and the achievement of individual autonomy.

Care of others, as a collective dimension of care of the self, takes shape in Fátima in the availability of knowledge and medical resources for women in situations of sex work and their children, in sessions of literature for blind people, and later in all the struggles for the defense of reproductive rights for women and the Black population's health, in addition to her interventions in the fields of genetics and bioethics. She includes preventative and curative strategies with all the propositions for public policies for governments or civil society.

The feeling of plenitude among the witnesses appears in internal peace that results from the commitment that they take on and that gives their lives meaning, in these insurgent intellectuals' consciousness of the impact of the relay between theoretical action and activist practice: they know what they chose and how to handle it. We have already seen this feeling in Edson's testimony; it also appears in Fátima's: "*I am extremely satisfied with my life. Very satisfied. Very, very. I think that for what I could contribute, the theoretical strength that I had, that I had the intellectual foundation for, I am aware that I've done it. That's that.*" This state of plenitude appears as a combination of various factors and various achievements: an autonomous subjectivity able to confront the mechanisms of subjection; knowledge that supports these emancipatory processes; and spaces of confrontation of powers, knowledge, and modes of subjectification from a perspective of emancipation of subordinated collectivities, notably Black people and women.

Sônia Nascimento, for her part, brings other lessons. This inscription appears on the prize she was most recently awarded, in the form of a silver plaque awarded by the Ordem dos Advogados do Brasil (OAB, Brazilian Bar Association):

> The Paulista Section of the Brazilian Bar Association has the honor of bestowing on the Hon. Dr. Sônia Maria Pereira Nascimento, Attorney in São Paulo, this humble award as a testament and tribute to her fraternal, charitable, and compassionate work for less privileged communities on the periphery of the capital.
>
> São Paulo, May 18, 2005
> President of the OAB–SP
> President of the OAB–SP Commission on the Recuperation of Memory

It's a faithful portrait of what has been for Sônia the translation of care of the self. A refined sense of social responsibility that she learned, internalized, and reproduced through different experiences and examples, especially the example of her mother. Education as care of the self finds its most precise translation in the words of dona Zilda, her mother: "*That we should help others because we always had someone who helped us, teach because we always had someone who taught us, give others a chance because we had many. You have to pass it on, have to spread it.*" She responded to the scholarly successes of her daughters with an inverted logic, refusing victimization and putting into action unswerving commitments that are due to our ancestry: "*You aren't doing anything more than your duty, we are survivors, our ancestors, who suffered terribly, came on horrible ships and survived so we could be successful here.*" "So we could be successful here" – this inversion is something extraordinary. Positioning a terrible experience of uprooting as a responsibility, a challenge, a test of humanity, of capacity for resistance and survival.

Sônia found in a Black woman, her teacher, the same form of support:

> *A Black teacher joined us, Dr. Clélia, the only one in the school, who was an advocate. I'd always been a leader, and she liked that about me, and practically adopted us, the two Black students in the class, Zélia and me. She would say: "They'll do anything to keep you from making it, but don't get discouraged, we're in it together, we're going to fight and we'll make it together."*

And she adds:

> *She encouraged us a lot, I think that's why I didn't know whether there was racism there, because I didn't feel it. There were many Black students, but the majority of them were boarders. There were few of us, the Black day students. She made me her assistant, I was the class representative, I began to study much more, she was our Portuguese professor. She frequently gave pop quizzes and I always had the lesson prepared; I knew everything and she was proud of me. She encouraged us a lot, but also asked a lot of the two of us. She would say that we had to know what it meant to be a leader, it was to be first, speak up, study, because we were Black girls and the world [*she laughs*] was conspiring against us.*

The Black teacher, who inspired her leadership as a youth, gave her the ways to react to this "conspiracy of the world" against Black people with a simple prescription: study, lead, resist epistemicide. Protect each other. From generous donation emerges the principle of reciprocity: "*We needed to repay her for that, so in Portuguese class we were always the top students in the class.*"

It is relevant to observe the outcomes that Sônia demonstrates here, in contrast to what Eliane Cavalleiro's research shows, in which examples of rejection of Black students proliferate, producing a decrease in self-esteem and cognitive capacity. In Sônia's experience, a welcoming educator, encouraging and conscious of the processes of racial exclusion present in the school and in society in general, produces in Black students a desire to perform their best in school.

A victim and a combatant in the apparatus's processes of subjection, Sônia makes law her instrument of promoting justice and citizenship historically denied to the Black population, especially Black women. This is the objective of one of the projects that is dearest to her among the many she has undertaken. It is PLPS, Promotoras Legais Populares (Women Public Prosecutors), a project of Geledés – Instituto da Mulher Negra (Geledés – Black Women's Institute) whose fundamental objective is empowering women. The project begins from the principle that information is power and that knowledge of the rights of citizenship is one of the most effective ways to empower yourself, precisely because, for a long time, Black women were excluded from the right to know, to learn, to be educated. This project aims to prepare women for community leadership in human rights and women's rights, with the goal that they will share this training with their communities, making use of it, strengthening it for the struggle for their citizenship rights. This experience has demonstrated that this investment gives women the capacity to develop organized interventions to demand essential services for their communities from public authorities, such as health clinics, schools, and daycare centers, and also strengthens them in their communities to act against domestic and sexual violence, pursuing the protection of their rights: human rights and state organization; women's rights; women's rights are human rights; laws, conventions, treaties; economic, social, and cultural rights, workers' rights; labor legislation, with an emphasis on equality in work relations; work and generating revenue.

These are the contents that are the subjects of PLPS courses that uncover new human rights and women's rights activists. Today they are educators, citizenship agents of innumerable other women on issues that until then they believed would depend on an attorney, such as child support; separation; salary adjustments (municipal employees); retirement; paternity investigation; violence against women, etc. They are an instrument of listening, guidance, liberation, and empowerment for other women. With these courses we venerate our religious tradition, according to which Black women have the role of guardians of our communities. These guardians are called Íyálòdès in the Yoruba tradition. The Black feminist Jurema Werneck describes them:

> in order for life to remain, so that *axé*[15] remains and multiplies, it is necessary for me to go beyond myself, searching for the best of myself. And of everyone. [. . .] among the Yorubas, the Íyálòdè was a women's representative, a community leader whose function was to take care that women's interests and the whole community's interests were attended to. Today, other women have the same task. We are the ones who take care of the community, the family, the children, who care for the sick. Restoring ethical trajectories also means self-protection, the protection of our children and all the community. We inherit the *axé* to be who we are. It is the legacy that we will leave to the future and fundamentally it is our decision. The choice is with each of us. [. . .] *Axé*![16]

It is to this tradition that Sônia, though a practicing Catholic, pays tribute, as the daughter of Oshun[17] that I know she is. And she does too.

The hundreds of women who have been empowered through this action are one of the reasons for the silver plaque that we mentioned above, awarded to Sônia, who frequently acts in partnership (instituted by her) between Geledés and the OAB–SP. We are lucky[18] that she is one of the board members of Geledés, after fulfilling two terms as president. As she relates, we enabled her retirement:

> *But I retired after twenty-seven years of service because of Geledés. Remember that the legal staff was leaving and you needed a lawyer? I was involved in activities from the beginning, but when I joined the organization, we worked so much, all of us, it was a revolution in my life, to be there, an integral time in the pioneering organization of stark raving mad Black women. Geledés's power, the example of the organization, the intense activities that we carried out were daunting for the time. The achievements, the events, the level of the talks, the first health event when we brought in the president of the Center for Black Women's Wellness from Atlanta, when Harlem Désir and Bryan Stevenson came, the participation in the Rio Eco-92 conference, one of ours in a conference panel at the Women's Tent, up there next to the officer. Participation in all the conferences: 1993 in Vienna, through Deise; 1994 in Cairo, with Edna; 1995, Niza in Beijing; 1995, the*

> *whole organization in Brasília for the Zumbi dos Palmares March, and us running the event. There I was at home, among my own, that was my place.*

In the end, there is a feeling of a full cup, of plenitude, of accomplishing the meaning of life that, as with Edson and Fátima, allows Sônia to declare: "*I'm finally a Black woman who has the courage to put a ring on her finger, enter a courtroom and expect to be treated well, because I never had an ounce of confidence in my legal practice, so I let a lot of things go.*"

Sônia bring up here the pattern of harms that Black women carry and to which Fátima is the counterpoint due to the special conditions that she experienced throughout her life. I feel the same insecurity and uncertainty about philosophy that she carries about law. We are, her, me, and many others, prisoners and combatants of the epistemicide that puts our capacity to think and act in check. We remain in a permanent state of doubt and alert. In my own case, here also as witness and author, I began to write out of fear, an insecurity to speak. The more I wrote to be able to speak, the more I was invited to speak. And the more I was speaking-writing, the more I was invited to write. In each of these acts, a birth with forceps. As with Sônia, it's a confidence that is constructed in the continual struggle against the apparatus's dynamic of inferiorization: "*I never wore it because I thought that I wasn't a good lawyer, and now I'm going to wear the ring, and now I speak up; I've had the experience of entering in a courtroom and the judge not looking me in the face [. . .].*"

It's the look of the hegemonic I instituting the Non-Being. An educational look that carries and makes explicit a truth about the Other, the nothing that constitutes them. And which our continual resistance refutes.

# Flowchart

## Functional Articulations among Knowledge, Resistance, and Race

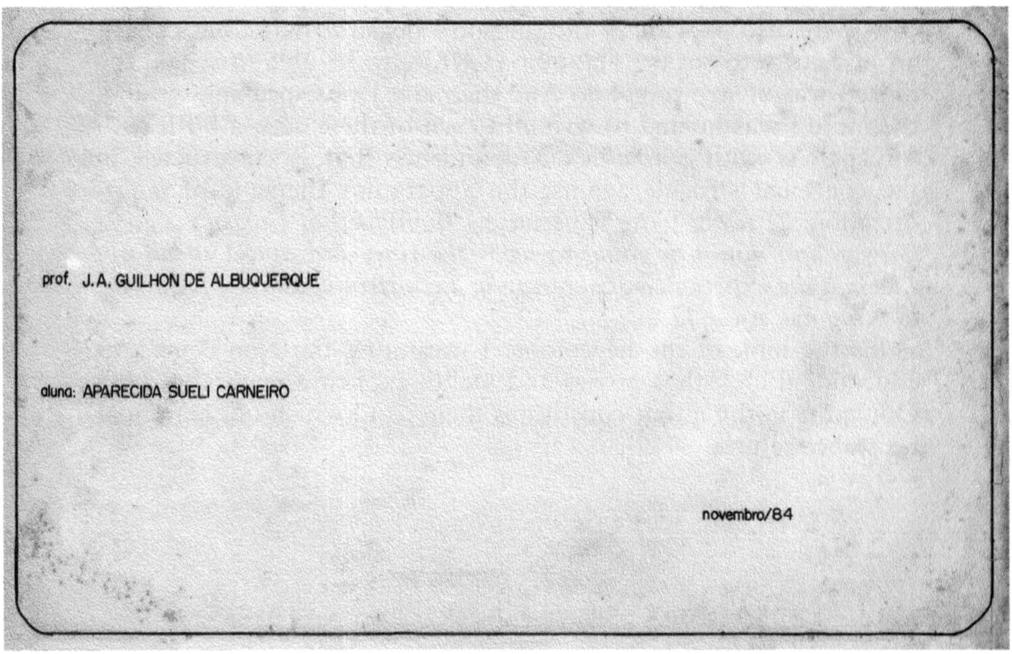
prof. J.A. GUILHON DE ALBUQUERQUE

aluna: APARECIDA SUELI CARNEIRO

novembro/84

# SUMÁRIO

# 1. DO DISPOSITIVO

ATRAVÉS DESTE TERMO TENTO DEMARCAR, EM PRIMEIRO LUGAR, U

**DISCURSOS,**

"Ouvi frequentemente em Dakar... que o africano era um homem que não tinha língua, tinha dialeto, não tinha filosofia, mas crenças, não tinha arte, e sim folclore" 2.

"Missionário profundamente embuído de sua missão civilizatória, Templs acredita poder estabelecer a cultura européia sobre a base cultural bantu de forma a conduzir o negro ao caminho do conhecimento, da civilização e da verdadeira religião" 3.

**INSTITUIÇÕES,**

"A expansão foi um empreendimento estatal, recomendado pelo Teoureiro Real exatamente porque os cofres do Estado estavam vazios. Custearam-se as expedições amoedando todo o ouro e a prata alcançáveis e empregando todos os recursos disponíveis do Estado e da Ordem de Cristo. Essa Ordem, herdeira das propriedades da dissolvida Ordem dos Templários, tornou-se uma instituição financeira para os empreendimentos estatais. Aos poucos, o açúcar da Madeira, o ouro e o negro africanos constituíram os principais elementos da formação do capital português" . 4

**ORGANIZAÇÕES A**

- Casa Grande

**MEDIDAS ADMINISTRATIVAS,**

"Sabe-se que aqui mesmo na capital mineira um diretor de empresa pública afastou sumariamente dos quadros funcionais de seu gabinete todos os elementos de cor, onde só admite funcionários brancos e de boa aparência. Louve-se, até certo ponto, essa preocupação estética, que vem modernizando e limpando dependências e instalações da repartição, a fim de que tenham uma aparência condigna e decente" 7

**ENUNCIADOS CIENTÍFIC**

"Foi naquele mesmo ano, aliás que Paul Broca, na França, e Galton, na Inglaterra, estabeleceram a ciência da medição dos crânios humanos, chegando a conclusão de que os crânios mais inadequados para conter um cérebro saudável seriam nesta ordem, os negros, os amarelos e, em último lugar, os judeus" 8

**PROPOSICÕE**

"Segundo a doutrina
vançados que dispun
cos e intelectuais
nestas regiões dorm
de explorar os bens
humanidade após a c
Por sua presença e
quada, o colonizado
vos letárgicos e os
lização e a verdade

EM SUMA, O DITO E O NÃO DITO SÃO OS ELEMENTOS DO DISPOSITIV
ELEMENTOS" 11

"...primeiro momento é da predominância de um OBJETIVO ESTRATÉGICO..."

1

...NTO DECIDIDAMENTE HETEROGÊNEO QUE ENGLOBA

...ÔNICAS.

DECISÕES REGULAMENTARES.

"A representação dos Comerciantes da Bahia, em 1757, defendia com ardor a exploração do comércio da Costa da Mina, embora preferissem os escravos desta os de Angola, porque os primeiros eram 'mais fortes e mais robustos'; estes eram 'mais domáveis e em melhor preço'. Daí o projeto de organização de uma Companhia de Comércio constituída com capitais formados no Brasil, e valendo-se da provisão de 30 de março 1756 que permitiria 'o uso franco da nagevação para a Costa da Mina a todos os que lá quisessem ir e mandar comerciar em embarcações que não excedessem o número de três mil rolos, como principal fundamento de ficarem sendo sendo contínuas as utilidades e de abundarem de escravos em preços cômodos o recôncavo, sertões e minas daquela dilatado continente" 5

LEIS.

"A corrente se tornando irresistível, minha mãe, que exercia a Regência na ausência do Imperador, não hesitou mais em seguir o impulso de seu coração. Sem desconhecer a gravidade do ato que realizava, mas colocando a caridade acima da política, ela assinou no dia 13 de maio de 1888, a lei submetida a sua sanção" 6

...ÓFICAS.

...os a- ...técni- ...rvir ...ca e ...toda ...do . ...ade - ...s po- ...civi-

MORAIS/FILANTRÓPICAS.

"A exemplo dos administradores e colonos, o missionário que ele é afirma ao menos duas teses, que a natureza sai das mãos de Deus e que pertence à comunidade dos melhores civilizar os irmãos inferiores, assim, o direito de colonização se desdobra de um dever natural e de uma missão espiritual" 10

...POSITIVO É A REDE QUE SE PODE ESTABELECER ENTRE ESTES

# 2. DO PREENCHIMENT
# ESTRATÉGICO

"Trouxeram o imigrante europeu, segundo o decreto lei nº 7967 de 1945, para preservar e desenvolver, na composição étnica da população, as característi-cas mais convenientes da sua ascendência européia. Por idênticas razões, um decreto de 28 de junho de 1890 concedia livre entrada no Brasil a todos os indivíduos aptos para o trabalho, excetuados os indígenas da Ásia ou da África" 13

**"Nós temos que redimir**
**redimir o negro do com**
**social"(tancredo neves**

"... ainda em pleno 1982 verificamos como tais teorias podem florescer até de maneira patológica, como a sugestão apresentada pelo Sr. Benedito Pio, ao Grupo de Assessoria do governo do Estado de São Paulo, anterior ao Sr. Franco Montouro. Propunha o ilustre assessor a esterilização de negros brasileiros, para evitar que estes, devido a seu crescimento demográfico, possam ascender democraticamente ao poder num futuro próximo" 16

"A visão s
gera ganh
pitalista
lhadores s
micos e nã
longo do t
çativa da
ples confi
inferiores
fato, o re
tas de sel
rencial do
classe que
prestígio

"EM SEGUIDA UM DISPOSITIVO SE CONSTITUI COMO TAL E CONTINUA A SER DISPOSITIVO... 12

**o complexo de cor, inferioridade**

"Sabe-se que aqui mesmo na capital mi - neira um diretor de empresa pública a- fastou sumariamente dos quadros funcio- nais de seu gabinete todos os elementos de cor, onde só admite funcionários brancos de boa aparência..." 15

l o racismo só
para a classe ca
todos os traba-
benefícios econô
acumulados ao
parcela signifi
anca pelo sim -
egro às posições
ia social. De
práticas racis -
é o acesso prefe
posições de
aior remuneração
". 17

"Desde a promulgação da lei, aqueles a- núncios cessaram, sendo realmente excep cional o caso de publicidade, como aque la aparecida na primeira página de um grande jornal, ainda em 1971, em que se diz precisar 'de babá de cor clara e meia idade' ou de 1972, em que se pede candidata a 'babá para casa de fino tra to que preencha o seguinte requisito : branca, jovem e muito prática...' e ou- tro convidando 'moça branca, até 20 a- nos' para 'auxiliar'. Surgiu, a partir de então, a exigência de 'boa aparên - cia' em todos os anúncios de emprego , não só de domésticas como de outras ca- tegorias; mas essa locução é, para mui- tos, apenas um eufemismo..." 18

# 3. DO SABER/PODER

- Centro de Estudos Africanos da Universidade de São Paulo.
- Instituto de Pesquisas e Estudos Afro-Brasileiro - PUC.SP.
- Centro de Estudos Afro-Asiáticos, Conjunto Universitário Cândido Mendes - RJ.
- Centro de Estudos Afro-Orientais, Universidade Federal da Bahia-
- SECNEB Bahia.
- Centro Afro Brasileiro de Cultura Religiosa Atim Lembá Furenã-SP.
- Centro de Estudos de Integração África-Brasil, Universidade Católica de Goiás.
- Centro de Estudos Afro-Brasileiro, Universidade Federal de Minas Gerais.
- Centro de Estudos Africanos, Universidade Eduardo Mondelane,Maputo.
- Caribbean, African and Afro-American Studies, Florida, USA.
- Centre de Recherches Africaines, Paris.
- Centro de Estudos Africanos - Lisboa, Portugal.
- CIDAF-Centro de Informacion y Documentacion Africanas, Madrid, Espanha.
- CELA- Centre d'Études des Littératures Africaines, Zaire.
- CARDAN- Centre d'Études Africaines, Paris, França.
- Centro de Estudos sobre a África, Lisboa, Portugal.
- Institute of African Studies, Ibadan, Nigéria.
- Instituto Cultural Brasil-Nigéria, Rio de Janeiro.
- Institute of African Studies, Legon, Gana.
- Institute für Afrika - kinde - Hamburg, República Federal Alemã.

20


ARAUJO, Cesa
Bahia. Rev
1939.

AUSTRAGÉSILO
co. In: —

AVELAR, Rome
Depto. Est.

ÁVILA, Bastos
In: — Estu

AZEVEDO, Fer
Rio de Jane

AZEVEDO, Fer
Nacional, 1

AZEVEDO, Lui
lítica. Rio

AZEVEDO, Tal
do Arquivo
1945.

AZEVEDO, Tha
1951.

AZEVEDO, Tal
pretos. In
da Univ. da

AZEVEDO, Tha
Cadernos B

AZEVEDO, Tha
neiro, Civi


"O PROBLEMA É QUE ATÉ AGORA NÃO CONSEGUIMOS ENCONTRAR NU
DOUTOR EM HISTÓRIA. POR MAIS QUE PROCURÁSSEMOS..." 22

"O FUNDAMENTAL DA ANÁLISE É QUE SABER E PODER SE IMPLICAM MUTUAMENTE: NÃO HÁ RELAÇÃO DE PODER SEM CONSTITUIÇÃO DE UM CAMPO DE SABER, COMO TAMBÉM, RECIPROCAMENTE, TODO SABER CONSTITUI NOVAS RELAÇÕES DE PODER. TODO PONTO DE EXERCÍCIO DO PODER É, AO MESMO TEMPO, UM LUGAR DE FORMAÇÃO DE SABER" 19


incidência da tuberculose no preto da
ogia da Bahia, Salvador, jul.-ago.

tiçagem no Brasil com o fator eugêni
s Afro-Brasileiros, op. cit. p. 325-333.

oi. In: — Figuras da terra. Maceió,
1963. p. 79-83.

ição ao estudo do índice de Lapicque.
leiro, op. cit. p. 29-38.

viais e engenhos na política do Brasil.
do Açúcar e do Álcool, 1948.

tura brasileira. São Paulo, Cia. Ed.

Música negra no nordeste. Cultura Po
(8): 183-186, 1945.

cto da mestiçagem na Bahia. Revista
São Paulo, São Paulo, 11 (101): 45-62,

ação e mestiçagem. Salvador, Progresso,

tamento verbal e efetivo para com os
de Antropologia Social. Bahia, Publ.
. p. 143-158.

ulo entre os escravos e o cidadão. In: -
op. cit. p. 27-30.

a e situação racial no Brasil. Rio de Ja
ileira, 1966.

CARDOSO, Fernando H. - Capitalismo e escravidão no Brasil meridional. O negro na sociedade escravocrata do Rio Grande do Sul. São Paulo, Difusão Européia do Livro, 1962.

CARDOSO, Fernando H. - Colour prejudice in Brazil. Presence Africaine, Paris, nº 25, 53: 120-128, 1965.

CARDOSO, Fernando H. - O negro e a expansão portuguêsa no Brasil meridional. Anhembi, São Paulo, 32 (94): 16-21, 1958.

CARDOSO, Fernando H. - O negro no Brasil meridional. O Estado de São Paulo, São Paulo, 12 jul., 1950.

CARDOSO, Fernando H. e IANNI, Octavio - Cor e mobilidade social em Florianópolis. São Paulo, Ed. Nacional, 1960.

CARDOSO, Fernando H.; MOREIRA, Renato e IANNI, Octavio - O estudo sociológico nas relações entre negros e brancos no Brasil meridional. In: — Revista Brasileira de Antropologia, 2, Bahia, Anais Bahia, Artes Gráficas, 1957. p. 213-229.

CARDOSO, M.S. - Slavery in Brazil as describes by americana, 1822-1888. Américas, Union Panamericana, nº 17-3: 241-260, 1961.

CARNEIRO, A.J. de Souza - Os mitos africanos no Brasil. São Paulo, Cia. Ed. Nacional, 1937.

CARNEIRO, Edison e FERRAZ, C.A. do Couto - Prefácio. In: — O negro no Brasil, op. cit., p. 7-11.

CARNEIRO, Edison - Antologia do negro brasileiro. Porto Alegre, Ed. Globo, 1950.

CARNEIRO, Edison - Assimilação e ascenção do negro escravo. In: — Reunião Brasileira de Antropologia, 3, Recife, Anais. Recife, IBEC, 1958.


21

S ELITISTA COMO O NOSSO, NENHUM NEGRO QUE SEJA

# 4. DA RESISTÊNCIA

SELVAGENS, SOLITÁRIAS, PLANEJADAS, ARRASTADAS, VIOLENTAS
FADADAS AO SACRIFÍCIO.

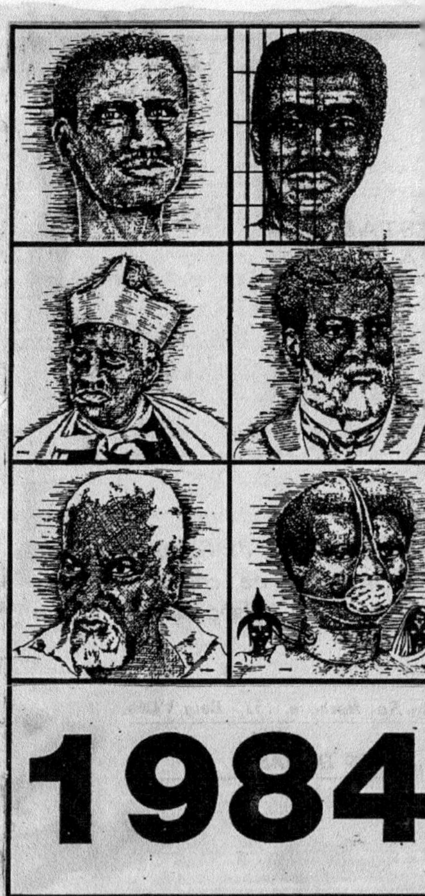


conselho da comunidade negra

ilê xoroquê

bloco afro alafiá

coletivo de mulheres negras

jb' sambar

ipeafro

MNU

legião rastafari

rua do samba

POR DEFINIÇÃO, NÃO PODEM EXISTIR A NÃO SER NO CAMPO ESTRA

TO, NÃO EXISTE, COM RESPEITO AO PODER, UM LUGAR DA GRANDE A- ALMA DA REVOLTA, FOCO DE TODAS AS REBELIÕES, LEI PURA OLUCIONÁRIO... MAS SIM RESISTÊNCIAS, NO PLURAL, QUE SÃO ÚNICOS: POSSÍVEIS, NECESSÁRIAS, IMPROVÁVEIS, ESPONTÂNEAS...

ICILIÁVEIS, PRONTAS AO COMPROMISSO, INTERESSADAS OU

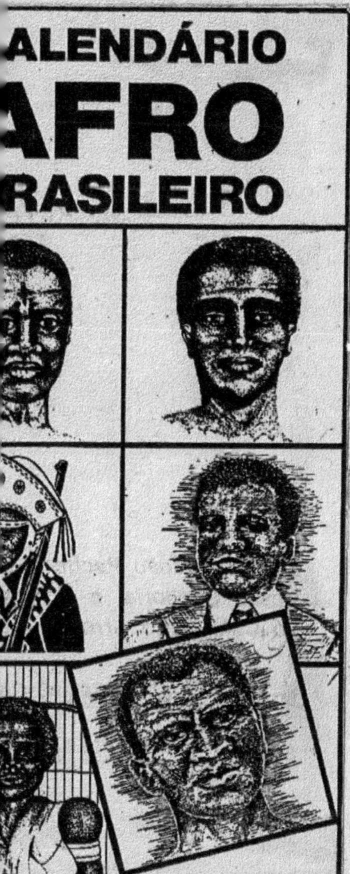


quilombhoje

feconezu

ilē aiyē

ilē opó afonjá

grupo negro da PUC

união das escolas de samba de são paulo

ARPAB

frente negra brasileira

união e consciência negra

DAS RELAÇÕES DE PODER.

## NOTAS

1. Michel Foucault. Microfísica do poder, p. 245.
2. V.Y. Mundimbe. Table ronde. In: Sommaire, nº 56, vol. IX, p. 16.
3. Louis Vicent Thomas. Table ronde. In: Sommaire, p. 4.
4. José Honório Rodrigues. Brasil e África - outro horizonte, p. 10.
5. idem, p. 25.
6. Paulo Sérgio Pinheiro. Abolição e Passadismo. Folha de São Paulo, 20.10.84, p. 40.
7. Thales de Azevedo. Democracia racial, p. 46.
8. Geraldo Mello Mourão. Marx, Freud e Darwin, o crepúsculo dos ídolos. Folha de São Paulo, 25.07.82.
9. V.Y. Mumdimbe. op.cit.
10. idem.
11. Michel Foucault. op.cit., p. 244.
12. idem, p. 245.
13. Abdias do Nascimento. 13 de maio: outra mentira cívica. Folha de São Paulo, 13.05.83, p. 3.
14. Tancredo Neves. Folha de São Paulo, 23.09.84, p. 8.
15. Thales de Azevedo, op.cit.
16. Abdias do Nascimento. op.cit.
17. Lélia Gonzales e Carlos Hasembalg. Lugar de negro, p. 80.
18. Thales de Azevedo, op.cit., p. 10.
19. Michel Foucault. op.cit., p. XXIII.
20. Solange M. Couceiro. Bibliografia sobre o negro brasileiro. Universidade de São Paulo, 1974.
21. Solange M. Couceiro. op.cit.
22. Revista Veja. 05.09.84, nº 835.
23. Michel Foucault. História da Sexualidade I - a vontade de saber, p.91.

# Postface

## Sueli Carneiro's Practical Philosophy

The book we finally have in our hands began to be conceived in 1984, when Sueli Carneiro intuited for the first time that Michel Foucault's concept of the apparatus could be a valuable resource to understand the dynamic of racial relations in Brazil. When she was thirty-four, she had finished her undergraduate degree in philosophy in the School of Philosophy, Literature, and Humanities at the University of São Paulo and had enrolled in the master's program. Two decades later, in 2005, this intuition gave form to her doctoral dissertation, directed by Roseli Fischmann and by the anti-racist and feminist political struggle begun during the period of military dictatorship. After she defended it in the School of Education at the University of São Paulo with the densely philosophical title of *A construção do outro como não-ser como fundamento do ser* (The Construction of the Other as Non-Being as the Foundation of Being), her thesis waited another two decades to become a book, which arrived in 2023, with its author already a septuagenarian in a Brazil still living in the shadow of authoritarian demons.

In the interim, Carneiro, always engaged in the feminist and anti-racist struggle, founded Geledés – Instituto da Mulher Negra (Geledés – Black Women's Institute) along with other colleagues, and also published a wide array of articles, talks, and newspaper columns, some of them collected in *Racismo, sexismo e desigualdade no Brasil* (Racism, Sexism, and Inequality in Brazil),[1] with a preface by Edson Cardoso Lopes, and in *Escritos de uma vida* (Life Writings)[2] with an introduction by Djamila Ribeiro and a preface by Conceição Evaristo. Written over three decades, they reveal the construction of a social theory with philosophy, oriented toward an understanding of the dynamics of oppression – and resistance – in a multiracial society with a colonial past profoundly marked by racism, sexism, and poverty.

We have in our hands one of the most relevant works of political philosophy written in Brazil. If philosophy is born of amazement, as we learn with Plato and Aristotle, Carneiro's is born of perplexity and indignation when faced with the permanence of racist ideas, discourses, and practices over the five centuries since the colonization of Brazil.[3] In *Dispositif of Raciality: The Construction of the Other as Non-Being*, Carneiro confronts this problem with a theoretical approach inspired by the philosophy of Foucault, who gives her the resources to approach raciality as a domain that produces power, knowledge, and subjectivities through the articulation of diverse elements.

However, it is not about the mere application of Brazilian realities to Foucauldian notions of the apparatus and biopower. Carneiro is inspired by Foucault but does not repeat him. She thus creates her own conceptual architecture that has at its center a new concept of her own making, that of the *apparatus of raciality*, developed to understand the heterogeneity and the articulation of practices and discourses engendered by Brazilian racism.

At the same time, Carneiro mobilizes the Foucauldian notion of biopower in its specific articulation with racism, to construct a diagnosis that underlines the extreme violence of racism in the Brazilian state. The thesis that "Once the State functions in the biopower mode, racism alone can justify the murderous function of the State"[4] fits Brazil like a glove. At first it seems absurd that biopower, whose principal function is to promote and administer life, would kill its own citizens. But it is not generic citizens whom biopower includes under the sign of death, but primarily the Others, who are Others because they are considered degenerates and of an inferior race. They are Others precisely because they confer an identity on the hegemonic I, included under the sign of life. In other terms, biopower promotes death when, articulated with the hostility that is socially consolidated against Black people in Brazil, racism finally operates as a legitimating element of the supposed right to kill, exercised by the state through action or omission, whether directly or indirectly.[5]

This thesis has empirical support, as Carneiro shows in Chapter 2. She also keeps in mind the effect of the social marker of gender, which, combined with race, allows us to see that although biopower inscribes Black people with the sign of death, it is imposed in different ways on Black men and Black women in post-abolition Brazil. Pure violence is reserved for Black men: without access to socially constructed assets, and with the majority of the formerly enslaved labor force outside the labor market, "violence becomes the constitutive grounds for the production of the Black masculine gender."[6] As far as Black women are concerned, the state simply lets them die by means of a health system that since the nineteenth century has functioned with a eugenicist orientation. The high maternal mortality rate for Black women and the high rate of preventable disease is, for Carneiro, a clear sign that there is a widespread perception that the value of life is different depending on the color of your skin.

And what about those who survive? The apparatus of raciality imposes on them assorted strategies of subjection, among which is epistemicide – a fundamental element in Carneiro's conceptual architecture – a term borrowed from Boaventura de Sousa Santos, and the topic of Chapter 3. Epistemicide is the result of debasing and sequestering Black people's reason, something that begins in school and extends through higher education, with devastating consequences for the few who are able to access university. By means of epistemicide, the apparatus of raciality more efficiently perpetuates racism by casting Black people as intellectually inferior and refusing their authority as knowing subjects. In addition to its violence, epistemicide generates a bad impression of Brazil, since various theoretical fields – from the social sciences to philosophy, passing through psychoanalysis and literature – have been exclusively occupied by white people convinced of their full authority to deal with these questions, including questions of racial oppression.

When applied to Brazil, the theory of apparatuses allows Carneiro to form a diagnosis that keeps in mind the diverse and heterogeneous strategies of the apparatus of raciality, which, when it does not kill directly, does so indirectly through multiple prohibitions: on Black people as knowing subjects, as moral subjects, and as political and legal subjects, the topic of Chapter 4. For European or American philosophical concepts to tell us something about Brazil – not just those of Foucault, but also Heidegger and Charles W. Mills – Carneiro puts them in dialogue with Abdias Nascimento's and Kabengele Munanga's work on Black people, with Isildinha Nogueira Batista's psychoanalytic theory, and with

Gislene Aparecida dos Santos's analysis of the contradictions of the Enlightenment. Though she is not cited in *Dispositif of Raciality*, I dare say that Léila Gonzalez, a key reference in other texts by Carneiro, is present from the first page to the last. An exegesis worthy of this work should be able to demonstrate that Carneiro's practical philosophy emerges from a tense dialogue with the Western tradition mediated through the interventions of Black Brazilian authors from different areas of knowledge.

## The Racial Contract

The heterogeneity of the apparatus of raciality is the very expression of a national project, the result of the way in which the social contract came about in Brazil. If it is Foucault who triggers the insight that formulates the concept of the apparatus of raciality, it is Charles W. Mills who offers Carneiro the conceptual resources to theorize the actual construction and structuration of raciality as an apparatus of power, something that begins for Brazilians long before the nineteenth century, when Foucault locates the emergence of the apparatus of sexuality. The theoretical articulation between Foucault and Mills is astonishingly original, and sustains one of the central theses of the book, namely, that the racial contract is the structuring element of the apparatus of raciality. The apparatus of raciality's point of emergence should be sought in European colonization, which kicked off the gradual consolidation of what Mills, without equivocation, calls "global white supremacy."[7]

It is worth remembering that at the end of the 1990s, with his *The Racial Contract*, Mills, inspired by Carole Pateman, made a U-turn in the tradition of contractualist theory. In *The Sexual Contract*,[8] Pateman had maintained that the contractualist theorists of the seventeenth and eighteenth centuries – Hobbes, Locke, Rousseau, and Kant, primarily – failed to mention that the social contract presupposes a sexual contract, just as the civil liberties established by the contract, which as we know are masculine privilege, presuppose patriarchal right. In her wake, Mills sought to show that the social contract also presupposes a racial contract. Just as Pateman helped us see that since the seventeenth century the contractualist theorists hid this other contract that underlies men's freedom and women's domination, Mills helps us see that the racial contract is similarly concealed, one which underlies white people's freedom and Black people's domination. As they are white men in their majority, the contractualist theorists' concealment of the real contracts that constitute white male supremacy is not surprising. That is why we had to wait for Pateman and Mills to enter the discussion for these recurrent exclusions of gender and race to be exposed.

At the beginning of the 2000s, when Carneiro was writing and defending her dissertation, Brazilian academia had scarcely heard of Mills. Only very recently – due to the attention that he has received from Black social scientists and philosophers – has he begun to attract attention. Carneiro was a pioneer in developing an analysis of the Brazilian social contract in Mills's terms, and what is more, in combining in such an original and unprecedented way Foucault's theory of apparatuses with the theory of the racial contract.

Once the racial contract – which is made among white people, imprisoning Black people in a state of nature – is the structuring element of the apparatus of raciality, the road to a real democracy is the establishment of new pacts that permit the inclusion of Black people as individuals and collectives.[9] It is important to note that throughout her trajectory, Carneiro has devoted herself to analyzing both the cultural and symbolic elements and the material aspects of the racial contract, as these are the elements that the apparatus of raciality articulates to perpetuate prohibitions. If poverty is "established as the chronic condition of Black existence,"[10] at the same time, "Support for racist ideology depends on its capacity to naturalize its conception of the Other."[11] This simultaneous attention to the field of the symbolic and that of the material leads Carneiro, in her 2003 article "Mulheres em movimento" (Women on the Move), republished in *Escritos de uma vida*, to an allegiance with Nancy Fraser and her theory of bidimensional justice, which encompasses both redistribution and recognition. The radicalization of democracy in the sense of correcting racial and gender injustices requires policies that combat not only the unequal distribution of material resources – which increased in neoliberalism – but also the lack of recognition, symbolic disregard, and both racial and gender stereotypes.

In *Dispositif of Raciality*, Carneiro deepens this diagnosis by showing that in Brazil the colonial education system is a fundamental strategic element of the apparatus of raciality,[12] since it institutes a racially hierarchical social order, simultaneously feeding Black poverty, epistemicide, and the ideal of whitening. This system is therefore at the base of the "multicides" to which Black people are subject by the multiple actions of the apparatus. This means that any democratic advance should involve the deconstruction of the colonial system of education.

It is interesting to note that by attributing this central role to education, Carneiro allies herself with a long tradition of woman philosophers – from Christine de Pizan to Mary Wollstonecraft, Angela Davis to bell hooks – for whom education is the necessary condition for concretely realizing liberty of action, autonomy of thought, and, more comprehensively, human emancipation.[13]

It's worth recalling that we are dealing with a text written in the first half of the 2000s, when Brazil was intensely discussing the Black Movement's proposal for racial quotas in public universities. And Carneiro, a key figure in this movement that culminated in the Ethnic-Racial Quota Law of 2012, spotted in the myth of racial democracy, as well as in the thesis of social apartheid, two important obstacles to its passage. For her, both needed (and still need) to be contested to construct an educational project – and, by extension, a democratic project – that is actually inclusive and universal. This happens by retelling our history and valorizing the Black struggles for emancipation as contents of "a liberatory cultural heritage,"[14] the spirit of the law 10.639/03, which established Afro-Brazilian culture and history as an obligatory subject in official school curricula.

## The Myth of Racial Democracy

The myth of racial democracy is a specific dimension of the Brazilian racial contract: by sustaining a "grand narrative" of harmony, it exercises a pacifying function on racial tensions and thus serves white hegemony.[15] Carneiro is especially interested in showing that by acknowledging the myth, an important sector of the progressive and leftist intelligentsia ends up exonerating itself from investigating "the complex mechanisms that historically determine the silence, denial, and invisibilization of the racial problematic."[16] The criticism stands.

In this way, whether consciously or not, we perpetuate the positive representation of racial mixing nourished by Sílvio Romero at the price of disguising racial violence, beginning with the colonial rape of Black and indigenous women. For Carneiro, the discourse exalting racial mixing tends to constitute itself as an instrument of whitening: it appears under the sign of diversity, when it is in fact the opposite. Brazil is not actually a country of diversity but rather of white hegemony, which reserves death, negation, and assimilation for Black people. It is necessary for the white intelligentsia to accept this fact, or it will continue to reproduce the position and the discourse of the "hegemonic I."

It is also necessary to abandon the insistence on the primacy of class oppression, which either does not consider racial oppression or relegates it to a secondary plane. Once race is a structural element in multiracial societies with a colonial past, declares Carneiro,

> The notion of social *apartheid* and the supremacy of the concept of social class championed by leftist thinkers, inheritors of historical dialectical materialism, do not account for – on the contrary, they erase or mask – the racial contradiction present in multiracial societies, considering that in such societies race/color/ethnicity (especially in Brazil) are variables that impact the very structure of classes.[17]

This is not an ideological dispute but an empirically based criticism: attention to statistics is a keynote in Carneiro's work throughout her trajectory, beginning with her pioneering study *Mulher negra* (Black Woman) in 1985.[18] By disaggregating indicators of race and gender, she showed that Black women were (and continue to be) disadvantaged in comparison to white women of all social classes, both in education and in the labor market. Based on the data obtained, she concludes two things: first, that the generalization that results from analyses that prioritize and isolate gender leads to the standardization of diverse experiences of oppression that women suffer, in detriment to race; and, second, and analogously, that the generalization that results from prioritizing social class leads to the standardization of diverse experiences of oppression that poor people suffer, in detriment to race. Both contradict the statistics that continue to show a racial hierarchy wherever you look: education, health, the labor market, the carceral system, police violence, and gender violence.

A more sophisticated and complete theory of oppression emerges from this diagnosis than those that give racial oppression secondary importance compared to class and gender. For Carneiro, as for Léila Gonzalez and Black feminist theorists of their generation – still insufficiently recognized in the field of Brazilian humanities – an understanding of the multiple oppressions in multiracial societies with colonial pasts and neoliberal presents requires attention to race, class, and gender.

## False Epistemology

There is a nexus between epistemology – a constitutive element of the apparatus of raciality in Brazil – the model of society projected by the racial contract, and the status of the Other in the Western philosophical tradition.[19] What links them is a paradigm that at once excludes Black people and kills diversity. Breaking this paradigm demands both a theoretical and a practical undertaking against the colonization that manifests, as we have seen, in the Brazilian education system,[20] as well as in an equally colonized way of doing philosophy here.

Carneiro teaches us that a practical philosophy engaged with Brazilian reality demands a critical revision to the tradition that, like Kant and Hegel (subjects of Chapter 3), strives to justify Black people's rational and moral inferiority. This tradition thus contributes to the fabrication of the Black person as a non-being and to a reiteration of the racism of Nina Rodrigues, who also detected in Black people a kind of "chronic cultural inadequacy."[21] What Carneiro is telling us is that, though we may insist, as we have done for decades in the sphere of academic philosophy, on exegeses that conceal the racism of the great minds of Western philosophical tradition, we will be intentionally or unintentionally contributing to epistemicide. We will also be contributing to what Mills called an "inverted epistemology": a pact to interpret the world incorrectly by sustaining myths and false representations about non-white people. A false, ignorant epistemology, but one stamped with the approval of so many Western philosophers. And excused by so many readers, trained in majority white academic spaces, and for that very reason, not liable to critically revise the canon, which is also white and masculine from one end to the other.

It is necessary to recognize how pioneering Carneiro is. If today, finally, Brazilian academic philosophy is beginning to open up to criticism of both the racism and the sexism of the Western philosophical canon, there was no one doing so in the early 2000s. Let it not go unnoticed that Carneiro did not find academic support to carry out this philosophical study in a field which, as majority white and male, was still acritically comfortable with resounding contempt for modern philosophy that considered women, African peoples, and the "savages" of the Americas. It will not be surprising that in Brazil, a Black woman would reveal the falseness of this epistemology.

If it weren't for the Quota Law and the democratization of our curricula and research programs precipitated by the admission of Black students to Brazilian public universities, would we be reading this *book* – which was left hidden in a thesis bank for twenty years – as a central work of Brazilian social and philosophical thought?

## For a Renewed Ethic

Criticism of the philosophical tradition does not imply, in Carneiro's case, leaping outside of philosophy, or even Western philosophy: with Foucault, she develops the concept of the apparatus of raciality; with Mills she rethinks contractualism; and appropriating a Heideggerian distinction between the ontic and the ontological, she explains racism as a reduction to the ontic, at the expense of the ontological dimension of being.

From a philosophical perspective on the construction of subjectivity, one of the strong theses of this book is that as with the production of madness and sexuality, the production and reproduction of raciality affects subjectification and has an ontological dimension, since the constitution of the standard subject depends on an Other, prohibited in their humanity and as a knowing, moral, political, or legal subject.[22] This is what Carneiro calls an ontological division, with echoes not only of Foucault but also of Isildinha Baptista Nogueira.

The ontological roots of the apparatus of raciality are explained by the fact that the most diverse practical and discursive manifestations of the apparatus ultimately depend on the dismissal of Black people's being. Or, in other terms, the construction of the (Black) Other as non-being is the foundation of the (white) Being, as the subtitle to the book says.[23] Because once it is established in subjectivity, this is the most profound dimension of the production of white hegemony in a country with a colonial and slaving past.

However, this is not Carneiro's entire theory of subjectification, which has yet another positive and ethical dimension, understood in the testimonies of leaders in the Black Movement – Edson Cardoso, Sônia Maria Pereira do Nascimento, and Fátima Oliveira, as well as the poet Arnaldo Xavier – included in Part II of the book and analyzed in Part III. These narratives are taken as the *content* of Sueli Carneiro's philosophical reflection,[24] just as Angela Davis based hers on the narrative of Frederick Douglass in *Lectures on Liberation*[25] to access an aspect of reality not captured by political philosophy in the Western tradition: Black resistance. It is a methodological innovation that seeks to correct the erasure of the concrete and real experiences of individual and collective struggle against subjugating and subjectifying methods. By taking insurgent experiences as the content for her philosophical reflection, Carneiro develops a certain phenomenology of Black resistance that signals a renewed ethic since, in the collective struggle, conditions are created such that care of the self is realized in care of the other.

Carneiro's notion of care of the self differs from Foucault's in that it is not based on ancient Greek experiences, but on other ones.[26] She goes beyond the individual and speaks of "the possibility of the construction of collective subjects freed from the processes of subjugation and subalternization,"[27] as well as the possibility of a *political* ethic, which would be realized in collective action and aims to re-signify both autonomy and emancipation. Here a field for recognition, identification, and belonging is constructed. With the other and not against the other. It is not by accident, as Edson Cardoso reminds us in his testimony, that "Brazilian society's greatest prohibition [is] on Black people getting together as such; there's a panic that for centuries has run through all of society."[28]

Thus this practical philosophy is able to move beyond the classical antagonism between theories of subjection (for example, in Foucault) and theories of emancipation (for example, in Habermas). Carneiro theorizes subjection without sacrificing agency and the concrete possibility of emancipation, and vice versa. She keeps an eye on each aspect of reality: on the power relations that subalternize and the experiences of resistance that point to their dismantling. It is true that, as in Foucault, resistance can imply a new reinsertion into the apparatus, but for Carneiro, it can also lead to profound and radical transformations, to new pacts, to the deactivation of the apparatus, to positive modes of subjectification, and, finally, to the construction of another ethical and political world. It's necessary to be political for this purpose.

It's worth noting, however, that this renewed ethic, which attributes an important and positive role to identification – and, therefore, to the contexts, particularities, and circumstances in which subjects find themselves – does not lead Carneiro to a rigorously particularist and anti-universalist philosophical position. Racism is indeed anti-universalist when it reduces Black people's being to their ontic (particular) dimension, denying them the ontological, human, and universal dimension. Curiously, she calls on the Heideggerian distinction between the ontic (which refers to particular entities) and the ontological (which concerns the being as such) to arrive at this definition of racism as a reduction to the ontic. Since race, color, culture, religion, ethnicity, are of the ontic order, enclosing the being in these particularities makes humanity itself incomplete. Or, to put it another way, the total reduction of the being to its particularities is binding. Out of this idea comes one of the most beautiful passages in the book. "In my interpretation," Carneiro says, "it is the idea of universality that emancipates the individual and allows them to express their specificity."[29] We will better understand the extent of this statement's significance in light of the 2002 text "Gênero e raça na sociedade brasileira" (Gender and Race in Brazilian Society), in which one of the most ancient philosophical questions – that of the relationship between the particular and the universal – is posed not by Heidegger but by Aimé Césaire, who once said that there are two ways to lose yourself: walled segregation in the particular or dilution in the universal. In Carneiro's words:

> The utopia we are chasing today consists of looking for a *shortcut* between a blackness that reduces the scale of humanity and a hegemonic Western universality that denies diversity. To be Black, without being only Black, to be a woman, without being only a woman, to be a Black woman, without being only a Black woman. The ultimate meaning of this struggle is to achieve equal rights and become fully human, full of possibilities and opportunities beyond the condition of race and gender.[30]

There is therefore another universalism in Carneiro, which is not substitutionalist (to use a convenient expression of the Turkish philosopher Seyla Benhabib[31]) because it does not take the experience of hegemonic groups as paradigmatic of human beings as such. A universalism allowing – instead of impeding – diversity to flourish, celebrated in "Tempo feminino" (Feminine Time) as "the greatest human heritage."[32]

## Democracy, Liberty, and Equality

To end this short postface, it's worth remembering that twenty years before the extreme right returned to power with Bolsonaro and authoritarianism returned to haunt us with all its might, Carneiro wrote:

> The women of my generation understand the meaning of the words liberty and equality in terms of the thirst that the lack of liberty and

> equality produced. It is this intense thirst that *transformed the notions of liberty and equality into the most dearly held principles of those of our generation*, because in addition to understanding that liberty and equality are *intrinsic and unnegotiable values for human beings*, we also discovered that in order to obtain them and maintain them we had to be very willing to fight and remain vigilant to defend them. This is because *liberty and equality are assets that are always being placed in danger* by authoritarian, fascist, neofascist ideologies, by different varieties of machismo, by racism and ethnic and racial discrimination, by religious fundamentalism, by neoliberalism, by globalization.[33]

This passage reveals that the diagnosis that the racial contract excludes Black people from liberty and equality, instead of leading Carneiro to discredit these ideals, leads her to affirm them as intrinsic and unnegotiable values for human beings. In the same way, the diagnosis that our rule of law excludes Black people, instead of leading her to find that law is inherently violent, makes her identify democracy as the only antidote we have against the different forms of authoritarianism present in the world. This practical philosophy is not at all susceptible to erasing the borders between dictatorship and democracy promoted by theories of the state of exception (and if they are equivalent, why bother fighting?); it also surpasses the limits of liberal and formalist models that reaffirm universal principles, but don't bother to make them real. In Carneiro's philosophy, the values of liberty and equality emerge *as principles* from the experience of the lack of liberty and equality: that is, they are not just norms, but something which one must constantly struggle to obtain, preserve, and expand.

Yara Frateschi
Professor of Ethics and Political Philosophy in the Department of Philosophy at the State University of Campinas (Unicamp) and author of *A física da política: Hobbes contra Aristóteles* (Ed. Unicamp, 2006) and *Liberdade, cidadania e ethos democrático: estudos anti-hobbesianos* (Alameda, 2021)

# Notes

## Foreword

1 Bianca Santana, *Continuo preta: A vida de Sueli Carneiro*, Companhia das Letras, 2021.
2 Juliana S. S. Bartholomeu, "Sueli Carneiro," in *Enciclopédia de Antropologia*, University of São Paulo, Department of Anthropology, 2019: http://ea.fflch.usp.br/autor/sueli-carneiro.
3 Lélia Gonzalez (1935–94) was an outspoken leader of the Black Movement in Brazil who helped found the MNU in 1978. A trained anthropologist, she also wrote extensively about the intersection of racism and sexism in Brazilian society and Latin America and authored many essays about the unique forms of oppression and inequality that Black women face in Brazilian society. Carneiro's relationship with Gonzalez is particularly important to her personal story. She often cites Gonzalez as the person who brought her to Black feminism and influenced her political and theoretical thinking. See, for example, her book on Gonzalez, *Lélia Gonzalez: Um retrato*, Zahar, 2024.
4 Santana, *Continuo preta*, p. 119.
5 The state of São Paulo organized this council in response to the call by the United Nations Council on the Status of Women to create commissions to explore women's issues in different countries.
6 Sueli Carneiro and Thereza Santos, *Mulher Negra: Política governamental e a mulher*, Livraria Nobel, 1985.
7 Geledés is a multifaceted institute focusing on social outreach, public education, public policy, and memory preservation. The organization has been recognized nationally and internationally by multiple entities,

including but not limited to the Ford Foundation, the Carlos Chagas Foundation, the Brazilian government, and the United Nations. For more information see their website: https://www.geledes.org.br/o-que-e-geledes/.

8 P. 1.

9 P. 4.

10 Sueli Carneiro, *Dispositivo de racialidade: A construção do outro como não ser como fundamento do ser*, Zahar, 2023.

11 Ann Laura Stoler, *Carnal Knowledge and Imperial Power: Race and the Intimate in Colonial Rule*, University of California Press, 2002.

12 Michel Foucault, *Discipline and Punish: The Birth of the Prison*, translated by Alan Sheridan, Pantheon, 1978.

13 Michel Foucault, *Society Must Be Defended: Lectures at the Collège de France, 1975–1976*, edited by Mauro Bertani and Alessandro Fontana, translated by David Macey, Picador, 2003.

14 P. 40.

15 P. 17.

16 Stuart Hall, "The Spectacle of the 'Other,'" in *Representation*, edited by Stuart Hall, Jessica Evans, and Sean Nixon, 2nd edition, SAGE, 2013.

17 See, for example, Carneiro's discussions of Alabama on pp. 48–9.

18 Charles W. Mills, *The Racial Contract*, Cornell University Press, 1997; Achille Mbembe, *Necropolitics*, Duke University Press, 2020.

19 Carneiro and I discuss this phenomenon in detail in my interview with her in season 2, episode 2 of the *Cite Black Women* podcast. This interview is transcribed and translated into English in "A Feminism So Complex and So Radical," in *Black Feminist Constellations: Dialogue and Translation across the Americas*, University of Texas Press, 2023, edited by myself and Lorraine Leu.

20 P. 30, original emphasis.

21 See, for example, my discussion on dialogic translation as Black feminist praxis with Lorraine Leu in our introduction to *Black Feminist Constellations*.

22 Cedric J. Robinson, *Black Marxism: The Making of the Black Radical Tradition*, revised and updated 3rd edition, University of North Carolina Press, 2020; Robin D. G. Kelley, "'But a Local Phase of a World Problem': Black History's Global Vision, 1883–1950," *The Journal of American History*, vol. 86, no. 3, 1999, pp. 1045–77; Carole Boyce Davies, "Sisters Outside: Tracing the Caribbean/Black Radical Intellectual Tradition," *small axe*, vol. 13, no. 1, 2009, pp. 217–29.

## Translator's Note

1 Michel Foucault, "Orders of Discourse," translated by Rupert Swyer, *Social Science Information*, vol. 10, no. 2, 1971, pp. 7–30.
2 P. 39.
3 Michel Foucault, *Society Must Be Defended: Lectures at the Collège de France, 1975–1976*, edited by Mauro Bertani and Alessandro Fontana, translated by David Macey, Picador, 2003, pp. 239–40.

## Prologue: Emancipation For All

1 Thomas S. Kuhn, *The Structure of Scientific Revolutions*, University of Chicago Press, 50th anniversary edition, 2012, pp. 46–7.
2 Roseli Fischmann, "Estratégias de superação da discriminação étnica e religiosa no Brasil," in *Direitos humanos no século XXI*, edited by Paulo Sérgio Pinheiro and Samuel Pinheiro Guimarães, IPRI, 1998, pp. 959–85.
3 *Translator's note.* Carneiro here and elsewhere draws on the social and lexical distinction among racial categories of *preto* (Black; sometimes used to distinguish from *pardo* and sometimes as a racial epithet), *pardo* (usually referring to people with lighter skin or of mixed racial heritage), and *negro* (people of African descent). As she notes, the social category of *negro* came to encompass other racial categories for people of African descent as an explicit recognition of shared experiences of racialization and discrimination. Any of these terms might be translated into English as "Black," reflecting the differing schemes of racialization in operation in the English-speaking world and in Brazil. I include the Portuguese terms to clarify when relevant.

## Introduction: Being and Other

1 Michel Foucault, *Society Must Be Defended: Lectures at the Collège de France, 1975–1976*, edited by Mauro Bertani and Alessandro Fontana, translated by David Macey, Picador, 2003, p. 256.
2 Michel Foucault and Gilles Deleuze, "Intellectuals and Power," in *Language, Counter-Memory, Practice: Selected Essays and Interviews by Michel Foucault*, edited by Donald Bouchard, Cornell University Press, 1977, p. 206.
3 Thomas S. Kuhn, *The Structure of Scientific Revolutions*, 50th anniversary edition, University of Chicago Press, 2012.
4 "First and foremost, I must clarify that I conceptualize 'paradigms of

the Other' on the basis of Thomas Kuhn and Emmanuel Levinas. The term 'paradigm' as it is used by Kuhn has a heuristic richness that is irreplaceable for our work. Analyzing the organization of the scientific world, Kuhn emphasizes that 'Scientists [. . .] never learn concepts, laws, and theories in the abstract and by themselves. Instead, these intellectual tools are from the start encountered in a historically and pedagogically prior unit that displays them with and through their applications' [ibid., pp. 46–7]. Establishing a parallel between the organization of scientific thought and the organization of everyday thought, I propose a hypothesis according to which the manifestations of prejudice, discrimination, and stigma have a 'historically and pedagogically prior unit,' from which would come an application. It would be, therefore, a modality of the 'paradigm of common sense,' and upon being articulated, would translate into expectations in terms of the behavior of the Other, configuring what I will call 'DPS syndrome,' frequently opening the way to the objective conditions that can confirm it, as in the processes of a 'self-fulfilling prophecy'" (Roseli Fischmann, "Estratégias de superação da discriminação étnica e religiosa no Brasil," in *Direitos humanos no século XXI*, edited by Paulo Sérgio Pinheiro and Samuel Pinheiro Guimarães, IPRI, 1998, pp. 973–4).

5 David Brion Davis, *The Problem of Slavery in Western Culture*, Cornell University Press, 1966, p. 90.

6 Ibid.

7 Ibid.

8 Martin Heidegger, *Being and Time: A Translation of Sein und Zeit*, translated by Joan Stambaugh, SUNY Press, 1996.

9 *Translator's note*. See Prologue n. 3 on uses of *preto* and *pardo* vs. *negro*. I include the Portuguese terms to clarify when relevant.

10 Antônio Sérgio Guimarães, *Racismo e anti-racismo no Brasil*, Editora 34/Fundação de Apoio à Universidade de São Paulo, 1999, p. 11.

11 Ibid.

12 Carlos Alfredo Hasenbalg, *Race Relations in Post-Abolition Brazil: The Smooth Preservation of Racial Inequalities*, dissertation, University of California, Berkeley, 1978, p. 232.

13 "The aim of the inquiries that will follow is to move less toward a 'theory' of power than toward an 'analytics' of power: that is, toward a definition of the specific domain formed by relations of power, and toward a determination of the instruments that will make possible its analysis" (Michel Foucault, *The History of Sexuality. Volume 1: An Introduction*, translated by Robert Hurley, Pantheon, 1978, p. 82).

14 *Translator's note*. Note that here Carneiro is playing with the close etymological relationship between *domínio* (domain, field) and *dominar* (both "to dominate" and "to master").

15 Foucault, *The History of Sexuality. Volume 1*, p. 98.

16 Caution is necessary regarding the legitimacy of secondary research sources. In debates about race relations, we can find various public pronouncements in the form of interviews or articles in newspapers and journals written by authors who are not always experts on the topic, but whose public authority, from an academic or intellectual point of view, turns them into opinion-makers with a significant impact on the public sphere. The debate on race as framed to society, especially with the emergence of policies of affirmative action and, particularly, racial quotas for the racial democratization of university access, invites various intellectuals to publicly weigh in, whether or not they are specialists on the topic of racial relations, even when they have not produced specific research on affirmative action and what is currently its most controversial dimension, quotas. While different, those public opinions (whether academically expert or not) will be dealt with on an equal footing.
17 Foucault and Deleuze, "Intellectuals and Power," p. 209.

## Chapter 1 On the Apparatus

1 Michel Foucault, "The Confession of the Flesh," in *Power/Knowledge*, edited and translated by Colin Gordon, Vintage, 1980, p. 194.
2 Ibid.
3 Ibid., pp. 194–5.
4 Ibid., p. 195.
5 Ibid.
6 Ibid., p. 196.
7 Michel Foucault, "Power and Sex," translated by David Parent, in *Politics, Philosophy, Culture: Interviews and Other Writings, 1977–1984*, edited by Lawrence Kritzman, Routledge, 1988, p. 111.
8 Michel Foucault, *The History of Sexuality. Volume 1: An Introduction*, translated by Robert Hurley, Pantheon, 1978, p. 121.
9 Ibid., p. 123.
10 Ibid.
11 Ibid.
12 Isildinha Baptista Nogueira, *Significações do corpo negro*, PhD thesis, IPUSP-USP, 1998, pp. 101–2.
13 Ibid., p. 42.
14 As Isildinha Baptista Nogueira emphasizes: "the physical attributes that characterize Black people, and particularly skin color, express the attributes that historically associate these physical characteristics with moral and/or intellectual attributes that correspond, on the spectrum of social typification, to that which is established in the realm of *the distant*, that is, that which expresses what is outside the set of values in which individuals recognize themselves. In this network, *Black* and

*white* are constituted as extremes, units of representation that correspond to the *distant* – the object of a gesture of remoteness – and the *proximate*, the object of a gesture of affiliation" (ibid., p. 44, original emphasis).

15 Ibid., p. 41.

16 As Foucault says in *The History of Sexuality. Volume 1*, this new class "which in the eighteenth century became hegemonic [. . .] provided itself with a body to be cared for, protected, cultivated, and preserved from the many dangers and contacts, to be isolated from others so that it would retain its differential value; and this, by equipping itself with – among other resources – a technology of sex" (p. 123).

17 "Let us not picture the bourgeoisie symbolically castrating itself the better to refuse others the right to have a sex and make use of it as they please. This class must be seen rather as being occupied, from the mid-eighteenth century on, with creating its own sexuality and forming a specific body based on it, a 'class' body with its health, hygiene, descent, and race: the autosexualization of its body, the incarnation of sex in its body, the endogamy of sex and the body. There were doubtless many reasons for this" (ibid., p. 124).

18 *Translator's note.* Foucault's terms *régularisation* (regularization) and *régulation* (regulation) are both, at times, translated as *regulamentação* in Portuguese.

19 That said, in their essay written as editors of Foucault's book *Society Must Be Defended: Lectures at the Collège de France, 1975–1976* (translated by David Macey, Picador, 2003), Alessandro Fontana and Mauro Bertani identify the articulation of racism with sexuality with the topic of *degeneration*, especially through the way in which psychiatry appropriates it: "As for racism, this was a theme that appeared and was dealt with in the seminars and lectures on psychiatry, punishment, the abnormals, and all the knowledges and practices associated with the medical theory of 'degeneracy,' the forensic theory of eugenicism and social Darwinism, and the penal theory of 'social defense,' which in the nineteenth century developed techniques for identifying, isolating, and normalizing 'dangerous' individuals: the early dawn of ethnic cleansings and labor camps (as Foucault himself reminds us, at the end of the nineteenth century, the French criminologist J. Léveillé advised his Russian colleagues to build labor camps in Siberia when he attended an international penitentiary conference held in St. Peterburg). A new racism was born when 'knowledge of heredity' – to which Foucault planned to devote his future research, as he explains in his candidacy presentation to the Collège de France – was combined with the psychiatric theory of degeneracy. Addressing his audience in the last (19 March 1975) of the 1974–75 course of lectures on 'The Abnormals,' Foucault said: 'You see how psychiatry can use this notion of degeneracy, these

analyses of heredity to establish a connection with, or rather give rise to a racism.' He added that Nazism had simply linked, in its turn, this new racism to the ethnic racism that was endemic in the nineteenth century, when it was used to provide an internal social defense against the abnormals" (pp. 285–6).

20 We learn with Foucault that "domination [. . .] is fixed, throughout its history, in rituals, in meticulous procedures that impose rights and obligations. It establishes marks of its power and engraves memories on things and even within bodies. It makes itself accountable for debts and gives rise to the universe of rules, which is by no means designed to temper violences, but rather to satisfy it" (Michel Foucault, "Nietzsche, Genealogy, History," in *Language, Counter-Memory, Practice: Selected Essays and Interviews by Michel Foucault*, edited by Donald Bouchard, translated by Donald Bouchard and Sherry Simon, Cornell University Press, 1977, p. 150).

21 Charles W. Mills, *The Racial Contract*, Cornell University Press, 1997, p. 20.

22 Ibid., p. 1.

23 Ibid.

24 Ibid., p. 3.

25 Ibid.

26 Ibid.

27 Ibid., pp. 13–14.

28 Ibid., pp. 4–5.

29 Ibid., p. 5.

30 Ibid., p. 4, original emphasis.

31 Ibid., p. 20.

32 Mills uses a periodization put forth by Anthony Pagden, according to which European imperialism is divided into two phases: one which corresponds to the colonization of the Americas, from 1492 to 1830, and another to the occupation of Asia, Africa, and the Pacific, which would go from 1790 to the post-World War II era and the processes of decolonization. The two periods represent two distinct moments of domination, which are, nonetheless, interdependent and maintain race as a common denominator and one which quickly comes to signify respective global positions of superiority and inferiority, of privilege and subordination.

33 Mills, *The Racial Contract*, pp. 20–1.

34 Hannah Arendt, *The Origins of Totalitarianism*, 2nd edition, Meridian Books, Inc., 1958, p. 221.

35 Ibid., p. 161.

36 Foucault, *Society Must Be Defended*.

37 We draw on Coulouris here because of her Foucauldian approach to gender relations. There is a long list of important theoretical works in this area (this author, as a Black feminist, has contributed to it), but we highlight Coulouris's Foucauldian analysis in particular because it helps

deduce the concept of an "apparatus of raciality" from an "apparatus of sexuality."

38 Daniella Georges Coulouris, "Ideologia, dominação e discurso de gênero: Reflexões possíveis sobre a discriminação da vítima em processos judiciais de estupro," *Mneme: Revista de Humanidades*, vol. 5, no. 11, 2010, p. 115.

39 "As a methodological instrument, [gender] seeks to make the comprehension of unequal social relations between men and women possible. As discursive practice, much of the research on this topic works to modify social relations that produce such undesirable outcomes as rape, child sexual abuse, and discrimination against women in families, school, workplaces, and the justice system" (ibid., p. 102).

40 Ibid., pp. 102–3.

41 See the interview with Fátima Oliveira in Chapter 7 of this book, which indicates that the healthcare field for Black populations was constructed by Black activism.

42 Ari Lima, "A legitimação do intelectual negro no meio acadêmico brasileiro: Negação de inferioridade, confronto ou assimilação intelectual?" *Revista Afro-Ásia*, no. 25–6, 2001, p. 284.

43 *Translator's note.* Alberto Guerreiro Ramos (1915–82): Brazilian sociologist of race and race relations. Luiz Gama (1830–82): abolitionist lawyer and poet. Abdias Nascimento (1914–2011): Brazilian playwright, activist, poet, and politician.

44 Coulouris, "Ideologia, dominação e discurso de gênero," p. 103.

45 Lima, "A legitimação do intelectual negro no meio acadêmico brasileiro," p. 284.

46 Coulouris, "Ideologia, dominação e discurso de gênero," p. 104

47 Kabengele Munanga, "Prefácio," in *Cem anos de bibliografia sobre o negro no Brasil*, vol. II, Fundação Cultural Palmares, 2000, pp. 9–10.

48 Mills, *The Racial Contract*, p. 2.

49 Ibid.

50 Ângela Figueiredo and Osmundo de Araújo Pinho, "Ideias fora de lugar e o lugar do negro," *Estudos Afro-Asiáticos*, vol. 24, no. 1, 2002, pp. 198, 206.

51 In *A invenção do ser negro: Um percurso das ideias que naturalizaram a inferioridade dos negros* (The Invention of the Black Being: A Journey through the Ideas that Naturalized Black Inferiority), Gislene Aparecida dos Santos undertakes an archeology of knowledge by illustrating raciality, thus establishing the ruptures and continuities that have developed about the idea of race since the eighteenth and nineteenth centuries, and the repercussions of these discourses for the Brazilian intelligentsia. I will return to this book in Chapter 4.

52 Muniz Sodré, *Claros e escuros: Identidade, povo e mídia no Brasil*, Vozes, 1999, p. 10.

53 Roberto Machado, "Introdução: Por uma genealogia do poder," in

Michel Foucault, *Microfísica do poder*, edited by Roberto Machado, Edições Graal, 2004, p. xxi.

54 And yet, if Nina Rodrigues to Oliveira Vianna, passing through Paulo Prado and Euclides da Cunha, among others, clearly deny that Black people are capable of sustaining the construction of a civilizing process, only one contribution is left for them before their desirable and inevitable extinction, which is that of serving as the object of knowledge.

55 *Translator's note.* Wilhelm Bleek (1827–75): a German linguist who documented Southern African languages.

56 *Translator's note. Senzala:* slave quarters.

57 Emphasis added.

58 *Translator's note. Moçambiques, benguelas, monjolos, congos, cabindas, caçangas*: ethnic and geographic identifiers among the enslaved.

59 Sílvio Romero quoted in Raymundo Nina Rodrigues, *Os africanos no Brasil*, Centro Edelstein de Pesquisas Sociais, 2010, p. 7, original emphasis except as noted above.

60 Dante Moreira Leite, *O caráter nacional brasileiro*, Pioneira, 1983.

61 "Como Diógenes: Comissão da Lei Áurea procura um negro," *Veja*, no. 835, September 5, 1984, p. 27.

62 Foucault, *The History of Sexuality. Volume I*, p. 98. [*Translator's note.* There is a slight discrepancy between the passage as Carneiro quotes it and as it appears in the Brazilian edition (Graal, 1988) that she cites. Her citation reads "*mecanismos de sujeição/opressão e subordinação*" while the Graal edition reads "*mecanismos de proibição.*" Both the Portuguese and the English translations (mechanisms of prohibition) closely follow the French (*méchanismes de prohibition*), thus we have quoted the English translation as published.]

63 Michel Foucault, "Orders of Discourse," translated by Rupert Swyer, *Social Science Information*, vol. 10, no. 2, 1971, p. 9, translation modified.

64 Ibid., p. 12.

65 Jessé Souza, "Multiculturalismo, racismo e democracia: Por que comparar Brasil e Estados Unidos?," in *Anais do Seminário Internacional Multiculturalismo e Racismo: O papel da ação afirmativa nos estados democráticos contemporâneos*, edited by Jessé Souza, Ministério da Justiça/Secretaria Nacional de Direitos Humanos, 1997, p. 31, original emphasis.

66 Ibid., p. 32.

67 Ibid., p. 34.

68 It seems that this is a specific aspect of our racial contract, epistemologically based, from Charles W. Mills's perspective, in the agreement on the rules of cognition that lead us to deny the situation of racial intolerance of Black people, though there are evident traces in the victims that it leaves along the way. We deal with this topic in more detail in Chapter 3.

69 Fernando Henrique Cardoso, "Entrevista," in *O presidente segundo*

*o sociólogo, a nódoa da escravidão*, interview by Roberto Toledo de Pompeu, Companhia das Letras, 1998, p. 13.

70 Ibid., p. 14.

71 Ibid.

72 Sueli Carneiro, "Raça, classe e identidade nacional," *Revista Thoth*, no. 2, Brasília, Informe de distribuição restrita do Senador Abdias Nascimento, Secretaria Especial de Editoração e Publicação do Senado Federal, 1997, p. 222.

73 Souza, "Multiculturalismo, racismo e democracia," p. 31.

74 Sílvio Romero, *História da Litteratura Brasileira*, 2nd edition, H. Garnier, 1902, pp. 4, 75. [*Translator's note.* There is a slight discrepancy between the source Carneiro cites and Romero's own text; for clarity, I have cited and translated directly from Romero here.]

75 *Translator's note. Correio Braziliense* (Braziliense Courrier): a Brasília-based newspaper.

76 Sueli Carneiro, "Miscigenação," *Correio Braziliense*, opinion, August 18, 2000.

77 Genetic research tells us that 61% of those who suppose themselves to be white in Brazilian society have the mark of a Black or indigenous female ancestor in their DNA, respectively, 28% and 33%. See Marcelo Leite, "Retrato molecular do Brasil," *Folha da São Paolo*, March 26, 2000.

78 *Translator's note. Caboclo* and *mameluco*: words used for people of mixed white and indigenous heritage. *Cafuzo*: used for a person of mixed Black and indigenous heritage. IBGE: Instituto Brasileiro de Geografia e Estatística (Brazilian Institute of Geography and Statistics). *Pardo*: term used broadly for people of color in Brazil.

79 For more on this topic, see Carlos Halsenbalg, *Discriminação e desigualdades raciais no Brasil*, Graal, 1979.

80 Kabengele Munanga, *Rediscutindo a mestiçagem do Brasil*, thesis to achieve the rank of *Livre-docente* in Anthropology, School of Philosophy, Letters, and Humanities, University of São Paulo, 1997.

81 Elisa Larkin do Nascimento, in *Sortilégio da cor: Identidade, raça e gênero no Brasil* (Summus, 2003), calls the inconclusive whiteness that describes the majority of white Brazilians "virtual whiteness." In Brazil, there is a nostalgia for a whiteness that is never fulfilled, a whiteness that is never fully realized except virtually. A depressed whiteness and a denied or rejected blackness.

82 Otávio Frias Filho, "Sociologia das loiras," *Folha de São Paulo*, December 9, 1999.

83 Ibid.

84 Sueli Carneiro, "Golpes de Caneta," *Correio Braziliense*, April 6, 2000.

85 By attempting to interpret the myth of racial democracy in light of religious tradition, also of undeniable importance in our cultural character, one could deduce that religion, among other elements, offers

a possible way to explain the model of racial hierarchy that appears in the myth. This does not alter the racialization of social hierarchy by eliminating conflict through converting it to tolerance. According to Jessé Souza, there is an interesting rapprochement between the "'elective democratic affinity' for the basic value of tolerance espoused by political liberalism and the hierarchical principle of the Church, which welcomes and guarantees a place for all" ("Multiculturalismo, racismo e democracia," p. 34). He adds: "the Church accepts and receives all individuals exactly as they are, establishing a hierarchy between them in accordance with the degree of spirituality and virtue that is possible for each person through Christian life. The concept of the Church includes the complementary notions of hierarchy and elitism" (ibid., p. 33). This architecture recognizes the cultural and racial supremacy of white and Western people and reiterates the lesser humanity that results in a subordinate position, through the necessity for permanent vigilance and training, since "social groups are fragile and need constant energy to keep functioning" (ibid.). As we have seen, for Western philosophers as much as Brazilian intellectuals, what distinguishes the character of Black people from other racial groups is a lack of the capacity for self-control. In his analysis of the myth of racial democracy, Contardo Calligaris will say that "the myth of racial democracy is found in a unilateral and white sense of comfort in interracial relations. This comfort is not an invention. It in fact exists: it is the effect of an uncontested dominant position. When I say uncontested regarding Brazilian society, I mean to say that it is not only an actual dominant position – more wealth, more power. It is more than that. It is an actual dominant position, but it is considered a position of right, that is, as an effect not of wealth but of a kind of caste hierarchy" (Contardo Calligaris, "Notas sobre os desafios do Brasil," in *Anais do Seminário Internacional Multiculturalismo e Racismo: O papel da ação afirmativa nos estados democráticos contemporâneos*, edited by Jessé Souza, Minstério da Justiça/Secretaria Nacional de Direitos Humanos, 1997, pp. 243–4).

86 *Translator's note*. Black Movement: Movimento Negro; a series of twentieth-century Black activist movements.

87 Souza, "Multiculturalismo, racismo e democracia," p. 34.

88 Ibid.

89 Ibid., pp. 31–2

90 Ibid., pp. 31.

91 Ibid., p. 32.

92 Ibid.

93 *Translator's note*. *Casa-Grande & Senzala* (1933) is the Portuguese title of Gilberto Freyre's canonical work analyzing Brazilian patriarchal society. *Casa-Grande* refers to the master's house, while *Senzala* is the word for slave quarters. The English translation uses the title

*The Masters and the Slaves: A Study in the Development of Brazilian Civilization* (translated by Samuel Putnam, Knopf, 1946); however, I keep the Portuguese title here for its importance to Carneiro's discussion of architecture.

94 *Translator's note*. *Quilombo*: community of fugitives from slavery. *Maloca*: community building or long house in indigenous communities in the Amazon; sometimes used as slang for a makeshift dwelling.

95 Luís Mir, *Guerra civil: Estado e trauma*, Geração Editorial, 2004, p. 71.

## Chapter 2 Biopower: Blackness under the Sign of Death

1 Michel Foucault, *Society Must Be Defended: Lectures at the Collège de France, 1975–1976*, edited by Mauro Bertani and Alessandro Fontana, translated by David Macey, Picador, 2003, p. 240.

2 Ibid., pp. 240–1.

3 Ibid., p. 247.

4 Ibid., p. 243.

5 Ibid., p. 249.

6 Ibid., pp. 242–3, emphasis added.

7 Ibid., p. 245.

8 As Foucault says, sexuality becomes a field of strategic importance in the nineteenth century for a variety of reasons, but "for these reasons in particular. On the one hand, sexuality, being an eminently corporeal mode of behavior, is a matter for individualizing disciplinary controls that take the form of permanent surveillance (and the famous controls that were, from the late eighteenth to the twentieth century, placed both at home and at school on children who masturbated represent precisely this aspect of the disciplinary control of sexuality). But because it also has procreative effects, sexuality is also inscribed, takes effect, in broad biological processes that concern not the bodies of individuals but the element, the multiple unity of the population. Sexuality exists at the point where body and population meet. And so it is a matter of discipline, but also a matter for regularization" (ibid., pp. 250–1).

9 Ibid., p. 253.

10 Ibid., p. 254.

11 Ibid., p. 255.

12 Ibid., original emphasis.

13 Ibid., p. 256.

14 Ibid.

15 Ibid., p. 255.

16 Ibid.

17 Michel Foucault, *The History of Sexuality. Volume 1: An Introduction*, translated by Robert Hurley, Pantheon, 1978, pp. 140–1.

18 In her doctoral dissertation on the relation between whiteness and power in public and private Brazilian businesses, Maria Aparecida Silva Bento uses the term "narcissistic pacts" for the way in which generally white employers prefer to choose white people for the best positions in the labor market (Maria Aparecida Silva Bento, *Pactos narcísicos no racismo: Branquitude e poder nas organizações empresariais e no poder público*, IPUSP-USP, 2002).
19 Foucault, *Society Must Be Defended*, p. 240.
20 For insight into this thesis, see Luís Mir's exhaustive study in *Guerra civil: Estado e trauma*, Geração Editorial, 2004.
21 Estela Maria Garcia de Pinho da Cunha, "Diferenciais na mortalidade de menores de um ano segundo raça: Novas constatações," *Encontro Nacional de Estudos Populacionais da ABEP*, 1998, p. 1776.
22 Audre Lorde, *A Burst of Light: Essays*, Firebrand Books, 1988, p. 60.
23 L. Alaerte Martins, *Mulheres negras e mortalidade materna no estado do Paraná, de 1993–1998*, DENSP-UEPG, master's thesis, 2000.
24 The data the study found are: (a) use of pain relief for childbirth: just 5.1% of white women did not receive anesthesia, versus 11.1% of Black women; (b) fetal heart monitoring: 97.6% of white women had fetal heart monitoring in all visits, versus 95.9% of Black women; (c) measuring the size of the uterus: 85.4% of white women responded that it had occurred, versus 91.9% of Black women; (d) responsiveness to concerns during prenatal visits: 73.1% of white women received information about signs of labor and 83.2% about appropriate nutrition during pregnancy, versus just, respectively, 62.5% and 73.4% of Black women; (e) permission to have a companion present before and during childbirth: 46.2% of white women could have someone present, versus just 27% of Black women.
25 Sabrina Petry, "Até na hora do parto a negra é discriminada," *Folha de São Paulo*, Cotidiano, May 26, 2002.
26 Ibid.
27 Ibid.
28 Fátima Oliveira, "O racismo mata, às escâncaras, todo dia," *O tempo*, April 10, 2002.
29 Ibid.
30 "Grávida e vítima de racismo em hospital," *Hoje em dia*, April 16, 2005.
31 Ibid.
32 Fátima Oliveira, *Saúde da população negra: Brasil, ano 2001*, Organização Pan-Americana de Saúde, 2002, p. 119.
33 Vera Cristina de Souza, *Mulher negra e miomas: Uma incursão na área de saúde, raça/etnia*, MA, PUC-SP, 1995, and *Sob o peso dos temores: Mulheres negras, miomas uterinos e histerectomia*, PhD, PUC-SP, 2002.
34 Fátima Oliveira, *Oficinas mulher negra e saúde*, Mazza Edições, 1998.

35 *Translator's note*. At that time, 8,000R$ would have been approximately $2,260.
36 *Translator's note*. See Prologue n. 3 on the use of *preto* and *pardo* (feminine forms *preta* and *parda*). As noted, *negro/a*, translated here as "Black" and used to encompass designations of *preto* and *pardo*, is Carneiro's preferred term for racialities associated with African descent to recognize a shared experience of discrimination.
37 SUS: Brazil's public health system.
38 De Souza, *Sob o peso dos temores*.
39 José Correia Leite and Cuti, . . . *E disse o velho militante José Correia Leite*, Secretaria Municipal de Cultura, 1992, p. 82.
40 *Translator's note*. Philippine Ordinances: the legal code that took effect in 1603 under King Phillip II of Portugal. It governed Brazil's legal system until well after independence in 1822.
41 *Translator's note*. *Roda* (literally, "wheel"): in capoeira, when practitioners form a circle, often playing music and singing, while two people come to the center to engage.
42 Lúcio Ronaldo Pereira Ribeiro, "Vadiagem," *Âmbito jurídico*, February 28, 2000, original emphasis: https://ambitojuridico.com.br/vadiagem/.
43 Ibid.
44 Ibid.
45 Ibid.
46 Ibid.
47 *Translator's note*. *Cafuzo*: historically used for people of mixed Black and indigenous heritage. *Mameluco*: historically, people of mixed white and indigenous heritage.
48 Ribeiro, "Vadiagem."
49 Ibid.
50 Fernando Henrique Cardoso, "Entrevista," in *O presidente segundo o sociólogo, a nódoa da escravidão*, interview by Roberto Toledo de Pompeu, Companhia das Letras, 1998, p. 15.
51 Gláucio Soares and Doriam Borges, "A cor da morte," *Ciência Hoje*, vol. 35, no. 209, October 2004, pp. 26–31.
52 Julio Jacobo Weiselfisz, *Mapa da violência IV: Os jovens do Brasil*, UNESCO, 2004: https://dspace.mj.gov.br/bitstream/1/10005/7/ue000080.pdf.
53 Foucault, *Society Must Be Defended*, p. 240.
54 Silvia Ramos and Leonarda Musumeci, *Elemento suspeito: Abordagem policial e estereótipos na cidade do Rio de Janeiro*, Civilização Brasileira, 2005.
55 This condition of suspicion that weighs on marginalized populations, notably Black populations, has given rise to studies like Ramos and Musumeci's *Elemento suspeito*. This study focuses on police checkpoints, or *blitzes*, a routine police activity carried out on the population by police. The study sought, on the one hand, to identify "the quality

and quantity of these experiences among different social segments" and, on the other, to "understand how they affect perceptions and opinions of police work" (ibid., p. 15). Among the conclusions are the persistence of mechanisms and relationships between the police and the Black population that date from a bygone era: that is, from the time the enslaved ceased to be enslaved and became the majority of delinquents.

56 James Cavallaro, *Police Brutality in Urban Brazil*, Human Rights Watch/Americas, 1997, p. 28. [*Translator's note*. The first sentence cited is drawn from Cavallaro's report. The second sentence is not found in the English version of the report we have been able to access; we leave it here as cited by Carneiro for consistency with her text.]

57 Sueli Carneiro, "O negro errado," *Correio Braziliense*, February 14, 2004, p. 19.

58 Ibid.

59 Sérgio Adorno's statement applies here when he refers to "the fabrication of life and the living as well as the fabrication of something monstrous, the possibility of unrestrainedly eliminating it through the dissemination of a virus, chemical weapons, war with no moral interdiction against 'the other races.' Etymologically, 'cide' is defined as 'the action of someone who kills or its results, [. . .] to bring someone down, to sacrifice'" (*Dicionário Houaiss*, Objetiva, 2001, p. 714).

60 Foucault, *Society Must Be Defended*, p. 258.

61 As Luís Mir states, restrictions on Black people comprising interethnic cooperation gives rise to "the institutionalization of a private club of ethnic groups with unclear rules of access, but with some non-negotiable conditions: culture, income, education and professional training, defined social and political groups. (Universal) cooperation and (interethnic) integration are annulled through European tribalism, with eugenic connotations. In the area of justice and internal security, there has never been any possibility for structures for interethnic cooperation, since these instruments were designed and built to be the engines of a process of ethnic and social selection" (Mir, *Guerra civil*, p. 71).

## Chapter 3 Epistemicide

1 Boaventura de Sousa Santos, *Pela mão de Alice: O social e o político na pós-modernidade*, Cortez, 1995, p. 328.

2 Ibid.

3 Immanuel Kant, *Immanuel Kant: Observations on the Feeling of the Beautiful and the Sublime and Other Writings*, edited and translated by Patrick R. Frierson and Paul Guyer, Cambridge University Press, 2011, pp. 58–9, emphasis added.

4 Thomas McCarthy, "On the Way to a World Republic? Kant on Race and Development," in *Politik, Moral und Religion – Gegensätze und*

*Ergänzungen*, edited by Lothar R. Waas, Duncker & Humblot GmbH, 2004, pp. 229–30.

5 Georg Wilhelm Friedrich Hegel, *Lectures on the Philosophy of World History: Introduction, Reason in History*, edited by Johannes Hoffmeister, translated by H. B. Nisbet, Cambridge University Press, 1975, p. 177, emphasis added.

6 Ibid., p. 184.

7 Ibid.

8 Charles W. Mills, *The Racial Contract*, Cornell University Press, 1997, p. 11.

9 Ibid., p. 17.

10 Ibid., p. 18.

11 Ibid., original emphasis.

12 Ibid., pp. 18–19, original emphasis.

13 Santos, *Pela mão de Alice*, p. 331.

14 Ibid., p. 329.

15 Roseli Fischmann, "Ensino religioso em escolas públicas: Subsídios para o estudo da identidade nacional e o direito do outro," in *Formação do educador, dever do estado, tarefa da universidade*, edited by Maria Aparecida Viggiani Bicudo and Celestino Alves da Silva Júnior, Unesp, 1996.

16 *Translator's note.* Sebastião José de Carvalho e Mello, Marquês de Pombal, was a reform-minded minister and *de facto* ruler of Portugal under King José I between 1750 and 1777 who oversaw the expulsion of the Jesuits from the Portuguese Empire in 1759.

17 *Translator's note.* Minas Gerais Conspiracy: an unsuccessful separatist movement in Minas Gerais, Brazil, in 1789.

18 *Translator's note.* Carneiro footnotes sociologist Fernando Azevedo, but Azevedo does not appear in the bibliography. Azevedo makes similar arguments to those Carneiro synthesizes in *A Cultura Brasileira: Introdução ao estudo da cultura no Brasil*, 7th edition, Edusp, 2010.

19 Cited in J. E. Martins Terra, *O negro e a igreja*, Loyola, 1984, p. 67.

20 Ibid.

21 "The truly humanistic consequences of Jesuit teaching in Brazil, beyond perhaps being less effective than is generally supposed, were thus indirect, and in great measure undesired. But in Brazilian culture's original nature there is, if not a religious character, at least a teleological one, and with all certainty a Trentine one (which would have profound repercussions over time, up to the nineteenth and twentieth centuries). Latin began to be taught in the colony at the same moment when Latin ceased to be the language of literature and culture [. . .] the Jesuits introduced the first books to the colony, but books of a special nature and with a restricted reach" (Wilson Martins, *História da inteligência brasileira*, Cultrix, 1977, pp. 14–15).

22 Roseli Fischmann, "Educação, democracia e a questão dos valores

culturais," in *Estratégias e políticas de combate à discriminação racial*, edited by Kabengele Munanga, Edusp, Estação Ciência, 1996, pp. 184–5.

23 *Translator's note*. Raymundo Nina Rodrigues (1862–1906): doctor and criminal anthropologist who studied Black culture in Brazil and promoted racialism.

24 Raymundo Nina Rodrigues, *Os africanos no Brasil*, Centro Edelstein de Pesquisas Sociais, 2010, p. 289.

25 Ibid., p. 291.

26 Ibid., p. 293.

27 Ibid. [*Translator's note*. Rodrigues cites *La questione dei negri: Nella storia e nella società nord-americana* (1898) by Italian historian Gennaro Mondaini (1874–1948).]

28 Rodrigues, *Os africanos no Brasil*, pp. 293–4, emphasis added. [*Translator's note*. Rodrigues cites British explorer Henry Morton Stanley (1841–1904), *The Autobiography of Sir Henry Morton Stanley*, edited by Dorothy Stanley, The Musson Book Company; Sampson Low, Marston and Co., 1909, p. 377; and French anthropologist Charles-Jean-Marie Letourneau (1831–1902), *Sociology Based upon Ethnography*, translated by Henry M. Trollope, Chapman and Hall, 1893, p. 555.]

29 Rodrigues, *Os africanos no Brasil*, p. 294. [*Translator's note*. Mondaini quotes Letourneau, *Science et Matérialisme*, C. Reinwald, 1879, p. 298.]

30 Ari Lima, "A legitimação do intelectual negro no meio acadêmico brasileiro: Negação de inferioridade, confronto ou assimilação intelectual?" *Revista Afro-Ásia*, 2001, p. 281.

31 *Translator's note*. Júlio Mesquita Filho (1892–1969), Brazilian journalist.

32 *Translator's note*. 1888: the date of the abolition of slavery in Brazil.

33 Júlio Mesquita Filho, "Descompasso entre as idéias e a realidade sócio-cultural," *O Estado de São Paulo*, National, April 20, 1977, p. 6.

34 *Translator's note*. Luiz Gama (1830–82): abolitionist lawyer and poet. The Rebouças brothers, André (1838–98) and Antônio (1839–74): engineers and abolitionists. Teodoro Sampaio (1855–1937): mathematician and engineer. Machado de Assis (1839–1908): Brazil's most distinguished nineteenth-century writer. Juliano Moreira (1872–1933): psychiatrist. Mário de Andrade (1893–1945): modernist poet. João da Cruz e Sousa (1861–98): Symbolist poet. Lima Barreto (1881–1922): twentieth-century novelist.

35 *Translator's note*. Carneiro cites the same editorial by Mesquita Filho here; however, the full citation is not included in the bibliography. The other two quotes by Mesquita Filho appear in a dossier of his work reprinted in 1977, eight years after his death, by the newspaper he owned, *O Estado de São Paulo*. However, this quote is not part of the

column in the dossier. I presume the column cited in 1977 is incomplete, but I have not had access the original.

36 Mesquita Filho, "Descompasso entre as idéias e a realidade sócio-cultural."

37 Fischmann, "Educação, democracia e a questão dos valores culturais," pp. 184–5.

38 José Correia Leite and Cuti, . . . *E disse o velho militante José Correia Leite*, Secretaria Municipal de Cultura, 1992, p. 26.

39 *Translator's note.* Frente Negra Brasileira: Brazil's first Black political party (1931–7).

40 Ricardo Henriques, *Raça e gênero no sistema de ensino: Limites das políticas universalistas*, UNESCO, UNDP, 2003, p. 93.

41 Ibid., p. 5.

42 *Desenvolvimento com justiça social: Esboço de uma agenda integrada para o Brasil*, Instituto de Estudos do Trabalho e Sociedade (IETS), 2001, pp. 14–15.

43 Muniz Sodré, *Claros e escuros: Identidade, povo e mídia no Brasil*, Vozes, 1999, p. 10.

44 *Pesquisa Nacional por Amostra de Domicílios* (National Domicile Research Sample), 1996. [*Translator's note.* IBGE: Instituto Brasileiro de Geografia e Estatística (Brazilian Institute of Geography and Statistics).]

45 Eliane Cavalleiro, *Do silêncio do lar ao silêncio escolar: Racismo, preconceito e discriminação na educação infantil*, Contexto, 2000.

46 Rebecca Reichmann, "Mulher negra brasileira: Um retrato," *Revista Estudos Feministas*, vol. 3, no. 2, 1995, p. 503.

47 Irene M. F. Barbosa, *Socialização e relações sociais: Um estudo de família negra em Campinas*, FFLCH/ USP, 1983, p. 34.

48 Reichmann, "Mulher negra brasileira," p. 503.

49 *Translator's note. Morena* (feminine form): lit. "brown-skinned," but not necessarily linked to a specific racial identity.

50 Reichmann, "Mulher negra brasileira," p. 504.

51 bell hooks and Cornel West, *Breaking Bread: Insurgent Black Intellectual Life*, Routledge, 2017, p. 150.

52 Ibid., pp. 151–2.

53 Ibid., p. 153.

54 Ibid., pp. 153–4.

55 Ibid., p. 157. While hooks acknowledges the importance of West's reflections about Black intellectual life, she is sure to observe the absence of any mention of Black women intellectuals in his works. For her, it would have been expected that West looked specifically at the intellectual lives of Black women, since "The Dilemma of the Black Intellectual" "was written at a historical moment when there was a feminist focus on gender that should have led any scholar to consider the impact of sex roles and sexism" (p. 150). hooks's article "Black

Women Intellectuals" also intends to correct this lack by reflecting on how the conflicts noted by West "seem particularly acute for Black women who must also fight against those racist/sexist stereotypes that continually lead others (and even ourselves) to question whether we are capable of intellectual excellence" (p. 157). [*Translator's note.* Note that hooks quotes West directly in the passage Carneiro includes.]

56 Ibid., p. 157. [*Translator's note.* Note the return to hooks's own words here.]

57 Ibid.

58 Ibid., p. 158.

59 We will delve into this question in the case of Brazil in Chapter 10.

60 hooks and West, *Breaking Bread*, p. 158. [*Translator's note.* Note hooks's direct citation of West here.]

61 Ibid., p. 161. [*Translator's note.* Note hooks's return to her own words here.]

62 Ibid. [*Translator's note.* Note hooks's direct citation of West here, with her commentary.]

63 Ibid., pp. 162–3. [*Translator's note.* Note hooks's return to her own words here.]

64 West, cited in ibid., p. 163.

65 Ibid.

66 Michel Foucault, *Society Must Be Defended: Lectures at the Collège de France, 1975–1976*, edited by Mauro Bertani and Alessandro Fontana, translated by David Macey, Picador, 2003, p. 10.

67 hooks and West, *Breaking Bread*, p. 160. [*Translator's note.* Note hooks's return to her own words here.]

68 Ibid., p. 161.

69 "When they are aware of their subalternity, Black intellectuals will discover the limits of their voice since before they are thinking agents they are "scientific objects." They will find out that though their subaltern consciousness authorizes them to speak about Black difference in Brazil, on the other hand, it looms over their degree of incorporation of universal scientific "objectivity," of adjusting to disciplinary tropes and appeals. It is their master, it is the authority that protects them as intellectuals from the lack of control of the feeling of difference and the insurgence that this feeling can represent, since, if it is possible to note the difference, they must keep silent about their deeper understanding, their deeper desires to reverse racial inequality and social injustice" (Lima, "A legitimação do intelectual negro no meio acadêmico brasileiro," pp. 282–3).

70 Foucault, *Society Must Be Defended*, p. 9.

71 Ruperake Petaia, "Kidnapped," in *Blue Rain*, USP Centre, Western Samoa, Publications and MANA Publications, 1980, pp. 10–11.

## Chapter 4 Prohibitions

1 Though inspired by Foucault, I use the term "prohibition" (*interdição/interdit*) in a more expansive way than he does. In "Orders of Discourse" (translated by Rupert Swyer, *Social Science Information*, vol. 10, no. 2, 1971, pp. 7–30), the term "prohibition" appears to explain one of the three discursive procedures of exclusion; the other two are division (between reason and madness) and the will to truth. As Foucault says, the production of discourse in a society is "at once controlled, selected, organized and redistributed according to a certain number of procedures, whose role is to avert its powers and its dangers, to cope with chance events, to evade its ponderous, awesome materiality" (p. 8). A prohibition is one of these procedures of exclusion, the most "obvious and familiar" (ibid.). In a discursive dimension, prohibition functions as exclusion insofar as "we cannot simply speak of anything, when we like or where we like; not just anyone, finally, may speak of just anything" (ibid.). As he further states, the regions where "this web is most tightly woven" are those of sexuality and politics: in the domain of sexuality, prohibitions reveal sexuality's link with desire; in the domain of politics, they reveal their link with power (ibid.). In this chapter, I speak of the multiple prohibitions that are imposed upon Black people and which have no other function than their exclusion, beginning with their exclusion from humanity itself.

2 Gislene Aparecida dos Santos, *A invenção do ser negro: Um percurso das ideias que naturalizaram a inferioridade dos negros*, Fapesp/Educ, 2002, p. 55.

3 Ibid., p. 60.

4 Michel Foucault, *Abnormal: Lectures at the Collège de France, 1974–1975*, edited by Valerio Marchetti and Antonella Salomoni, translated by Graham Burchell, Picador, 1999, p. 56

5 *Translator's note. Negão/Negrões*: augmentative for "negro," and deployed in Brazil as racial epithets.

6 Joel Rufino, "Vera, Clara dos Anjos, Iládio," in *Atrás do muro da noite: Dinâmica das culturas afro-brasileiras*, edited by Wilson do Nascimento Barbosa and Joel Rufino, Minstério da Cultura, Fundação de Palmares, 1994, p. 161.

7 *Translator's note*. João Guimarães Rosa (1908–67): modernist writer from Brazil; *Dão-lalalão* (1965): a novella by Guimarães Rosa.

8 Rufino, "Vera, Clara dos Anjos, Iládio," p. 169.

9 Ibid.

10 Ibid.

11 Ibid.

12 Marco Frenette, *Preto e branco: A importância da cor da pele*, Publisher Brasil, 2000, p. 38.

13 Foucault, *Abnormal*, p. 58.
14 Ibid.
15 Ibid., p. 8.
16 Ibid., p. 7.
17 Ibid., p. 14.
18 Ibid.
19 Ibid., p. 7.
20 Though in Foucault the notion of a "panopticon" refers to the architectural description of institutions, derived from "a new eye" and which emerged with Jeremy Bentham's carceral project, here we use it to illustrate the perception of the permanent surveillance of blackness. It is also a principle of visibility of blackness that in Brazil represents a specific territorial allocation in which the principle of privacy is excluded, as occurs, for example, in favelas.
21 Michel Foucault, "Truth and Juridical Forms," in *The Essential Works of Foucault, 1954–1984. III. Power*, edited by James D. Faubion, translated by Robert Hurley and others, vol. III, New Press, 2000, pp. 70–1.
22 Frenette, *Preto e branco*, p. 22.
23 Eliane Cavalleiro, *Do silêncio do lar ao silêncio escolar: Racismo, preconceito e discriminação na educação infantil*, Contexto, 2000, p. 91.
24 Foucault, *Abnormal*, p. 15.
25 *Translator's note*. See Prologue n. 3 on uses of *pardo* and *negro*. I include the Portuguese terms to clarify when relevant.
26 Sérgio Adorno, "Racismo e discriminação," in *Novas faces da cidadania: Identidades políticas e estratégias culturais*, Cadernos de Pesquisa No. 4, Centro Brasileiro de Análise de Planejamento (Cebrap), Entrelinhas, 1996, pp. 86–7.
27 Foucault, *Abnormal*, p. 8.
28 *Translator's note*. See Prologue n. 3 on uses of *preto* to mean "Black"; *pretinho*: diminutive of *preto*; the context makes clear the derogatory use of the term.
29 Frenette, *Preto e branco*, p. 22.
30 Ibid., pp. 22–3.
31 Ibid., p. 50.
32 Ibid., p. 54.
33 Liv Sovik, "Alô, alô, mestiçagem," Geledés – Instituto da Mulher Negra, July 16, 2010: https://www.geledes.org.br/alo-alo-mesticagem/.
34 Moema de Poli Teixeira, *Negros na universidade: Identidades e trajetórias de ascensão social no Rio de Janeiro*, Pallas, 2003, pp. 139–40.
35 Milton Santos, "No Brasil, hipocrisia marca questão racial," *Folha de São Paulo*, May 7, 2000.
36 *Translator's note*. Wilson Simonal (1938–2000): a Black pop star of the 1960s and 1970s. During Brazil's military dictatorship (1964–85),

after Simonal fired his accountant, the accountant accused Simonal of informing on him to the secret police, leading to his imprisonment and torture. Simonal was convicted of extortion by means of kidnapping.

37 Nelson Motta in Pedro Alexandre Sanches, "O julgamento de Simonal: OAB quer reparar memória de músico que passou de ídolo popular a acusado de 'dedo duro' no regime militar," *Folha de São Paulo*, October 16, 2003.

38 *Translator's note.* The title of Carneiro's article "Meu irmão, meu limoeiro" (My Brother, My Lemon Tree), plays with the title of Simonal's song "Meu limão, meu limoeiro" (My Lemon, My Lemon Tree). She describes a famous 1969 concert by Simonal at Rio de Janeiro's Maracanãzinho stadium.

39 Sueli Carneiro, "Meu irmão, meu limoeiro," *Correio Braziliense*, October 24, 2003.

40 *Translator's note. Dedo-duro*: literally, "hard finger"; a police informant.

41 *Translator's note.* Ziraldo Alves Pinto (1932–2024): author, cartoonist, and journalist, known as Ziraldo.

42 Sanches, "O julgamento de Simonal."

43 *Translator's note.* Caetano Veloso (1942– ): a musician and writer who was exiled for his political activism against Brazil's military dictatorship.

44 Sanches, "O julgamento de Simonal."

45 *Translator's note.* Jaguar: the pseudonym of Sérgio de Magalhães Gomes Jaguaribe (1932–2025), cartoonist and comics artist and one of the founders of *O Pasquim* in 1969.

46 Sanches, "O julgamento de Simonal."

## Part II Prologue

1 Michel Foucault, *The History of Sexuality. Volume 1: An Introduction*, translated by Robert Hurley, Pantheon, 1978, pp. 95–6.

2 Hannah Arendt, *The Origins of Totalitarianism*, 2nd edition, Meridian Books, Inc., 1958.

3 Other authors – researchers, poets, artists – deal with different aspects of this resistance, with whom we dialogue here, such as, among others, Marcos Antônio Cardoso, *O movimento negro em Belo Horizonte: 1978–1998*, Mazza Edições, 2002.

4 Here we are dealing with the strict observance of a fundamentally Foucauldian principle as Deleuze attributes it to Foucault in "Intellectuals and Power." Deleuze considers Foucault to be "the first – in [his] books and in the practical sphere – to teach us something absolutely fundamental: the indignity of speaking for others" ("Intellectuals and Power: A Conversation between Michel Foucault and Gilles Deleuze," in *Language, Counter-Memory, Practice: Selected Essays and Interviews*

*by Michel Foucault*, edited by Donald Bouchard, Cornell University Press, 1977, p. 209).

5 Since raciality is inscribed in the dynamic of an apparatus of power, discourses, as the locus of the attainment of knowledge, power, and subjectivities, in Foucault's view, have the same legitimacy wherever they come from, since behind them there are no truths to be revealed. They carry within them the truths produced in each correlation of forces that constitutes the apparatus, whether from the position of exercising power or the place of resistance that it engenders. This takes place insofar as in their strategies of exercising power and resistance, "victims" and "executioners" find themselves sometimes simultaneously implicated in the same side of a strategic position, and at other times in dispute.

6 Márcio Seligmann-Silva, *O local da diferença: Ensaios sobre memória, arte, literatura e tradução*, Editora 34, 2005, p. 183.

7 Ibid., p. 185.

8 Ibid., p. 192.

9 Ibid., p. 186.

10 Ibid., p. 193.

11 *Translator's note*. Zumbi dos Palmares: the leader of Palmares, Brazil's largest community of fugitives from slavery in the seventeenth century, and also a contemporary symbol of Black consciousness.

12 Conceição Aparecida de Jesus, *Atos de resistência cultural e educação: Discurso e expectativas para além de Zumbi dos Palmares*, PhD, FE-USP, 2001, p. 12.

13 Not all the witnesses agreed to declare their ages. However, they are all my contemporaries. I am currently fifty-five years old. [*Translator's note*. Carneiro was born in 1950; the interviews date from her PhD dissertation, completed in 2005.]

14 *Translator's note*. Note the photographs of the witnesses date to the era of Carneiro's PhD dissertation in 2005.

15 Ministério de Justiça/Comissão Nacional dos Direitos da Mulher (Ministry of Justice/ National Commision on Women's Rights).

16 Pan-American Health Organization – World Health Organization – Brazil.

## Chapter 5 Edson Cardoso

1 The following testimony was granted in 2004.

2 *Translator's note*. Santo Amaro: a municipality in the region of Recôncavo, on the Bahia de Todos-os-Santos, close to the city of Salvador in the state of Bahia.

3 *Translator's note*. Feira de Santana: a city in the state of Bahia.

4 *Translator's note*. We use the Portuguese terms to keep the specificity of Brazil's educational system. In Brazil prior to 1971, *ginásio* included the years between elementary and pre-university education (high school), ages

eleven to fourteen, and often required an entrance exam. It lasted four years, while *colégio*, high school, was the final three years of secondary education. *Científico* (science-related) was a specialized *colégio* curriculum.

5 *Translator's note*. Ação Popular (People's Action): a leftist political organization in the 1960s–70s with roots in Jesuit student activism.

6 *Translator's note*. Luiz Orlando da Silva (1945–2006), intellectual and activist who organized a network of *cineclubes* (cinema clubs) focused on Black history in the 1970s and 1980s.

7 *Translator's note*. Abdias Nascimento (1914–2011): Brazilian playwright, activist, poet, and politician.

8 *Translator's note*. *Vestibular*: Brazil's university entrance exam, taken for a specific area of study.

9 *Translator's note*. AI-5: Institutional Act No. 5, an act passed in 1968 by the Brazilian military dictatorship that severely curtailed civil rights.

10 *Translator's note*. ICBA: Goethe-Institut Brasilien Theater.

11 *Translator's note*. Jorge Amado (1912–2001): one of Brazil's most famous modernist writers, from Bahia.

12 *Translator's note*. *Veja* (Look): a weekly news and culture magazine.

13 *Translator's note*. Dom Jerônimo Tomé da Silva (1849–1924): archbishop of Salvador da Bahia from 1893 to 1924.

14 *Translator's note*. Transdroga: a cargo transport company.

15 *Translator's note*. Edvaldo Pereira de Brito (1937– ): a noted lawyer and law professor from Bahia.

16 *Translator's note*. Edison Carneiro (1912–72): Brazilian ethnologist and historian from Salvador da Bahia who focused on Black Brazilian culture. Nelson Carneiro (1910–96): Brazilian politician and journalist, and brother to Edison.

17 *Translator's note*. MNU: Movimento Negro Unificado (Unified Black Movement).

18 *Translator's note*. Leonel Brizola (1922–2004): a governor of the state of Rio Grande do Sul who resisted Brazil's military dictatorship; he went into exile and was elected governor of Rio de Janeiro after his return.

19 *Translator's note*. João da Cruz e Sousa (1861–98): Symbolist poet.

20 *Translator's note*. Palmares: a complex seventeenth-century network of communities of fugitives from slavery in Northeast Brazil, famed for its resistance against Portuguese and Dutch military conquering forces. Palmares's most famous leader, Zumbi dos Palmares (1655–95), remains a symbol of Black resistance in Brazil.

21 *Translator's note*. Zumbi Day: now formally the Day of Black Consciousness, celebrated on November 20 since the 1970s, and formally recognized by the federal government in 2003.

22 *Translator's note*. Instituto C&A (C&A Institute): non-profit organization focused on youth education and entrepreneurship.

23 *Translator's note*. Yvonne Maggie (1944– ): Brazilian anthropologist who supported affirmative action in Brazil's universities.

24 *O Presidente negro* (The Black President) (1926): a eugenicist and segregationist speculative/science fiction novel by Monteiro Lobato (1882–1948), set in the United States. It concludes with the elimination of the Black population through involuntary sterilization.
25 *Translator's note. Retrato do Brasil* (1928): a study of Brazil's development and character by modernist writer Paulo Prado (1869–1943).
26 *Translator's note.* Whitening (*embranqueamento*): a nineteenth- and twentieth-century ideology that was common in Latin America. Derived from scientific racism, it promoted racial miscegenation as a "solution" to the "problem" of Black presence in slavery and post-slavery societies, with the goal of "whitening" the Black population and eventually eliminating it.
27 *Translator's note.* Luis Fernando Verissimo (1936–2025): a Brazilian satirical writer. The book being referred to here is *O opositor* (The Opponent) (2004).
28 *Translator's note. Quilombo*: community of fugitives from slavery.
29 *Translator's note.* Caetano Veloso (1942– ): a musician and writer who was exiled for his political activism against Brazil's military dictatorship.
30 *Translator's note.* Cardoso refers to Caetano Veloso's album *Noites do Norte* (Northern Nights), which takes as its theme Brazil's history of slavery. The lyrics of the song "Noites do Norte" are comprised of selections from Brazilian abolitionist Joaquim Nabuco's autobiography; Nabuco saw abolitionism as a project of Brazil's political and economic elite, and a mark of its belonging to the "civilized" world. The lyrics of "Zumbi," written by Jorge Ben and performed by Caetano, celebrate Zumbi dos Palmares as a warrior who will vindicate the enslaved.
31 *Translator's note.* Candomblé: an Afro-Brazilian religion that originated among the enslaved. It was suppressed or carefully controlled by authorities for most of its history.
32 *Translator's note.* Xangô: one of the Orixás, or divine beings, worshiped in Candomblé and other African diasporic religions with origins in Yoruba. *Terreiros*: physical sites of worship as well as communities of practice.
33 *Translator's note. Ogã*: describes various functions assigned to men in Candomblé rituals; during rituals, when other participants are possessed by Orixás, *ogãs* are not, though they do have other liturgical roles.
34 *Translator's note.* In 1822, Brazil gained its independence from Portugal, but until 1889, when it became a republic, Brazil was an imperial monarchy. It maintained slavery until 1888.
35 *Translator's note.* The Rebouças brothers, André (1838–98) and Antônio (1839–74): engineers and abolitionists.
36 *Translator's note.* Malê Revolt (1835): a revolt that took place in 1835

led by Muslim enslaved persons whose leaders were literate and made written plans in Arabic.

37 *Translator's note.* Lima Barreto (1881–1922): twentieth-century novelist.

38 *Translator's note.* Manoel da Motta Monteiro Lopes (1867–1910): one of Brazil's first Black legislators.

39 David Raimundo dos Santos, "Frei David" (1943– ): Franciscan priest dedicated to promoting Black students' access to higher education in Brazil, including through affirmative action.

40 *Translator's note.* IAPI: a neighborhood in Salvador named for and created by the Instituto de Aposentadoria e Pensões dos Industriários (IAPI, Institute of Industry Retirees and Pensioners).

41 *Translator's note.* Seu: *senhor* (Mr.).

42 *Translator's note.* Petrobras: Brazil's state energy company.

43 *Translator's note.* Ìrohìn – Centro de Documentação, Comunicação e Memória Afro-brasileira (Ìrohìn – Center for Afro-Brazilian Documentation, Communication, and Memory): an institution dedicated to the preservation and dissemination of the history of the Black Movement in Brazil. The center is named for the Yoruba term for "news."

44 *Translator's note.* Federal law 10.639 (2003) requires that Afro-Brazilian history and culture be taught in schools.

45 *Translator's note.* Frente Negra Brasileira: Brazil's first Black political party (1931–7).

46 *Translator's note.* Presumably Fernando Pessoa (1888–1935): "*Todo o conhecimento vem dos ou pelos sentidos*" (all knowledge comes from or through the senses), from "O conhecimento e a sensaçao," in *A procura da verdade oculta: Textos filosóficos e esotéricos*, edited by António Quadros, Europa-América, 1986, p. 78.

47 *Translator's note.* Doudou Diène (1941– ): a lawyer from Senegal and the United Nations' Special Rapporteur on contemporary forms of racism, racial discrimination, xenophobia, and related intolerance from 2002 to 2008.

48 *Translator's note.* Caio Prado Júnior (1907–90) and Gilberto Freyre (1900–87): two intellectuals who wrote influential works on Brazil's cultural, political, and economic formation. Freyre's work was associated with the concept of Brazil as a "racial democracy" supposedly absent of the racism that plagued other post-slavery societies. See Chapter 1 n. 85.

49 IBGE: Instituto Brasileiro de Geografia e Estatística (Brazilian Institute of Geography and Statistics).

## Chapter 6 Sônia Maria Pereira Nascimento

1 *Translator's note.* Queen Nzinga (c. 1583–1663): a famed ruler of Ndongo and Matamba in present-day Angola.
2 Testimony granted on December 8, 2004, the Day of Justice, which the interviewee made a point of emphasizing.
3 *Translator's note.* Aparecida do Norte: a municipality in São Paulo state, named for the patron saint of Brazil.
4 *Translator's note.* Macumba: term used for several different African diasporic religions in Brazil.
5 *Translator's note.* In Brazil prior to 1971, *ginásio* included the years between elementary and pre-university education (high school), ages eleven to fourteen, and often required an entrance exam. It lasted four years.
6 *Translator's note. Colégio*, high school, was the final three years of secondary education.
7 *Translator's note.* In Brazil in the mid- to late twentieth century, subject and career specialization began in "*colégio.*"
8 *Translator's note. Vestibular*: Brazil's university entrance exam, taken for a specific area of study.
9 *Translator's note.* José "Zé" Dirceu (1946– ), Aloysio Ferreira (1945– ), and Luís Travassos (1945–82): leftist activists who participated in armed resistance against the Brazilian military dictatorship. Travassos and Dirceu were imprisoned by the dictatorship. All three went into exile, and returned to Brazil following the political amnesty law of 1979.
10 *Translator's note. Estadão*: A São Paulo daily newspaper.
11 *Translator's note.* Only people over eighteen can attend a trial in Brazil.
12 *Translator's note.* Pinah (Maria da Penha Ferreira Ayoub): an accomplished samba dancer with the Beija-Flor samba school who often wears her hair shaved. *Passista*: samba dancer.
13 *Translator's note.* "There I'm a friend of the king's" is a verse from the poem "Vou-me embora pra Pasárgada" ("Pasárgada") (1930) by Brazilian modernist poet Manuel Bandeira.
14 *Translator's note.* Arcadas: Nascimento is likely referring to the influential student alumni association of the USP's Law School, the "Antigos Alunos das Arcadas" (Ex-Students of the Arcades), named for the distinctive arcades of the law building.
15 *Translator's note.* Antônio Frederico de Castro Alves (1847–71): one of Brazil's leading abolitionists and Romantic poets.
16 *Translator's note.* Harlem Désir (1959– ): French leftist politician and the first president of the anti-racist organization SOS Racisme. Bryan Stevenson (1959– ): American lawyer and founder of the Equal

Justice Initiative, a nonprofit that provides free legal representation. Rio Eco-92: the United Nations Conference on Environment and Development held in Rio in 1992, a conference on sustainable development. Women's Tent (Planeta Fêmea): a sector of the NGO Global Forum, an event that was part of the Rio Eco-92 conference, focused on women's roles in sustainable development.

17 *Translator's note.* World Conference on Human Rights, Vienna, 1993; International Conference on Population and Development, Cairo, 1994; Fourth World Conference on Women, Beijing, 1995.

18 *Translator's note.* OAB–SP: Ordem dos Advogados do Brasil – Secção São Paulo (Brazilian Bar Association – São Paulo section).

19 *Translator's note.* Banespa: State Bank of São Paulo.

20 *Translator's note.* See Prologue n. 3 on uses of *preto* to mean "Black." The context makes clear that it is used as an epithet.

21 *Translator's note.* See the discussion of Flávio Ferreira Santana, a young Black dentist murdered by military police, in Ch. 2, pp. 57–8.

22 *Translator's note.* SOS Racismo: anti-racist legal aid organization that began as part of Geledés.

23 *Translator's note. Pátria minha*: Brazilian soap opera that aired from 1994 to 1995 on the network Rede Globo. After portraying a scene where a white employer used racial epithets to falsely accuse a Black gardener of stealing, Geledés filed legal action against Rede Globo with the complaint that the program portrayed the Black character as quietly submitting to the racist attack, reinforcing an undignified racial stereotype and promoting racial prejudice. As part of the settlement, Rede Globo changed the plot of *Pátria minha* and aired a new program centered on a Black middle-class family. See Armando Antenore, "Negros vão à Justiça contra 'Pátria minha'," *Folha de São Paulo*, July 11, 1994; "Trama terá família de negros," *Folha de São Paulo*, March 13, 1995; Armando Antenore, "Personagem negra faz discurso anti-racismo," *Folha de São Paulo*, December 14, 1994.

24 *Translator's note.* Antônio Delfim Netto (1928–2024): Brazilian economist and politician.

25 *Translator's note.* José Bernardo Cabral (1932– ): Brazilian lawyer and politician.

26 *Translator's note.* May 13: date commemorating the legal abolition of slavery in Brazil in 1888.

27 *Translator's note.* Article 140 of the Brazilian Penal Code refers to the crime of defamation, and Article 3 provides for more severe penalties when the offense refers to race, color, ethnicity, religion, origin, age, or disability.

28 *Translator's note.* In 2004, the São Paulo state Febem (Fundação Estadual para o Bem-Estar do Menor) was replaced by the Fundação Centro de Atendimento Socioeducativo ao Adolescente (Fundação CASA/SP; Center for Socio-Educational Services for Youth Foundation).

29 *Translator's note.* Alexandre de Moraes (1968– ): Brazilian Supreme Court Justice and professor at USP. The book referred to here is his *Direito constitucional*, Editora Atlas, 1997 (41st edition, 2025).

30 *Translator's note. Coronelismo*: political and social power exercised by rural landowners.

31 *Translator's note.* Eduardo de Oliveira e Oliveira (1923–80): a Black sociologist who specialized in racial issues, a key figure in Brazil's Black Movement, and a member of the GTPLUN (Grupo de Trabalho de Profissionais Liberais e Universitários Negros; Working Group of Black Professionals and University Students), a group that promoted the Black population's access to university education, professionalization, and concomitant economic mobility. Iracema de Almeida (1921–2004): one of Brazil's first Black women to become a doctor, as well as the founder and president of the GTPLUN in 1972.

32 *Translator's note.* Igreja Nossa Senhora do Rosário dos Homens Pretos (Church of Our Lady of the Rosary of the Blacks) in Paissandú Square in São Paulo: originally built as a chapel for enslaved people in 1721 by the Irmandade dos Pretos (Brotherhood of the Blacks), a lay Catholic confraternity. After the land was appropriated by the city of São Paulo in 1903, the Brotherhood rebuilt the church in its current location. In using "Blacks" as a noun here, I follow Miguel Valerio's translation. See Miguel A. Valerio, "Architects of Their Own Humanity: Race, Devotion, and Artistic Agency in Afro-Brazilian Confraternal Churches in Eighteenth-Century Salvador and Ouro Preto," *Colonial Latin American Review*, vol. 30, no. 2, 2021, p. 245.

33 *Translator's note.* Joel Rufino (1941–2015): a celebrated writer, historian, and professor at the Federal University of Río de Janeiro (UFRJ), and one of the authors of the *História Nova do Brasil*, a coauthored Brazilian history series of textbooks for secondary education published in 1964 and subsequently banned by the Brazilian dictatorship.

34 *Translator's note.* Marina Colasanti (1937–2025): an Italian-Brazilian author and feminist who served on Brazil's first National Women's Rights Council in 1985. She was awarded Brazil's most prestigious literary award, the Prêmio Machado de Assis, in 2023.

35 *Translator's note. Janista*: followers of Jânio Quadros (1917–92), a populist politician who ran on an anti-corruption campaign using the emblem of a broom, and served as mayor of the city of São Paulo from 1953 to 1955, governor of São Paulo state from 1955 to 1959, and president of Brazil for seven months in 1961 before resigning. *Adherista:* a follower of Adhemar Pereira de Barros (1901–69), a populist governor of São Paulo state between 1947 and 1951 (when he was defeated by Jânio Quadros), mayor of the city of São Paulo from 1957 to 1961, and governor again from 1963 to 1966. Widely believed

to be corrupt, his followers used the slogan "*rouba, mas faz*" (he steals, but he gets things done).

36 *Translator's note*. Adalberto Camargo (1923–2008): the first Black politician to be elected to federal Congress in São Paulo, where he served four terms between 1966 and 1982. Theodosina Ribeiro (1930–2020): the first Black woman elected to São Paulo's city council, and the first Black woman to be elected to the São Paulo state legislature, as well as a recognized civil rights lawyer.

37 *Translator's note*. *Santinhos* (literally "little saints"): electoral propaganda cards used to campaign for a particular candidate.

38 *Translator's note*. Helio de Souza Santos (1945– ): an activist in the Black Movement in the 1970s and professor at the Visconde de Cairu Foundation, where his work specializes in diversity and inclusion, and sustainable development. Chico Whitaker Ferreira (1931– ): an architect and social justice activist who served in the São Paulo Municipal Chamber from 1989 to 1993.

39 *Translator's note*. PT: Partido dos Trabalhadores (Workers' Party): center-left political party in Brazil.

## Chapter 7 Fátima Oliveira

1 Fátima Oliveira died on November 5, 2017. Geledés provided an overview of her published articles: http://www.geledes.org.br/fatima-oliveira-uma-nova-estrela-no-orun/. Testimony recorded on December 21, 2004 in Belo Horizonte, Minas Gerais.

2 *Translator's note*. *Sertão*: the dry outback in Brazil's Northeast, an overwhelmingly rural part of the country.

3 *Translator's note*. *Vestibular*: Brazil's university entrance exam, taken for a specific area of study.

4 *Translator's note*. Mangalarga Marchadore is Brazil's national horse breed.

5 *Translator's note*. *Quilombo*: community of fugitives from slavery.

6 *Translator's note*. Seu: *senhor* (Mr.).

7 *Translator's note*. Coluna Prestes: literally, "Prestes column," a revolutionary movement headed by members of the military and named for Luís Carlos Prestes. The group marched on Brazil between 1925 and 1927 to foment rebellion and demand greater political representation and an end to corruption. They went into exile in Bolivia in 1927.

8 *Translator's note*: *A Pacotilha*: a "trinket" or collection of poorly made goods.

9 *Translator's note*. In Brazil prior to 1971, *ginásio* included the years between elementary and pre-university education (high school), ages eleven to fourteen, and often required an entrance exam. It lasted four years.

10 *Translator's note. Jornal Nacional* (National News): the nightly news program on Rede Globo, Brazil's largest network, at 8:00 p.m.
11 *Translator's note. Científico* and *magistério*: two specialized curricula for the last three years of secondary education in Brazil prior to 1971.
12 *Translator's note.* Cimo: a Brazilian furniture manufacturer that operated for most of the twentieth century.
13 *Translator's note. Cachaça*: a liquor made from sugarcane.
14 *Translator's note. Voz do Brasil*: a state radio program focused on news and politics that airs on every radio station in Brazil.
15 *Translator's note. Cuscuz do Norte* (literally couscous from the North): a Northeastern regional dish made with corn or rice meal, coconut milk, and sugar, and served for breakfast.
16 *Translator's note.* JOC: a movement founded in Belgium in 1912 to train factory, trade, agricultural, and other workers to evangelize in their workplaces.
17 *Translator's note.* Araguaia Guerrilla: an armed guerrilla movement associated with the PCdoB and centered in the area of Brazil's Araguaia River that during its years of operation (1967–74) sought to overturn the military dictatorship.
18 *Translator's note. Geografia da fome* (1936): a seminal work by Brazilian physician Josué de Castro that argues that hunger is caused not by scarcity of resources but by the unequal distribution of them.
19 *Translator's note.* PDT: Partido Democrático Trabalhista (Democratic Labor Party): leftist political party. Constitutional representative (*deputado constituinte*): an elected representative to the body that writes or updates Brazil's constitution; in this context, in the 1980s, the 1988 constitution that was ratified after the military dictatorship.
20 *Translator's note.* Elsimar Coutinho (1930–2020): Brazilian gynecologist and professor who made discoveries leading to injectable contraceptives for women and founded Brazil's Centro de Pesquisas e Assistência em Reprodução Humana (CEPARH, Center for Human Reproductive Research and Assistance) in Bahia in 1981. Coutinho supported the sterilization of women living in poverty, and the CEPARH under his direction was accused of scientific experimentation especially on poor and Black women without adequate warning about the risks and consequences of the procedures.
21 *Translator's note.* On the use of the terms *preto* and *negro* (feminine forms *preta* and *negra*), see Prologue n. 3. *Moreno* (feminine form *morena*): typically used to designate someone as non-white, but closer to whiteness on Brazil's racial spectrum.
22 *Translator's note.* A reference to the International Conference on Population and Development, Cairo, 1994.
23 *Translator's note.* Luiza Erundina (1934– ): founding member of the PT (Workers' Party) and mayor of São Paulo from 1989 to 1993.

24 *Translator's note*. Parlatino: the Latin American Parliament, permanently located in São Paulo.
25 *Translator's note*. Fábio Júnior (1953– ): Popular Brazilian singer and actor. In the 1992 telenovela *Pedra sobre Pedra* (Stone Over Stone), Fábio Júnior's character, Jorge Tadeu, urinated daily on a plant; he would then appear to whoever ate the leaves.
26 *Translator's note*. Mackenzie Presbyterian University, a private university whose main campus is in São Paulo.
27 *Translator's note*. Note that Oliveira's testimony was given in 2004; the Declaration of Helsinki was subsequently updated in 2004, 2008, 2013, and 2024.
28 *Translator's note*. As Oliveira predicts, the provisions she mentions were in fact increasingly weakened in each subsequent update to the Declaration of Helsinki. The relevant guidelines on the use of placebo and provision for follow-up care, as of the 2024 update, require only that participants not "be subject to additional risks of serious or irreversible harm as a result of not receiving the best proven intervention" (Article 33); and that "post-trial provisions must be arranged by sponsors and researchers to be provided [. . .] for all participants who still need an intervention identified as beneficial and reasonably safe in the trial. Exceptions to this requirement must be approved by a research ethics committee" (Article 34). See: https://www.wma.net/policies-post/wma-declaration-of-helsinki/.
29 Doctoral dissertation, Medical School, Federal University of Minas Gerais, 1998.

## Chapter 8 Arnaldo Xavier, the Poet (in Memoriam)

1 *Translator's note*. *Cangaço*: rural banditry in the *sertão* region of Northeast Brazil in the nineteenth and early twentieth centuries. *Coronelismo*: political and social power exercised by rural landowners. *Voto de cabresto* (literally "vote by halter"): a practice of forcibly compelling votes for large landowners during Brazil's first republic at the end of the nineteenth century and beginning of the twentieth. *Bachelarismo*: social and professional privilege awarded to those who earn a *bacharel*, an undergraduate degree. *Latifúndios*: large rural estates.
2 *Translator's note*. Ossanha: one of the *Orixás* (spirits or deities) associated with medicinal herbs and sacred leaves in many African-diasporic religions in the Americas. Babalorixá: *pai de santo*, or a priest in African diasporic religions in Brazil.
3 *Translator's note*. *Cordel* (plural: *cordéis*): cheaply printed pamphlets of narrative verse, typical of Brazil's Northeast, recounting folk histories, political commentary, etc.

4 *Translator's note. Sertanejo*: rural.
5 *Translator's note.* UNE: União Nacional dos Estudantes (National Students' Union).
6 *Translator's note. Dancin' Days*: a Brazilian soap opera from the late 1970s.
7 *Translator's note.* Poem/process (poema/processo): poetic and artistic movement (1967–72) focused on visual and non-verbal poems, and founded by Wlademir Dias-Pino (1927–2018), Moacy Cirne (1943–2014), Neide Sá (1940– ), and Álvaro de Sá (1935–2001).
8 *Translator's note.* Key figures in Brazilian literature and culture.
9 Poemas, 1974.
10 Poemas de envelope, 1975.
11 ECE Antologia, 1976.
12 Coletânea das Edições Pindaíba, 1977.
13 Arnaldo Xavier, *Contramão*, Edições Pindaíba, 1978, pp. 19–20.
14 *Translator's note. Nordestino*: from Brazil's Northeast.
15 *Translator's note.* "Bodarrada": the popular title for Gama's poem "Quem sou eu?" (Who am I?) (1859), in which the poet plays with the word *bode* – literally "goat," but also used at the time as a slur for Black people. "Bodarrada" is a neologism that implies a group or party of *bodes*.
16 *Translator's note. Axébedoria*: a portmanteau of *axé* (roughly "life force" in African diasporic religions such as Candomblé) and *sabedoria* (wisdom).
17 *Translator's note. Crioulo*: literally, "Creole," the word was sometimes used as a pejorative for "Black." Xavier here is playing with the similarity between *crioulo* and *criou* (created).
18 *Translator's note.* "*Tupi or not tupi*": a play on Shakespeare's "To be or not to be" from Oswald de Andrade's modernist 1928 essay "Manifesto Antrópofago" (Cannibalist Manifesto), which defended a notion of "artistic cannibalism" of foreign cultures to "digest them" and thus create a Brazilian identity. Critics have seen this movement as contributing to a notion of "racial democracy," and thus to ideological whitening/erasure of blackness. Tupi: an indigenous group in Brazil that practiced anthropophagy. *Ori*: in Candomblé and other African diasporic religions, the head, intelligence, thought.

## Part III Prologue

1 Boaventura de Sousa Santos, *Pela mão de Alice: O social e o político na pós-modernidade*, Cortez, 1995, p. 328.
2 Fábio Wanderley Reis, "Mito e valor da democracia racial," in *Multiculturalismo e racismo: Uma comparação Brasil-Estados Unidos*, edited by Jessé Souza, Paralelo 15, 1997, p. 227, n. 5, original emphasis.

## Chapter 9 Education: Negation and Affirmation

1 Eliane Cavalleiro, *Do silêncio do lar ao silêncio escolar: Racismo, preconceito e discriminação na educação infantil*, Contexto, 2000.
2 We have decided to put all citations of our testimonies in italics to facilitate their visualization, as the sources of our reflections in this and the next chapter. All the citations of testimonies by Edson Cardoso, Sônia Nascimento, and Fátima Oliveira are drawn from, respectively, Chapters 5, 6, and 7.
3 *Translator's note.* "Years of lead" (*anos de chumbo*): the years of the worst political repression between 1968 and 1974 under Brazil's military dictatorship.
4 This happens in both the public and private spheres. See the case of Wilson Simonal recounted in Chapter 4.
5 This relates to Erving Goffman's idea in *Stigma: Notes on the Management of Spoiled Identity*, Simon & Schuster, 1986.
6 Ricardo Paes de Barros, *Erradicar a pobreza: Compartilhar o desafio*, CARE Brasil, 2001.
7 See the warm applause for the few or only Black people in graduation ceremonies, as though to enshrine surprise and even the impropriety of their presence. Roseli Fischmann, "Identidade, identidades – indivíduo, escola: Passividade, ruptura, construção," in *Multiculturalismo: Mil e uma faces da escola*, edited by Azoilda L. Trindade and Rafael Santos, DP&A, 1999.
8 The testimony in this passage says: "*He was Black and he wasn't doing high school, high school was interrupted for him. I didn't understand why, so he was what, then? He was nothing.*"
9 In one of the classes I had to take to complete my postgraduate requirements, a professor spoke ironically and aggressively in referring to the celebrations around the National Day of Black Consciousness, November 20, which pays homage to Zumbi dos Palmares. The focus of her criticism was precisely the celebration of Black consciousness in a country that was, for her, a mixed-race one. I felt her gesticulation, the looks in my direction, and her encouragement of the class's complicity as a provocation. Certainly, she knew that there was an activist before her, for that matter the only Black person in the room, and used the authority of her speech that resulted from her position as a graduate school professor to make arguments that disqualified Black people's mobilization around raciality. She used an image itself, for me one of an Afro-Brazilian woman, for her the expression of a true national identity, to reinforce her arguments. This makes one suppose that the discourses celebrating racial mixing, as a foundation of national identity that circulated uncritically in schools, conspired to deny legitimacy to Black mobilization for the political struggle for

equality. Through these discourses, the existence of inequalities based on race are denied, inequalities that motivate the demands that bring Black people to political organizing as Black people. The principle of equality that schools also reiterate, whether from a religious point of view or from liberal political concepts, is equally useful to denying the legitimacy of Black identity to constitute itself based on protest and demands. In both cases, a strategy of demobilizing Black identity is manifest.

10 In Chapter 10, we will seek to demonstrate how other paths to the Black social movement are forged.

11 Note how, in this conversation, the witness simultaneously dialogues with the interviewer and the hegemonic I, masterfully expressed in this "They." In this instance, we add single quotation marks to analytically demarcate the remarks that the witness directs to the hegemonic I.

12 We reiterate here, as in the Introduction, Foucault's lesson recalled by Deleuze: "Practice is a set of relays from one theoretical point to another. No theory can develop without eventually encountering a wall, and practice is necessary for piercing this wall" (Deleuze, in Michel Foucault and Gilles Deleuze, "Intellectuals and Power," in *Language, Counter-Memory, Practice: Selected Essays and Interviews by Michel Foucault*, edited by Donald Bouchard, Cornell University Press, 1977, p. 206).

## Chapter 10 Education and Care of the Self

1 Frantz Fanon, *Black Skin, White Masks*, translated by Richard Philcox, Grove Press, 2008.

2 *Translator's note. Pai Tomás*: from the Portuguese translation of Harriet Beecher Stowe's infamous novel *Uncle Tom's Cabin*, *A cabana do Pai Tomás*.

3 *Translator's note. Menor*: a reference to how Black children and youths are criminalized by descriptions (e.g. in media) as "minors" rather than, for example, "children."

4 In an interview from 1984 (Raúl Fornet-Betancourt et al., "The Ethic of Care for the Self as a Practice of Freedom: An Interview with Michel Foucault on January 20, 1984," *Philosophy & Social Criticism*, vol. 12, no. 2–3, July 1987, pp. 112–31), Foucault explains that the notion of "care for the self" – of fundamental importance for an understanding of the last phase of his intellectual trajectory – emerges from the observation of a little-studied phenomenon, but one quite relevant in the Greco-Roman era: the practice of the self. Practices of the self did not have the sense of a morality of abstention, as they later came to have, but rather were an "exercise of self upon self by which one

tries to work out, to transform one's self and to attain a certain mode of being" (ibid., p. 113). What interests Foucault is that, especially for the Greeks, "in order to behave properly, in order to practice freedom properly, it was necessary to care for self" (ibid., p. 116). My notion of "care of the self" – in agreement with which care of the self is realized in care of the other – has a political and collective dimension and emerges not in the discovery of a phenomenon from the Greco-Roman world, but in the testimonies of Edson Cardoso, Sônia Maria Pereira Nascimento, and Fátima Oliveira.

5 Nelson Mandela, *Long Walk to Freedom: The Autobiography of Nelson Mandela*, Little, Brown, 1994, p. 543.

6 *Translator's note*. In this sentence, Carneiro's text identifies *The Struggle Is My Life* as the subtitle of Mandela's autobiography. The phrase, which is taken from Mandela's speech given on June 26, 1961, appears as as the subtitle of the Portuguese translation of his collection of speeches and writings published while he was still in prison, and as the title of the original English-language edition. To avoid confusion, we have identified the phrase here as the title instead of the subtitle. See Nelson Mandela, *The Struggle Is My Life: His Speeches and Writings Brought Together with Historical Documents and Accounts of Mandela in Prison by Fellow-Prisoners*, International Defence and Aid Fund for Southern Africa, 1986, and *Nelson Mandela: A luta é a minha vida*, translated by Celso Nogueira, Globo, 1988.

7 He is referring to Abdias Nascimento, the godfather of the contemporary Black Movement.

8 This process of being "led by the hand" by a peer is repeated with Fátima Oliveira and Sônia Nascimento.

9 This topic seems full of significance for education; however, exploring them would go beyond the parameters of this text. It is worth citing Frantz Fanon as one of the principal authors who are pioneers on the topic of decolonization.

10 Emmanuel Levinas, *Totality and Infinity: An Essay on Exteriority*, translated by Alphonso Lingis, Duquesne University Press, 1969, p. 23.

11 See the prologue of Part II of this book.

12 Fátima Oliveira, *Bioética: Uma face da cidadania*, 8th edition, Moderna, 2004, p. 82.

13 Michel Foucault, *Discipline and Punish: The Birth of the Prison*, translated by Alan Sheridan, Pantheon, 1978.

14 *Translator's note*. These passages do not appear verbatim in the published version of Fátima Oliveira's testimony.

15 *Translator's note*. *Axé*: roughly "life force."

16 Jurema Werneck, "O desafio das ialodês: Mulheres negras e a epidemia de HIV/AIDS," In *O livro da saúde das mulheres negras: Nossos passos vêm de longe*, edited by Jurema Werneck et al., Pallas/Criola, 2000, p. 102.

17 *Translator's note.* Oshun: in Yoruba and associated African diasporic religions, the deity of love and abundance.
18 Allow me the license to refer to "us" in this context, since I am also the director of the organization, of which I am so proud.

## Postface: Sueli Carneiro's Practical Philosophy

1 Sueli Carneiro, *Racismo, sexismo e desigualdade no Brasil*, Selo Negro Edições, 2011.
2 Sueli Carneiro, *Escritos de uma vida*, Editora Jandaíra, 2019.
3 See, for example, pp. 2–3.
4 Michel Foucault, *Society Must Be Defended: Lectures at the Collège de France, 1975–1976*, edited by Mauro Bertani and Alessandro Fontana, translated by David Macey, Picador, 2003, p. 256.
5 See p. 42.
6 P. 56.
7 Charles W. Mills, *The Racial Contract*, Cornell University Press, 1997, p. 20; Carneiro, this volume, see Part I.
8 Carole Pateman, *The Sexual Contract*, Polity, 1988.
9 P. 21.
10 P. 37.
11 P. 7.
12 PP. 72–3.
13 P. 245.
14 P. 233.
15 P. 31.
16 P. 31.
17 P. 7.
18 Sueli Carneiro and Thereza Santos, *Mulher negra: Política governamental e a mulher*, Livraria Nobel, 1985.
19 P. 50.
20 P. 68.
21 P. 70.
22 PP. 5–6.
23 *Translator's note.* Carneiro's original work in Portuguese has a longer subtitle than this English edition: *A construção do outro como não ser como fundamento do ser* (The Construction of the Other as Non-Being as the Foundation of Being).
24 PP. 89–90.
25 Frederick Douglass, *Narrative of the Life of Frederick Douglass, An American Slave, Written by Himself*, a new critical edition by Angela Y. Davis including her "Lectures on Liberation," City Lights, 2010.
26 Chapter 10 n. 4, pp. 327–8.
27 P. 251.

28 P. 125.
29 P. 6.
30 Carneiro, *Escritos de uma vida*, p. 184, original emphasis.
31 Seyla Benhabib, *Situating the Self: Gender, Community and Postmodernism in Contemporary Ethics*, Polity, 1992.
32 Carneiro, *Escritos de uma vida*, p. 115.
33 Ibid., pp. 108–9, emphasis added.

# Index